Globalization and Democratization in Asia

An impressive cast of contributors plus a multi-layered conceptionalization of the changing interface between globalization dynamics, democratic developments and identity constructions.

(Professor Samuel Kim, Columbia University)

Globalization is a defining feature of our times, covering everything from economic and political issues to the spread of Western culture. However, its status is controversial, with some viewing it as leading to greater development for all, and others as a threat to national cultures and democratic political life. This book shows how simplified such binary views are, and examines how various globalizing forces have affected Asian societies. It discusses the relationship between globalization, identity and democratic developments in Asia, both theoretically and empirically, and aims at understanding how economic, political and social forces interact and are mutually reinforced in Asian societies

All the chapters show the volatile nature of the relationship between the global and the local in Asia. Together they provide a picture of Asia characterized both by global flows of capital, information and people, and by localized contextual historical interpretations of such flows. It is at this nexus of the global and the local that identity, as social relations, becomes the missing link for understanding globalization and democratization in Asia. The book contains a range of in-depth case studies focusing on a variety of Asian countries, including China, India, Japan, Indonesia, South Korea, Laos, Vietnam, Thailand and Malaysia.

Catarina Kinnvall is Assistant Professor at the Department of Political Science, Lund University, Sweden. She has written extensively on globalization and identity in India and China. She is also the author of *Cultural Diffusion and Political Learning: The Democratization of China* and *Globalization and the Construction of Identity: Democracy, Diversity and Nationhood in India.*

Kristina Jönsson is a Lecturer at the Department of Political Science, Lund University, Sweden. She is currently researching how foreign ideas and policies are spread and translated into domestic practices, with special focus on the pharmaceutical sector in Laos and Vietnam.

Globalization and Democratization in Asia

The construction of identity

**Edited by Catarina Kinnvall
and Kristina Jönsson**

London and New York

First published 2002
by Routledge
11 New Fetter Lane, London EC4P 4EE

Simultaneously published in the USA and Canada
by Routledge
29 West 35th Street, New York, NY 10001

Routledge is an imprint of the Taylor & Francis Group

© 2002 Selection and editorial material Catarina Kinnvall and
Kristina Jönsson, individual chapters, the contributors

Typeset in Times by Taylor and Francis Books Ltd
Printed and bound in Great Britain by MPG Books Ltd, Bodmin

British Library Cataloguing in Publication Data
A catalogue record for this book is available from the British Library

Library of Congress Cataloging in Publication Data
A catalogue record for this title has been requested

ISBN   0–415–27730–2 (hbk)
ISBN   0–415–27731–0 (pbk)

Contents

Contributors

Lowell Dittmer, Professor of Political Science at the University of California at Berkeley, has written, among other things, *Sino-Soviet Normalization and Its International Implications* (1992), *China's Quest for National Identity* (1993) (with S. Kim), *China Under Reform* (1994), *Liu Shaoqi and the Chinese Cultural Revolution* (rev. edn. 1997), and *Informal Politics in East Asia* (2000) (with H. Fukui and P. N. S. Lee).

Hugo Dobson is Lecturer in Japan's International Relations, the School of East Asian Studies at the University of Sheffield. He is the author of several articles and the co-author of *Japan's International Relations: Politics, Economics and Security* (2001). He is the sole author of *Japan and United Nations Peacekeeping: Pressures and Responses* (forthcoming).

Edward Friedman, Professor of Political Science at the University of Wisconsin-Madison, is a specialist on Chinese politics who has focused on how cultures construct understandings of authoritarian regimes and democratization. His work deconstructs the political interests in opposing the West, treated as the native land of democracy/imperialism, and has appeared in numerous books and journals. His most recent book is *What if China Doesn't Democratize? Implications for War and Peace* (2000) (with Barret L. McCormick).

Geir Helgesen is a cultural sociologist. Based at the Center for Pacific Asia Studies at Stockholm University, he is engaged in the project "Korean Democracy in the 21st Century. The Normative Basis for the Political Process. Politics between Localism and Globalism." His present research continues from the book *Democracy and Authority in Korea. The Cultural Dimension in Korean Politics* (1998).

Michael Jacobsen is currently a Research Fellow at the Southeast Asia Research Center, City University of Hong Kong. Before that he was a Nordic-Netherlands Research Fellow at the International Institute of Asian Studies in Leiden, and a guest researcher at the Center for Development Research in Copenhagen. He is co-editor of the book *Human Rights and Asian Values. Contesting National Identities and Cultural Representations in Asia* (2000) (with O. Bruun).

Kristina Jönsson is a Lecturer at the Department of Political Science at Lund University, Sweden, researching how foreign ideas and policies are spread and translated into domestic practices, with special focus on the pharmaceutical sector in Laos and Vietnam. She is author of "Democratic Values—Universal or Contextual?", in G. Hydén (ed.), *Democratization in the Third World* (1998, in Swedish).

Catarina Kinnvall is Assistant Professor at the Department of Political Science at Lund University, Sweden. She has written extensively on globalization and identity in India and China. Publications include *Cultural Diffusion and Political Learning: The Democratization of China* (1995), and *Globalization and the Construction of Identity: Democracy, Diversity and Nationhood in India* (forthcoming).

Bishnu N. Mohapatra is Associate Professor at the Center for Political Studies at the Jawaharlal Nehru University in New Delhi, India. He is the author of a number of articles including *Ways of Belonging: The Kanchi Kaveri Legend and the Construction of Oriya Identity* (1996) and *Colonialism, Culture and Making of an Identity: Orissa 1900–1936* (forthcoming).

Aswini K. Ray is Professor at the Center for Political Studies at the Jawaharlal Nehru University in New Delhi, India. He has published a number of books and articles, including *Domestic Compulsions and Foreign Policy* (1975), *The Global System: A View from the Periphery* (1996), and "The Islamic Bomb and India's National Security," in V. Grover and R. Arora (eds.), *Partition of India, Indo-Pak Wars and the UNO* (1999).

Richard Robison is Professor of Asian and International Politics at the School of Politics and International Studies at Murdoch University. He has written extensively on economic and political regimes in Southeast Asia, particularly Indonesia. His latest book is *The Political Economy of Southeast Asia: Conflict, Crises and Change* (2001) (co-edited with G. Rodan and K. Hewison).

Shamsul A. B. is Professor of Social Anthropology and, currently, Director of the Institute of the Malay World and Civilization, Universiti Kebangsaan Malaysia, Bangi. His latest book, in English, is *Japanese Anthropologists, Malaysian Society* (1998) (co-edited with T. Uesugi). At present he is finalizing a manuscript on "Identity Formation and Contestation in Malaysia."

Vivienne Shue is Professor of Chinese Government at Cornell University and Director of the Cornell East Asia Program. Publications include *State Power and Social Forces: Domination and Transformation in the Third World* (1994) (co-edited with J. Migdal and A. Kohli), *Tethered Deer: Government and Economy in a Chinese County* (1994) (co-authored with M. Blecher), and *The Reach of the State: Sketches of the Chinese Body Politic* (1998).

Anders Uhlin is Associate Professor at Södertörns högskola, University College, Stockholm. His current research focuses on transnational civil society relations and problems of democratization. Recent publications include *Indonesia and the "Third Wave" of Democratization* (1997) and a number of book chapters and articles on Southeast Asian politics.

Abbreviations

AAR	Association for Aid and Relief
ACFOD	Asian Cultural Forum on Development
AFC	Asian Financial Crisis
AMF	Asian Monetary Fund
APEC	Asia-Pacific Economic Cooperation
ARF	ASEAN Regional Forum
ASEAN	Association for Southeast Asian Nations
BJP	Bharatiya Janata Party
EPCReN	Eurasia Political Culture Research Network
EU	European Union
FDI	Foreign Direct Investment
GATT	General Agreement on Tariffs and Trade
GDP	Gross Domestic Product
GNP	Gross National Product
IMF	International Monetary Fund
IRRI	International Rice Research Institute
ISA	International Security Act
KDB	Korean Democracy Barometer
LDP	Liberal Democratic Party
MNC	Multinational Corporation
NAFTA	North American Free Trade Agreement
NGO	Non-Governmental Organization
NIC	Newly Industrialized Country
NPO	Non-Profit Organization
OBC	Other Backward Caste
PRC	People's Republic of China
SAARC	South Asia Association for Regional Cooperation
SOE	State-Owned Enterprise
TMD	Theatre Missile Defense
UMNO	United Malay National Organization
UN	United Nations
UNCED	United Nations Conference on Environment and Development
USAID	United States Agency for International Development
WTO	World Trade Organization

Acknowledgments

Many people have contributed to this volume. We would like to express our gratitude, both as editors and authors, to all those who have taken their time reading and commenting and who in other ways have helped us in our work. The idea for this book grew out of a conference on globalization and democratic developments in Asia, held at Lund University in May 2000, and in which the majority of the authors participated. Since then a long process of editing and rewriting has taken place, and we are most thankful to all the authors of this book, who have contributed their work and positive attitudes in completing this volume. We are also thankful to Samuel Kim, Ian Manners, and an anonymous referee for their valuable inputs into this project. Finally we would like to thank the Crafoord Foundation, The Swedish Research Council (HSFR), Sida/SAREC, Center for East and Southeast Asian Studies and the Department of Political Science, Lund University, for generously financing the conference and thus making this book possible.

Catarina Kinnvall and Kristina Jönsson, editors
Lund, October 2001

Part I
Introduction

1 Analyzing the global–local nexus

Catarina Kinnvall

Globalization has become the all-inclusive, all-enveloping catchword of our times. An endless number of books and articles have been devoted to the subject, covering a number of issues from the EU, the IMF, and the role of the World Bank to endless speculations about the movement of capital, finance and multinational corporations. But it is not only economic factors that are associated with globalization. Migration, refugee flows and the so-called "brain drain" from the developing world is often described as a consequence of globalization, and so is the spread of Western (often American) "culture" in the forms of soap operas, music, fashions and similar trends. Newspaper columnists, economists and political analysts are, on the one hand, all apt to warn about being left behind as the global train is leaving, and the issue of catching up is on everybody's lips. On the other hand, we have a number of hesitant voices being heard, doubting the value of the term "globalization" and pointing to the negative effects of global and international forces, both between and within societies.

In academia, the debate on globalization has similarly taken many forms and scholars have focused on a number of issues. Depending on discipline, studies have been concentrated on aspects such as the future of national identities and cultures, the rethinking of ideas of modernity, religion and world history, the localization of the global and the transformation of state-centric assumptions in the social sciences in general. In its more popular version, globalization is often viewed as the path leading to greater development of all people (that is, toward a global market as conceived by contemporary neo-liberals), while others paint a bleak and threatening picture of globalization as the new hegemony of capital markets, the evil that is to destroy national cultures, reduce democratic political life, and make the state redundant. In this latter sense it is often seen as an unstoppable process which affects all areas of economic, political and social life, and is often associated with, or even viewed as identical to, "Americanization."[1]

This book shows how simplified such opposing views are for describing some very complex processes that are currently taking place around the world. Asian societies, as in other parts of the world, have been affected by various globalizing forces. However, this has not happened in a consistent pattern or in a similar fashion, nor have these societies been purely helpless victims in the process. Globalization, as clarified below and illustrated in the following chapters, should be understood in relation to economic, political and social context, and must be conceptualized as a *relationship* between the global and the local. Hence local action has to be understood with reference to the meanings that the action has for the actors and for its audience—be it local or global (see Deutsch and Kinnvall 2001; Kinnvall forthcoming). Human action, as Giddens (1984, 1991) has argued, is rooted in intersubjective contexts of communication, in intersubjective practices and forms of life which have distinctive historical origins. What this means is that we cannot possibly explain the various outcomes of, for instance, the Asian Financial Crisis (AFC), for different societies, without investigating how local cultural and institutional patterns of behavior differed in relation to various global flows. Why, for example, did Hong Kong, China, Taiwan, Singapore and India fare so much better in the crisis than South Korea, Thailand, Malaysia and Indonesia? Or how can we explain democratization in South Korea, Taiwan and Indonesia, while other societies such as China, Vietnam and Laos are still one-party states. Or why is it that India, Malaysia and Indonesia have experienced recurring clashes between different communities, while other multicultural societies such as Singapore and China have had few such communal conflicts (which is not to say that these societies have lacked other conflicts)?

These and many other issues are raised and dealt with in this volume. In doing this we bring together studies of East and Southeast Asia with those of South Asia, at the same time as we bridge the gap between studies of globalization and democratization. The latter is done by introducing the issue of identity as providing the missing link in much of this literature. Below I identify and explain how this is the case, by first discussing the issue of globalization—definitions, approaches and problems with the term. Second, I investigate its relationship to democracy, democratization and to the issue of civil society. And, finally I turn to the complex issues of identity and citizenship which, I argue, are necessary ingredients for the "glocalization" cake, providing both substance and symbolism to the theoretical and empirical debate. Each section is followed by a brief overview of the corresponding chapters as dealt with in Parts II, III and IV of the book. Part II of the book is thus concerned primarily with the phenomenon of globalization in Asia—its consequences and effects. Part III is more specifically interested in the relationship between globalization, democracy and civil society in Asia, while Part IV relates this debate to issues of identity, culture and citizenship in Asian societies. Part V, the conclusion, attempts finally to bring the various threads, ideas and questions together by revisiting the global–local nexus in Asia as dealt with in the various chapters.

Globalization and its effects: unification and fragmentation

Globalization is often discussed in terms of three processes: *scale, speed,* and *cognition.* The first, *scale,* involves a discussion of magnitude—the extent to which the number of economic, political, social and human linkages between societies are greater than at any previous time in history. The second, *speed,* has to do with how globalization is conceptualized in time and space—the argument here is that globalization is not a new phenomenon but involves a compression of time and space never previously experienced. The third, *cognition,* involves an increased awareness of the globe as a smaller place—that events elsewhere may have consequences for our everyday political, social and economic lives and may affect individuals' sense of being (Kinnvall 1995: 244ff.). In a general sense we understand globalization as a combination of these processes, i.e., not as something new but as a deepening of the extent to which relations transcending geographical borders are now possible; the increased speed with which such relations are now taking place; and the consequences of such intensification of relations on political, economic and social levels. Globalization thus involves the reduced significance of barriers such as borders, distances and states to global flows of both tangible and intangible factors such as goods, services, technology, people and ideas.

A number of such interrelated global flows can be identified (Manners 2000). Some such flows are mainly economic, such as the global flow of production, found in the increasingly mobile economic activities of multinational companies, and the global flow of finance through billions of dollars, euros and yen crossing the globe. Another set of flows is more directly political, as in geography, which is being changed and shaped as borders and boundaries of a physical and political nature are being crossed. Global flows concerning authority and governance also belong to this set, where demands for local autonomy compete with regional attempts to create supranational structures as the state's hold on sovereignty is questioned. Finally, we have global flows of a more social and human nature. Here the rapid diffusion of information and knowledge is both connected to and dependent on advances in technology which have facilitated communication. Global flows of people through migration, travel and tourism are closely connected to global flows of culture, understood in its broadest sense as historically transmitted (constructed and reconstructed) thoughts, values, and ideas which come embodied both in a symbolic and material form as well as in social practice (Kinnvall 1995). As discussed below, it is important to point out that most of these flows are spread unevenly and not in a one-way direction as is often assumed.

In relation to such flows, globalization is also discussed in terms of homogenization versus heterogenization (or unification versus fragmentation), and is here linked to discussions of modernization and development (see for example Robertson 1992; Featherstone 1995; Hall 1997). As mentioned earlier, the modernist, often neo-liberal, approach tends to view globalization as the solution and underdevelopment, backwardness and provincialism as the problems. Here, the main arguments in favor of globalization have to do with the pace of

economic and communicative transformations. The pace of economic transformation, it is argued, has created a new "world politics" as states are no
longer able to control their economies. Electronic communications have
altered previous relational structures as we live increasingly in a world where
events in one location can be observed elsewhere. It is further argued that a
new global cosmopolitan culture is emerging, a "global village,"[2] as the world
is becoming more homogeneous and time and space are undermined by the
speed of modern communications and media.

The so-called "anti-modernists," in comparison, often portray globalization as the problem and localization as the solution.[3] Globalization is only
another term for Western colonialization and a buzzword to denote the
latest phase of capitalism. The world economy is not global as there is no
shift of finance and capital from the developed to the underdeveloped
worlds; rather, trade, investment and financial flows are concentrated in
Europe, North America and Japan. Also, it is argued, globalization is very
uneven in its effects, and only a small minority of the world's population is
actually directly affected. In a similar vein, critics of globalization argue that
the forces that are being globalized are, conveniently, those found in the
Western world and that non-Western values have no place within this
process. Moreover, there are considerable losers within the globalization
process and globalization may only allow for more efficient exploitation of
less well-off nations in the name of liberal openness.

Both pictures give but a limited view of globalization as they fail to problematize culture and identity adequately and instead continue to see
modernity as a universalizing hegemony originating in the West and then
spreading around the globe. The tendency is to take for granted that global
flows continue to be constituted as one-way traffic from the "West to the rest."
Also, though the predominant flow of cultural discourse is from the West to
the East and from North to South, this should not necessarily be understood
as a form of domination. Finally, it is unclear that globalization is simply a
process of homogenization since the processes of fragmentation and hybridity
are equally strong (Barker 1999). In other words, it is not only American
culture affecting the rest of the world, as often portrayed in mass media and,
at times, also in academia. As eloquently demonstrated by Friedman in
Chapter 4, Asian cultural practices have, for instance, become increasingly
influential in many parts of the Western world. In addition, the fact that
American products, such as Coke, McDonald's and American soap operas,
are sold and shown in remote villages of Asia and Africa does not automatically result in the creation of a global cultural unit. As a matter of fact it is
not uncommon that the inflow of such products are interpreted and given
different meanings depending on local context (Ong 1999). As a number of
postcolonial writers have suggested (see for example Spivak 1993; Bhaba 1990,
1996; Chatterjee 1993), what we see are various competing centers bringing
about shifts in the global balance of power between state and nonstate actors
that together forge new sets of interdependencies. The result is not the creation

of equality between these participants, but mainly that a number of new actors are demanding to be heard, locally and regionally, as well as globally.

Pointing to regionalism also highlights the need to move away from a tendency to think of the global and the local as dichotomies. Regionalism may be part of the homogenizing or unifying effects of globalization but it can simultaneously be a response to such homogenizing forces. Hence at the same time that Asia, and the world, is being shaped by global flows, it is also part of a trend toward creating regional blocs which may be of an economic, military, political, and/or social nature. In this sense regionalism is a process of both unification and fragmentation. Regionalism is mostly thought of as a number of interacting states enjoying institutional cooperation through a formal multilateral structure, such as the EU, ASEAN or SAARC. However, regionalism can easily be thought of in much looser terms, such as the triadic nature of world affairs where the Triad is said to consist of three regions—Northern America, the EU and Japan (Ohmae 1985)—with the possible arrival of a fourth global economic superpower, China, and the emergence of the Quad. Regardless of whether either the Triad or the Quad is a good description of the current world structure, both continue to represent regionalism as state interaction and/or institutional arrangements. But regionalism can also signify regional cooperation within a state or between regions in several states, which brings it closer to processes of localization. In comparison to regional unification, such processes often aim at increasing differences or heterogeneity as they accentuate claims to distinctiveness through culture, economics and politics, presenting both globalization and regionalization with a local dimension.

The local dimension of globalization is at the heart of all of the chapters in this volume. This, and the fact that globalization is not a new phenomenon, is amply illustrated in Part II. Both Lowell Dittmer and Aswini Ray show how globalization in East, Southeast and South Asia has long been a real part of people's lives in these societies. In Chapter 2 Dittmer outlines the political and economic changes in East and Southeast Asia and their relationship to globalization. Of particular importance is how recent developments, such as the AFC, have reconfigured the role of the nation-state in this region. By emphasizing the local dimension of globalization, Dittmer suggests that we look at how the forces of globalization have interacted with serious weaknesses in domestic, economic and political structures in the various countries in the region.

Chapter 3 similarly places globalization in a localized historical context by looking at the role of colonialization and de-colonialization in South Asia. Ray argues that it becomes difficult to understand current issues of democracy and conflict in South Asia, without considering how these are historically rooted in the distortions of the colonial process of globalization and reinforced by the cold war. He also shows how globalization, as a phenomenon, has altered speed and space and how this has affected democratic governance in India from 1991 and onward.

Globalization and democracy

From what to where? Importing and exporting values in a globalized world

To understand how global processes of democratization are being established, deepened or rejected in Asia it is important to connect discussions of democratic development to issues of culture and context. Both culture and context are at the heart of the notion of identity as a contested concept, emphasizing how (implicitly) identity provides the missing link in much literature on democracy and civil society.

This involves first of all a problematization of the liberal, institutional view of democracy which tends to assume that once a certain democratic framework is in place, a democratic content will more or less automatically fill the void. The liberal tendency to equal liberalization with democratization and to see both as unidirectional processes that will eventually occur in an evolutionary fashion is problematic to say the least.

Second, and related, it involves a critical discussion of strands of revisionist modernism which tends to emphasize a direct causal relationship between modernization and development, on the one hand, and between modernization and democratization, on the other. In the modernist version, as discussed above, globalization is often viewed as the path leading to the greater development of all people. The spread of the global market, it is argued, will eventually create a middle class who will demand liberal voting procedures and liberal democratic institutions. As most contributors to this volume suggest, this has clearly not been the case in many parts of Asia and elsewhere, and even in places where liberal democracy has been the chosen form of government, it may be very different from its Western counterparts (see for example Hewison *et al.* 1993; Clarke 1998). Globalization is related to changing forms of governance and authority, and liberal democracy may be one outcome of this process. It is not, however, a natural consequence of either economic or political liberalization, or the only form of chosen government. Rather, political rule may take many forms and is context-dependent.

Here it is important to remain critical of a large part of the transition literature which tends to argue, in line with the spread of the global market, that ongoing struggles in Asia and elsewhere are against authoritarian rule and for democratic developments (see for example O'Donnell *et al.* 1986; Diamond 1994). However, as a number of authors have pointed out in connection with Asia, such transition processes are occurring but they are not the only ones that are taking place and they may not happen in a linear fashion (Hewison *et al.* 1993; Rodan 1996). We do not, in other words, have authoritarian rule one day and democracy the next as political processes are clearly far more complex than that. The tendency in much of the transition literature to focus on élites, and the strategic choices made by such élites, as determining the transition process is, if possible, even more problematic. By focusing on élites, short-term tactical maneuvering becomes central to the analysis while structural and cultural factors are excluded from it. As Levine (1988) argues, the examination of élites in isolation necessarily ignores the day-to-day societal struggles whereby issues are framed and legitimating arguments advanced. Furthermore, the global capitalist market is not always antagonistic to authoritarianism or supportive of democracy, but may benefit from the presence of a strong state in certain circumstances. At the same time, however, there is a great likelihood that the global capitalist market may weaken the power of the state and increase the likelihood of political struggle and contestation.

Third, and finally, we can only really understand this relationship if we complicate notions of culture and identity by moving away from the tendency among liberal theorists to keep liberal democracy as the main point of reference while letting culture assume the role of obstacle. Ironically, as Rodan points out (1996: 4), such attempts often resonate with the message of authoritarian leaders concerning so-called "Asian values." Hence the concept of culture has been widely used in a fundamental way to generalize patterns of political development where culture has been viewed as either preventing or facilitating a democratic transition. Liberal theorists also tend to regard the middle class as a cultural unit, similar to the Western notion of the middle class as rational individualists, thus disregarding that the middle class may have a number of internal divisions and competing value claims (Jones 1997; Robison and Goodman 1996). Globalization complicates such simple readings of culture and identity as it redefines power relations in society, but it does not do so in a linear direction.

Part III of the book attempts to refute this tendency to view democracy and democratic developments in relation to culture as unproblematic and linear. Hence in Chapter 4, Edward Friedman starts by asking the question of what Western democracy actually is? In answering this question he shows how culture is always complex and how, in fact, all societies are multicultural, and how democratic practice is always idiosyncratic. Friedman's chapter is an excellent example of how globalization and the spread of democracy cannot be viewed as a one-way process but must be understood in localized terms, making institutional and ideational borrowing a two-way process.

Geir Helgesen makes a similar point in Chapter 5. Focusing on South Korea, Helgesen proceeds from the premise that the liberal model of democracy entails both a conceptual misrepresentation of this model and a huge practical problem by being elevated to the position of universal truth. Helgesen relies on survey analyses to understand why it is that the idea of democracy has always commanded a strong power of attraction in Korea, while in practice it has had significant problems. Because of different cultural traditions there is, Helgesen argues, an inherent problem in measuring Korean democracy against some absolute Western model as it will always come out as second best.

While both Friedman and Helgesen discuss the meaning of democracy and emphasize how the spread of democratic and other values is uneven and idiosyncratic, Richard Robison is more directly concerned with the structural components of power in relation to political regimes. Focusing on

Indonesia in Chapter 6, Robison proposes that the process of democratic consolidation in Indonesia is nothing less than a fundamental contest to reorganize social power in the aftermath of the crisis and the fall of Soeharto. Similar to the previous chapter, Robison is critical of the "demo-cratic preconditions" argument, whether this is based on a rational actor approach, cultural determinants, the rise of civil society, or the assumed affinities between markets and democracy.

In comparison to both Robison's and Helgesen's emphases on democratic consolidation and its problems, fewer studies are devoted to societies that show no or very few signs of democratic developments. Chapter 7 is concerned with two such societies, Vietnam and Laos. In the chapter, Kristina Jönsson proceeds from a critical discussion of the relationship between global-ization and liberalization, on the one hand, and between liberalization and democratization, on the other. Jönsson argues that these relationships are by no means unidirectional, or for that matter mutually co-existent in the frame-work of authoritarian societies. Instead she shows, and discusses the implications of, how Vietnam and Laos are trying to combine their one-party systems with a market economy in an increasingly globalized world.

Coming from various perspectives, what unites these chapters is their critical reading of much literature on democratization, transition and democratic consolidation. However, they are also united by their wish to make a difference, to understand and analyze complex processes through intricate rather than simplified arguments. This is at the heart of all the chapters of this book, as globalization and its relationship to democracy can only be understood if structural, cultural and contextual processes are properly analyzed.

The role of civil society in a globalized world

Globalization, it has been argued, involves changing relations between state and society, often resulting in state decentralization and increased nonstate forms of organization. However, the liberal emphasis on the rise of a middle class and the emergence of civil society in opposition to the state remains problematic, as it tends to romanticize civil society by viewing it as a natural domain of personal and group freedom in contrast to the state as a coercive institution (see Rodan 1996; Robison and Goodman 1996). Here it is impor-tant to re-emphasize that globalization is not a linear process, but may take many forms resulting in global processes of resistance and dominance. Hence, civil society may be both illiberal and anti-capitalist.

Global processes of marketization, privatization and structural adjust-ment policies are affecting societies in Asia and elsewhere. However, as argued by Rodan (1996: 7–8; see also Hewison *et al.* 1993: 2–8), the result of these processes is best understood as the opening up of political space rather than as a struggle between state and civil society. Economic and rapid social change throws up a variety of challenges, produced not just by new forms of social wealth and social power, but also by those marginalized by the new forms of development who want to resist or reverse these changes and return to idealized traditional situations. Some of these struggles may involve attempts to expand civil society without doing so in a liberal democratic fashion or they can involve attempts to establish space for political struggle in arenas other than civil society (Rodan 1996: 7–8). Such struggles or movements may be based on various forms of collective cultural identity or may be religious organizations, professional bodies, trade unions, or any other kind of nongovernmental organization, national or transnational. Political changes taking place in Asia and elsewhere are thus more than just transitional processes from authoritarianism to democracy as they involve complex manifestations of identity and culture.

Such manifestations involve the rise of nonstate actors as a result of the expansion of civil society. This is the focus of Chapter 8. In this chapter Hugo Dobson explores the relationship between democracy and the pursuit of economic developments in postwar Japan through an analysis of globalization and the changing relationship between state and society. Arguing against the view of Japan as a top-down authoritarian model of democracy, Dobson demonstrates how incomplete such a picture is by describing flourishing bottom-up activity on a number of transnational issues such as the environment and gender issues, at the same time recognizing how some NGOs have provided a safety net against too radical a change.

This latter emphasis corresponds with Anders Uhlin's focus in Chapter 9 on transnational issues and mediating domestic structures when discussing the effects of globalization. Comparing Thailand and Malaysia, Uhlin shows how the semi-authoritarian state in Malaysia has been able to keep its restrictions on civil society despite embracing economic globalization, while political space for civil society in Thailand has fluctuated quite significantly. This discussion is extended to account for the emergence of transnational civil society as a response to such mediating domestic structures.

Dobson and Uhlin both bring an important dimension to the civil society debate by highlighting the limitations to perspectives that separate the domain of the state from that of society. In doing so they bring to the forefront civil society's transnational border-crossing character. Of significance for their arguments is how social movements are not separate phenomena requiring a distinct analytical framework (see Rodan 1996: 19), but how they exist in relation to the states and to other forces in national and transnational civil society. The fact that such movements are constituted around certain domestic and/or transnational issue areas re-emphasizes how identity and culture are crucial for understanding the meaning of these movements in response to global transformative flows—the global–local nexus.

Globalization, democracy and identity

Here it is important to point out that even when the struggle for liberal democracy is taking place, democratization may not necessarily result in intergroup harmony and cooperation. Instead, it may result in a destabilization of previous societal structures. Constitutional guarantees of freedom of association and expression provide, for instance, political and cultural space not only to democratic forces, but also to extremist organizations which may be openly anti-democratic, divisive and violent (Kolodner 1995). Global processes of democratization also expose asymmetries in power and knowledge and thus provide a basis for new cultures of resistance among previously marginalized groups, such as women, low-caste groups, religious or other minorities. Part IV of this volume focuses on the growth of such identity-based groups in relation to a rapidly changing environment and the democratization and liberalization of politics.

Several of the chapters in this and the previous parts of the book are thus directly or indirectly concerned with how globalization and/or the democratic electoral process may be instrumental for the mobilization of groups that have previously been rather passive and weak, as it provides opportunities for leaders to polarize issues in order to attract political followers. A tension, in other words, has been created between democracy and the pursuit of economic development (Calhoun 1994: 306). On the one hand, as the political legitimacy of the state declines in favor of regional dominant classes and communities, the state may possibly respond by strengthening its internal security apparatus and may indulge in indiscriminate political repression, including a declaration of some sort of emergency. This obviously threatens the social foundation of democracy. On the other hand, democracy itself has, as argued above, served to give voice to divisive forces (cf. Parekh 1995).

The media and improved communication in general have increased the magnitude of such mobilization, as political leaders now have the possibility to propagate their messages to vast audiences. This, in turn, is likely to further increase dislocation and facilitate tensions between various societal groups as growth in information sharing also reduces the isolation of one community from another (Kolodner 1995). The media also produce demonstration effects, implying that modern media not only record and distribute information about reality, but also construct that reality.

Globalizing identity: the role of the state and the individual quest for security

The above is all directly related to the impact of globalization. One of the most significant features of globalization has to do with the reduced power of the state. Of interest is the extent to which the drive for global competitiveness has reduced the economic and political role of the state and how this has affected the government's image as protector of citizens' welfare. Studies have shown, for instance, how a decreased role of the state may produce an authority vacuum in which new groups emerge in response to individuals' desire for security and welfare (see for example Giddens 1990; Alam 1999).

The spread of the global market may thus produce social and economic dislocation as well as personal uncertainty and insecurity. Citizens may respond to this crisis by turning to leaders who they hope will solve their problems of material deprivation, psychological uncertainty, and ideological absence (Kolodner 1995). Of particular importance is the extent to which ethnic, gender, national and other identities have served to challenge the existing state structure in these societies. It is important to note that the state itself may react to the threat of global competition by trying to strengthen its threatened role in society. The state, similar to newly established groups, may thus play the ethnic, nationalist or religious card in these circumstances.

Culture, in its various definitions and shapes, is likely to become a political weapon in this process. It becomes the means to recover, within its arena, what is lost through law, politics and struggle. A curious aspect here, as pointed out by Alam (1999: 68), is that those who engage in this kind of politics tend to feel a genuine sense of loss. As such it points to the destabilizing effects of the interplay between the global and the local. This suggests that constructed cultural attributes provide not only the symbolic references or resources but they also provide for the revival of some or other aspects of a collective past. They can, in other words, act as a source of revivalism, fundamentalism, and national chauvinism. It is within this process that neat distinctions are created between concepts, such as modern and traditional, or secular and religious, though in reality they are a lot more complex than these dichotomies imply. Hence, it remains important that we complicate the view of globalization as a one-sided Western project.

At the same time, however, one must take seriously the extent to which domination has often worked, and still does, to favor global capital. Here the connection between globalization and modernity as represented by the spread of capitalism and the development of a new form of social alienation (using Marxist terminology) is essential. Modernity, Peter L. Berger (in Pathak 1998: 22) argues, has to do with the spread of an "engineering mentality" as it deprives human beings of a natural relationship with the world. The abstract character of public institutions with their implicit anonymity causes alienation and the pluralistic structures of modern society have made the life of more and more individuals migratory, ever-changing and mobile as they are uprooted from their social milieu. It is at such times of economic, social and ideological uncertainty that the state, as a legally constituted institution, is supposed to come in to provide its residents with protection from internal insecurity and external aggression. But, as noted above, this is clearly not what is happening in today's world, where the state, rather than gaining legitimacy in the traditional sense of the term, seems to lose power in relation to individuals, groups, companies and organizations. One result of such developments has been that the world of identity— nationalism, ethnicity, race, gender and various other "politics of difference"—has taken a hesitant step into the realm of academic discourses on democracy and globalization.

Globalizing citizenship: nation, state and issues of transnationality

This relationship between globalization and group conflict tends to have been largely neglected in literature on the transition to democracy or democracy literature in general. As a relationship it has mostly been analyzed and dealt with in separation from the larger issue of democracy (Calhoun 1994: 304ff.). Hence nationalism and group conflict have been treated as something to be avoided, instead of as a central dimension of the subject of democracy, regardless of the fact that nationalism and group conflict are fundamentally involved in questions about the social foundations for democracy. Often forgotten is the fact that states remain the most crucial vehicles to achieve self-determination, which means that nationalism or the search for a lost identity becomes the solution to the privatizing effects of the market (ibid.).

This is clearly connected to discussions concerning state and citizenship: "Membership in a territorially demarcated, 'sovereign' political unit is still the relevant precondition for citizenship rights; membership in the 'human race' does not yet translate into universal human rights which would incorporate political, economic, social or ecological citizenship rights" (Axtmann 1996: 4). The problem, however, is that globalization challenges clearly defined national boundaries which have traditionally demarcated the basis on which individuals are included and excluded from participation in decisions affecting their lives. Social, economic and political movements of goods, ideas and people create problems as it brings into question which "relevant community" is supposed to speak on behalf of the state. This raises questions for any political system in terms of *representation*, who should represent whom and on what basis, and in terms of *political participation*, who should participate and in what way (Held and McGrew 1999)?

The question of citizenship brings identity issues to the forefront as it puts into focus the politics of resistance and empowerment. On the one hand it points to those groups excluded from traditional (national) political communities, such as refugees, migrants (short- or long-term), women (in some societies), or members of various economic networks, all of whom may challenge the state structure in its present form. On the other hand it also gives significance to (new) social movements of a more transnational character, such as environment, women, and peace movements. These latter movements are often compared to the "old" social movements, like organized labor, and are viewed as playing an important role in global democracy (ibid.). However, similar to the previous discussion of civil society, not all transnational forces are democratic, but transnational phenomena also include illegal drug business, the international arms trade, the trafficking of women and children, and the transnationalization of the sex trade in general. Political power is becoming reconceptualized as a result of these less territorially based power systems making traditional mechanisms of political accountability and regulation less effective. This, in turn, is likely to prove a challenge to notions of citizenship as conventionally understood.

All these issues are dealt with from a number of perspectives in Part IV of this volume. An extended discussion of the relationship between citizenship and democracy is, for instance, found in the chapter by Bishnu Mohapatra, Chapter 10. In this broadly framed chapter Mohapatra proceeds from a discussion of how, in the framework of Indian democracy, the debate on minority rights encompasses several heterogeneous claims. Of particular importance for Mohapatra's argument is how the role of the state and politics must be at the center of one's understanding of minority rights/identity in postcolonial societies such as India. The important question following from this argument is how India accommodates diverse ethnic demands and what the mechanisms are by which they do this?

This latter aspect is also the focus of Chapter 11, in which Shamsul A. B. studies the relationship between development, globalization and the growth of identity-based movements in Southeast Asia. Here the main concern is the formation of new social movements around major social concerns, such as "environmentalism" and "fundamentalism." The author shows how such movements have risen in Southeast Asia in general and in Malaysia in particular, as a result of the weakening of the nation-state by globalization. Of particular importance are the uncertainties and distress brought about as a result of the limits of developmentalism and the increasing selectivity of globalization.

This relationship between feelings of uncertainty and social decay in connection with globalization is further illustrated by Vivienne Shue in Chapter 12, as she problematizes issues of past and present, myth and history, reality and imagination. Shue shows how the search for "the essence of Chineseness" has become a contested domain in relation to the marketizing and privatizing effects of China's crypto-capitalist reforms, and the role of Falun Gong in this process. By providing a different picture of morality and truthfulness, Falun Gong is challenging the Chinese state's moral hegemony.

Similar to Shue's description of how Falun Gong has threatened the Chinese state's moral superiority, Michael Jacobsen in Chapter 13 illustrates how states may conceive of ethnic groups as a threat to their national unity and state sovereignty. By critically analyzing identity formation among the Minahasa in contemporary Indonesia, Jacobsen demonstrates how processes of globalization indirectly influence Minahasa identity formation by engaging directly in the current transformation of the Indonesian state and nation.

Though the chapters in Part IV differ in their approach toward the relationship between globalization and identity, what brings them together is their willingness to question identity as a primordial, singular and unitary phenomenon. Instead all the authors discuss identity construction as a project which may take many forms and which is closely related to global destabilizing forces. This latter aspect is intimately connected to the emotional and affective dimensions of identity construction and identity mobilization in times of rapid change. This is one of the core themes running through all the chapters of this volume, even when it is not addressed directly or analyzed in full. Identity, culture and the question of citizenship remain, as Kratochwil (1996: 18) has argued, "a prism for investigating the problem of inclusion and exclusion that is fundamental to the problem of political order." Hence all the chapters in this volume explore how issues of identity in forms of essentialized dichotomies, such as we and them, East and West, state and society, national and international, affect our perceptions and analyses of Asian societies. In this they all bring in culture and identity as a project, a link that may shape the current rethinking of globalization, democratization and issues of civil society and citizenship.

In Part V, the concluding chapter brings together and critically analyzes the patterns that have emerged in the mixture of theoretical approaches and empirical case studies in the three empirical parts of the volume (Parts II, III and IV). Continuing from the introductory chapter, this final chapter is particularly concerned with analyzing how, first, global–local linkages have affected democratic developments, the role of the state and issues of civil society in a nonlinear direction in the regions, and second, how globalization has been tied to issues of identity, citizenship and the pronunciation of difference, and how these have had both positive and negative consequences in the various case studies. The concluding chapter is not purely evaluative, however, but is also an attempt to suggest ways of analyzing the relationship between globalization, democratic developments and identity in a more comprehensive manner than is commonly the case in much empirically based literature on Asia. In doing so it returns to the issue of constructing Asia through the empirical discussions and narratives provided.

Notes

1   For general accounts of globalization, see for example John Baylis and Steve Smith (1997), and David Held and Anthony McGrew (1999). For more skeptical accounts of globalization, see Paul Hirst and Grahame Thompson (1996), and Alan Scott (ed.) (1997). For more critical accounts, see Douglas Kellner (1998), Jan Aart Scholte (2000), and Anthony King (ed.) (1997). For globalization and International Relations theory and discussions of globalization and the nation-state, see Gerald Clarke (1998), B. McSweeney (1999), Robert J. Holton (1998), and Kenichi Ohmae (1985). For the relationship between modernity and globalization see for example Andrew Linklater (1998), Anthony Giddens (1990), Javeed Alam (1999), and Stuart Hall and Bram Gieben (eds.) (1992). For a more explicit structural account of globalization in relation to the postcolonial world, see for example Ankie Hoogvelt (2001).

2   The notion of the "Global Village" was developed already in the 1960s by the media theorist Marshall McLuhan, but has recently experienced something of a revival (see Mackay 2000: 55). See for instance a recent issue of *Understanding Global Issues 98/7*, which is devoted to an article on "The Global Village: Challenges for a Shrinking Planet." For more general accounts of how globalization entails the Westernization of the world and the spread of capitalism, see Serge Latouche (1996).

3   For general accounts of the relationship between modernity and postmodernity in relation to globalization, see for example Anthony King (ed.) (1997), Mike Featherstone (1995), Roland Robertson (1992), David Harvey (1989), and Fredric Jameson (1991).

References

Alam, J. (1999) *India: Living with Modernity*, Delhi: Oxford University Press.

Axtmann, R. (1996) *Globalization and Europe*, London: Pinter.

Barker, C. (1999) *Television, Globalization and Cultural Identities*, Buckingham: Open University Press.

Baylis, J. and Smith, S. (1997) *The Globalization of Politics*, Oxford: Oxford University Press.

Bhaba, H. (ed.) (1990) *Nation and Narration*, London and New York: Routledge.

—— (1996) "The Other Question: Difference, Discrimination and the Discourse of Colonialism," in F. Barker (ed.), *Literature, Politics and Theory*, London: Methuen.

Calhoun, C. (ed.) (1994) *Social Theory and the Politics of Identity*, Oxford: Blackwell.

Chatterjee, P. (1993) *The Nation and Its Fragments: Colonial and Postcolonial Histories*, Princeton: Princeton University Press.

Clarke, G. (1998) *The Politics of NGOs in Southeast Asia: Participation and Protest in the Philippines*, London: Routledge.

Deutsch, M. and Kinnvall, C. (2001) "What is Political Psychology," in K. Monroe (ed.), *Political Psychology*, United States: Erlbaum Publishers.

Diamond, L. (ed.) (1994) *Political Culture & Democracy in Developing Societies*, Boulder: Lynne Rienner.

Featherstone, M. (1995) *Undoing Culture: Globalization, Postmodernism and Identity*, London: Sage Publications.

Giddens, A. (1984) *The Constitution of Society*, Berkeley: University of California Press.

—— (1990) *The Consequences of Modernity*, Stanford: Stanford University Press.

—— (1991) *Modernity and Self-Identity: Self and Society in the Late Modern Age*, Cambridge: Polity Press.

Hall, S. (ed.) (1997) *Representation: Cultural Representations and Signifying Practices*, London: Sage Publications.

Hall, S. and Gieben, B. (eds.) (1992) *Formations of Modernity*, Cambridge: Polity Press.

Harvey, D. (1989) *The Condition of Postmodernity*, Oxford: Blackwell.

Held, D. and McGrew, A. (1999) *Global Transformations*, Stanford: Stanford University Press.

Hewison, K., Robison, R. and Rodan, G. (eds.) (1993) *Southeast Asia in the 1990s: Authoritarianism, Democracy and Capitalism*, St. Leonards: Allen & Unwin.

Hirst, P. and Thompson, G. (1996) *Globalization in Question*, Cambridge: Polity Press.

Holton, R. J. (1998) *Globalization and the Nation-State*, Basingstoke: Macmillan.

Hoogvelt, A. (2001) *Globalization and the Postcolonial World: The New Political Economy of Development*, Basingstoke: Palgrave.

Jameson, F. (1991) *Postmodernism or the Cultural Logic of Late Capitalism*, Durham: Duke University Press.

Jones, D. M. (1997) *Political Developments in Pacific Asia*, Cambridge: Polity Press.

Kellner, D. (1998) "Globalization and the Postmodern Turn," in R. Axtmann (ed.), *Globalization and Europe*, London: Pinter.

King, A. D. (ed.) (1997) *Culture, Globalization and the World-System: Contemporary Conditions for the Representation of Identity*, London: Macmillan.

Kinnvall, C. (1995) *Cultural Diffusion and Political Learning: The Democratization of China*, Lund: Lund University Press.

—— (forthcoming) *Globalization and the Construction of Identity: Democracy, Diversity and Nationhood in India*, London and New Delhi: Sage Publications.

Kolodner, E. (1995) "The Political Economy of the Rise and Fall(?) of Hindu Nationalism," *Journal of Contemporary Asia*, 25, 2: 233–253.

Kratochwil, F. (1996) "Revisiting the 'National': Toward An Identity Agenda in Neo-realism," in Y. Lapid and F. Kratochwil (eds.), *The Return of Culture and Identity in IR Theory*, Boulder: Lynne Rienner.

Latouche, S. (1996) *The Westernization of the World*, Cambridge: Polity Press.

Levine, D.H. (1988) "Paradigm Lost: Dependence to Democracy," *World Politics*, 40: 377–394.

Linklater, A. (1998) *The Transformation of Political Community*, Cambridge: Polity Press.

Mackay, H. (2000) "The Globalization of Culture?", in D. Held (ed.) *A Globalizing World? Culture, Economics, Politics*, New York and London: Routledge.

Manners, I. (2000) "Europe and the World: The Impact of Globalisation," in R. Sakwa and A. Stevens (eds.), *Contemporary Europe*, Basingstoke: Macmillan.

McSweeney, B. (1999) *Security, Identity and Interests: A Sociology of International Relations*, Cambridge: Cambridge University Press.

O'Donnell, G., Schmitter, P. and Whitehead, L. (1986) *Transitions from Authoritarian Rule*, Baltimore: Johns Hopkins University Press.

Ohmae, K. (1985) *The End of the Nation-State: The Rise of Regional Economies*, London: HarperCollins Publishers.

Ong, A. (1999) *Flexible Citizenship—The Cultural Logics of Transnationality*, Durham and London: Duke University Press.

Parekh, B. (1995) "Ethnocentricity of the Nationalist Discourse," *Nations and Nationalism*, 1, 1: 25–52.

Pathak, A. (1998) *Indian Modernity: Contradictions, Paradoxes and Possibilities*, New Delhi: Gyan Publishing House.

Robertson, R. (1992) *Social Theory and Global Culture*, London: Sage Publications.

Robison, R. and Goodman, D. (eds.) (1996) *The New Rich in Asia: Mobile Phones, McDonald's and Middle Class Revolution*, London and New York: Routledge.

Rodan, G. (ed.) (1996) *Political Oppositions in Industrializing Asia*, London and New York: Routledge.

Scholte, J. A. (2000) *Globalization: A Critical Introduction*, Basingstoke: Macmillan.

Scott, A. (ed.) (1997) *The Limits of Globalization*, London: Routledge.

Spivak, G. C. (1993) "Can the Subaltern Speak?", in P. Williams and L. Chrismaw (eds.), *Colonial Discourse and Postcolonial Theory*, London: Harvester Wheatsheaf.

Part II
Approaching globalization

2 Globalization and the twilight of Asian exceptionalism

Lowell Dittmer

"Globalization" is defined here in terms of the increasing scale and speed of exchanges of people, products, services, capital, and ideas across international borders. Economics is the vanguard and most basic driving force in this dynamic, and among economic factors finance is most important, because of the great fluidity and fungibility of money. Some $1.2 trillion in currency currently changes hands daily in foreign exchange markets, six times the amount of a decade ago and 85 per cent of total government foreign exchange reserves (Auguste 1998). Economic globalization entails a relative derogation of political institutions and the enhancement of markets as an alternative means of facilitating transnational activity, with regional and international markets subsuming and integrating national markets (Weber 2000). Commodities follow cash, facilitated by the declining unit costs of communication and transportation in the international arena and by the consequent economic advantage of moving factors of production from place to place. Since 1945, average ocean freight charges have fallen by 50 per cent, air transportation costs by 80 per cent, and transatlantic telephone calling charges by 99 per cent. International trade has assumed unprecedented scale and geographic reach: its share of world GDP has doubled since 1950 and will continue to increase more rapidly than other economic indices. Economic and cultural globalization has proven impossible to disentangle, given the commoditization and digitization of symbolism (for example, electronic entertainment is now the second largest American export). Thus globalization, spurred by opportunities for generating both inflated MNC profits at the micro level and superior GNP growth prospects at the macro level, continues to gather momentum (Frenkel and Peetz 1998).

Globalization is by no means a new phenomenon: idea systems such as Islam or Marxism have had transnational appeal for centuries, and commodities and personnel have long been mobile (for example, there was greater demographic mobility in the late nineteenth and early twentieth centuries than today). But global mobility has since the end of the cold war become unprecedented in speed, range, density, and compression. This has notoriously been facilitated by recent technological innovations in cybernetics and telecommunications. But of at least equal importance have been various political watersheds, such as the successive rounds of the GATT, followed in 1995 by WTO talks; the "demonstration effect" exercised by those developing countries which shifted successfully from import substitution growth to export promotion (for example, the Asian NICs, and more recently the People's Republic of China), and by the end of the cold war, which shattered all remaining "iron curtains." Globalization's intensification, coming at a time when the political and military forces that formerly dominated the world have suffered something of a crisis of faith, has made this perhaps the dominant postmodern trend, elevating the G8, IMF, WTO and other international economic institutions above strategic arms control or disarmament talks as central fora of élite international discourse.

What is the relationship between globalization and East Asian moderniza-tion? Our central argument is that globalization has been moving in counterpoint with the Asian attempt to maintain a distinctive normative regime and political-economic culture. This argument must take into account a number of paradoxes. Many of the most successful Asian developing states have been enthusiastic globalizers in the economic dimension we deem to be the prime mover in this process, having some of the highest trade dependency ratios in the world. And why not? East Asia has been a conspicuous beneficiary of economic globalization. Here is the poster child of the World Bank's 1993 publication, *The East Asian Miracle*, which told us how eight nations—Japan, Korea, Hong Kong, Singapore, Taiwan, Indonesia, Malaysia, and Thailand—had since 1960 grown faster than all other regions of the world, accelerating their pace between 1980 and 1995 to a rate nearly three times that of the world economy. The share of global trade for which Asia (excluding Japan) accounted rose from 9 to 15 per cent between 1980–1991, while the developed countries' proportion shrank from 72 to 63 per cent (McNally 1998). Thus it is hardly surprising that opposi-tion to economic globalization has been far less marked in Bangkok or Beijing than in Seattle or London. Yet Asian adoption of globalization has always been highly selective. The realm of ultimate values has typically been excepted, in part to preserve indigenous cultural traditions, partly in deference to the inter-ests of political and social élites. The result has been a distinctively Asian hybrid of pell-mell economic globalization and political-cultural exceptionalism. This hybrid approach has been formulated in different ways, from the "Chinese learning as the core [ti], Western learning as applied method [yong]" of China's "self-strengtheners" at the end of the nineteenth century, to Mahathir's endorse-ment of "Asian values" in the 1990s. Globalism's inherent homogenizing tendencies—increasing competition leading to an equalization of costs (albeit not of incomes[1]) and techniques, and on toward institutional convergence, as economic institutions respond to the same functional requisites—were not particularly welcome in a region of revitalized nationalism. This is not only because these tendencies are identified with Western imperialism but because the successful Asian modernizers had evolved their own institutional alterna-tives, to which various socioeconomic interests became attached in the course of successful development. It was the 1997–1999 AFC that gave these hybrid glob-alizers their first sharp setback. The crisis subjected those institutions most exposed to the forces of globalism to a sort of trial by ordeal, severely damaging many of them and in the process forcing a reassessment of the hybrid approach that had evolved over the preceding decades. The immediate (if controversial) impact was to enhance the power of the IMF as international lifeguard, whose rescue package reinforced the homogenizing impact of the globalizing trends that had precipitated the crisis. Yet the impact of the AFC has been not only economic but political and to some extent even cultural, subjecting the attempt to exclude and preserve a privileged realm of ultimate values from the forces of globalization to its severest test.

Not all of the affected countries have taken this "lesson" equally to heart, for various reasons having to do with institutional momentum, political vested interests, and in some cases serious intellectual disagreement. Yet the outlook is that, barring a radical disjuncture from dominant recent trends in the international economic environment, those countries subscribing to such prescriptions will make the most robust recovery from the crisis. At the same time it should be noted that even if globalization and the international financial institutions allied with it emerge from the AFC as a sort of international switchman in the railway station to Asia's economic future, this is not necessarily to say that such an outcome would necessarily be in any broader sense "right" or "just." Inherent in the emergent network of intensified and all but unregulated globalization trends is not only the prospect of accelerated growth but the danger of sudden, unanticipated financial panics and crashes. For the AFC is but the latest in a series of financial crises, including the reverses in 1990–1993 (in Finland, Norway, and Sweden), 1992–1993 (Europe), 1994–1995 (Mexico), and May 1998 (Russia). All these came in the wake of the financial liberalization that swept the globe following the collapse of the Bretton Woods agreement in 1972. After the "big bang" reforms of October 1986 in Margaret Thatcher's Great Britain, to be adopted in France, Germany, Belgium, and the Netherlands shortly thereafter, rapid liberalization of financial markets ensued. This resulted in daily transactions at the ten main stock markets of the world reaching $900 million per day by 1992, rising to $1.3 billion per day in 1995. Much of this money is speculative, so it can move quickly, with either benign or disastrous economic consequences for the host economy. Those who argue that the distinctive Asian approach to modernization is an innocent victim to a random drive-by shooting by irrational international financial forces can thus make a quite plausible case.

Yet the victims of the AFC were not entirely blameless, as we shall see. In any event the Asian approach to modernization has generally been quite pragmatic, when substantial interests are at stake. So what seems likely to make the difference in the long run is not the question of right or wrong but of who (which forces) won or lost.

The crisis

The AFC, which according to conventional periodization began with the collapse of the Thai baht in July 1997, is noteworthy in a number of respects.

As Radelet and Sachs put it: "It has prompted the largest financial bailouts in history. It is the sharpest financial crisis to hit the developing world since the 1982 debt crisis. It is the least anticipated financial crisis in years" (Radelet and Sachs 1998). The AFC is the third-largest economic collapse in the twentieth century, after the 1929 crash and the 1973 first oil shock. Like most crises, the AFC struck without warning: the early-warning macroeconomic indicators that were relevant for the 1994–1995 Mexican peso crisis—too much consumption (too little saving), persistent budget deficits, and a high rate of inflation—did not apply in the East Asian cases.[2] Right up to the eve of the crisis, traditional growth indicators remained sound, as the region retained savings and invest-ment levels reaching one-third of its GDP. In the immediate pre-crisis period, the five most severely stricken economies (Thailand, Malaysia, Indonesia, South Korea, and the Philippines) had low inflation rates (less than 10 per cent), budgets generally in surplus, and declining government foreign debt (as a fraction of GDP). During the 1990s, these governments seemed to engage in responsible credit creation and monetary expansion, and unemployment rates remained low. For example, Indonesia boasted 10.4 per cent export growth in 1996, its government budget was in surplus each of the previous four years, and its current account deficit was only 3 per cent to 5 per cent of GDP.

In retrospect it has however become clear there were serious structural prob-lems in the crisis economies, including a high reliance on external capital, a poorly developed banking system, cronyism between the financial sector and high-ranking government officials, and a lack of transparency in the workings of financial institutions. Rapid and sweeping capital market liberalization beginning in the late 1980s led to massive influxes of foreign capital, which was used to fuel many questionable investments (for example, Tommy Soeharto's "National Car" project in Indonesia). The region had been exhibiting a "bubble economy syndrome" and fighting a tendency to overheat since the early 1990s. While these economies had become dependent on export growth in the 20 to 40 per cent range to sustain full employment, between the summer of 1995 and the summer of 1996 they lost global competitiveness as their export growth declined. Southeast Asian firms had saturated many of their traditional export sectors such as clothing, footwear, and household electronics. They were also facing increasing competition from other low-wage producers such as China, which following the 1994 devaluation of the renminbi by 35 per cent was able to undersell its competitors, resulting in a surge in China's share of East Asian exports to the United States from 6 per cent to 26 per cent (in the course of the 1990s). This exacerbated Japan's economic troubles, so in the summer of 1995 Tokyo allowed its currency to depreciate (the yen fell 60 per cent against the dollar between April 1995 and April 1997), thereby increasing Japan's export competitiveness. The Southeast Asian countries, whose currency remained pegged against the now overvalued dollar, found themselves priced out of their most lucrative export market, and export growth fell from 30 per cent in early 1995 to zero by mid-1996. At the same time, trade liberalization, strong currencies, and rising domestic demand spurred a growth in imports, which combined with sagging export growth to generate high trade deficits and low current account balances. Whereas long-term sovereign debt was kept under control, the ratio of short-term debt to foreign exchange reserves in Thailand, Korea, and Indonesia exceeded 1.0 beginning in 1994. Thailand's current account deficit surged to 8 per cent of GDP in 1995, while Malaysia's reached 5 per cent of GDP and Indonesia's exceeded 4 per cent. The current account deficits were financed by inflows of foreign capital, which in turn exerted pressure to keep currency values (and interest rates) high. South Korea, in contrast, did not have a serious current account problem (though the current account rose temporarily in 1996 because of the crash of the world semiconductor market, by 1997 Korea was heading back toward current account balance); its problem was weak bank supervision, allowing short-term foreign liabilities to exceed foreign exchange reserves.

Though not generally associated with the AFC, the first events leading to the crisis were failures of certain large South Korean *chaebols*. In January 1997, Hanbo Steel declared bankruptcy, the first bankruptcy of a leading Korean conglomerate in a decade. This was followed in March 1997 by the failure of Sammi Steel, and by rumors of the imminent collapse of Kia, Korea's third-largest auto maker. Meanwhile, in Thailand, Samprasong Land, a finance company burdened by large, bad real estate loans, missed its February deadline for payment on its foreign debt. The Thai government was expected to step in with a rescue package, but after promising to do so on March 10, it reneged, leading to the collapse of Samprasong and thence to the bankruptcy of Thailand's largest finance company, Finance One, on May 23. After repeated assurances that the baht would not be devalued, on July 2 the Bank of Thailand announced it would allow it to float, and the baht promptly lost a third of its value. Immediately, the Philippine peso came under attack, followed a few days later by the Malaysian ringgit. The Indonesian rupiah did not come under severe pressure until mid-August; by late January 1998, it had lost 80 per cent of its value against the dollar.

By November, the Korean won began losing value. As the crisis reached its peak, foreign exchange rates approached free fall, and by October the crisis had spread to the stock markets as well (for example in Hong Kong and Korea). South Korea entered a recession in early 1998 (with a record high 1.2 million people unemployed), and the impact of the crisis in Indonesia was even worse, with a 7–8 per cent GDP contraction, a 45 per cent inflation rate (April 1997–April 1998), and an official estimate (unduly optimistic) of 10 per cent unemployment. An averaging of all these economies suggests that an Asian asset worth $100 in June 1997 was worth $25 by September 1998. That loss of 75 per cent compares with the American crash of 1929–1932, when Standard & Poor's index declined 87 per cent. Beyond the immediate region, Australia and New Zealand incurred losses in export and tourist markets that had become increasingly dependent on East Asia, and Russia was obliged to devalue the ruble in August 1998. Even American and European banks and MNCs faced reduced sales and bad debts, leading the IMF to conclude that world economic growth in 1998 would be 1 per cent lower than predicted, and others to imagine worldwide deflation (*Financial Times* January 13 and 15, 1998).

Causes

As noted above, the conception of the AFC as an innocent casualty of financial globalization has considerable empirical support.[3] American equity markets were awash in liquidity in the early 1990s for a variety of reasons: the tendency of investors to shift from low-velocity real estate to high-velocity stocks and bonds, and the consequent proliferation of "emerging market" funds, Japan's need to recycle the proceeds from the trade surplus it continued to collect from most of its trade partners, even the massive capital flight from post-communist Russia seeking remunerative external investment opportunities (*qua* "money laundering"). Thus while in 1990 the inflow of FDI into less developed countries was $44 billion, by 1996 it had reached $244 billion. Over this seven-year period, cumulative inflows totaled $938 billion (see Garg *et al.* 1997). In 1995, East Asia alone received two-thirds of total FDI outflows to developing countries; in 1996, total private capital inflows to Southeast Asia were estimated at around $93 billion (UNTAC 1996). But what goes up can come down: by 1997, this had changed to a net outflow of $12 billion, and an additional negative $4 billion in 1998, amounting to nearly 11 per cent of the GDP of the countries involved. In terms of the value of listed companies' shares on the stock market, Southeast Asia's market capitalization was valued at $565 billion in January 1997; by mid-1998 the value had fallen to $160 billion (*Straits Times* August 16, 1998).

When foreign investors began moving their money out of (initially) Thailand, because they were concerned about the Thai ability to repay, the central bank responded by buying baht with its dollar reserves and raising interest rates. The increase in interest rates drove down prices for stocks and land, which excited suspicion about the value of loan collateral; it became evident that the banking system was swamped with unpaid loans. When the Thai central bank ran out of dollars to support the baht, the financial system collapsed. And then, the peso, ringgit, rupiah, and won toppled in value like so many dominos. The IMF arranged emergency rescue packages of $17.2 billion for Thailand, $43 billion for Indonesia, and $58 billion for Korea (Poon and Perry 1999).

It was this indiscriminate, contagious pattern of capital flight that supported the thesis of a blind reversal of the forces of globalization that had created the bubble in the first place. In an investment climate lacking transparency, investors seek to allocate a stock of wealth globally among national assets that are increasingly substitutable with one another. When news or the pressure of events leads them to reallocate their assets, the resulting short-term demands on a country's foreign exchange reserves far exceed anything encountered in the old regime of limited capital mobility. If the blindness of globalized financial flows helps to explain the precipitate pattern of capital flight, how are we to understand why these economies became host to the sort of blind investment that will leave in a hurry? The problem in Asia in 1997 was twofold: debt was concentrated in short-term liabilities; and reserve assets were low. In Korea, for example, foreign indebtedness was actually relatively moderate, but large portions of the private debt were short-term loans. At the beginning of 1997, Korea's reserves were less than half of its short-term liabilities, and a large portion of apparent reserves was committed to other purposes. Because the emerging Asian economies, following Japan's lead, favor banks over equity markets for financial intermediation, little public debt is available to be traded. The economies hurt most by the crisis had long histories of problems with their banking systems, and were in the midst of financial reform and liberalization as part of their move to full capital mobility when liberalization created opportunities for excessive risk taking by inexperienced bankers supervised by inexperienced regulators. South Korea, for example, abolished its Economic Planning Board in 1996, thereby relaxing virtually all controls over financial institutions. Such errors are likely in the context of "crony capitalism," typically leading to excessive investment in marginal projects. Thus cronyism tends to result in a "highly geared" corporate sector (characterized by a high debt-to-equity ratio), which is financially fragile and vulnerable to interest rate shocks.

In crony capitalism, tied together by insider "connections" and hearsay, the markets lacked adequate information about the true financial status of the corporations and the banks. If unpleasant economic information (for example, the weaknesses of the central banks' international reserve positions) were to be publicly exposed, this might lead to a collapse of confidence, possibly manifested in a run on the banks. The lack of transparency, and implicit faith in sovereign loan guarantees, gave rise to "moral hazard." In Korea, for example, opacity had become so systemic that corrective action came too late and ultimately could not prevent the collapse of market confidence. The IMF was finally authorized to intervene just days before potential bankruptcy. Financial cronyism and lack of transparency also exacerbated capital flight when the balloon was finally punctured: Given that investors knew so little about the financial soundness of the economy, they were liable to panic at the first rumor of trouble.

While the blind forces of globalism certainly made a bad situation worse, there are several problems with any attempt to attribute the AFC exclusively to globalism. For one thing, if globalism alone were adequate to account for the crisis, such financial crises would be far more pandemic than they are—the globalism thesis fails to answer the questions: Why here? Why now? Clearly Asia was more vulnerable to crisis than other regions because of specific Asian distortions of the market model. At the same time, it is not easy to identify exactly what the Asians did wrong. There is some question about the adequacy of full transparency in ensuring against currency crises, as both Germany and Japan have analogous constraints on transparency, but neither has been frequently susceptible to bank panics (though Japan currently has problems with bad loans and other financial problems analogous to those faced by the AFC victims). India's corporate sector is also highly geared, second only to that of Korea (that is, more so than Malaysia's or Indonesia's), yet it escaped financial crisis. Currency crises are seemingly endemic to capitalism and can occur with or without transparency; for example, though the financial sector in the Scandinavian countries is high in international transparency, in the early 1990s they had a banking crisis with serious effects on the real economy. Moreover, if cronyism and financial opacity were necessary and sufficient conditions for financial crises, how were the Asian economies able to prosper for so many years before crashing? Even if the Asian financial syndrome is economically ill advised and may be said to constitute a predisposition to crisis, there is inadequate evidence to deem this the necessary and sufficient cause of the crisis.

Our thesis is that while globalization makes host countries more acutely vulnerable than before to forces beyond national control, in direct proportion to their exposure to short-term cash infusions, which proffer both accelerated prosperity when times are good and the prospect of sudden disaster in case of panic, the basic cause of crisis *hic et nunc* is specific financial and political conditions in the host country or set of economically linked countries. In the case of the AFC, weak regulation combined with implicit deposit guarantees (based on "moral hazard") had left local bankers free to gamble with the money that global capital markets had gladly poured into their coffers. Endemic weaknesses in the financial sector were exacerbated by the timing of the crisis, which coincided with financial reform and liberalization when the new institutions set up to regulate the market economy were still weak. Panic set in when foreign depositors realized that there were not enough dollar reserves left to cover their debts. This realization hit home when specific large foreign-invested firms began to default in early 1997 and the government failed to intervene to protect investors. The result was not a cascade in which one default logically implied another, but a region-wide "herd" response to subtle danger signals amid an absence of hard financial information.

It fits our argument ascribing primary responsibility to the host regimes that even within the adversely affected East Asian region we find that some countries did much better than others. Those countries that did best had three things in common: high foreign exchange reserves; positive current account balances; and relatively low levels of debt. Taiwan and Singapore had the highest level of international reserves, and both registered positive current account surpluses for all the years in the 1990s. The Hong Kong and Taiwan economies are largely driven by small and medium-sized firms (in contrast to, say, Japan or Korea), accounting for the low exposure to foreign loans. In Singapore's case, the high level of foreign ownership, mainly in the form of branch offices of leading MNCs, reduces exposure to debt; also, the domestically owned sector is dominated by government-linked companies, constraining the accumulation of offshore debt. Singapore and Taiwan suffered only relatively minor currency devaluations of some 20 to 30 per cent (compared with 40 to 75 per cent for their neighbors), while the Hong Kong dollar was insulated by its peg to the US dollar (though Hong Kong equity markets were hit). The PRC is a special case: China has enormous excess capacity, a declining return on loans, and big property bubbles. Debt–equity ratios in China's SOEs, once low, now approach a ratio of 6:1, higher than in South Korea. From 1978 to 1995, tax revenues declined from 35 per cent of GDP to 11 per cent, largely due to lower tax revenues from SOEs, more than half of which have been operating in the red. China's financial sector is in serious difficulty, with a high proportion of nonperforming loans. The solution will require massive corporate restructuring, resulting in rising unemployment and political volatility. Yet China has remained almost completely immune to the AFC. There are at least four reasons for this: its inconvertible currency; substantial foreign exchange reserves (about $150 billion); a large, protected domestic market; and a heavy influx of FDI, very little of which is short-term portfolio investment subject to quick withdrawal.

Consequences

The most direct, immediate impact of the crisis was to strengthen the role of international financial institutions, specifically the IMF, which entered the scene as a lender of last resort to save these countries from the brink of bankruptcy. When Thailand's appeals for bilateral American or Japanese assistance were rebuffed, Bangkok appealed to the IMF on July 28, 1997, which responded with a US$17.2 billion emergency international rescue package, to which Japan's ExIm Bank pledged to contribute $4 billion and China $1 billion. Thailand in return agreed to accept an IMF austerity package consisting of draconian fiscal cuts and a tight monetary policy (to stop authorities from printing money to rescue failing financial and property companies). The IMF imposed similarly austere conditions on its emergency rescue packages of $43 billion for Indonesia and $58 billion for Korea. The recipients greeted the rescue with considerable ambivalence, partly because the IMF demanded conditions (for example, transparency) the organization itself scarcely displayed, and partly because they viewed it a Trojan Horse for Western neo-imperialism. Indeed it appears to be the case that Western economic interests were well served by the IMF, whose rescue package forced Asian debtor regimes to repay for the most part Western creditors. Western financial interests were enabled to make major inroads into the region's banking sectors: in the first four months of 1998, there were 479 mergers and acquisitions in Asia amounting to US$35 billion, and these buyouts were dominated by Western banks, MNCs and financiers (for example, Citibank took a majority share in a major Thai bank, after December 1998 American firms made major inroads into the Korean financial sector, and GE Capital has been a beneficiary of bargains to be had at East Asian "fire sales"). The advisability of the IMF rescue package has also stirred controversy among economists, with US Treasury Secretary Lawrence Summers leading the applause and Harvard's Jeffery Sachs (*inter alia*) sounding the alarm. The critics argued on the one hand that tight money and fiscal austerity dried up the investment pool and precipitated cash crunches or bankruptcies among companies with high debt exposure who might otherwise have survived, meanwhile precipitating a "stampede mentality" among foreign creditors. Other critics argued from the opposite perspective that the package created moral hazard and soft budget constraint by bailing out irresponsibly bankrupt firms.

Whereas economic globalization had been popular in the region, the AFC "flu" and the IMF's bitter medicine clearly demonstrated that globalization has at least two faces, evoking intense resentment, even conspiracy theories in some quarters (for example, Malaysia). Nevertheless, the rescue package seems to have turned the tide, as those afflicted economies which accepted IMF assistance for the most part accepted the accompanying strictures in good faith and experienced at least partial remission with surprising swiftness. Equity markets in Korea, Tokyo, Hong Kong, and Indonesia had already made an impressive rebound by 1999. South Korea seems to have made the most spectacular economic recovery: after a contraction of 5.8 per cent in 1998, it grew by between 7 and 8 per cent in 1999, despite falling consumer prices and a very high level of government debt (*c.*19 per cent of GDP in 1998, vs. 11 per cent in 1997, by conservative estimates)—though the following year their failure to reform the *chaebol* caught up with them, as the economy slowed (GDP growth, 5 per cent) and unemployment swelled (to 5 per cent). Even Indonesia, hardest hit by the crisis, registered 4.8 per cent growth in 2000. According to preliminary estimates, GDP was expected to increase in Asia by 4.4 per cent in 1999 and by 5.9 per cent in 2000, with Beijing leading the growth sweepstakes. Yet partly because they had been lured into complacency by their swift recoveries, many of these countries failed to carry through and hence descended into recession in 2001–2002.

The political impact of the AFC was relatively inimical, so far as regional institutions were concerned. But at the same time the crisis had a stimulatory impact on nationalism. Let us first look at the impact on regional institutions, then consider the repercussions at the level of the nation-state.

Regional institutions were diminished by the crisis. The only visible impact on the twenty-one member APEC forum was to stall the process of intramural trade liberalization held responsible for financial contagion. There was a sense at the 1998 Kuala Lumpur meetings—the first regional forum for chiefs of state to be held since the 1993 APEC summit in Seattle—that APEC conferences were losing their relevance. Likewise, the ARF, a meeting of Asian foreign ministers launched in 1994 to discuss regional security issues, disqualified itself from dealing with a crisis lacking direct security relevance. While existing regional organizations were not financially equipped to deal with the crisis, it proved difficult to cobble together a regional consensus in short order to organize such institutions. In the spring of 1999, Japanese Prime Minister Obuchi Keizo, following a proposal by Japan's Ministry of International Trade and Industry, called for a free trade zone in Northeast Asia, taking the lead in a bilateral agreement with Korea, later to be extended to include Hong Kong, China, and ASEAN. It was pointed out that two-thirds of the 134 WTO members already belonged to regional trade organizations such as the EU or NAFTA, making East Asia one of the few regions lacking such arrangements. The Japanese Institute of International Monetary Affairs, with the Asian Development Bank Institute, has also been studying the feasibility of a single currency system for Asia. ASEAN also proposed in late 1997 to set up a regional equivalent of the IMF, an Asian monetary fund, the AMF, consisting solely of Asian states, which would provide emergency regional support and thus avoid the humiliation of future IMF bailouts. Tokyo promptly promised to underwrite the fund, with support from Hong Kong and Singapore, to be initially capitalized at US$100 billion. It remains to be seen what will become of such proposals, but the immediate fallout has not been encouraging. The AMF was opposed by China, the United States, and the IMF, and by the time of the Manila APEC meeting in November 1997 had become a dead letter, for the time being at least. While a regional institution of this sort would in theory have much to recommend it, Japan's seriously overextended banking sector, rife with nonperforming loans, undermined its financial credibility, and the strategic implications of placing Tokyo at the financial center of East Asia were troubling to regional rivals (and former victims of Japanese aggression). It was also noted that the AMF would have been in Japan's financial interest, as its banks hold large proportions of Southeast Asian foreign debt (nearly 50 per cent in Thailand and 40 per cent in Indonesia), thanks to its consistently steep imbalance of trade with that region.

If regional institutions could at least in theory claim relevance to the AFC's solution, the crisis, by dint of its regional and international ramifications, to a considerable extent transcended the sphere of competence of the nation-state. But just as the crisis varied widely in its intensity, contingent upon specific local political-economic factors, national remedial responses varied in their appropriateness and efficacy. Whether democratic or authoritarian regimes were most effective at coping with the crisis has occasioned some debate. Some aspects of the functioning of these still relatively immature democratic regimes could well be said to have contributed to AFC vulnerability: whereas authoritarian regimes could decree interest rates and taxes almost at will, democracies are typically beholden to the business community and responsive to its demands. Thailand's series of coalition governments (five in six years), frequent general elections, and extensive buying ($1.1 billion in the November 1996 election) made it particularly vulnerable to vested interests. Democracy was also closely tied to the crony capitalism in South Korea, where under the financial deregulation launched under Kim Young Sam, the leading *chaebol* were able to borrow huge sums of investment capital at government-subsidized interest rates and to pay off the politicians who served their interests, resulting in the amassing of enormous slush funds by former presidents Chun Doo Huan (1981–1987) and Roh Tae Woo (1988–1992) that resulted in their successful prosecution. Yet China and Indonesia were proof enough that corruption was hardly peculiar to democracies. A preliminary accounting suggests that both authoritarian and democratic regime types were perhaps equally susceptible (AFC victims included both Malaysia and Indonesia on the authoritarian side and Thailand and South Korea on the democratic side). This can be illustrated by comparing the cases of Singapore and Malaysia, both with parallel colonial histories and Westminster parliamentary structures masking single-party authoritarianism, but Malaysia was both significantly more corrupt (cf. the tendency to favor UMNO party connections in public–private infrastructure projects, resulting in several scandals which President Mahathir later blamed on former vice president Anwar Ibrahim), and harder hit by the crisis.

Yet if the AFC hit democracies and dictatorships alike, democratic regimes proved to be rather more flexible in adapting to economic exigencies. This was largely because they could more easily scapegoat incumbents and rotate politi cians, thereby reversing course without damage to regime legitimacy. Thus Thailand elected the much more competent Chuan Leekpai regime, and South Korea elected its first opposition candidate, Kim Dae Jung, both of whom negotiated salvation from the IMF and promptly implemented reforms. Indonesia in contrast took over a year to respond, largely because of the diffi-culty of removing the well-entrenched authoritarian leadership of Soeharto. Whether democracies are any more qualified to implement the structural reforms necessary to forestall a recurrence of financial turmoil remains to be seen. The democratic Philippines, for example, forced out the honest and competent Fidel Ramos in 1998 based on term limits, only to elect the thor-oughly corruptible ex-movie star Joseph Estrada, by a landslide.

National responses to the crisis tended to diverge into two patterns. On the one hand, such states as South Korea and Thailand plunged into international capital markets as a way of subjecting their entrepreneurial sectors to interna-tional market discipline, using what we might call a homeopathic remedy (that is, globalization must be cured by still more globalization). In Thailand the crisis contributed to the fall of the weak Chavalit six-party coalition govern-ment, bringing the opposition Democrats to power under Chuan Leekpai, who dealt quite effectively with failing finance companies and passed a constitu-tional revision addressed to the institutional problems that had hitherto weakened governmental regulatory capacity. In South Korea, newly elected President Kim Dae Jung opened capital markets to foreign investors (attracting a record US$8.9 billion in 1998), inaugurated a new electronic stock market (KOSDAQ, patterned after NASDAQ), and initiated extensive privatization, including selling stakes in state-run steel and electricity companies to foreign investors. Efforts to break up the *chaebol* network have however met with deter-mined resistance, except in worst-case scenarios such as Daewoo. On the other hand, Malaysia joined North Korea and Vietnam in reintroducing tight capital controls and deferring further financial opening. The economic results in both models have thus far been surprisingly positive, though foreign investment in Malaysia has fallen sharply and it remains to be seen how an economy that had previously enjoyed substantial FDI will adjust to a more self-reliant growth pattern. China's response fell somewhere in between, temporarily postponing currency convertibility and further market opening measures but meanwhile negotiating for entrance into the WTO on the most favorable possible terms.

One significant strategic implication of the crisis has been to enhance the relative importance of People's Republic of China in the regional economy. The PRC decided quite early not to devalue the renminbi again, as it had in 1994. Beijing was in a position to do this not only because it had large foreign exchange reserves, but also because its large internal market made it less dependent on international cyclical dynamics. Moreover, Beijing did not wish to jeopardize the "peg" of Hong Kong currency to the US dollar so near the time of retrocession (July 1, 1997). So China became what US Treasury Secretary Robert Rubin called an "island of stability" in Asia. The result was that Washington for the first time worked in tandem with China rather than Japan in a major economic crisis. In June 1998, when the yen seemed to be falling below 150 to the dollar, Chinese officials expressed concern, hinting that they might have to devalue. This subtle warning was enough to prompt Japan to reverse course and support the yen. Some have seen this as China's first effective intervention in global financial policy making, with conceivably important implications for the triangular balance among the three countries. Along with such slights as President Clinton's refusal, at Beijing's behest, to include a Tokyo stopover in his June 1998 China summit trip, and the contretemps during Sino-Japanese summit in Tokyo later the same year, China's successful debut in international financial policy making circles has aroused Japanese status anxiety.

Though generally speaking the AFC was not the nation-state's finest hour, the Asian regimes have compensated by responding to growing social unrest with an onset of nationalist rhetoric. The impact of the AFC, together with the new militancy of Japan's neighbors (notably North Korea's firing of a Taepodong I over Japanese territory on August 31, 1998, but also perhaps including China's repeated demands for war guilt apologies), seems to have induced Japan to embrace more nationalist foreign and defense policies. This shift was expressed by the readoption of the second world war "rising sun" battle flag and national anthem, and by Tokyo's agreements to an expanded interpretation of the Japanese-American Security Alliance (in 1997) and to cooperate with the United States in the development of TMD technology. China's most high-profile expression of assertive nationalism antedated the crisis (in the form of its 1995–1996 saber-rattling confrontation with Taiwan), but Beijing has continued its long series of double-digit annual increases in defense spending, including massive purchases of high-tech Soviet weaponry. China's case is however exceptional: the other East Asian states, more severely constrained fiscally by the AFC, have curtailed the arms spending they indulged during their heyday of high-speed growth. Taiwan has also become more nationalistic, as evinced by greater popular identification with Taiwanese (as opposed to "Chinese" or "Chinese and Taiwanese") ethnicity, the growing public use of the local dialect, and finally by the election of DPP candidate Chen Shui-bian, an erstwhile advocate of Taiwan Independence, to the presidency in March 2000.

Conclusions

In our analysis of the impact of globalization on East and Southeast Asia, we find that we actually have at least three globalizations: the expansive globalization of the 1960s through the 1990s; the capital-flight crash global-ization of the AFC; and the austerity globalization superimposed by the IMF. So we may measure the impact on the region of an unusually diverse array of independent exogenous variables, arriving in three installments.

During phase I, East Asia was an unalloyed and conspicuous beneficiary (if not free rider) of the international political-economic conjuncture. This is makes the Asian experience a somewhat unusual one, distinguishable in this respect from that of most developing countries. Whereas Latin America or Africa could plausibly (whether accurately or not is another story) conceive globalization to be humiliating and exploitative, the "development of under-development," this stereotype has had very little currency in East Asia, where the NICs shifted smoothly into a neo-mercantilist mode and grew by expanding their export sectors and entering the great American market. This is not to say that all benefited equally—Papua New Guinea, Burma, *et al.*, have had considerably more difficulty—but Japan and the NICs had a demonstration effect that Malaysia, Thailand, Indonesia and the Philippines seemed to be emulating successfully. We have referred to this as a hybrid adaptation pattern inasmuch as economic free-riding went in tandem with the preservation of distinctively Asian political and cultural values: authori-tarian, often seniority-based government, and social stability patterned around the kinship system. Though deriving from an equally ancient but entirely different civilization from the West, Asian values seemed to mesh well with the functional requisites of industrialization: Confucian respect for authority reinforced a disciplined industrial labor force and coherent corpo-rate hierarchy; reverence for learning was conducive to acquiring the necessary educational qualifications and meritocratic validation procedures; traditional frugality and diligence facilitated capital formation and produc-tivity. Max Weber to the contrary notwithstanding, Confucianism seemed no less compatible with the industrial revolution than the Protestant ethic.

Yet the resulting prosperity was perhaps too good to be true. The East Asian pattern of adaptation to globalization had been one-sided and partial, promoting exports while barring imports, grafting export-led growth onto continuing import substitution. Under a form of state *dirigisme* that systemati-cally manipulated prices and exchange rates to bar imports, these export platforms failed to develop financial sectors. Yet they welcomed foreign invest-ment, and as growth accelerated, footloose capital started to flood their still primitive financial networks, only to exit even more swiftly at the first sign of risk. The Asian values that had facilitated the Asian miracle were now seen to be a double-edged sword. The tight family structure that fostered achievement-oriented socialization and a voluntary welfare safety net was also conducive to nepotism and cronyism. The bonds of community that underpinned social stability and civility also gave rise to corporatism, lack of transparency, and moral hazard. The respect for authority so conducive to industrial discipline also permitted blind obedience to élite corruption. Paradoxically, the same cultural values that made Asia the late twentieth century's miracle of non-Western modernization suddenly seemed to be a grave liability, giving rise to a highly effective but clearly flawed form of capitalism.

It is obviously not logically possible for the same phenomenon to be both the source of Asian hypergrowth and the principal reason for the crisis that brought that growth to a halt, and when the AFC struck it occasioned considerable consternation, even outrage. How could the same values upon which our success had been built now betray us? One possible reaction was to absolve Asian values and lay the blame squarely upon the forces of globalism. But this was a minority response, adopted at the state level only in Malaysia. The more typical response, as we have seen, was to accept, however grudgingly, the bitter medicine prescribed by the IMF. And because the prescription appeared to "work," the IMF appears to have been redeemed—at least until the next time. Globalism still seems to have greater credibility in most of these countries than it has in the West.

The fate of the other term of this dialectic, Asian exceptionalism, is more problematic. The Asian "way" will necessarily have to be painfully dissected and reassessed, for of course it is true that it defies the rules of contradiction to assume that the same thing can be both the source of triumph and ruin. The term must be unpacked. Some Asian cultural values—respect for learning, diligence, frugality (savings average 30 per cent in the region)—are indeed conducive to modernization and probably have very little to do with the Asian "flu." Other aspects of Asian culture as it has become bundled with the Asian growth model have however given rise to a lopsided pattern of growth that is not entirely proof against the sometimes stormy tides of globalism. Like values everywhere, it was found that such "Asian" values as filial piety, family loyalty and in-group solidarity could be overdone or inappropriately applied. Authoritarian government seems to have been most severely mauled by the crisis, surviving intact among crisis-impacted countries only in Malaysia. While the Asian "tigers" made the immediate emergency adjustments necessary to qualify for IMF loans, the more basic structural changes required to build financial immunity against future financial gyrations will take time and effort, particularly when the status quo is interwoven with vested interests and values. Thus far it must be said that these reforms have not yet been fully undertaken in any of the AFC-stricken countries. In some it may even be said that the recovery came too soon, prematurely stemming the incentive for reform.

Yet even if the structural reforms recommended by the IMF and the community of professional economic advisers are not successfully carried through, this is not necessarily to say that Asia is doomed to a second crash. These countries have now become fully immersed in the forces of globalism, which will hereafter impose market discipline in virtually all of life's mundane transactions. The old Asian model of a "capitalist developmental state" has been sufficiently discredited by the AFC (and by the continuing travails of Japan) to be forced to adapt. This is not to envisage a future Chicago on the Irawaddy or a Shanghai Wall Street, but rather some form of compromise between economic growth and political discipline. It would appear, however, that market forces have gained the upper hand, and will play an increasingly prominent role not only in economic transactions but also in the commercialization of politics and even culture. Available indicators suggest a race in many of these countries between enthusiastic, even reckless, marketization on the one hand, and élite efforts to buttress culturally appropriate and effective market regulatory institutions on the other.

Notes

1   The rise of several East Asian economies, notably the "four small dragons" (Hong Kong, Singapore, South Korea, and Taiwan), to income levels of a developed country and the rapid growth rates in China are cited hopefully as examples. Such convergence in incomes may eventually occur, but the overall recent trend has been more toward polarization than convergence. Whereas in 1965, 52 of 108 developing countries had per capita incomes 20 per cent or less than that of the rich countries, in 1995 the corresponding proportion was 88 of 108 (Auguste 1998).
2   Neither the 1929 nor the 1987 stock market crash had an obvious precipitating event (in contrast to the sharp market declines in the fall of 1973 and 1980, which were caused by OPEC's announcement of its oil embargo and the fall from power of the Shah of Iran, respectively). Similarly, the 1992 crisis in the European exchange rate mechanism and the recent Mexican crisis did not have clear triggers.
3   For example, see Malaysian Prime Minister Mahathir Mohamad's jeremiad: "Asian countries will prosper again but not as Asian countries. Their economies would be dominated and run by the huge foreign corporations, practically all owned and managed by non-Asians. Southeast Asia will provide a base for the production of low-cost products to compete with those of certain large Asian economies which refused to be controlled. In the end these countries too will give in." As cited in *Straits Times* (Singapore), June 7, 1998.

References

Auguste, Byron C. (1998) "What's So New about Globalization?", *New Perspectives Quarterly*, 15, 1: 16–21.
Frenkel, S. J. and Peetz, D. (1998) "Globalization and Industrial Relations in East Asia," *Industrial Relations*, 37, 3: 282–310.
Garg, R., Kim, S. H. and Swinnerton, E. (1999) "The Asian Financial Crisis of 1997 and its Consequences," *Multinational Business Review*, 7, 2: 32–36.
McNally, D. (1998) "Globalization on Trial," *Monthly Review*, 50, 4: 1–14.
Poon, J. P. H. and Perry, M. (1999) "The Asian Economic 'Flu': A Geography of Crisis?", *Professional Geographer*, 51, 2: 184 ff.
Radelet, S. and Sachs, J. (1998) *The Onset of the East Asian Financial Crisis*, Cambridge: National Bureau of Economic Research, WBER Working Paper No. 6680, internet version.
Weber, S., (2000) "Introduction," in Weber (ed.), *Globalization and European Political Economy*, New York: Colombia University Press.

3 Globalization and democratic governance

The Indian experience

Aswini K. Ray

Postcolonial political economy

Globalization, in the sense of the interweaving linkages of the factors of production, consumption and lifestyle across the territorial boundaries of sovereign states, is at least as old as the global expansion of European civilization through conquests, proselytization, trade, commerce, mass migration, industrial capitalism, and colonialism. All of South America, Australia, and New Zealand are among the various versions of globalization through mass migration; North America, particularly the United States and Canada, are among its most finished versions.

The colonial mode of production structurally linked Europe with Asia. In South Asia, including India, transfer of capital to, and migration of indentured labor, and soldiers, across the global British empire have left their trail of complexities which have long survived, reinforced by the cold war. For example, the unresolved Kashmir dispute between India and Pakistan, and the ethnic conflicts in Sri Lanka as well as in most other countries of South Asia, are historically rooted in the distortions of the colonial process of globalization and the cold war, still surviving beyond its end in Europe. That may explain why what is often claimed in the Western hemisphere as the "end of history" has little resonance in much of the third world.

Admittedly, the end of the cold war—rather than the collapse of the Soviet Union—eliminated the most organized military, economic and ideological challenge to the unfettered expansion of postwar globalization of the United States' "power élite" through the world capitalist market. This reality, along with the quantum leap in technology and communications, has brought the spatial limits of the entire universe within this homogenized version of globalization through the world market, with one hegemonic power now also encompassing the cultural domain. This is historically unique. So that, historically, while the process of globalization is not a new phenomenon, what is new in the postcold war era is its pace and scale, range and sweep; also, its techniques of enforcing the rules of the game.

This is important, because while globalization has always been within the terms and conditions of the dominant player laying down the rules of the game, the absence of any single hegemonic power provided enough space for diversity in the overarching process of globalization in the earlier phases. For example, within the colonial phase of globalization, the British, French, Dutch, Portuguese, Spanish versions, or the American version of globalization of the "Banana Republics," the Japanese colonial globalization in East Asia, or the globalization of Central Asia and Eastern Europe under Soviet domination all were significantly different in terms of the techniques and instruments of dominance and impact. But in the postcold war era, the existence of a single hegemonic power has meant its impact is of a globally homogenizing type. Obviously, this version of globalization has asymmetrical levels of impact and resistance in different societies, varying with levels of asymmetry with the hegemonic power. This may explain partially the abiding resistance against globalization in its many historical versions in societies with long continuous civilizations, for example India. But Europe, more familiar with its own globalization in the colonial era, and with the hegemonic power in the period after the cold war, is more receptive to the new rules of globalization than countries like India and China, the historical targets of the process.

For India, by the time the postcolonial sovereign state emerged at the cost of partition of the Subcontinent, the overarching cold war process of globalization through military alliances was vying for space in South Asia. The objective priorities of India's postcolonial nation-building agenda were at sharp variance with the goals, instruments and techniques of the process. For example, the distortions on India's political economy of two centuries of the colonial mode of production had to be corrected, along with economic development (Thorner 1982). These distortions were at various tiers, political, economic and sociological (Bagchi 1982; Bardhan 1986).

In politics, the colonial political economy spawned multiple tiers of duality. First, between the relatively developed state apparatus created by a modern industrial power like the British colonial government, and the predominantly traditional, deeply segmented, indigenous, civil society. Second, within the state apparatus, between its relatively developed coercive component compared with the democratic instruments of conflict resolution. Political democracy in the absence of a civil society, linking these dualities through universal adult suffrage, from its inception spawned a range of problems in sharp variance with the historical trajectory of Western liberal democracies. In fact, many of these variations distinguished the structural attributes of "postcolonial democracies" like India from Western liberal democracies despite their comparable formal institutions of governance.[1]

Third, since the colonial liberation struggle was concerned with the right to self-determination of nations as communities, the social base of democratic consciousness around the rights of citizens as individuals was relatively limited in most such "postcolonial democracies." Fourth, in the specific case of India, the democratic state emerged in the midst of a massive communal upsurge within civil society (the result of partition and mass migration on communal lines), and an adversarial relationship with neighboring, theocratic, Pakistan, soon under military dictatorship, underwritten by the cold war era's dominant economic and military power.

In the sphere of economics, along with underdevelopment there was the more daunting problem of distorted development during the colonial era: the duality between the relatively small modern sector linked with international trade—predominantly, plantations, minerals, low-technology consumer products and services, overwhelmingly owned and/or catering to the needs of colonial rulers—and the large agrarian sector with its primitive tenurial, technological and managerial structure (Bagchi 1975). Also a problem was the wide-ranging regional diversity between the coastal areas and around port towns, and the vast hinterland of landmass and population still derisively referred to as India's "cow-belt." The existence of an urban–rural sociological disparity (Gupta 1991) between the metropolitan centers, hill stations and cantonments, and the rest of the country, a contradiction referred to by some modernized peasant leaders as the "India versus Bharat" syndrome (Joshi 1989). Many of these sociological disparities encompassed almost all components of the contemporary indices of human development, such as literacy, income, life expectancy, health care, environment and human rights, with long-term impact on democratic governance in the postcolonial era.

There were also the historical "untouchables" within the caste structure of India's predominantly Hindu population, now called the *Dalits* (oppressed) (Gupta 1984, 2000); the tribals, now called *Adivasis* (original inhabitants), and the *Vanavasis* (forest dwellers); the disparate diversity of ascriptive identities, such as religion, language, caste, ethnicity, part of the inheritance of a long and continuous history. The developmental complexities of such wide-ranging diversities continue to have considerable salience for modern India's democratic governance, more so in the present phase of globalization.

The developmental imperatives of India's postcolonial state were shaped by the mass struggle for national liberation. Consequently, the economic development agenda under universal adult franchise had a built-in bias in favor of the social transformation of the overwhelming majority of the rural people, as well as the traditionally deprived and the socially oppressed, irrespective of its impact on the overall rate of growth (Desai 1948). These goals were to be pursued within the secular, democratic institutions of governance, a structural imperative of nation-building given India's demographic diversity. These and the institutions of nation-building constituted the core concern of India's national security, alongside external threat.

But such goals were also at sharp variance with the aims and priorities of postwar reconstruction of Europe, Japan and the United States, the dominant players of the global market in the postwar era. It was the United States that spawned the "realist paradigm" of national security, with its emphasis on military deterrence against an identified external threat. Whilst this version of national security conformed to the structural imperatives of postwar reconstruction of the industrial societies of Western democracies, it did not tally with those of postcolonial democracies such as India (Ray 1989, 1996). The contradictions manifested themselves in many ways within India's developmental politics, including through its foreign policy of nonalignment.

India's emphasis on economic development through "self-reliance" and substitution through foreign imports, in sharp contrast with the export-led growth strategy advocated for the third world by Western developmental agencies, was another important manifestation of this structural contradiction. In fact, this contradiction, and its reciprocal operational responses, constitutes the core area of India's postcolonial developmental politics. At the macro level this history underscores, on the one hand, India's assertion of national sovereignty in order to pursue its indigenous developmental priorities, based on self-reliance; and on the other hand, pressure from Western agencies—both direct and indirect—to globalize and pursue a policy of export-led growth, as imposed on other military allies across the world, including nearby Pakistan. In this historical contest of unequals within the world capitalist market, between nonaligned India and the advanced industrial democracies, the resilience of India's secular democratic instruments of governance has proven to be the major political dividing line.

All this took place during the cold war era of the "military-bureaucratic élite" as the main vehicle of "third world modernization" through military alliances and export-led growth, as envisaged by Western funding agencies.[2] And this is what makes the Indian case so distinctive: from the inception of its republican era, India has generally conformed with the institutional imperatives of democratic governance, including universal adult franchise, but not with the Western strategy of "third world modernization". The Western plea for "interdependence" has had small appeal in India's political culture of resurgent postcolonial nationalism, which perceived them instead as imposing "dependence." In this confrontation, empirically, there has been a direct positive correlation between India's ability to resist Western pressures—and allurements—to globalize, and the relative strength of its democratic institutions of governance. Weak political leadership, and dented democratic institutions of governance, have generally been more vulnerable to such external pressures, and vice versa. This trend can be seen clearly throughout the entire phase of India's planned developmental politics, from its beginnings in the early 1950s until the 1991 move toward economic liberalization and structural adjustment to promote globalization. The historical balance sheet shows India reinforcing the structural underpinnings of democratic governance. Paradoxically, this move also spawned space for the more strident phase of globalization of India's political economy in more recent times. The trajectory of this balance sheet is important for any future projection about the impact of globalization on democratic governance in India.

Goal of "self-reliance" in the cold war era

Historically, the second five-year Plan launched in 1956 spelled out the basic goals and priorities of India's postcolonial nation-building agenda (Roy 1965). It envisaged a public sector dominating the "commanding heights of the economy," consisting of "heavy, key and basic industries;" carrying forward the infrastructural reforms of the colonial political economy in both agriculture and industry; a concerted program to create a reservoir of skilled technical personnel as human resource; and strict import control and foreign exchange restrictions geared toward industrial development and food self-sufficiency. Difficult to enforce within the democratic structure, unlike in China, India aimed, like China, at promoting long-term "self-reliant growth" of the economy, in defense of national security and territorial integrity. But also unlike China, India's pursuit of development-led national security was at the cost of military build-up.

Initially, the postwar Western alliance led by the United States opposed the goals and priorities of the Plan. The president of the World Bank called it "unrealistic and over-ambitious," and pleaded for a strategy of export-led growth, while the United States refused any aid to the public sector (Roy 1965). The Indian prime minister only had to "leak" the contents of the Bank president's letter for an outraged Indian public opinion to rally against such "Western interference" in postcolonial India's domestic policy and immediately endorse the Plan priorities. In 1957, a serious foreign exchange crisis sparked off another round of similar Bank initiatives and Indian response (Kurien 1966). The second general election in India in 1957 was also a referendum of the second Plan, and the over-whelming electoral verdict in favor of the Congress Party, its author, was a democratic endorsement of the party's goal of "self-reliant growth." The triumph of democratic governance was highlighted with the first military coup in neighboring Pakistan in 1958, which aborted India's historic adversary's first visualized general elections. America's endorsement of the coup, and its diplomatic, military and economic support of Pakistan's "military-bureaucratic clique," coupled with general Western support for Pakistan's case in the Kashmir dispute, undermined the credibility in India of the Western alliance and its advocated strategy of development. In 1958, the Western alliance constituted the "Aid India consortium", under World Bank sponsorship, to "coordinate" its aid strategy for India, largely along the lines previously visualized. However, from inception such strategies (and the institutions promoting them) were perceived in India as complementary to the pursuit of the "global military containment" of communism. In a context of resurgent postcolonial nationalism, such efforts constituted an attempt by the West to introduce "imperialism through the backdoor."[3]

The Sino-Indian border war of 1962 provided the first opportunity for the Western alliance to undermine the Nehruvian concept of "national security" with a substantial increase in India's defense budget at the cost of its economic development on planned lines. The Fund Bank and its Western alliance partners provided massive aid to ensure this shift in Indian policy on national security toward the "realist paradigm." This immediately helped improve the image of the West in India, but soon the Soviet Union, for its own cold war reasons, outdid the West in bolstering India's defense build-up. This process fueled the arms race in South Asia between India and Pakistan, ultimately leading to their mutual nuclear deterrence capabilities in 1998. Nonetheless, throughout the 1960s, and despite considerable modifications in defense allocations, Nehru's death (1964) and another two rounds of the Indo-Pakistan war (1964 and 1965), India's macro-level Plan priorities remained unchanged. In fact, as a consequence, the goal of "self-reliance" was extended to the sphere of defense production.

The Fund Bank and the Western alliance continued to pressurize India along the same lines at all crisis points: for example, immediately after Nehru's death, and in the aftermath of the wars against Pakistan which resulted in a balance-of-payments problem (see Roy 1965; Kurien 1966). But the domestic political consensus, and Soviet support for Plan priorities, provided the political and economic underpinnings in defense of India's indigenous developmental goal of "self-reliant growth," and its vision of relative autonomy from the hazards of an inequitable global economic order dominated by the leaders of the world capitalist market, including the former colonial powers.

In 1966, and for the first time, Fund Bank pressure paid dividends when one of the periodic foreign exchange crises coincided with a major political battle for succession for the post of India's prime minister. The ruling Congress Party controlled by a "syndicate" of regional bosses was reluctant to endorse the candidature of the politically powerful Morarji; instead they supported a politically weak Indira Gandhi who announced the devaluation of the Indian currency to promote exports as her first policy step.

The consequent popular resentment against this "capitulation" to perceived Western pressures led the new prime minister to jettison her finance minister as scapegoat. She also quickly rid herself of the "syndicate," split the Congress Party, and established her authority over India's democratic politics, which, in the prevalent political culture, involved a dose of populist nationalism (the rhetoric of "anti-imperialism," and "threat" of "foreign hands"). She even defied the United States by intervening militarily in the disintegration of Pakistan, an American ally, and helping in the creation of Bangladesh after the war of 1971. The Western realist paradigm of national security had spawned its Frankenstein in the person of the new Indian prime minister; but this was a monster whose charismatic appeal contributed also to the stability of India's political democracy.

In the sphere of nuclear weapons, the Western model had to await its ultimate denouement until 1998, with successive explosions in India and Pakistan taking place against a backdrop of strident economic globalization. Ironically, by this point Western development strategy for the third world had dramatically transformed from its "national security"-based "realism" to the neo-realist neo-liberalism emphasizing human development, human rights, and human security alongside democracy.

By 1974, the emergence of dynastic "extra-constitutional authority" in the ruling Congress Party and the government had undermined the autonomy of most democratic institutions of governance. In 1975 the formal declaration of a "national emergency" put a moratorium on the functioning of political democracy. With the press censored, opposition leaders arrested, and freedom of speech denied, the economic policy of the Emergency regime shifted to boost exports, liberalize imports, and encourage foreign investments, without any formal change of earlier policy (Selbourne 1977). The Western powers and the Fund Bank turned a blind eye to India's Emergency regime, as did the Soviet Union, both for reasons of global power politics. Unsurprisingly therefore, successive Indian regimes have operationally conformed to the compulsions of the post-Emergency political economy by providing greater incentives to export, import liberalization, and foreign investment, all sharply at variance with earlier policy based on national consensus; none of the regimes have instituted a formal change of policy.

There have been some token gestures of defiance against the West. For example, the faction-ridden coalition government, after the elections of 1977, sought to reinforce its political legitimacy by periodic symbolic gestures against powerful American MNCs such as IBM and Coca-Cola.

In 1980 Indira Gandhi was back in power after again splitting the ruling Congress Party. This time she openly continued her economic policies of the Emergency era, reinforcing them with a second devaluation of the Indian currency; in foreign economic policy she was more in tandem with Soviet diplomacy. This operational version of "nonalignment" provided a new external scaffolding for the domestic viability of Indian regimes. Her assassination in 1984, unrelated to her economic policies, brought about a wave of sympathy, and contributed to the massive electoral mandate in favor of her son Rajiv Gandhi in the general elections following. His political support base, and coterie, consisted of high-profile corporate technocrats and computer whizz-kids, all committed to the Western version of "third world modernization." This regime, committed to "economic reforms" and "modernization"—as political euphemisms for a total reversal of earlier economic policies—was also the most hyped in the Western media and its political élite. His assassination however paved the way for the beginning of the long era of weak coalition governments, lasting until the present day and threatening political stability. It was also the era of India's formal entry into the process of globalization, in conformity with long-standing Western strategy.

It was one such minority government led by a weak leader that confronted the newly elected Indian parliament with "Hobson's choice" of endorsing a new economic "reform" plan or facing a general election. The members of India's parliament elected in 1991, predictably, ensured against the risk of a general election. Most of the parties in the parliament also ensured that they were politically correct. For example, the erstwhile opponents of economic "reform," particularly the numerically significant parties of the "left," opted to abstain from voting in its favor, rather than voting against it. This governmental strategy ensured parliamentary endorsement for its "reform" package for which, until then, there was no electoral mandate. In fact, no political party had even suggested these "reforms" in their election manifesto.

The "reforms," suggested as "conditionalities" of the Fund Bank, consisted of measures which were a total reversal of earlier economic policies, and ensured conformity with Western "advice," in a situation comparable to the foreign exchange crises affecting balance of payments. Additional pressure was provided by the collapse of the Soviet Union and India's economic crutch. This scenario provided the economic backdrop to the request for an IMF bailout by the Indian government, and the IMF's response outlining conditions for its aid. The package was negotiated by Mammohan Singh, an academic turned economic technocrat of the Indira Gandhi era, but with long formal association with the Fund Bank and its affiliate institutions. He was soon appointed finance minister and portrayed as a future prime minister. His political profile in 1991, when compared with his counterpart's fate during the devaluation of 1966, would be a reasonable indicator of the transformation of India's political economy in the intervening period, and the social base of the new political élite viewing the world as its oyster, in sharp contrast to its counterpart in the aftermath of national liberation.

The political conjuncture of a weak leadership in a minority government was also typical of earlier regimes vulnerable to such Fund Bank "advice." This political scenario, rather than the periodic balance-of-payment difficulties, appears causally more related to the political decision to accept the "conditionalities" involving economic liberalization and structural adjustment to the process of globalization. The subterfuge of "reform" to this project involving a total reversal of existing policies was a conceptual mystification of policies without any democratic mandate and historically suspect. Not only the policy, but all its advocates were either political nondescripts or suffered from weak political legitimacy.

Admittedly, many of the domestic "vehicles" of India's reform package improved their political image later, when the general thrust of the reforms garnered an implicit ex-post-facto consensus among the mainstream political parties. At any rate, the cost of reversal of the reforms was increasing with time. But when the structural adjustment program of economic liberalization was initiated in 1991, neither the policy nor its advocates in India had any significant democratic legitimacy; and the Fund Bank, as the main architect of the "conditionalities," was historically suspect in India's political culture. In this sense the political support base of India's dramatic decision to move toward globalization of its economy has remained inauspicious from its inception, for purpose of democratic governance of the country. Besides, India's economic liberalization began in an era of considerable de-liberalization of its political democracy and atrophy of the postcolonial democratic institutions. In fact, historically, as already described, the very contest for political space within this externally inspired policy of globaliza-tion in India can be dialectically linked with the dent in India's liberal institutions of democratic governance.

Unrelated to the Indian scenario, this phase of global politics also coin-cided with the collapse of the socialist world, and the emergence within the global order of normative concerns like democracy, human rights, gender justice, environment and ecology. These events and concerns have also had their impact on democratic governance after economic globalization, influ-encing the latter's pace, scale, and impact in India.

Impact of economic liberalization

It has been over a decade since the structural reforms for economic liberal-ization were initiated in India's political economy. It is important to assess empirically the economic balance sheet of this phase to enable us to make any political projections about its impact on the future of democratic gover-nance in the country. It is also important to assess this balance sheet in comparative terms, between the earlier phase, when the external pressure for globalization was resisted in India, and the phase of political capitulation to such pressures in 1991. This would enable an assessment of the political viability of the new policy within the democratic process.

India's National Sample Survey (NSS) has recently published data (*The Times* April 10, 2000) which are quite revealing in this context. According to the survey, the reforms have produced unprecedented economic growth. Before the reforms in 1991, the rate of economic growth remained constant at around 3 per cent, which was popularly described as the "Hindu" rate of growth. But by the mid-1990s, GDP growth exceeded 7.5 per cent annually; agricultural growth also remained high; and social indicators like literacy and infant mortality and longevity also improved.

Paradoxically, this high rate of growth, distributed inequitably, has led to an increase in the number of poor people, and also to the widening of the regional disparity of the colonial era. The comparative figures of the period before and after the reforms are more revealing in this context. At the height of the era of controlled economy, rationing, price controls and nationaliza-tion of the 1970s and 1980s, poverty actually declined 2 per cent annually. By contrast, there was hardly any reduction in poverty between 1991 and 1997. The survey conducted in 1997 show that every third person—34.4 per cent of the population—lived in conditions of absolute poverty, the same as in 1990. It also showed that the decline in poverty was marked in the period 1994/95–1997, despite the high GDP growth rate.

NSS data on poverty between 1951 and 1997 is equally useful. This shows that between 1951 and 1955, more than half of all Indians (53 per cent) existed below the poverty line; the situation remained largely unchanged until 1971–1974. But from 1973–1977 to 1986–1987, poverty declined steadily to 38 per cent; and, between 1989–1990 it declined still further to 34.07 per cent. In July 1991, when the reforms were launched, 36.34 per cent of Indians were poor, and at the end of 1997, 34.4 per cent were still poor, the same as in 1990, shortly before the reforms. These figures do not provide a particularly inspiring argument to sustain or widen the political will in favor of the reforms in a political democracy with universal adult suffrage.

Another "thin" survey with a smaller sample carried out by the NSS in 1998 (*The Times* April 20, 2000) reveals the contrast between the period before and after the reforms more sharply. In fact, it suggests that the number of people existing below the poverty line has actually increased to approximately 40 per cent. Along with "anecdotal evidence" of "immiseration" in some regions of the country, it underscores the plight among the relatively poorer sections of landless laborers in rural areas, who are also inequitably adversely affected by inflation and rising food prices.

An economic commentator[4] (*The Times* April 30, 2000) highlights the wide-ranging variations in the impact of economic reforms in India. While the industrially more advanced states like Gujerat, Maharashtra and Tamilnadu have prospered, the relatively poorer states like Bihar and Uttar Pradesh—with their very high electoral strength—have suffered declining economic growth and greater poverty since the reforms. The two poorer states account for a quarter of the country's total population and over one-third of the country's poor.

The same survey also reveals that poverty trends in the five traditionally poorer states of Bihar, Uttar Pradesh, Orissa, Rajasthan and Madhya Pradesh worsened after 1990. More interestingly, Bihar and Uttar Pradesh had grown much faster in the 1980s, before the reforms, and actually experienced reduced poverty.

The per capita income growth in these five states (NSS, World Bank, TOI; *Times* 30 April 2000, quoting World Bank and NSS) in the period between 1981–1991 and 1992–1997 show similar trends. In Uttar Pradesh, it declined from 2.6 per cent to 0.7 per cent; in Rajasthan from 4.7 per cent to 2.9 per cent. Even in some of the relatively more prosperous states it declined: for exmple, in Punjab growth declined from 3.3 per cent to 2.8 per cent; in Haryana, from 3.9 per cent to 2.6 per cent. Meanwhile the prosperous states of Maharashtra, Gujerat and Tamilnadu boomed, along with Karnataka, Andhra Pradesh, West Bengal and Orissa.

This uninspiring economic reality has to be viewed in the context of the pressures of the "conditionalities" of reform on fiscal policies, such as budget deficit, subsidies for the welfare of the vulnerable sections, poverty alleviation, the social sector, defense needs, etc. For example, the Union Budget for 2000 seeks to reduce subsidies for energy, transport, communication, education, the public distribution system and agricultural inputs, and also to accelerate the reduction of existing investments in the public sector. At least in the short term, the incidence of hardship under such policies is inequitably harsh on the relatively poor and the deprived. While the politically organized working class, rich farmers and the urban middle class, with their larger operational leverage within the democratic institutions, are able to pressurize for "safety nets," the vast mass of unorganized rural and urban poor are at greater risk. This generally tends to undermine the cumulative political will in favor of reforms within a democratic system based on universal adult suffrage. There are winners and losers, with sharp cleavages between the two.

The patent regime of the WTO, one of the principal institutional agencies of the globalized international order, has also attracted adverse political attention in India by allowing traditional Indian food, spices, and medicines such as *Neem*, *Haldi* and *Basmati* rice to be patented by enterprising foreigners, thereby stoking the fading embers of India's postcolonial nationalism. This pro-nationalist movement has been reinforced by the inequitable global information order enabling an inundation of Western pop culture through films, satellite TV channels and other mass media, along with the brand-named jeans and fast foods. The numbers of disaffected, drawn from India's traditional society in opposition to globalization, are significantly large within the political democracy to be managed by its party system and atrophying postcolonial democratic instruments of conflict resolution. There are reports of suicides by retrenched workers of disinvested public-sector enterprises and municipal corporations denied welfare subsidies. There are also reports of the suicides of farmers unable to bear the failure of cotton crops in farms employing expensive genetically engineered seeds of American multinationals. Such events have not helped to make new converts to globalization in India's political democracy, which is faced with a quantum leap in the level of social and political violence, even before economic liberalization, which has merely stoked them further.

With the decline of the Congress Party, which spearheaded the national liberation, and the waning ideological appeal of communism, political parties are moving increasingly toward regionalism, based on one or another of India's myriad ascriptive social identities. Attempts by the BJP, the single largest party in the present parliament, to provide a national alternative to the Congress Party through a homogenized version of Hindu nationalist ideology have, predictably, floundered. India's democratic diversity—even within its macro-level Hindu majority—of language, caste, tribe ethnicity, and spatial location is simply too disparate for any single ascriptive identity to represent it. Even the ideological appeal of communism in India has been regionally specific.

Consequently, coalition governments consisting of political parties representing regional and sectional interests have become the rule, rather than the exception, and are likely to be so in the foreseeable future. The economic impact of the process of globalization, by widening the regional and sectional disparity is, on the one hand, reinforcing the structural imperative toward coalition governments and, on the other hand, making them difficult to manage. The fiscal incentives, and disincentives—"conditionalities" of globalization—inequitably affect the different constituents of India's system of universal adult franchise. For example, withdrawal of subsidies for the public distribution system, or for fuel used by the poor, and for transport or agricultural inputs are affecting food prices; similarly, withdrawal of subsidies from education affect the middle-class youth. Tax incentives to boost exports and the stock market also affect existing regional and sectoral disparity, making the complexity difficult to manage through coalition governments within a democratic system with weak institutions of conflict resolution.

The Congress Party which, as the minority leader of the erstwhile coalition, initiated the process of globalization, is already under internal pressure to be less enthusiastic about some of the fiscal imperatives of the globalization process and its "conditionalities." The BJP, the present leader of the new coalition government implementing the reforms, is faced with similar contradictions. The present finance minister of the ruling coalition government has done his bit of tightrope-walking under such compulsions: first announcing strict fiscal constraints, then rolling some of them back as democratic concessions to public demands. But there are severe limits to such gamesmanship, particularly with regard to the ever-increasing allocation to the defense sector, a result of relations with Pakistan. This part of the "conditionalities" of the reform process toward globalization is likely to remain unfulfilled within India's democratic structure, at least for the foreseeable future. Even on other problems, exacerbated by the existing impact of globalization and its fiscal pressures, four former prime ministers before the era of reforms have already joined hands, along with parties of the left, to provide a "third front," envisaging a slower and more cautious pace of globalization, allowing for allocations for poverty alleviation, social welfare for the weaker sections, safety nets for redundant workers and deceleration of public-sector disinvestment, subsidized public distribution systems for the urban poor, etc. An all-India strike of Bank and other public-sector employees was held on March 11, 2000, many more such strikes have been threatened. The political culture of the era of the planned welfare state of the pre-globalized period is reasserting itself off the backlash of the immediate effects of the reform.

There are also institutional constraints against a faster pace of globalization. The colonial legal system and its civil and criminal code are already overextended in dealing with the increasing level of social and political violence. The proliferation of new instruments, and laws, for coercive resolution of such conflicts by the state is creating problems: economic costs are creating fiscal pressure on the budget; the state's actions are resented by domestic civil rights groups with global networks, thereby attracting attention from funding agencies who are under democratic pressure at home.

In the upper-class urban areas, elderly relatives at home, deserted by the younger, skilled, professionals attracted by globalized employment opportunities, are increasingly becoming the victims of crimes by the vast army of the local urban unemployed. In rural areas, remittance economies are creating new spheres of social tensions. Global human rights consciousness around bonded and child labor, gender equality, and environment are also creating new problems, paradoxically in the exporting industries, the principal beneficiaries of the globalization process, which are now faced with concerns of "business ethics" and "social audit." The institutions of democracy, including the machinery of law and order, are inadequately equipped to respond to the new challenge and are under pressure.

While funding agencies attribute the problems, causally, not to the reforms per se but to their inadequacy, thereby urging faster and more reforms, the domestic political will to accelerate its pace and scale remains weak, as yet at least. But even the present level of globalization, alongside its losers, has also created new winners, who are among the strong political pillars of the ongoing process of globalization. Those associated with computer software, telecommunications, food-processing industries and the burgeoning service sector, though still numerically marginal, remain the political vested interest for the ongoing process of globalization. However slow, faltering, or reluctant, the process of reversal has already become quite expensive. In fact, all political parties, implicitly at least, acknowledge this. And this is the basis of the ex-post-facto political consensus around the general thrust of globalization.

In the specific historical reality of the Indian experience as discussed here, any reckless increase in the pace of globalization has endemic risks for democratic governance, which is dialectically linked with the national security and territorial integrity of the country.

Notes

1 See "Towards the Concept of a Post-Colonial Democracy" (1989).
2 A case study of Pakistan has been made in Ray (1975).
3 Both Ajit Roy (1965) and K. Mathew Kurien (1966) provide empirical details of the developmental politics in the era.
4 *Swaminomics* is the by-line of Swaminathan A. Iyer.

References

Bagchi, A. (1982) *Political Economy of Underdevelopment*, Cambridge: Cambridge University Press.

Bagchi, A. K. (1975) *Private Investment in India 1900–1939*, New Delhi: Orient Longmans.

Bardhan, P. K. (1986) *Political Economy of Development*, New Delhi: Oxford University Press.

Desai, A.R. (1948) *Social Background of Indian Nationalism*, Bombay: Popular Prakashan.

Gupta, D. (1984) "Continuous Hierarchies and Discrete Castes," *Economic and Political Weekly*, November 17 and December 1.

—— (1991) "Country–Town Nexus," in K. L. Sharma and D. Gupta (eds.), *Studies in Social Transformation in Contemporary India*, Jaipur: Rawat Publications.

—— (2000) *Interrogating Caste*, London: Penguin.

Joshi, S. (1989) *Bharat Speaks Out*, Build Documentation Centre, Bombay, Occasional Paper No. 3.

Kurien, K. M. (1966) *Impact of Foreign Capital on Indian Economy*, New Delhi: Manas.

Ray, A. K. (1975) *Domestic Compulsions and Foreign Policy*, New Delhi: Manas.

—— (1989) "Insecurity and Instability in the Third World: A Critique of Western Perspective," in J. Bandyopadhaya, A. K. Banerjee, Basu and A. D. Mukherjee (eds), *Dimensions of Strategy, Some Indian Perspectives*, Calcutta: Jadavpur University.

—— (1996) *The Global System in a Historical Perspective: A View From the Periphery*, Institute of Developing Economies, Tokyo, VRS Monograph Series No. 272.

Roy, A. (1965) *Planning in India: Achievements and Problems*, Calcutta: Jadavpur University.

Selbourne, D. (1977) *An Eye to India*, London: Penguin.

Thorner, A. (1982) "Semi-feudalism and Capitalism? Contemporary Debate on Classes and Modes of Production in India", *Economic and Political Weekly*.

"Towards the Concept of a Post-Colonial Democracy" (1989) in Z. Hasan, S. N. Jha and R. Khan (eds.) *The State, Political Processes and Identity*, New Delhi: Sage Publications.

The Times of India, New Delhi, April 10, 20 and 30, 2000.

Part III

Globalization, democracy and civil society

The three "Ts"—Transitional, Transformational and Transnational democracy in Asia

4   On alien Western democracy

Edward Friedman

> still less do we want that Western-style stuff ... multiparty elections....
>
> (Deng Xiaoping)

What is "Western" democracy? What is at stake when a political system, democratic or Leninist, is found to be non-indigenous, other, alien?

Essentializing the West

One standard answer to the question "What is 'Western' democracy?" is to reject the question, to insist that there is no such thing as "Western" democracy. After all, democracy is but a set of political institutions. Just as any political system—divine monarchy, military tyranny, Leninist Party dictatorship—democracy too can develop in any and every region of the earth. Indeed it has.

If the fledgling democracy in Indonesia institutionalizes, then three of the four most populous democracies in the planet—India, Indonesia and Japan—will be Asian. When a democracy movement spread through China in 1989, its participants were aware that democracy was sweeping Asia, first the Philippines, then South Korea, and most recently the Republic of China on Taiwan. And Mongolia soon followed.

Some people, however, contend that a democratic polity rests on a very peculiar democratic culture. Data proves such people are wrong. Authoritarian cultures of course flourish in authoritarian polities. Democracy must first rise within an authoritarian culture. Democracy has won out in all cultures despite that obstacle. Studies indicate not that a democratic people creates a democratic political system, but that living a democratic politics engenders democratic consciousness, shaping citizens with democratic attitudes. Living in a democratic polity can strengthen elements of democratic culture. That democracies tend to have democratic cultures is a consequence of democratization, not a cause.

The notion that democracy is a peculiar Protestant Europe cultural product is belied by the strength of democracy all over Asia. Typical of the viewpoint stigmatizing China as culturally anti-democratic is the important book *China Wakes* by otherwise insightful *New York Times* reporters Cheryl

WuDunn and Nicholas Kristof. They imagine a deep Western cultural discourse uniquely suited to democracy.

> In the West, we have the tradition of Antigone, of the righteous person who is obstinate and unreasonable and ultimately pursues justice until enveloped by disaster.... The Chinese, by contrast, appear to be more sympathetic to unprincipled reasonableness.
>
> (Kristof and WuDunn 1994: 262)

These intelligent journalists argue for an essential difference between East and West without investigating the issue. East–West polar binaries have been put forth in diverse ways for centuries. A look at the startling mutations of these binaries shows that little is fixed, that much is political. There was a time when East and West were contrasted precisely the reverse of the way claimed by the just-cited reporters.

When a pre-modern Asia confronted European gunboat diplomacy, the Chinese understood the West to be as "barbaric Mongols and Manchus," primordial, fierce and practical, having adopted all the great innovations of China that had once made China the world's technology leader for more than a millennium. In contrast to the opportunistically practical West, Asian civilizations were understood as too spiritual, "unpractical and other worldly" (Duara 1997: 1041), the exact reverse of our reporters' essentialist imaginary of East and West. As with the Chinese, similarly Iranians contrasted an Orient contemplating the true with a worldly materialistic West (Borbujerdi 1996: 64).

To many nineteenth century Chinese worried about China's decline from great power predominance, the expanding West looked like the expansive China of Han and Tang, like the Ming emperors Hungwu and Yongle, like an open China which had once marched south, opened land and moved in settlers (Duara 1997: 104, 105). The West was doing as the East had long done.

No serious historian should invoke a discourse that treats the East as one, unchangeable unprogressive cultural category, as did the above-quoted American reporters. Japanese-born Masao Miyoshi dismisses as racist those who propound essentialist binaries that deny the East a democratic potential, who "claim that the ancient Greek and modern European languages are the only languages capable of rational discourse and democracy" (Friedman 1994: 15). One should not forget that the influential eighteenth-century *philosophe* Rousseau despised democratic Athens and embraced militaristic Sparta, that Rousseau's discourse with its intolerance for pluralism helped spawn the Robespierre–Lenin project which legitimated single-party dictatorship as true democracy in China and East Germany, in Czechoslovakia and Cuba. The West is neither single-stranded nor uniquely democratic.

However, Professor Miyoshi overlooked how the dismissal by some Europeans of others as culturally unsuited to democracy began within Europe. It was an intra-European chauvinism. European Protestants found

European Catholics culturally hierarchical and authoritarian, and therefore incapable of democracy. Some Anglo-Americans still touted the democratic virtues of Anglo-Saxon Protestantism in the 1990s, making invisible the tragedy of Irish Catholics in Protestant Britain, the long history of Protestant KKK racism in America, and the power of Dutch Protestantism in South Africa in legitimating the racist tyranny of apartheid. By the early twenty-first century democracy flourished in Catholic countries from the Philippines through Spain to Argentina.

Still, cultural arguments are often psychologically appealing even when they are devoid of merit. Reason never defeated the prejudice about Catholic culture. Appeals to stereotypes appear as palpable truth, beyond argument to holders of such views.

French anti-democrats of the nineteenth century loved the argument that democracy required a Protestant culture. That bias allowed French Catholic authoritarians to find that democracy was alien, unsuited for moral people such as, French Catholics insisted, the French Catholics. By 1870 even many French democrats believed that democracy required an individualistic culture of sacred consciences as supposedly existed only in Protestant Europe. How else can one explain the failure of the French to establish constitutional republics in 1789, 1830 and 1848? The great French historian of a failed French quest for freedom, Michelet, bemoaned France's supposedly deeply structured failure, treating a correlation as a cause, blaming France's bureaucratic despotism on land-locked continentalism. He concluded, "The Ocean is English. It makes me sad to think that this sublime field of liberty belongs to another nation" (Friedman 1994: 13). While globalized commercialization may facilitate republicanism (Moore 1966), the French tended to believe that France inherently could not be democratic, believed it, that is, until *after* France democratized. Therefore, phenomonologically, it may not be easy to persuade the Chinese in an authoritarian polity of their democratic potential, that is, until after China has a democratic breakthrough.

Not essentializing the East

Cultural arguments about democracy as alien appeal to biases that seem facts. Only after change gives the lie to the prejudice does the prejudice weaken. Entering the twenty-first century, Muslims in a democratizing Indonesia increasingly imagine their religious culture as deeply democratic. But only after Indonesia opened itself to a democratic politics.

Entering the twenty-first century, ever more Chinese have been persuaded that human rights is an alien discourse. Politically conscious villagers have been persuaded that human rights is an excuse for anti-Chinese interventions by Americans and have persuaded themselves that, whereas Western culture may embrace abstract rights, Chinese culture is rooted in human feelings and relations. Authoritarian China is morally superior. On their college campuses, Chinese students tend to keep away from foreign students, experiencing the foreigners as alien, virtually incomprehensible. Yet this does not stop Chinese villagers from organizing and demonstrating for fair treatment, understood as institutionalizing a politics where they have a political voice and leaders can be rendered accountable. Culture is not determinative of democratic advancement.

Thomas Jefferson's supporters in early nineteenth-century America never believed that democracy was a seed that sprouted only in English and Dutch Protestant soil. Jefferson's political support base included discriminated-against Irish Catholics and dissenting Protestant sects that suffered at the hands of Protestant establishment bigots from Massachusetts to Virginia. Many Jeffersonians were descendants of families that had fled from Protestant England to escape its undemocratic religious discrimination and persecution in the mid-seventeenth century. When the Jeffersonians looked for a people truly tolerant on religious freedom, they found one democratic culture worth emulating—the Hindus. India, they noted, historically has been more open and pluralist (Friedman 1999b: 348).

Of course India, as any other site, also is replete with intolerant tendencies. While there is, as Rajmohan Gandhi points out, a cultural stream going at least as far back as Guatama Buddha and running through the emperor Asoka, "the Bhakti poets; the Sufi saints; the Mogul ruler Akbar; the Sikh guru Nanoki; and, of course, Mahatma Gandhi," which lends itself to reconciliation, there are also in India, as everywhere, cultural strands which are vengeful (Shah 2000). Political struggle decides whether the victor is a pluralist secularist such as Nehru or a Hindu revivalist such as the BJP.

In the Indian subcontinent in the sixteenth century Hindus saw Europeans as intolerant, repressive, and authoritarian. This was the age of Torquemada and the Inquisition, when savage Europeans burned witches and fought barbarous religious wars. The West too contains contradictory tendencies, both democratic and anti-democratic forces. Each site's history is fraught with contested possibilities.

With Ireland now a member of the EU, it is easy to imagine a deeply shared Western culture and to forget that it was not so long ago that English Protestants considered Irish Catholics subhuman savages and slaughtered them. Harvard University long excluded Irish. Mid-nineteenth century English racist anthropology considered Africans as subhuman and Irish as sub-African. Eastern and Western cultures are not mere categories of an analytical social science. Homogenizing East or West does a disservice to the complexity of both.

Imagining a nondemocratic Chineseness

Modern Chinese at the turn into the twenty-first century, in debating how to envision their past, are, as all peoples, inventing tradition, a term imported into China only in the late nineteenth century. Chinese who imagine China as inherently authoritarian tend to see a 5,000-year history of pure blood decent from a mythical Yellow Emperor and a Xia dynasty. In contrast, Chinese democrats tend to find Chinese glory in openness, exchange via the Silk Road and the South China Sea. The contemporary Chinese writer Yu Jie, translated on a Web site, notes,

> During the Han and then during the Tang dynasties, China had a position in the world something like America has today. These dynasties also were very open. They enjoyed things from all over the world ... China in the Qing became very closed.... The Chinese locked themselves up like someone with an epidemic disease.

Yu Jie adds,

> Amartya Sen, an Indian is an expert on famine. His research demonstrates that democratic countries with freedom of expression ... avoid [massive] famine....

In contrast, in China, during Mao Zedong's murderous great leap forward, "Thirty million [Chinese] people died. They didn't just die of starvation ... they died from having lost the ability to express themselves." Democracy allows a gored ox to cry out its pain and call attention to its plight. Chinese would benefit from successful democratization.

The Chinese critic Liang Xiaosheng finds that China's Communist Party tries to "make ordinary people feel 'if only we had another good emperor everything would be fine'." Liang mocks the authoritarian prejudice that "China's conditions weren't mature enough for democracy ... [While] Chinese wait ... South Africa is already democratic and Cambodia is heading the same way. And you begin to wonder, is the level of our people that much lower than the people in those countries?" (Lawrence 1999). China's authoritarian apologists sound like Japan's Emperor Hirohito, Japan's "most ... influential political actor" at the end of the second world war, who, in opposing democratization, argued that "the Japanese people's cultural level is still low" (Dower 1999: 22). Such arguments demean a people.

Why not find rather that China's Leninist party dictatorship is alien? China's post-1949 governing system is a result of importing the political institutions of Stalin's Soviet Union. Chinese analysts by 2000 knew that czarist "feudalism and authoritarianism" became the "Stalin model [which] ... fit this kind of traditional political culture" (Lu 2000: 113). Back on September 25, 1930, the great Indian intellectual Rabandranath Tagore, after touring the USSR, informed its Communist Party newspaper that "for the sake of humanity I hope that you may never create a vicious force of violence which will go on weaving an interminable chain of violence and cruelty. Already you have inherited much of this legacy from the [Russian] czarist regime. It is the worst legacy you could possibly have" (Dutton and

Robison 1997: 125). Are Chinese authoritarians suggesting that the glories of Confucian civilization are no different than the shriveled feudal despotism of czarist Russia?

Authoritarian feudal Leninism is palpably foreign. It promotes political loyalists, ignores people with merit, and negates the glorious legacy of the Chinese who invented the merit civil service exam. Which alien political system, Leninism or democracy, is more suited to a globalized economy infused with knowledge-based enterprises?

Confucianism and democracy

It is not easy to counter the pseudo-realists who ridicule earthbound folk who believe humans can fly, that is, until after the Wright brothers actually flew. There is a contest pitting believers in a better future against cynics fixated on an essentialized, one-dimensional interpretation of the limits of the past, reifiers who leave no space for creative human agency, people who fear to see their own people empowered and liberated.

Yet South Korea, the most Confucian society in the world *is* democratic. So are Confucian-infused democratic Japan and Taiwan. The argument that Confucians could not be democrats was virtually hegemonic in these places before they democratized. But Korea, Taiwan and Japan are Buddhist too. They also diversely contain strong elements of Christianity, Taoism, or Shinto. Culture is complex and multi-stranded. As Indian political scientist Ashis Nandy put it, referring to claims that the leaders of little Malaysia and tinier Singapore embodied mammoth Asia's authoritarian essence, "Asian values are not just about Mahatir and Lee Kuan Yew but also the Dalai Lama, Aung San Suu Kyi and Gandhi as well." Each culture contains all the human—and inhuman—possibilities.

Yet numerous analysts invoke the category of Western democracy. But what is it that democratic France, Germany and the United States of America share that distinguishes them from democratic Japan, South Korea and India? "Westerners who assert that Western models should not be applied to the developing world are not ... in solidarity with non-Westerners, but are taking one side in a debate among non-Westerners." " ... democracies ... outside the West ... are based on the principles of ... liberal democracy ... .There is of course 'Asian-style democracy—but the leaders of Singapore and Malaysia, are not actually democrats—they do not subject their rule to the consent of the governed through free and fair elections" (Carothers 1999: 99–100).

Institutions of constitutional freedom can be crafted to suit any culture. What could it mean to say that Taiwan is a *Western* democracy? The island enjoys a Buddhist revival. Taiwanese vote for legislators on the basis of a system invented in the Japanese Taisho era, single nontransferable votes, multi-member districts (SNTV MMD). Executive officials—mayors, county heads and the president—are elected on a first past-the-post basis, as in Britain and the United States. The constitutional structure, a so-called cohabitation system with both president and prime minister is modeled after France, as is South Korea. Taiwan's constitution added reserved seats for descendants of the original Austronesian settlers scattered throughout the island, something not done for indigenous peoples in the West. Taiwan's democracy is both as democratic and Taiwanese as Germany's is German and democratic.

The East versus the West

While the potential for democracy is universal, its practice is idiosyncratic. Every democracy is *sui generis*. If a democracy is not indigenized to fit particularities of culture, history and society, a democracy would never flourish. Fair elections in a nation with America's racial legacy could not be the same as fair elections in China. There is no Western democratic model to export to China.

While the concept of "Western" democracy is incoherent, it is no secret which Asian countries copy the nineteenth-century French authoritarians who dubbed democracy "alien". Stigmatizing democracy as alien is not peculiarly Chinese. German anti-democrats, right into the Hitlerean 1930s, acting as Asian authoritarians subsequently, insisted that democracy was so conflictfully individualistic and atomizing as to be alien to their (non-Western German) culture. Democracy was said to be at odds with the Germans' alleged unique sense of a warm, humane, caring, organic community. The German novelist Thomas Mann claimed in 1914, "Whoever would aspire to transform Germany into a middle-class democracy in the Western-Roman sense and spirit would wish to take away from her all that is best ... to take away ... [what] really makes up her nationality; he would make her dull, shallow, stupid and un-German, and he would therefore be antinationalist who insisted that Germany became a [democratic] nation ... " (Friedman 1999a: 67). After that war, Mann added, "I don't want the trafficking of parliament and parties ... I want impartiality, order, and propriety ... If it is German, then I want it in God's name to be called German" (Heilbrunn 2000: 89).

If French and Germans have denied they are Western, then who is? The East–West binary of authoritarianism versus democracy hides the long history of authoritarianism in the West. Germany, the center of Europe, did not become a democracy for all Germans until the 1990s.

Germany's Weimar democracy was defeated by Germans who rejected what they denounced as Western political culture. Many leading American intellectuals in the 1920s and 1930s accepted the view that Italy and Germany were better off without democracy. The American diplomat George Kennan agreed that "Benevolent despotism had greater possibilities for good" than democracy, even suggesting that America too should travel "along the road ... to the authoritarian state" (Mazower 1998: 27). In fact, if you compare post-Second World War surveys in Germany with those in Japan, more Germans than Japanese still found so-called Western democracy unsuited to their people. Consequently a senior British civil servant concluded in 1952 that "it is unlikely democracy will develop in Germany in the near future" (Mazower 1998: 241). Yet, Samuel Huntington in 1956 predicted that military rule would soon win out in *"samurai" "bushido"* Japan. The Chinese view that "In Germany, Nazism was completely liquidated after World War II, but in Japan the same did not take place with respect to militarism" (Wu 2000: 300) is a myth, the standard misleading privileging of an allegedly uniquely tolerant and democratic West. The "neo-right in Germany is more worrisome than anything that has happened in Japan" (Cumings 1999: 224).

The East–West binary clearly is blinding. Japan's Post-Second World War democratic state has little in common with that of India. Its institutions are most like those of France. Categories of Western or Eastern democracy are vacuous.

In the 1990s fledgling democracies, from South Africa to Russia, borrowed from the electoral innovations of Germany. No one found anything useful in England, once dubbed "the mother of parliaments." Britain and Germany had little in common. Britain was an over-centralized state where the dominant party in the lower house of the legislature appointed the chief executive for regional governments, imposing leaders opposed to the dominant local politics. In contrast, a decentralized federal Germany had its national upper house elected by regional legislatures. There is no homogeneous "Western" democracy to copy. New democracies borrow whatever usefully fits the particular needs of local realities. Democracy, if it is to sink roots and blossom, is never alien.

The enemies of democracy

Asia's great democratic political leaders have skewered Asian authoritarian apologists who talk about democracy as Western. Burma's Nobel Prize winner Aung San Suu Kyi wrote, "There is nothing new in ... governments seeking to justify and perpetuate authoritarian rule by denouncing liberal democratic principles as alien." "Patriotism ... the vital love and care of a people for their land, is debased into a smokescreen of hysteria to hide the injustices of authoritarian rulers who define the interests of the state in terms of their own limited interests" (Aung San Suu Kyi 1991: 167, 174). The description of democracy as Western is the self-serving language of authoritarian rulers.

In pinpointing what blocked democratization elsewhere in Asia, South Korea's president-to-be Kim Dae Jung wrote, "The biggest obstacle is not its [Asia's] cultural heritage but the resistance of authoritarian rulers and their apologists" (1994: 194). Authoritarian apologists in Asia self-interestedly invented the notion of an Asian developmental dictatorship as a good world in contrast to so-called alien Western democracy, chauvinistically and maliciously portrayed as a bearer of social decay and economic decline.

Proper policies and institutions are actually the major determinants of growth. Yet democracy is far more successful than authoritarianism in fostering patience and stability by persuading citizens that pain is being shared fairly in adapting to the imperatives of globalization and economic restructuring. Consequently, a China still needing to complete the painful process of reforming out of Leninist economic trammels should do far better in winning its people's patience and maintaining stable legitimacy were China a democracy. Treating democracy as alien hurts both polity and economy, while distorting history.

Democrats in Asia, such as Aung San Suu Kyi and Kim Dae Jung have pointed out that all cultures are replete with strands that can be woven into a democratic political fabric. Buddhist and Confucian cultures may actually have more of these democratic elements than did Greco-Christian culture.

As the philosopher of freedom Karl Popper and others have pointed out, the Greek progenitors of the Western political tradition, Aristotle and Plato, insisted that some groups had slave natures by birth, an anti-democratic notion that never appears in the works of the progenitors of Confucianism or of the founders of Buddhism. Some scholars in Asian democracies therefore ask if the democratic transitions in Taiwan and South Korea were "relatively smooth," lacking the long, painful difficulties of France and Germany in part because Asian cultures are far more suitable to democracy, lacking the "religious and class conflicts" of Europe (Kim Byung-Kook 1998: 175). Daniel Chirot suggests that the monotheistic cultures of European religions with their jealous gods are more "capable of inspiring massacres and persecutions on a large scale" than other cultures (Chirot 1994: 413) and, as with the Rousseau–Robespierre–Lenin tradition mentioned earlier, the Marxist–Stalinist disaster in China was the bearer of this Western culture.

It is tempting to reverse the East West binary. After all, rights in Europe were for most of European history not protections of freedom but absolute prerogatives of office, from God's total dominion to the feudal lord's right to deflower daughters of serfs. Much of the West's imagining of its past involves great creative forgetting, interpretation, myth making.

Borrowing best practices

Yet I do not want to throw out the concept of "Western" democracy. Rather, I embrace the idea of democracy as Western, but in a way that the tyrants and the apologists for tyrants in France, Germany, Indonesia etc. never did. The point is to understand why Western democracy was not alien to France or Germany or to any people.

As the Jeffersonian defenders of religious freedom in the United States took inspiration from the tolerant practices of Hindus, so each of us should learn from the good in all cultures. Exchange can be enriching. That is why long-distance trade has existed from time immemorial. To close one's doors to learning from others is to make oneself stupid. Not to be open to learning from others is to have to reinvent the wheel, to act as if one small piece of humanity can invent all that is good and important. One reason I enjoy visiting China is that there are so many able people to learn from.

Taiwan rose while Maoist China stagnated because, among other reasons, Taiwan built on the best that American, Japanese and Chinese influences offered, because Taiwan opened to the world and plugged into its best practices, while, in contrast, Mao Zedong hid behind a Great Wall and made the Chinese people miserable and ignorant. To be pure is to be poor.

The rising blood identity in twenty-first century China which presents Chinese as a pure race, not a member of the one human species that emerged from Africa, has ominous foreign policy implications. Chinese chauvinists rage at Taiwanese as traitors for feeling fortunate in benefiting from the good in Japanese culture. Actually China's modern political discourse is also replete with borrowings from Japan, concepts such as police, tradition and socialism. Karaoke, Nintendo, manga (comic strip books) and Japanese fashion are also popular on the Chinese mainland.

My own life is infused with Asian culture, the blessings of the age-old saga of globalization. In preparing to write this chapter, I sat on the veranda of my bungalow in my silk pajamas reading Tang poetry, sipping tea (or was it Java?) out of my good Chinaware while listening on my Sony Walkman to sitar music. All these things—veranda, bungalow, pajamas, silk, tea, Tang poetry, Java, Chinaware, Sony Walkman, sitar music—are Asian creations. Yet I did not feel I had lost my cultural essence, whatever that might be, in availing myself of a minute fraction of the great creations of Asia. Borrowing enriches.

Democracy's Western origins

It is true that the institutions of modern democracy were invented in a few spots in northwest Europe abutting the Atlantic. Why that is so is debated. Some see it as a peace pact of religiously intolerant Christian people whose internecine religious wars were devastating. Democracy is a way to end the war. Democracy pacifies the conflicts of groups, interests and values and offers a prospect of stable, peaceful progress. With crime, violence and instability spreading in China, can that nation afford to reject the democratic institutions of stable, peaceful progress because they originated elsewhere?

Some see democracy not as a peace pact between previously warring groups but as the result of an historical power balance and compromise of fast-rising international commercial groups capable of checking weak authoritarian centers. This was the view cited earlier of the French historian Michelet. In contrast to benighted Europe, prospering Asia, in pre-modern times, lacked prolonged, bloody religious strife and successfully built much stronger, more capable centralized states, as Moore (1966) has detailed. Strong Asian polities were not so easily challenged by commercial groups.

Some historians offer a third approach to democracy's Western origins. They relate the origin of democracy to the expensive early modern military revolution in Europe which so enormously raised the cost of war that rulers surrendered some power and allowed representation in order to obtain the tax revenues required for state survival. Whatever the contingent historical origins, democratic institutions of representation, toleration and procedural balance were, in fact, first crafted in places like Holland and England. As with steam engines or wireless communication, or compass and printing, intelligent people borrow what works better wherever it originates. To be closed to borrowing in our globalized age is to hurt oneself very much.

The price of chauvinism

The United States tends to be somewhat open to importing what works, from the northwest European institutions of political freedom to able people from India to Taiwan, creators who have mastered computer technologies. Half the start-up firms in California's Silicon Valley in the 1990s were begun by people from India. As in Jefferson's time, Asia still enriches America.

To be sure America too is chauvinist. Because of the arrogance of their automobile manufacturers, American car firms refused to learn the superior ways of Japan's Toyota for some twenty years, costing hundreds of thousands of American workers their jobs. Chauvinism is very expensive for any people, East or West.

For a long time, students in Asia have scored far higher than American students on standardized math and science tests. On May 15, 2000 in my morning Madison, Wisconsin daily, a front-page headline announced, "U.S. Teachers Turn to Singapore Texts for Math Lessons" (Dizon 2000). The story described how a math teacher at the Madison County Day School had been using Singaporean texts for the last three years and how superior they were. In like manner, for the last couple of years, educational delegations have been sent from Japan and Singapore to look at American schools to learn how to better succeed at encouraging the creativity of their students, an imperative in an age where knowledge and innovation drive an economy. Exchange is mutually beneficial. .

People who are afraid of openness, learning and the creativity of others wound themselves. A joke circulated to that effect in 2000 among democrats in China about how chauvinistic Chinese are learning the wrong lessons, inventing a self-wounding tradition for rejecting democracy and human rights, preferring nativism to breaking down barriers to a better world. This semi-humorous tale is about a chap named Ah Q, a character invented by the early twentieth-century Chinese writer Lu Hsun. Ah Q is an anti-hero who misreads happy meanings into deadly events.

One day Ah Q goes from his humiliating daily life in a repressive state toward a beautiful green park promising a better world. At the park entrance is a racist sign, "No dogs or Chinese allowed." Instead of hating the barrier and insisting on entrance into the better world of the verdant park, Ah Q proclaims, "Good! I am best off never entering the park."

Had Ah Q raised his eyes, he would have found the park named "Human Rights Park." But Ah Q never lifts his eyes to see what he is missing. His shriveled identity precludes liberating human possibilities.

Interpreting patriotism

Clashes over national identity are a constant challenge. The experience of post-Second World War Japan can be taken as paradigmatic. On the one hand, very conservative forces controlled the Ministry of Education and wanted students taught history so as to inculcate pride in the nation's past achievements. Telling the story of one's nation in a most positive way slighted Japan's brutal aggression in Asia. Euphemisms were invented to obscure Japan's colonial conquest and cruel exploitation of Korea and to minimize Japan's long and destructive war on China, including the Nanjing Massacre, Nazi-like medical experiments on living Chinese, sex slavery and the use of internationally outlawed poison gas.

Japan's post-war leaders were not alone in stressing the positive so that young people would grow up to be proud patriots. The same is true of China and America.

Teachers and their unions in Japan responded to the whitewash. They believed that for Japan to avoid repeating the inhumanities of the past, it was best to remember them, to discuss them, to make students not forget what horrors the Showa era imperium had committed before Japan democratized after the Second World War and set itself on a peaceful path of freedom and prosperity through international trade. Thus, they taught what the textbooks omitted. When, in America, the issue is barbarous slavery, or in China the issue is the waste of life, treasure and time in the Mao era, do teachers act as honorably as teachers in Japan?

The Government of the PRC continually criticizes Japan's conservatives in the Ministry of Education for not telling the truth in school textbooks. But many Chinese in the post-Mao era do not want to be reminded of how Mao's policies wounded the Chinese people and locked them into stagnant misery in the collectivist era from 1953 to 1977. They do not want to focus on dark spots in their nation's history, matters such as military support for the genocidal Pol Pot regime. Indeed, in response to the pains of reform and to the fears of globalization, a nostalgia for Mao era policies grew in China. There may be more amnesia in China about twentieth-century cruelties perpetrated by Chinese than among Japanese about their historical inhumanities. Clearly the job of educators is to tell their students the truth, not to hide the truth for political reasons. But what is historical truth?

Whenever a political entity sets out on a new path, its education officials are confronted with a need to reimagine the past in order to legitimate a very different future. The prior history suddenly seems an absurd lie to many who embrace the new understanding. Yet the old view still appeals as eternal truth to some. Globalization speeds up this conflictful process.

As humanity enters the twenty-first century, governments from Australia to Mexico have asked their people to reimagine their history. Australia is rethinking its history to stress how much it is part of an economically rising Asia and not merely the offspring of the decayed British Empire. In like manner, the Government of Mexico, in order to persuade its people that their better future lies not, as they previously thought and were taught, in closing the door to so-called Yankee imperalists, but in opening up to NAFTA, has begun to reimagine Mexican history so that national heroes are not anti-foreign chauvinists but instead are confident patriots who understand that the only way to ensure continued economic progress is to be open to learning from the highest achievement of all humanity.

Yesterday's hero becomes tomorrow's villain. So it has been with China's Taiping rebellion leader Hong Xiuquan, who was presented in the Mao era as an auger of a utopian future for China's peasants, but who, by the end of the twentieth century, seemed to most knowledgeable Chinese to be the leader of an impossible quest which caused the unnecessary loss of millions of Chinese lives. However stable it seems at any moment, identity is inevitably ambiguous and contestable. Chinese are not frozen into understandings that stigmatize democracy as alien.

Reinterpreting openness and multiculturalism

Anti-imperalist nativists would praise people for no longer using borrowed words. Yet no people prospers as an isolated entity. Europe did not become Arabic when it adopted Arabic numerals. Nor did China. International borrowing empowers. Yet nativists resist it. The cost of such resistance rises in the age of globalization.

Patriots who understand that prosperity requires openness to the wisdom of all humanity call attention to the benefits to one's nation of being able to command foreign languages. Xenophobes do not find it easy to understand that being comfortable with diverse foreign cultures is good for one's own people, facilitating earnings from tourism—the world's leading industry—and easy access to the achievements of the human species.

Nativists, instead, see meaning, value and national identity as an indigenous commodity. They cannot comprehend a link between openness and greatness. When they are told to be open to the world, they feel they are being asked to betray their people. While such tendencies pervade China, it is not alone in this regard.

Many French are offended when asked to confront murderous French collaboration with the Nazis, asking, "Why open old wounds?" They resist an education which explores past evils and explains how much all peoples, including theirs, benefit from truthful self-awareness, openness to and interchange with all the people and wisdom of the world. The better fate of a nation, therefore, is a heavy responsibility for educators whose task it is not to satisfy the narrow-minded and short-sighted who rage against all other peoples and singularly praise their own. It is wrong when the Japanese Ministry of Education does it. It is dangerous to the peace and prosperity of one's people, whoever practices narrow nativism.

Chauvinists tend to believe that the myths of their nation that they had imbibed early on are the only basis for a moral and patriotic life. They are inordinately uncomfortable on hearing a retelling of their people's history to fit the new imperatives of globalization and international openness. That reimagining of the past seems to them to be arrant nonsense, a guarantee of immorality among the young and destabilizing and unethical chaos for society. Nativists in power experience truth-tellers as immoral traitors. Chinese patriots are prevented from encountering the truth of their complicity in the origin of the Korean War revealed in Soviet Russian archives. China is always innocent, always wronged by malicious foreigners. Consequently, as in Japan, educators everywhere tend to be subject periodically to great political pressures to stick with apparently ancient verities and to find new perspectives as faddish or foreign nonsense. This self-censorship seems far more prevalent in China than in Japan.

In America, Eurocentrists lash out at multiculturalists who introduce the achievements of, and discrimination against, all America's people, including Chinese immigrants who were victims of cruel racism. American Eurocentrists, as do their Chinese counterparts, imagine dreadful consequences such as disintegration were the purist myth discarded or discredited.

Taiwanese also felt these conflicting pressures from proponents of old and new histories at the end of the twentieth century. Since the arrival of Chiang Kai-shek's Nationalist Party on Taiwan at the end of the 1940s, island students were taught to be proud of mainland China's 5,000-year history. This historical identity was meant to legitimate power for Chiang's dictatorial party. Then, in the 1990s, with the Taiwanization of the ruling party and democratization, most Taiwanese began to discover and to discuss a 400-year history. Here is how the new history read in the 1994 Taiwan bestseller by Zeng Liangping, *The Leap Month of August 1995*:

> Taiwan has been a Dutch colony, an anti-Qing Dynasty base for Zheng Cheng'gong to use to resurrect the Ming Dynasty, and a base for Japan to use to march South ... the people of Taiwan became alienated from the mainland ... Using brainwashing methods, the Nationalist Party indoctrinated Taiwan's people with the idea that only the mainland enjoyed natural beauty ...

The author Zeng errs in the notion of "brainwashing." Nativists believed they were telling the truth, even about the absurdity that nothing was beautiful on the supposedly primitive wasteland of Taiwan. I remember, from 1964–1966, while a graduate student on Taiwan, a mainlander correcting me when I appreciated a beautiful flower. "Beautiful? Beautiful? If you want to see beauty, go to China. In China there are beautiful flowers. Not here!"

Yet at the end of the twentieth century, Taiwanese are proud of the world-class beauty they have created, from computer designs to smash hit movies that are enjoyed all over the world. The old nativist history in which only China had beauty now seems silly to most Taiwanese.

The new Taiwan history, however, soon came under attack for hiding how the early arrivals from China, the Hakka and the Hokklo, oppressed the indigenous Austronesians who had dwelled on the island for millennia, pushing the original settlers off good land and into the mountains. The government on Taiwan therefore has to rewrite elementary school textbooks. Reinterpretation is endless.

Reconstructing Chinese identity

A similarly huge change in national identity may be beginning in post-Mao China. The attractiveness of globalization leads Chinese to recall a history in conflict with the one of continental cultural purity propagated by the regime. For many years, the city of Xian celebrated the archeology of Qin Shi Huang to proclaim how the people of China, as in the building of parts of the Great Wall, sacrificed to keep alien dangers outside. But in the post-Mao era, Xian built a new museum. It celebrated, not the narrow racist history propagandized from the state center, but a story of international exchange via the Silk Road. China's better future is a story which can show how much Chinese, as all people, gain from imbibing the best from all humanity. Democracy too can be made Chinese.

It is discombobulating for nativists to be told that there were numerous great civilizations even in China itself, where in addition to the Zhongyuan, there were the Chu and the Wuyue and the Bashu as well as others, each and all infused and enriched by exchanges with non-Chinese. In the post-Mao era, Chinese are increasingly aware that their people are a mixture of many centers of civilization. Each of these six to nine cores benefited from exchanges with the advances of other peoples. Keels for ships came from the Malays. Cotton came from Hindus. Wet rice came from Champuchae. Buddhism came from India. As did Europe much later, so China rose because it was open to borrowing from the advances of all peoples.

In addition, China was not united, as the official discourse claims, because one superior civilization was peacefully accepted by peoples convinced of their own inferiority. War, blood and conquest in China, as everywhere, enlarged an empire. The great ancient civilization of Chu crushed the Yue. The Han defeated the Nanyue. In the Hong Kong region, in 1197 the Lating people on Lantou Island were slaughtered. And in 1580 the Ming defeat at Luowan Island included yet another blood-letting. Much Chinese blood was shed because of nonpeaceful ways of making transitions of power and because of nonplural ways of living with each other.

Chinese chauvinists instead embrace a tale of the modern era beginning with China's vicitimization by imperialist forces in the Opium War. But it is

dangerous to imagine one's contemporary era in terms of one's pure inno-
cence and total victimization by others. Many Japanese like to think of the
Second World War as beginning with American atomic bombs dropping on
mere civilians—women, children and the elderly—in Hiroshima and
Nagasaki. The Chinese know better about Japan's aggressive militarism:
Showa era imperial armies shipped out from Hiroshima to conquer Asia.

A quest for militaristic purity and keeping out the alien is an ordinary—
and inhuman—consequence of conceptualizing one's history as born in
innocence and victimization in which one's own people could not possibly be
complicit with evil. To act responsibly, any nation, whether Japan or China
or America, must remind itself of how it seems to other nations. Certainly
people in a Korea or a Vietnam will not forget whose armies invaded in the
past. Nativism, by blinding a great people as to how it looks to smaller or
weaker nations, can cause misunderstanding, unnecessary clashes, destruction, and even self-destruction. In an age of globalization, democratization
open to critical self-understanding may be a requisite for peace.

Instead of dangerous nativism, post-Mao Chinese reformer Deng
Xiaoping asked why China, once the world leader in science in technology
from about 450 to 1450, was so weak in 1839 that it could not defend itself
against a small part of the British navy. Deng reminded Chinese of their
ocean prowess at the start of Ming Era when Admiral Zheng He's massive
fleet could sail to East Africa.[1] But the Ming, China's most nativistic
dynasty, and Mao's favorite, smashed the fleet, destroyed blueprints for the
ships and abandoned ocean links to world progress. Consequently, China
cut itself off from the advances of the early industrial revolution and the
scientific revolution. China made itself weak by making itself ignorant.
Closing one's doors to the supposedly alien actually closes one's mind and
society from the dynamism of human progress.

The nativistic Ming hated things foreign and sought to purify China under
an unpolluted, super-Confucian tyranny. In contrast, the Tang Dynasty's greatness was based on openness to the world, both via the Silk Road to Changan
and across the South China Sea to the great river ports of Hangzhou and
Yangzhou. Much of Japanese cultural strength involved borrowing from the
Tang era's open Wuyue culture of the economically dynamic Jiangnan region
in China's south. Paintings from the Tang look much like Japan more than a
millennium later. The way to rise is to borrow the best from the advanced. The
rise of Hong Kong through international openness is well known.

Europe too, when it rose along the Atlantic Ocean coastlines of Europe's
northwest, strengthened itself by being open to the great achievements of
much of the rest of the world. This was not just a matter of borrowing
compass, gunpowder and printing from China. Europe also borrowed from
Hindu civilization and Islamic peoples both in North Africa and in West
Asia. Sustainable greatness involves openness to learning from others.
Nativists are enemies of the prosperity of their own people. Malaysia's
Premier Mahathir makes this point over and over.

The vicissitudes of globalization

So why is it so difficult to tell the history of the achievements of openness in an era which cries out for openness? The major lesson on entering the twenty-first century among nationalistic Chinese ruling groups about China's loss from cutting itself off from ocean-going international exchange is that China must build the military needed to gain control of nearby blue waters. It has become pre-suppositional in Chinese politics that China must incorporate the entire South China Sea right up to the borders of Vietnam, the Philippines and Indonesia, that it must conquer the Taiwan Straits and take the East China Sea and the Senkaku islets that belong to Japan. Instead of singularly fostering openness, exchange and mutual benefit, globalization in China has strengthened also an expansive chauvinism.

The vicissitudes of the painful transition to the postmodern can unleash vengeful, narrow nationalist forces everywhere. Globalism begets tribalism. In Europe, post-modernists are trying to forge a common market that enriches by crossing and largely erasing former national divisions, only to be met by a backlash from European nativists—indeed, virtual racists and fascists—who seek to exclude the alien, seen first as Muslims from Turkey and North Africa, said to be incapable of harmony with Christian European civilization. The postmodern era brings hope and fear, promise and anxiety, greater inclusiveness and stronger nativism. As in the past, all peoples contain better and worse potentials. As always, politics will decide. In China, the politics of chauvinism has long easily trumped democratization.

To comprehend the historical logic of national identity crises requires exploring the meaning of the era. The modern era was marked by a quest to build strong, centralized states using steel to build railroads and the artifacts of war, from tanks to planes. The new era of globalization, in contrast, is marked by the relative decline of the heavy industry sector and the rise of information industries. Volvo gives way to Ericsson in Sweden. A communications revolution is undoing a pillar of the modern centralized state. The advent of instantaneous satellite communication, of fax, email, cordless phones and the like diminishes the monopolistic role of a strong center. News can be obtained anywhere by pushing a button. One no longer waits for a centralized printing press to publish, with the information then transported from the center to the peripheries. In the postmodern, people and information more readily cross borders. Walls no longer block. All of this frightens rulers in Beijing who see societal forces spinning out of control. They are still trying to complete the modern project of building the centralized nation-state while trying to compete economically in the new age of globalization.

Postmodern changes come quickly. Many cannot comprehend or absorb the mutations. They feel dizzy. They search for old roots. They become nostalgic. They imagine a warm past of human caring and sharing. They see treasured values threatened by the new, new thing. They welcome nativism. They become chauvinists. The challenge of the postmodern is so frightening to some that they fight against it as if life itself depended on not losing old verities. In China, this creates popular forces which share the anxieties, hates and ambitions of chauvinists.

The frightened are not bad people. They seek simply the security of a known home. They fear the open-ended, fast-changing postmodern story which does not guarantee a happy ending. Demagogues, from militias in America to Islamicists in Pakistan to nativists anywhere and everywhere, can appeal to popular unease about postmodern progress and turn people against the too new, the postmodern. The danger is quotidian. It is very strong in China. The backlash to the problems of globalization may only be beginning.

Everywhere a struggle is underway between postmodernists and neo-nativists. In Japan, nativists imagine a pure Japanese people, descendants of united family cooperation in cultivating rice, the sacred essence of the people. The new multiculturalists and pluralists in Japan who are open to the postmodern, in contrast, imagine Japan as the consequence of a diversi-fied economy which long benefited from contacts with foreigners such as the Chinese or the Dutch. This is a Japan of fishermen and goat herders, of merchants and traders, as well as rice farmers.

East and West, nations debate how to imagine their history in a global-ized age of extraordinarily rapid transition from the modern to the postmodern. Since many in all countries flee the imperatives of this histor-ical advance, preferring to hold on to their roots, it makes little sense to condemn such people. Their plight is pan-human. Humanity must grapple with and transcend this crisis. People in regions of China that have barely begun to modernize readily imagine those who prosper in a postmodern economy as alien and undeservedly rich. The dangerous is quotidian. It makes Chinese welcoming of a most racist reimagining of their people, one not polluted (that is, enriched) by others (Sautman 2001).

People who feel themselves defeated by or excluded from the blessings of the postmodern invariably see the new forces as unjust. They are not all wrong. The new and extensive financial powers that are hard to control by centralized governments seem immorally wealthy, while too many other peoples seem stuck or even moving backward. Those threatened will lash out against the new wealth as if it is in fact unjust. Nativists could win. Humanity could lose, in China, in the Unites States, everywhere. If some equity is not maintained, demagogues are likely to mobilize a populist and nativistic backlash against the wealth of the postmodern. But in a China in transition from Leninist command economy irrationalities, not enough tax revenue is available to build the social safety nets necessary to cushion the shocks. Democracy could do so much better for China if the nativist notion of "alien Western democracy" were abjured.

In China, otherwise, the poorer hinterland will declare political war on open coastal wealth from Guangzhou to Taipei. The defeat and incorpora-tion of the immorally advanced by the moral but backward will be seen as the real story of Chinese history. One can already hear such people begin-ning to tell this story, reminding Chinese in Hong Kong and elsewhere of how Sun Yat-sen's progressive forces were defeated by the more backward Beiyang warlords, of how advanced coastal and valley wealth was next defeated by Mao's peasant armies raised in a traditionalistic northern hinterland. In imagining better and worse futures, people seek continuity. They see the inland Han of central China, not the south coast or the non-Han borderland peripheries, as the core of the Chinese race which sacrificed for millennia to hold back marauding nomads and then lost millions of good people in resisting cruel Japanese invaders, and yet who again, in the age of reform, benefit least and last.

Identity is constructed, contested, deconstructed and reconstructed forever. The identity crisis attendant to postmodern globalization in China has strengthened both democratically open and repressive political forces.

Benefits of global cooperation

The prospects of victory for the more open and postmodern forces may be aided by significant international cooperation on restructuring the architecture of international finance. That mutuality is not easy in an age of nativistic backlash against the fast-moving, usually incomprehensible and often polarizing forces of the postmodern, experienced as the alien. Yet, there may be no alternative to neo-nativism other than international cooperation in the interest of equity.

In the post-Bretton Woods new economy of frighteningly volatile international finance, chauvinistic scapegoating is on the rise, East and West. The burgeoning Asian international economy is quite complex and diverse. Japan is a major force in East and Southeast Asia. So are Chinese ethnic networks, which constitute a major factor of great concern to the Japanese. The United States is not an all-powerful economic hegemon in Asia. No one is. All are anxious about alien power in the age of globalization.

Chinese rulers imagined out-of-control international financial volatility helping to end the Soeharto kleptocracy in Indonesia. Rulers in Beijing are concerned about a similar trajectory in China. Chauvinistic authoritarianism can seem an attractive alternative in this frightening new age. That is why, sadly, using the idea of "Western" democracy to stigmatize is still alive in China. It also metastasizes in the so-called West, as indicated by the rise of skinheads and the normalization of the Nazi era in Germany, by Haider in Austria, by Le Pen in France, and by the Oklahoma City bombing in the United States. A truly open, tolerant and inclusive notion of democracy consequently is never easy to achieve anywhere, East or West. But it may be especially difficult in the new economy of this age of globalization with its out-of-control herd money. Thus, while democratization is a universal potential, challenges to democracy are also universal. It is my fervent hope that people in Asia, especially in a riven China of the turbulent twenty-first century, succeed better than did people in Europe, the French of the nineteenth century and the Germans in the twentieth century (Mazower 1998), in grappling with the fearsome challenges that still lie ahead for the contradictory forces of globalization as they impact on the promise of democracy.

Note

1   Deng did not notice what Indonesians see, and indeed are taught in their history texts, that Zheng He was a destructive invader.

References

Aung San Suu Kyi (1991) *Freedom from Fear*, New York: Penguin.
Borbujerdi, M. (1996) *Iranian Intellectuals and the West*, Syracuse: Syracuse University Press.
Carothers, T. (1999) *Aiding Democracy Abroad*, Washington, DC: Carnegie Endowment for International Peace.
Chirot, D. (1994) *Modern Tyrants*, Princeton: Princeton University Press.
Cumings, B. (1999) *Parallax Visions*, Durham: Duke University Press.
Dizon, N. Z. (2000) "US Teachers Turn to Singapore Texts for Math Lessons," *Wisconsin State Journal*, May 15.
Dower, J. (1999) "A Message from the Showa Emperor," *Bulletin of Concerned Asian Scholars*, 31, 4: 19–24.
Duara, P. (1997) "Transnationalism and the Predicament of Sovereignty," *American Historical Review*, 102, 4: 1030–1051.
Dutton, K. and Robinson A. (eds.) (1997) *Rabandranath Tagore: An Anthology*, New York: St. Martin's Press.
Friedman, E. (1994) *The Politics of Democratization*, Boulder: Westview.
—— (1999a) "Asia as a Fount of Universal Human Rights," in P. Van Ness (ed.), *Debating Human Rights*, New York: Routledge.
—— (1999b) "Does China Have the Cultural Preconditions for Democracy?", *Philosophy East and West*, 49, 3: 346–359.
Heilbrunn, J. (2000) "Germany's Illiberal Fictions," *The National Interest*, Summer: 84–94.
Kim, Byung-Kook (1998) "Korea's Crisis of Success," in D. Larry and M. Plattner (eds.), *Democracy in East Asia*, Baltimore: Johns Hopkins University Press, pp. 113–132.
Kim Dae Jung (1994) "Is Culture Destiny?", *Foreign Affairs*, November/December: 189–194.
Kristof, N. and WuDunn, C. (1994) *China Wakes*, New York: New York Times Books.
Lawrence, S. (1999) "Imperial Yoke," *Far Eastern Economic Review*, September 9: 63–65.
Lu, N. (2000) "Chinese Views of the New Russia," in S. Garnett (ed.), *Rapprochment or Rivalry*, Washington, DC: Carnegie Endowment for International Peace, pp. 99–116.
Mazower, M. (1998) *Dark Continent*, New York: Random House.
Moore, Barrington, Jr. (1966) *Social Origins of Dictatorship and Democracy*, Boston: Beacon Press.
Sautman, B (2001) "Peking Man and the Politics of Paleoanthropological Nationalism in China," *Journal of Asian Studies*, 60, 1: 95–124.
Shah, A. (2000) "Review of Rajmohan Gandhi, Revenge and Reconciliation," *Foreign Policy*, Summer: 139–142.
Wu, X. (2000) "The Security Dimension of Sino-Japanese Relations," *Asian Survey*, 40, 2: 296–310.

5 Imported democracy

The South Korean experience

Geir Helgesen

Democracy came to South Korea through American liberation cum occupation forces after 1945 as an offer that could not be refused. The élite of that time capable of and ready to work with the US forces subsequently established "democracy" as a system encompassing whatever people found to be good and desirable, to the extent that "every political practice, institution and formula [had to be] legitimized by its consistency with democracy", as Hahm Pyong-choon wrote in 1969, adding that this modern political myth making was remarkably successful (Hahm 1986: 192–193). Despite the institutionalization of democratic rituals, South Korean politics were deeply imbedded in the traditional social order, that is, a strict patriarchal hierarchy expecting and producing benevolent leaders and obedient subjects.

The political élite in Korea has apparently struggled ever since to bridge the distance between myth and reality on the different political scenes.[1] Liberal democracy was delivered and received on a turnkey basis (Ahn *et al.* 1988: 4), but political actors and their followers continued to operate the system their way. The core content of this "way" was rationalized in a political culture permeated by Confucianism and transmitted through institutionalized upbringing and education. Data from value surveys conducted throughout the 1970s reveal that democratic ideas and values were well recognized, but the political attitudes and behaviors of the majority of Koreans were still anti-democratic and authoritarian, based on values "inherited from the country's Confucian past" (Lee 1985: 83).[2]

Traditional values thus prevented comfortable accommodation with the imported political system, as did the postwar division of the country, which linked the two parts of the nation to one or the other of the two antagonistic "world systems" of the time. The division of the country and the ensuing extremely hostile relationship with the Northern regime—fellow countrymen operating as communists within that ideological block—made the South Korean political system a make-believe system up until 1987. As part of the "free world," or rather as a base for that part of the world under a bipolar division, authoritarian rulers with military backing staged a democratic showcase in order not to embarass their allies.

Despite its past in Korea as a disguise for military authoritarianism during the cold-war ideological conflict, the idea of democracy has always commanded a surprisingly strong power of attraction,[3] and still does. Recent surveys reveal an almost unanimous support for democracy, including human rights.[4] It might be difficult to understand therefore why it apparently remains hard to practice this system in Korea.[5] A clue is offered, however, in the response to the following statement in one of the above-mentioned surveys: "The ideologies and lifestyle of the West, such as individualism and materialism, threaten to destroy the Korean society." Large majorities agreed to that statement—85 per cent in 1990 and 78 per cent in 1995 (Helgesen 1998: 128). The seemingly contradictory fact that democracy is strongly supported, yet weak in practice is the subject of this chapter, where reasons for this state of affairs will be discussed. The possibility of combining modern (Western-oriented) and traditional ("indigenous") attitudes will also be touched upon. For obvious political reasons, the external point of reference in South Korea's modernization and democratization process is the United States. This is reflected upon in the discussion below.

Politics and social values

With the end of the cold war, the liberal model of democracy has been elevated to the position of a universal truth. This is, however, a conceptual misrepresentation as well as a huge practical problem. A model developed in one part of the world, based on one particular set of conditions in one particular period of history, cannot—as a matter of course—claim to have general validity. To do so would be acceptable if human beings were not only created alike, but furthermore that people in all parts of the world develop the same hopes and aspirations, the same ideas about good and evil, the same emotional needs, dreams and desires. But this is not the case. Biologically, people may be created equal and alike, albeit with different predispositions and abilities. But from the time of creation, the given circumstances have always been different in different parts of the world. For this reason, people actually develop distinctly different values and norms which guide their world views. These values and norms include important preferences with relation to political viewpoints.

Given the premise that every political system is a unique, socially constructed creation within the confines of a cultural context, which to a greater or lesser degree shapes the pattern of human interaction in the system, politics in the West may currently have lost some of its cultural touch. This may in part be due to the weakened position of religion in many Western countries, (if one perceives of religion in the Durkheimian sense, as a system of beliefs and rituals with reference to the sacred which binds people together into social groups). Many of the great problems that can be observed in Western politics and society may thus emanate from the disappearance of a transcendent source of morality. When the sacred source has evaporated, total freedom may remain, but it carries insecurity and alienation with it. This kind of freedom implies a lack of meaning in life. The Asian values argument was also, albeit not exclusively, an attempt to respond to this alienation, which threatened to destroy the social fabric of societies which were modernizing toward the Western way.

This East Asian vision of good government challenges the liberal "cult of the individual." A good political system, which is acceptable in relation to the values and mores of Asia and able to take root in Asian societies, is characterized by a number of reciprocal relations:

- personal freedom requires individual responsibility;
- initiative presupposes discipline;
- individual rights must be seen in relation to collective obligations;
- the condition for social welfare is individual unselfishness.

(Sopiee 1993)

This morally founded reciprocal social system emphasizes the *balance* between the individual and the community, between rights and duties, between personal happiness and the common welfare of society. It is the obligation of the state to secure this balance, to secure the *right* to social order, and to secure *freedom* from anarchy and chaos. A weak or passive state is unable to maintain such a system, whereas a morally strong state can maintain it. In this perspective, the state is viewed as a body capable of establishing the framework to secure a balance between the rights and duties of the individual and those of the collective. These considerations are basic to the survival of any political system and any society, not only in the East Asian context. Therefore, they should be brought to the forefront of the global political agenda.

Asian (or non-Western) critiques of Western democracy apply, first and foremost, to the United States. Such criticism is often focused on aspects that are viewed as negative social consequences of the democratic system. Former Singaporean Prime Minister Lee Kuan Yew is an outspoken critic of American-style "Western democracy." As a critic he may have discredited himself to a large extent by treating his own opposition less benevolently than he ought to have, by his own set standards. However, he is not the only political leader whose practices do not measure up to his ideas, and his critique is to the point when he claims that:

The expansion of the right of the individual to behave or misbehave as he pleases has come at the expense of orderly society. In the East the main object is to have a well-ordered society so that everybody can have maximum enjoyment of his freedom.

(Zakaria 1994: 112)

Similar arguments are forwarded by Kishore Mahbubani, another Singaporean scholar-official who criticizes the direction of an American society with a democracy that has experienced serious problems of its own in *reconciling individual rights with the interests of the larger community*. He underlines that a well-ordered society needs to plant clear constraints on behavior in the minds of its citizens, not to suppress their freedom, but to make individual freedom possible. The American way, according to Mahbubani, is to liberate the individual to such an extent that society becomes imprisoned (1994: 5–23).

This critique, as well as the one forwarded by Lee, reflects the fact that judgments based on fundamentals of one political culture apparently lose their validity when applied to the reality of another. Whether or not one recognizes this critique, it seems clear that both Lee and Mahbubani take for granted that the state, through its political powerholders, has the ultimate responsibility for the population at large. In the American version of Western liberal democracy, this responsibility has been especially discon-nected from the political system, and the Asian critique is thus perceived as misplaced, irrelevant and even anti-democratic.

From the perspective of a liberal version of democracy, the individual is the point of departure in politics and social life, and the strength of democracy lies in the belief that it aggregates individual choices (often confused with freedom). It is, moreover, a clear position in liberalism that the free pursuit of individual self-interest in a free market economy will ultimately maximize the common good. The state is not in a position to secure the common good using programs and legislation. Less state, more freedom, more democracy, seems to be the mantra of "the libertarians," as they are labeled by Amitai Etzioni, one of the proponents of a communi-tarian democracy. He traces the American liberalist anti-social tendency, their fear that the community may suppress dissent and minorities, and ultimately violate individual and civil rights, to "the roots of the American existence, a society fashioned by dissenters escaping dogma" (incidentally, he adds that this is "a legitimate concern for all democracies") (Etzioni 1992: 531). A fundamental and decisive difference between the libertarian and the communitarian position is with regard to the individual human being: "communitarians argue that persons are social creatures" (ibid.: 533). Relating to this, Etzioni has forwarded a practical and down to earth argument. He argues that while there might be little need for community values, consensus and social virtues in a frontier society in which everyone must find his or her own way in unsettled territories, the list of matters of collective concern to be dealt with collectively in a modern, urbanized society is very long. In such a society "[i]ndividual rights do not rest on individuals, somehow born or endowed with them, but on a community-shared morality that legitimates and otherwise sustains them "(ibid.: 536). Individuals in society are, according to the communitarian position, guided by a commonly held moral compass which provides "persons and social institutions with direction as they grapple with the economic, political, and social issues of the day" (ibid.: 533). A brief overview of the latest rise and descent of a South Korean president will cast some light on this.

Korean political culture and democracy

After nearly fifty years of trial and error, in 1997 Korea finally elected a celebrated fighter for democracy to the highest office. Kim Dae Jung was already internationally acknowledged for his untiring efforts to truly bring Korea into the democratic camp. A man who has endured jail, torture, and continuous personal harassment—to the point of putting his own life at stake for democracy and human rights—obviously came with solid credentials.[6] Moreover, he engaged in the so-called "Asian values" debate at an early stage by challenging Singapore's Lee Kuan Yew in an article in *Foreign Affairs* (Kim 1994), formed as a commentary to an interview with Lee in the same journal (March–April 1994). In a direct, sharp tone not often seen in print in Korea, Kim accuses Lee of promoting self-serving arguments, using culture as a pretext for maintaining his grip on power. Discussing obstacles for democracy in Asia, he suggests that "[T]he biggest obstacle is not its cultural heritage but the resistance of authoritarian rulers and their apologists" (p. 5, Internet version). In Korea, the present ruler is the very same Kim.

John Larkin of the *Far Eastern Economic Review* points to the gap between promises and realities as the main reason for President Kim's recent nosedive in popularity ratings. "He promised in 1997 that the country's democracy would be burnished and its shattered economy remodelled, but voters see next to no change" writes Larkin (2001: 18). This professional observer of the Korean political scene refers to a growing wave of negative sentiments against a leader who promised to be different but is "ruling in the same high-handed manner" (ibid.). Political scientist Hahm Chai Bong, in an interview with Larkin, says that the problems started immediately after the 1997 election when Kim, lacking a parliamentary majority, "chose the old tactic of poaching opposition lawmakers" (ibid.: 20). Furthermore, he reinforced the strong and destructive regional animosity by appointing loyalists from his own region. The prosecutor's office and the national tax office are still under the government's influence (which means the president's influence). Party candidates are still selected by the top man, which "creates parties of 'yes-men,' and candidates are sometimes chosen for their chequebooks" (ibid.). This gloomy picture is supported by David Steinberg, director of Asian Studies at Georgetown University and a long-term Korea observer, who says that "I've heard from people in the Blue House[7] that nobody can disagree with Kim Dae Jung" (ibid.). The latest rumors from political corridors in Seoul whisper that *King* Dae Jung is the new nickname of the incumbent.

Larkin suggests that the crisis engulfing Kim's government is due to "the president's failure to bring South Korea's destructive political culture into step with a more sophisticated electorate" (ibid.: 18). It is not easy to prove Larkin's viewpoint right or wrong, but it cannot merely be dismissed. His views are absolutely in tune with a generally held conviction (in Korea as elsewhere) that necessary change and societal reforms will have to be implemented by the younger generations. It is, however, difficult to follow his line of argument. Should the electorate in Korea be generally more politically mature and democratically minded than the president? Though the president is elderly, he is not just any old Korean, but became a Nobel laureate for his tireless struggle for peace and democracy.[8] Kim Dae Jung is the East Asian leader who has most forcefully attacked proponents of the idea that Asian values should be alien to democracy. In a personal conversation some years ago he flatly denied that there were any reasons to modify or adjust democracy in order for it to be operational in his country. Regardless of cultural differences, he stated that there is only one democracy: liberal democracy.[9]

This position notwithstanding, politics is embedded in culture inasmuch as political actors are socialized human beings, or "cultured animals." Sustainable development, in economy as well as in politics, presupposes a certain level of concordance between political thinking, institutional setup and political actions, on the one hand, and the cultural values and norms widely accepted in society, on the other. In the case of Korea, where democracy has been the name of the game for half a century, a strong cultural tradition has made it extremely difficult for people to accept democratic procedures. A central question is thus: how persistent are the values and norms stemming from traditional culture and to what extent do they guide people's behavior in present-day Korea?

Recent survey data on good government

Some results from recent surveys, conducted by the author in collaboration with Korean colleagues,[10] will be presented in the following account. These surveys have been designed to measure attitudes toward society, politics and cultural issues such as values and norms that are supposed to influence people's opinions in daily life. Brief references will be made to data and analyses based on the Korea Democracy Barometer (KDB) program (1988–1999) reported by Doh Chull Shin (Shin 2000).

The target groups in the surveys conducted in 1990 and 1995 can generally be characterized as modern, urban, educated, articulate, politically aware and concerned, well informed and experienced in international matters. Many of them had acquired parts of their education from Western universities. About 90 per cent agreed on the following three statements:

1   "A better future depends on the social morality in society."
2   "Democracy is seeking harmonious social relations."
3   "The ideal society is like a family."

(Helgesen 1998)

The people questioned in these surveys are actually the sophisticated electorate mentioned by Larkin above, or rather, the élite of this sophisticated electorate. The unambiguous attitudes above may thus reflect a general positive notion of morality and harmony among Koreans. Whether this is connected to a particular traditional trait is difficult to substantiate. Other issues have a more clear cultural link. In both surveys, more than 75 per cent of the respondents agreed on all of the three following statements:

1   "Respect for one's ancestors will surely survive modernization in Korea."
2   "Good morals and a humanistic attitude are the most important qualities in politics."
3   "Korean democracy must take the traditional culture as its point of departure."

(ibid.)

The last statement seems to summarize the general attitude. While the first set of statements were somewhat vague and general, this second set have a more forceful and direct wording and meaning: the majority supports a moral position that has been rationalized in Korean Confucianism. Based on the positive response to all the statements above, a distinction between tradition and modernity seems obsolete, no longer a relevant dichotomy (if it ever was) in this post-cold war era. Rejecting this dichotomy, the stage opens up for other forms of social practices, including other forms of good governance. The coexistence of different values—traditional and modern—operating on different levels corresponds with simple observations of daily life in most societies. Among the very few solid studies offering empirical evidence in support of such observations, Ronald Inglehart's World Values Surveys stands out. Inglehart maintains that, even if economic development tends to move societies in a common direction, traditions everywhere die hard: "distinctive cultural zones continue to persist two centuries after the industrial revolution was launched" (Inglehart 2000: 88).

In East Asia tradition exists within modernity, and traditions seems more vital here than in most Western countries. When it comes to the relevance of traditional values as guidelines for political views, some might be basic while others are of less significance. To distinguish the basic from the less significant is a delicate problem, but even if the above themes only have an indirect bearing on the respondents' political affiliations, one can already sense where the obstacle to liberal democracy is anchored. A cautious conclusion based on the response to the six statements above suggests that "moral politics" is preferred by a strong majority of the respondents in the two surveys conducted in Korea in 1990 and 1995. Of particular importance for this discussion is that there were no significant differences in views between younger and older respondents; neither were there any differences due to social status, educational background, or sex.

It thus seem to make good sense to suggest that Korean democracy must take traditional culture as its point of departure, regardless of how it should be practiced.

According to the KDB 1998/1999 survey, 91 per cent embraced the idea of democracy, and 88 per cent wanted the limited existing democracy expanded (Shin 2000: 47). This suggests that both central traditional values and a Western-type understanding of democracy command support in Korea. The two surveys of the élite recorded a 90 per cent agreement on the idea that democracy means "to secure harmonious social relations." The 2000 sample survey (EPCReN forthcoming) had a similar formulation, stating that: "[T]he objective of good government is to maintain harmonious social relations." The agreement rate here was 91 per cent. On the statement: "[T]he ideal society is like a family," 90 per cent agreed in the 1990/1995 surveys, and 87 per cent agreed in the 2000 survey. These responses show a close agreement between the surveyed élite and the general populace. The question then is what kind of harmony is wished for in such statements, and what it means to see the ideal society as a family?

It is important to note, though rather obvious, that both *harmony* and *family* are culture-specific phenomena. Every human being has acquired a clear notion of these things during childhood years, more as a result of how life is lived than of direct indoctrination. Though there are differences within every culture between social classes, urban and rural practices (which are often depicted as modern versus traditional), as well as differences from family to family (and even within families), there are also general characteristics. The general understanding within the culture is often rationalized in educational material used in civic or moral education in primary and secondary schools.

Moral education is a standard, compulsory subject on the curriculum in the educational systems of all East Asian and several other Asian countries. Ideological ideas of the governing élites are here revealed. Here, the world view of the political authorities, or at least the world view with which they wish to imbue the populace, is formulated. Until recently, moral education was an ideological battlefield in Korea, because the subject contained a mixture of ideological indoctrination and a somewhat modernized version of traditional social morality (Helgesen 1998: 158–177). This was changed during the latest democratization process, which started in 1987. From then on, ideological indoctrination was dramatically downscaled, while education in morals remained the same. In the 1991 edition of South Korean moral educational textbooks, commissioned by the Ministry of Education, the family is presented as the nucleus of the nation, and the nation as an extended family. The idea of ancestor worship and filial piety is explained as a blood-based relationship characterized by a feeling of being *one and the same*. Generations are linked not only by sharing a name and a common history and destiny, they are of the same flesh and blood. The textbook explanation is that:

the relationship between parents and children is an inseparable physical one in which they share bones, flesh, and blood. It is a relationship in which both parents and children feel inside each other.

(Moral Education, Seventh Grade, Seoul 1991: 60–61)

This description of ancestor worship and filial piety, the mainstay of Confucianism, is extended to a moral and blood-based nationalism. As a whole, people can be divided into children, parents and ancestors.

[A]ncestral worship, which is only a part of our unique tradition, has great vitality that enable us to belong and depend on our family as well as our people, nation, and race.

(ibid.: 81)

From a Western, individualistic point of view the wording may seem turgid and archaic; nevertheless, it depicts a widely held view among Koreans, which was demonstrated in the survey responses above. The family referred to in the moral educational texts is a patriarchal family where the father is the natural authority. Great changes in daily life due to urbanization, such as families living in apartments rather than houses, which effectively block the ideal of three generations (or more) under the same roof, have not basically changed the family ideology. Furthermore, even where these changes may have seriously undermined the traditional ideology as a moral guideline for daily life, its importance for the political sphere is still dominant.

When society is seen as the family writ large, the next logical inference is to see the leader in the role of a father. The leadership cult in North Korea is consciously linked to this traditional Confucian notion. Through moral education, children are taught to love the leader as the father of the whole nation, and to see themselves as his children, and thus his subjects. Though it is not as blatant in South Korea, the logic is similar. The leaders in the South are not eternal, but replaceable, which actually might cause some concern, because good leadership is held in extremely high esteem. This is clearly revealed below, where the response pattern to questions related to leadership in the 2000 survey is presented. The figures in parentheses denote agreement in percentages:

- A leader should care for the people as parents care for their children (89).
- A group of people without a leader means chaos (82).
- We can leave everything to a morally upright leader (75).

(EPCReN forthcoming)

If one has a morally upright leader, what rationale could there be for replacing him? Replacement of fathers rarely occurs in Korea. If the

objective of good government is the maintenance of harmonious social relations—as accepted by 90 per cent of the respondents—it is hardly a surprise
that 94 per cent agree to a statement claiming that "[G]ood political leaders
should maintain harmony in the society." Political debates in Korea do
reveal differences in opinion over issues, but ideologically based debates are
rare. Visions of a new and better world are linked to a leader rather than to
the ideology of the party he represents. This is reflected in the following
statement: "The moral and human qualities of a political leader are more
important than his ideas," agreed to by 85 per cent of the respondents.
Asked which qualities of a political candidate are most important in
deciding one's vote, 94 per cent point to moral character. Almost as many
(90 per cent) find it important that he appear to be a strong leader. Strong
here is obviously not a physical attribute. Asked directly whether "the
quality of politicians is more important than laws and institutions," 74 per
cent of the respondents say yes (ibid.: 2000).

Political parties are traditionally formed to represent different ideas and
interests. Parties are supposed to give different social forces a voice and a
political instrument through which they can articulate their opinions and
operate on the political scene as potential caretakers of state affairs. This
line of thinking may not be easy to digest in a nation where the state is
depicted as some kind of parent body for the whole of society, and where
this society is understood as an extended family. In such a context, political
parties as interest organizations may be an alien invention. This is under-
lined by the fact that 74 per cent of the respondents in the EPCReN survey
feel that strong differences of opinion may undermine social order. The 1997
KDB survey found that a majority of about 65 per cent of the respondents
feared that too many competing groups would disturb social harmony, and
that too many diverse opinions would disturb social order (Shin 2000: 55).
Where harmony is attributed the highest importance as a political goal, it
may indeed seem strange to promote and organize contrasting viewpoints.

This notwithstanding, the political scene in Korea does have political
parties, a government (appointed by the president) and a parliament, to
which members are elected in parliamentary elections. Still, these institutions play a secondary role, more as supporting bodies to strong leaders
than anything else. The parliament may impede initiatives from the president's office, but should not take independent initiatives in the reform
process. As mentioned in the first part of this chapter, a president lacking
parliamentary majority will, democrat or not, start poaching opposition
lawmakers to solve this "technical" problem. In his own camp he has mainly
yes-men, and even the prime minister may perceive himself as such a yes-
man.[11] All this is no secret in Korean society. Asked about their trust in
political, social and other institutions (the parliament, political parties, trade
unions, media, the legal system, public offices, police, armed forces, major
companies), with the exception of the armed forces, a majority of more than
70 per cent expressed little or no trust in these institutions. The military was

trusted by 42.5 per cent of the respondents, while the parliament commanded the least trust (6.4 per cent), followed by political parties (11.1 per cent). A similar though not identical pattern was found in the KDB 1997 survey, in which 72 per cent of the respondents had some trust in the military, but in which only around 20 per cent expressed any trust in the National Assembly and the political parties. "Evident from this finding," writes Shin, "is that the two fundamental institutions of representative democracy are trusted least by the Korean people" (Shin 2000: 52).

From a Western—liberal democratic—position, the above data paint a gloomy picture of the often-celebrated young Korean democracy. The data presented may be interpreted in several ways, and other questions would reveal different attitudes and opinions. There is a clear trend, though, emphasizing politics as extraordinarily leader-oriented, with leadership modeled after the traditional, patriarchal father figure. Despite a grave lack of trust in political organizations and institutions, a majority of 78 per cent thinks that the government should be more active (EPCrEN 2002). People expressing such views may actually be thinking *leader* when they say *government*. Not that they automatically hail the leader. The general view is, to the contrary, very critical, if not directly negative, when it comes to political leaders. A majority of 75 per cent of the respondents agrees to a statement claiming that "the people we elect stop thinking about the interests of the people after taking office" (ibid.). In contrast, as much as 58 per cent agrees with the following: "It is more important to have an outstanding political leader than political democracy" (ibid.). The paradoxical relations between leaders and followers is often confusing for observers of Korean politics. In his *Asian Power and Politics. The Cultural Dimensions of Authority* Lucian W. Pye summarizes the complicated essence of leadership in Korea:

> Korean rulers, like Korean fathers, are expected to be embattled, needing to prove themselves in adversary contacts; but they are also expected to be masterful at all times, for like the Chinese leader-father, the Korean is supposed to be an aloof, lonely authority figure, able to cope single-handedly with all of his problems and demanding total adherence to his wishes. Yet again like the Japanese leader-father, he is expected to be sympathetic, nurturing, and sensitive to wishes of his followers' family, though at the same time vicious and aggressive in fighting external foes.
>
> (Pye 1985: 67)

This richly faceted description is meaningful within a traditional cultural context, and in the case of Korea, we can see how this context informs present-day leadership and perceptions of leadership. The overly high expectations are transformed—when promises are broken in the vortex of real-life politics—into equally strong disappointments.

It is foreseeable that the ambivalence in people's attitudes toward leadership affects their views about the political system as such. However difficult to measure and inaccurate the result, we tried to rate general satisfaction with the system by asking: "How well do you think your country's political system is working?" On a scale from 0 (very badly) to 10 (very well), 82 per cent of the respondents marked between 0 and 5 (inclusive) (EPCReN forthcoming). The KDB survey tested a similar question from 1994 through 1999, and Professor Shin reports that while 58 per cent found the system to be functioning satisfactorily in 1994, only 36 per cent expressed this view in 1999. The author's conclusion is that "there has been a steady and significant regression in the democratization of political beliefs and values. This is the most notable characteristic of Korean democratization in recent years" (Shin 2000: 59).

The data reported above suggest that both central traditional values and a Western-type understanding of democracy command support in present-day Korea. It is a prevalent opinion, also shared by Professor Shin, that the postwar military dictatorships must be blamed for the widespread nondemocratic values and political practices (ibid.: 54). To explain the prevalence, even the growing strength, of cultural values unfavorable to democracy he refers to a downward trend in cultural democratization. Yet he states, "For a large majority of the Korean people, the current regime fails to meet their standards for democratic political order"(ibid.: 59).

A basic problem in this seems to be that while people want democracy, more democracy than they have today, the same people are not much committed to the practice of democratic governance, having little trust in the institutions designed to make democracy possible. If this reluctance is due to authoritarian schooling during military dictatorships, time may be the remedy. However, if the culprit is Confucius rather than Park Chung-hee, a comparatively quick solution may be much less likely. With reference to the moral education program mentioned above, and to the Confucian undercurrent—even within the modernized moral teaching—my suggestion is that the values, norms and social attitudes which conflict with liberal democratic ideas in Korean society are more deep-rooted than a life under thirty plus years of military dictatorships could possibly make them.

Prospects for a culturally acceptable mode of government

In the process of globalization, the concept of democracy has to be reconsidered not only in East Asia but in the West as well. It is not a matter of finding the ultimate model, but of realizing the simple truth that the divergence between ideal democracy and the existing reality seems to be increasing.

Democracy as government *of* the people, *for* the people, and *by* the people is more and more of an illusion in most Western countries. Politics have developed from people's power into a trade for specialists. Instead of being a dialog between leaders and the led, the discussion between advocates

of alternative solutions to political problems is guided by commercial advertisement companies. Elected politicians are hunted by lobbyists paid by large
organizations and huge private firms, and the time horizon for a politician is
limited to the period between two elections. The outcome of election
campaigns increasingly depends on money and public relations consultan-
cies, which leaves neither room nor reason for popular political
participation. Instead of providing public information to qualify for democratic participation, the mass media have become sources of entertainment.
Thus political apathy and alienation among "the grassroots" is prevalent.
Whether this situation is solely due to the intrusion of market "rationality"
into politics, or whether one must look for other reasons as well, lies outside
the scope of this chapter. But regardless of the reasons, Western politics—
and not only the American version of it—seem to be steadily developing in a
less and less democratic direction.

The political scene in Korea and other parts of East Asia also has
changed remarkably in the past few years. Still, no country in the region is
likely to succeed in making a liberal system, identical to those established in
the West, work in their country. Political pluralism has taken root, but
democratization is not an uncontested development. By emphasizing the
importance of culture and cultural differences, which will increasingly play
an important role in world politics, the above discussion consequently rejects
the idea that liberal democracy is "the only game in town."

In relation to our present discussion, one of Samuel Huntington's observations concerning Asia deserves special attention. Though a controversial
figure in political science, his contribution to reintroducing the cultural
perspective in studies of international politics deserves acclaim. He points to
the dominant-party system as an interesting consequence of the strong trend
of continuity in East Asian political culture. The dominant-party system
involves competition for power without alternation of power holders, and
participation in elections for all but participation in office only for the mainstream party (Huntington 1991: 306). He suggests that such a system may be
seen as representing "an adaption of Western democratic practice to serve
Asian or Confucian political values. Democratic institutions work not to
promote Western values of competition and change but to enhance
Confucian values of consensus and stability" (ibid.). From a Western point
of view this may not be at all acceptable. Proponents of democracy, as it has
hitherto been known, might wish to reserve the concept for political systems
with more clear-cut definitions, systems which live up to some basic aspects
delineated in the liberalist tradition. The problem with this view is that we
then will have to continue operating with *the West, against the rest.*

Challenges of the twenty-first century include the apparent shrinkage of
the globe by means of communication, transportation, and marketization.
The "global village" has been a catchword for a while, depicting the
unknown with a familiar and safe-sounding concept. A more salient feature
of globalization is that huge companies now operate and dominate the

global market. Commercialized global networks in the information and entertainment industries promote standardization/regimentation through *infotainment*, undermining the social fabric of all societies by promoting the gospel of an individualism de-linked from social responsibilities. The total dominance of a market economy results in a growing gap between the rich and the poor areas of the world. Tu Wei-ming depicts the "global village" as "at best an imagined community" (Harrison and Huntington 2000: 259), and continues that:

> The world has never been so divided in terms of wealth, power, and accessibility to information and knowledge. Social disintegration at all levels, from family to nation, is a serious concern throughout the world. Even if liberal democracy as an ideal is widely accepted as a universal aspiration by the rest of the world, the claim that it will automatically become the only dominant discourse in international politics is wishful thinking.
>
> (ibid.)

In Korea, globalization became a relevant topic for the former administration to tackle, and a strategy for the country's active participation in the globalization process was developed.[12] The present administration seems to be following up on this, restructuring Korea's economy according to present global demands. Restructuring is, however, not only taking place in economic spheres. Late in 1998 one could read about the "new intellectuals' movement" in Korea, designed to produce permanent changes in people's cultural attitudes. By favoring creativity over schooling and innovation over hierarchy, the movement's aim was said to "de-Confucianize" Korean public life.[13] This may prove a tremendous challenge and could also turn out to be counterproductive to the reason behind the formation of the movement, which was *to strengthen Korea in the globalization process*.

For more than half a millennium, the traditional state ideology and social morality was Confucian. Throughout that extended period, Confucianism was inculcated in the population. Education and enculturation were the way, tutoring and self-discipline, moral behavior performed as ritual and reverence for age and tradition were the messages, and social harmony the goal.

Korea's modernization after the war has been marked by a peculiar dualism with regard to political socialization: traditional culture has been perceived both as an obstacle to development and as a necessary, even positive, point of departure in the modernization process. Civic and moral education have clearly been marked by these two positions. In the curriculum, social morality was basically Confucian, using the ideal patriarchal, hierarchical family as the point of departure and explaining all other social relations within the same contextual frame. Ideally, this framework was meant to extend to the national level, with the president as its head. At the same time, when politics and civic studies were introduced into the curriculum, the liberal version of democracy, as idealized in American political ideology, became the model. It is evident that these two ideals—Confucian social morality and liberal democracy—contrast with each other, and so if moral education has had any effect at all on those who received it (in my understanding it has, and still does), the outcome might be the formation of divided minds.

In later years tradition and modernity have been rationalized as basically generational differences, and it has been regarded as only a question of time until the change is complete and the division resolved—that is, until modernization is completed. In defending this viewpoint, many observers, including social scientists, have overestimated the importance of obvious and often articulated differences in purely political viewpoints, related to the generational "gap." By focusing on generational differences (and hoping for change) they have overlooked the possibility that beneath these political differences, there may lie a general common understanding about more fundamental but less visible matters, the basic values and norms which lay the foundation for the overall political orientation.

A strong support for traditional values and norms surfaced in the reported survey results. A rational and reasonable thing would be to accept this state of affairs. Instead of trying to uproot values based on Confucian morality, it would be more reasonable to consider them a necessary point of departure for any modernization strategy. This might prove to be more realistic as well as more effective. It might even open up for necessary adjustments and modernization of some problematic aspects of the widely accepted, traditionally informed (political) culture. It is widely known that the emphasis on the well-being of the collective as opposed to the personal interests of the individual often translates into political demands for obedience to the government as a means to true social harmony. This notwithstanding, a father-like leader is an acceptable concept to almost all Koreans. It goes without saying that some kind of checks and balances might be relevant.

The Western-oriented modernization of Korea has been a process of trial and error for more than fifty years. Several of the basic aspects of the democratic process, as well as the fundamental institutions of a representative political system, are not yet fully accepted. However, to suggest that an impersonal (party-based) representative political system is *not yet* rooted in Korea presumes that this is an ongoing process that will succeed one day. One could just as well consider the possibility that this process, after the end of the cold war, might transform into a search for more indigenous ways as a reaction against globalization. There are at any rate good reasons to do so. One reason is that as long as the Korean political system is measured against a Western model it will, because of different cultural traditions, continue to come out as second best. Another reason might be that as long as cultural traditions are perceived from a modernization perspective—which is a Western perspective as well—Korea's cultural traits will always seem problematic in relation to the preferred direction of development, which more often than not is toward the realization of liberal democracy—where the rights of the individual are the most central and seldom-contested aspect.

Concluding remarks

Individualism and liberal democracy are no panacea. Even in the most individualized of the liberal democracies there is, as discussed above, currently a search for communal values. *Too many rights and too few obligations:* for years this has been the complaint forwarded by Amitai Etzioni and the communalist intellectuals in the United States, who feel that their country is falling apart. In less individualized societies, such as the Nordic countries, there is a growing interest in the role of values in modern society. This tendency is a reaction to a growing uncertainty concerning the direction and the speed of development in our times, a process that many feel is beyond human control. A general clarity in life, a more manageable social and political environment, space for emotions in human relations, and time to reflect upon the meaning of life are felt to be lacking.

Realizing that political ideologies are in deep crisis and that many people in the modern world are experiencing a value vacuum which sometimes causes social and mental alienation, it is time to question whether the market qualifies as the only and basic value measurement. In his article "East Asia as Conservative Civilization: Restoration and Preservation as Political Processes" Robert E. Bedeski suggests that "Western liberal ideas and society remain alien to the sinic world and its epigones—not because they are not understood, but because they are understood—and rejected" (Bedeski 2001: 99). This rejection might be deliberately formulated, as it has been by Mr Lee in Singapore, or it might on the contrary be subdued, as has been the case in Korea.

It still seems clear that Korea's imported democracy has failed to accommodate the community-shared values which are based in the traditional political order and rationalized in a Confucian, family oriented social morality. Or, to formulate it differently: the present, commonly shared social morality in Korea does not support a liberalist version of democracy which hails individual freedom, freedom of choice, and political pluralism as the supreme good. Empirical evidence from several surveys, some of them reported in this chapter, as well as simple observation of social interaction in Korea—inside and outside the political sphere—substantiates that there is a discrepancy between the existing social morality and the liberal democratic ideology. Politics, as the concept encompassing the whole system of power relations in a society, is not independent of the general social pattern. Our Korean data suggest that cultural traditions make a difference. To establish a well-functioning political system it seems crucial to consider the links between politics and culture. Implicit in this view is that liberal democracy as a universally applicable political model has no future.

The most precious thing for a human being is another human being. How we relate to each other, both on the personal level and globally, ranks among the most important political questions of our times. Thus, it may not be the individual per se, but the relations between each individual and any other individual that really matters. The rules of such relations cannot—in a society—be everybody's free choice. In that case individual freedom may result in the opposite for others. Constraints on the individual and the need for some social conformity must be understood as a necessary means to maintain an orderly community, stressing mutual responsibility for the well-being of all. The particular way of promoting such constraints and their character as well as the pattern of social conformity differs from place to place, and changes—albeit slowly—over time. In his "Multiple Modernities", Tu Wei-ming suggests that "Asian values" such as sympathy, distributive justice, consciousness of duty, ritual, public spiritedness, and group orientation, are universalizable modern values (Harrison and Huntington 2000: 264). Whether these values are particularly Asian can be discussed. Those traits we have found to characterize Korean political culture can be found within several other cultures as well. Perhaps East Asian Confucianism, which clearly impacts Korean politics and daily life, may, in a modernized version, be congruent with communitarian as well as European social-democratic welfare ideas—and thus have a message for the world at large on its long journey toward true universalism.

Notes

1 This revamping of the social infrastructure combined with the need for general political education was high on the agenda both before and after Park Chung-hee's military rule from 1961 to 1979. It is interesting to note that Park actually criticized what was labelled democracy in Korea at that time by calling the process a "compulsory transplantation of a blindly imitated, lame, imported democracy" (Park 1962: 15).

2 In addition to the survey conducted by Lee Nam Young 1973–1974 and reported in 1985, Lee Hong-koo, Hong Sung-chik, Lee Young-ho, Oh In-hwan, Kim Bun-woong and others tried to conduct surveys, despite the harsh political climate which obviously affected the outcome. This could be seen, for example, by the high rate of "no answer/don't know" recorded in their studies.

3 In 1975 a former minister of education recalled that "in the euphoria of post-liberation excitement, we were all blindly optimistic about the prospects of our nation. Whatever each of us may have understood by the term democracy, we were all convinced that democracy was what we wanted and would get. Perhaps it was an illusion to think so, but I must say it was a great illusion while it lasted" (Min 1975: 2).

4 Surveys conducted in 1990 and 1995 reveal that 99 and 98 per cent respectively agreed to a statement claiming that "Without human rights there is no democracy" and 95 per cent in both surveys accepted a statement claiming "Essential to democracy is people's participation" (Helgesen 1998).

5 In the following Korea means South Korea.

6 In South Korea the notorious dissident Kim Dae Jung was, against all odds, elected president of the country in 1997. Barely escaping a death penalty in 1980 as the alleged mastermind behind the Kwangju uprising, which remains one of

the difficult wounds to heal in Korea's postwar political history, this regional leader and lifelong fighter for democracy, human rights and reconciliation with North Korea outmaneuvered the hitherto ruling élite. He reached his goal by forming an alliance with Kim Jong-pil, heading the right-wing United Liberal Democrats. This Kim was the former head of the Korean CIA and the very person who signed Kim Dae Jung's death sentence.

7 The Blue House is, little surprise, a Koreanization of The White House. In Korea white is the mourners' color, blue that of the King.

8 When the Nobel comittee in Oslo awarded Kim Dae Jung the Nobel Peace Prize 2000, the South Korean president was granted the finest honor and proof of political sincerity globally available.

9 Personal exchange with Kim Dae Jung in Copenhagen, summer 1995.

10 Two surveys conducted in 1990 and 1995 (N:500 and 838 respectively) were carried out with strong support from Professor Kim Uichol, Chung-ang University, and Professor Park Young Shin, Inchon University. The 2000 survey is a part of an international study on Good Government conducted by researchers from EPCReN, the Eurasia Political Culture Research Network. The main investigator of the Korea survey was Lew Seok-choon from Yonsei University. The 2000 national sample survey was administered by the Korea Gallup.

11 Personal communication at a former prime minister's office in Seoul, September 1997.

12 An example is "The Segyehwa Policy of Korea under President Kim Young Sam," an official pamphlet published by the Korean Overseas Information Service, 1995.

13 This was reported in *Newsreview*, December 19, 1998, and commented upon by columnist Robert J. Fouser in his regular contribution "Cultural Dimensions," pp.14–15.

References

Ahn, B. M., Kil, S. H. and Kim, K. W (1988) *Elections in Korea*, Seoul: Seoul Computer Press.

Bedeski, R. E. (2001) "East Asia as Conservative Civilization: Restoration and Preservation as Political Processes," *Korea Observer*, 32, 1: 83–110

EPCReN (forthcoming) *Good Government, East Asian and Nordic Perspectives, 1999–2001*, Eurasia Political Culture Research Network, NIAS/Curzon Press.

Etzioni, A. (1992) "On the Place of Virtues in a Pluralistic Democracy," *American Behavioral Scientist*, 35, 4/5.

Fouser, R. J. (1998) "Cultural Dimensions," *Newsreview*, December 19: 14–15.

Hahm, P. C. (1986) *Korean Jurisprudence, Politics and Culture*, Seoul: Yonsei University Press.

Harrison, L. E. and Huntington, S. P. (2000) *Culture Matters. How Values Shape Human Progress*, New York: Basic Books.

Helgesen, G. (1998) *Democracy and Authority in Korea. The Cultural Dimension in Korean Politics*, Richmond and New York: Curzon/St. Martins.

Huntington, S. P. (1991) *The Third Wave. Democratization in the Late Twentieth Century*, Norman and London: University of Oklahoma Press.

Inglehart, R. (2000) "Culture and Democracy", in L. E. Harrison and S. P. Huntington (eds.), *Culture Matters*, New York: Basic Books, pp. 80–97.

Kim, D. J. (1994) "Is Culture Destiny? The Myth of Asia's Anti-Democratic Values," *Foreign Affairs*, 73, 6.

Larkin, J. (2001) "Kim Dae Jung Comes Up Short," *Far Eastern Economic Review*, May 24: 18–24.

Lee, N. Y. (1985) "The Democratic Belief System: A Study of the Political Culture in South Korea," *Korean Social Science Journal*, XII: 46–89.

Mahbubani, K. (1994) "The United States: 'Go East, Young Man'," *Washington Quarterly*, Spring.

Min, K. S. (1975) *Personal Reflections on Democracy in Korea*. Honolulu: Center for Korean Studies Colloqium Paper No. 3.

Moral Education Textbooks (1991) (in Korean) Ministry of Education, Seoul, Republic of Korea.

Park, C. H. (1962) *Our Nation's Path*, Seoul: Dong-A Publishing Company Ltd.

Pye, L. W. (1985) *Asian Power and Politics. The Cultural Dimensions of Authority*, Cambridge: The Belknap Press of Harvard University Press.

Shin, D. C. (2000) "Monitoring the Dynamics of Democratization in Korea. The Korea Democracy Barometer Surveys", *International Journal of Korean Studies*, IV, 1: 37–66.

Sopiee, N. (1993) *Towards a New Asia*, A Report of the Commission for a New Asia, Malaysia (no publisher recorded).

Tu, W. M. (2000) "Multiple Modernities: 'A Preliminary Inquiry into the Implications of East Asian Modernity'," in L. E. Harrison and S. P. Huntington (eds.), *Culture Matters*, New York: Basic Books, pp. 256–266.

Zakaria, F. (1994) "Culture is Destiny—A Conversation with Lee Kuan Yew," *Foreign Affairs*, 73, 2.

6 What sort of democracy? Predatory and neo-liberal agendas in Indonesia

Richard Robison

Asia's recent financial crisis has been more than just an economic shock. In several key instances it has unraveled entrenched economic and political regimes. Faced with collapsing currencies, fiscal crisis and rapidly spreading public and private debt, beleaguered governments in Thailand, South Korea and Indonesia have found themselves forced into agreements with the IMF requiring extensive deregulation in trade and investment and the reform of public and corporate governance (Robison *et al.* 2000; Pempel 1999). Banks were closed and recapitalized and corporate groups forced to write down debt, moves that threatened the financial regimes holding together privileged leagues of private oligarchies. As capital flight took hold, governments had little choice but to accede to the IMF demands. As IMF Chief, Camdessus observed, those who benefit from global capital markets must also observe its disciplines (*Asiaweek* October 3, 1997: 62, 63).

But it was not only economic arrangements that were to be overturned. As governments in Thailand, South Korea and Indonesia struggled to contain the gathering pace of economic decline, corporate collapse, unemployment and debt, they were also to unravel from within, a process hastened by a surge of popular protest. These events promised more than a change in government. They appeared to signal an end to systems of rule beholden to powerful officials, provincial bosses, corporate cartels and politico-business oligarchies. It was in Indonesia, however, that the most dramatic transition was to take place. Unlike Thailand, where market reforms and the increasing clamor of popular resentment in the 1980s had resulted in the opening of the political system, in Indonesia the authoritarian state remained intact after market deregulations in the same period. State capitalism was simply transformed into a form of private oligarchic capitalism guaranteed by the same authoritarian state. Yet, this seemingly invulnerable political regime was to unravel in 1998. Facing a fiscal crisis and with its corporate sector and banks mired in debt, the Soeharto regime was abandoned by its own lieutenants as angry and resentful citizens filled the streets. The old centralized authoritarian regime was dismantled and quickly replaced with a system where parliament and parties became the new arenas of power.

Yet, these events were to be no grand triumph of liberal markets and democratic politics. In both Thailand and South Korea, the pace of market reform has stalled and old power groups returned to center stage in political life. The recent election of Prime Minister Thaksin in Thailand has seen a return to a system of money politics on a scale even beyond that which characterized the pre-crisis Banharn government. In Indonesia too, electoral and parliamentary politics is caught between the entrenched remnants of the old state apparatus; its military, state corporations and courts, and a spiraling descent into the unconstrained politics of populism, localism and gangsters. Early champions of democratic reform now complain that democracy has grown too fast. For Amien Rais, Head of the People's Consultative Assembly and a leading figure in the democratic movement throughout the 1990s, democracy had outpaced the spread of democratic values and culture. Persisting remnants of feudal mentality hijacked the new institutions (*Straits Times* May 12, 2001). As we shall see, amongst neo-liberal economists and investors, too, the instability and chaos of the new democracy has invoked some nostalgia for the orderly rule of the Soeharto era.

The primary question for Indonesia is not whether democracy will become consolidated but what sort of democracy will emerge. What factors drive the apparent surge toward a predatory democracy that preserves the power relations of the old regime? Is this development a consequence of a weak civil society and a fragile middle class, the consequences of four decades of authoritarian rule? Or is it a consequence of poor strategies and weak leadership in the reformist camp? What I will argue in this chapter is that the struggle to shape the institutions that define the new democracy is dominated by the same broad alliances and coalitions of state power and social interest that dominated the Soeharto regime. It is not the weakness of Indonesia's bourgeoisie or middle classes but their preference for predatory authority that is decisive. At the same time, political pressures emanating from global markets drive a neo-liberal agenda that shrinks from a democracy that gives license to distributional coalitions. Their preference is to isolate the state and its technocratic decision makers from predatory raids by vested interests. Hence, the struggle in Indonesia is between predatory and regulatory forms of democracy.

Theoretical issues

To a large extent, the questions currently being raised about regime changes are replays of those that emerged in the 1980s as a wave of democratic transitions spread across southern Europe, Latin America and Asia, in Thailand, South Korea and Taiwan, sweeping away long-established authoritarian regimes. Such developments appeared to confirm for liberal theorists the inexorable progress of the liberal juggernaut and the proposition that the rise of capitalism and the emergence of market economies inevitably require the replacement of absolutist and arbitrary forms of state power with democratic rule. Resurgent modernization theorists argued that the globalization of markets and the emergence of a middle class and a technically educated population had created centers of power and systems of science and technology unable to be accommodated within authoritarian rule.[1] The interregnum of authoritarian rule as the surrogate of the middle classes (Huntington 1968) had ended. Thus, in Lucien Pye's view, the world of technocratic decision making, the constraining power of economics and technology must yield to "politics" and the stability of society sought in learning how to manage the disorderliness of politics (Pye 1990: 9).

Within the Marxist tradition, too, the rise of capitalism and the bourgeois interest provided the conditions for democratic transition. As the bourgeoisie are drawn to participate in the global economy, they feel the constraints of state capitalism and predatory dictators. They now seek to ensure "… an accountability of public officials and expenditure," and that "the common interests of capital shape the important policies of the state" (Harris 1988: 247). In this context, democracy becomes the "best possible shell" for capital (Jessop 1983). At the same time, economic growth provides the conditions in which the working class and peasantry are drawn away from the violence of revolution into the politics of democracy and trade unions (Becker 1984).

But new democracies, as with earlier democratic regimes in Malaysia, the Philippines and Pakistan, did not represent a liberal democratic convergence. They opened the door to the ascendancy of cliques and cartels of wealth and power, their legislative institutions the auction halls of politics, patronage and state favor (Hewison 1993; Handley 1997: 98; Anderson 1990; Gomez and Jomo 1997: 117–166). In Thailand, as Hewison has pointed out, the democratic reforms at the end of the 1980s can be seen less as mechanisms of popular sovereignty than as tools for powerful new political entrepreneurs to appropriate state power and capture networks of pork-barreling. Amongst the middle classes, so supportive of reform, there emerged, in Hewison's view, a fear of the "dark forces" unleashed by formal democracy. Similarly, in the Philippines, Anderson (1988) argued that *cacique* democracy emerging in the wake of Marcos' fall has served primarily to reinstate the rule of powerful families and entrench oligarchy, patronage and money politics. At the other end of the spectrum, the illiberal democracies of Singapore, and to some degree Malaysia, are played out in the shadow of a powerful central state and are dominated by a single party where civil rights are exchanged in a Hobbesian bargain for order and stability (Rodan 1993). Representative politics carried out within laws that guarantee free expression and association is overridden in the latter case by the authority of the state, and in the former by its inability to enforce those rules.

At one level, these might be explained as stages in the long process of democratic evolution. After all, the sort of democracies that existed in eighteenth-century Britain or in nineteenth century America; the rotten

boroughs and Tammany Halls, possessed some remarkable structural similarities with the sort of democracy now emerging in Indonesia. Indonesia, in
this view, still possessed a weak middle class and a civil society disorganized
and deformed by decades of suffocating authoritarian rule. It was an interregnum to be swept away as markets replaced "political capitalism," as civil
society asserted itself and as individuals and groups "learned" how to seek
and organize power in the new parliamentary and electoral institutions. But
there are difficulties in sustaining the idea that predatory democracy might
be explained as a consequence of immature capitalism, where the deepening
of capitalist development, more intense integration with global markets and
the increasing power of private business interests is so evident.

At one level the paradox is explained in terms of different and immutable
cultural traditions transcending time and the structures of society and
economy. Samuel Huntington, for example, concluded that some cultures
simply do not value democracy: "In contrast to the Western model, another
culture's image of the good society may be of a society that is simple,
austere, hierarchical, authoritarian, disciplined and martial" (1987: 25).
Such explanations were welcomed by a range of Asian political leaders
anxious to justify their own political regimes as specifically "Asian" forms of
democracy in the face of criticisms over human rights and civil freedoms
that came often from Western sources. It was argued that strong states and
social discipline were functionally superior mechanisms for organizing
markets and economic growth (Robison 1996; Rodan 1996).

The apparent disjuncture between assumed social preconditions and
democratic transition led a range of rational choice theorists to dispense
entirely with socio-structural explanations of democratic transition and
consolidation. It was proposed instead that these were driven by the
rational calculations of rising and declining élites facing rising costs of
suppressing opponents and forced to seek a new political format that,
while second best, is preferable to the prospect of mutual destruction
(Diamond 1993: 3). Decisive in the success of the transitions are the
specific twists and turns of micro-level political maneuverings between
conservative hard-liners and reforming élites in the negotiation of the new
regimes: the appropriateness of strategies adopted, capacities of leaders,
and the coincidences and confusion that intervene in the process. Hence,
transitions may be crafted and manufactured, even in the most arid of
social environments (O'Donnell *et al.* 1986; Diamond 1989). Identifying
the interests of classes and groups involved in any situation, argues
Przeworski (1986: 48), has no predictive value. "... objective conditions do
not delimit the possibilities inherent in a given historical situation and,
therefore, they are not crucial."[2]

Transition theory recognized that democracies might harbor the same
predatory power relations that were nurtured under authoritarian rule.[3] One
logical outcome of these observations is to ask whether regimes are relevant.
Is it really true, as O'Donnell *et al.* have argued, that even where transitions

are achieved at the cost of leaving the economic and political power of incumbent ruling classes intact the regularized rules and procedures of democracy will provide a framework for change?[4] Linz (1997: 408) has argued that "... even bad democracies are better than authoritarian rule or chaos since we can assume that they may undergo processes of re-equilibration, and with improved conditions and leadership may become fully consolidated." Emphasis is shifted to the problems of democratic consolidation and to a voluntarism in policy agendas focused on supplying the institutions and constitutional arrangements within which change may be facilitated.

But democracies harboring repressive, corrupt and rapacious systems of social power have shown a great capacity for survival. Philippine democracy has provided a shell for oligarchic rule for over fifty years now, as has democracy in Pakistan. There is little sign in either of these examples that a "re-equilibrium ... with improved conditions of leadership" is going to occur. Nor is there any sign that the illiberal democracy of Singapore is about to spawn a vibrant and progressive civil society that will release the grip of state power. The mere existence of democratic institutions has not automatically provided the pathway for workers or other politically marginalized groups to secure a political foothold. Transition theorists offer little to explain this except in terms of game theoretic abstractions that focus on poor leadership, ineffective strategies or unrelated coincidence.

The emphasis on agency over structure, however, obscures the circumstances in which choices are made. Élites are both constrained by configurations of power and interest and are themselves embedded in such structures in various ways. Political regimes and the institutions that define them are not just about efficiency, stability, order and integration. They are also about the concentration of power and its distribution. It is critical within the process of democratic consolidation whether parliament has authority over the coercive apparatus of the state, whether cartels of wealth and power are subject to rule of law, whether representation and civil rights prevail over the apparatchiks of centralized party apparatus. Some rational choice theorists accept the importance of social interest. They propose that "[w]hile social interests and relations do not determine the prospects for democracy ... Analysis of socio-economic structure is essential for identifying politically relevant groups and their policy preferences and for understanding political alignments and conflicts" (Haggard and Kaufman 1995: 6). This neo-pluralist vision, however, provides no sense of the vast historical shifts and overarching power relationships within which these interests are caught, nor how social interest is translated into political power.

In contrast, I propose that regimes are forged in processes of social conflict. In such conflicts, the bourgeois, middle classes and civil society play different roles, supporting fascist or predatory regimes in some historical cases and driving liberal reform in others. In Indonesia, capitalism and the bourgeoisie were nurtured within the state and dependent upon a relationship that kept the market, rule of law and democracy at bay. It is true that the economic crisis dramatically shifted the equation of power. It fractured the alliances that underpinned the Soeharto regime. Unable to rule in the same way, their survival required that they reorganize their ascendancy within the new democratic institutions and within new social alliances. In the specific circumstances, the interest of Indonesia's largest corporate moguls lay in perpetuating predatory arrangements, not least because international and domestic creditors were in hot pursuit. The new party leaders also recognized that entrenched state institutions were best able to provide the extra-budgetary funds required for political victory in the new electoral arena. At the same time, while the economic crisis strengthened the hand of reformist interests intent on introducing a rule based system, the neo-liberal alliances that emerged shared with their predatory opponents a profound distrust of open politics. International investors and financial institutions seek to construct systems of governance that provide certainty and predictability for investors by regulating markets, at the same time insulating "technocratic" decision makers from distributional coalitions (Jayasuriya 2000).

The Indonesian case

For over three decades, Indonesia's President Soeharto wielded power over Asia's most stable capitalist dictatorship. He ruled partly through a highly developed security apparatus, imposing an efficient regime of repression and control on political activity and expression. At the same time he constructed a vast corporatist structure encompassing all political and social organization within state-sanctioned political parties and front groups. The regime permitted no legitimate political association or political activity outside the state apparatus—civil society was effectively disorganized. Such a system was supported by an ideology of organic statism in which the state operated as the integrating cement of the national interest while opposition was not only denied legitimacy but was regarded as dysfunctional to the organic interest (Reeve 1990; Robison 1993). But the New Order did not rest exclusively upon repressive and political institutions. Within its structures it encompassed a vast and complex alliance of state officials, politico-business families and business interests that extended from Jakarta down to the regions and villages of Indonesia. A system of predatory power relations provided the cement of such an alliance focusing around a corps of power holders within the state apparatus itself who stood as gatekeepers to the allocation of the monopolies and contracts that constituted the currency of economic life in Indonesia (Robison 1986).

This seemingly invulnerable regime was to unravel rapidly in the wake of the financial crisis of 1997. Not only were its corporate moguls and banks paralyzed by huge levels of debt, what distinguished the Indonesian case was that its financial and economic crisis quickly unraveled the political regime itself. By May 1998, Soeharto had fallen. Unable, on the one hand, to stem the downward spiral of the rupiah and the wave of corporate and banking collapses that followed or, on the other hand, to resist the structural reforms demanded by the IMF, Soeharto's capacity to control events had evaporated. The apparatus of state power and ideological control built up over the past decades was to prove ineffectual in the face of the economic disaster and social unrest let loose by the crisis. For international governments and financiers, Soeharto had become the main obstacle to a cohesive agenda for economic recovery. For increasingly restive domestic critics he became the focus of resentment and the primary target of political action. The man who had created the complex and highly centralized apparatus of state power that constituted the New Order now became its greatest liability (Robison and Rosser 1998).

Attempts by elements in the military and the bureaucracy to channel anti-regime sentiment into racial and religious violence or to raise the specter of anti-foreign xenophobia were unable to prevent the unraveling of the regime. It soon became clear to the entrenched élites that they could no longer rule in the old way. Indeed, their survival now looked to be best ensured if they could successfully join and colonize the democratization movement. Deserted by his closest lieutenants, Soeharto handed power to his vice president, Habibie. Though this transfer of power was not generally regarded as a real break with the past, Habibie had little choice but to embark on a course that would introduce a new political regime to Indonesia. Changes to the laws on politics and elections opened the door to the free establishment of political parties and ideological platforms where previously only those sponsored and approved by the government had been permitted. An electoral process that had been totally manipulated now became disarmingly open and transparent. Military representation in the parliament was slashed and civil servants could vote freely for any party. Nor could the president easily control the composition of the MPR—the People's Consultative Assembly (the body that elected the president) by determining the appointment of most of its members as Soeharto had done.[5]

The elections of 1999 were the first since 1955 where the outcome was uncertain and the prospects for a change in government real. Golkar saw its vote drop from over 70 per cent to 21 per cent. Whereas the election of Soeharto by the MPR had been a mere formality in previous years, a complex process of political negotiation and maneuvering now preceded the election of the new president. In a volatile and often bitter contest, interim president Habibie and the leader of the largest party, Megawati Soekarnoputri, were defeated by moderate Muslim leader Abdurrahman Wahid, whose political party, PKB, had received only 13 per cent of votes in the election. Nevertheless, his election as president was greeted within Indonesia with almost universal acclaim, not least because he was acceptable to the broad range of Muslim and more secular nationalist forces as well as liberal and progressive elements. He represented what many believed to be the only chance for national leadership where deep ideological and sectarian divides threatened ongoing civil violence.

Internationally, the momentous changes in Indonesia were welcomed as constituting the long-awaited shift from authoritarianism to democracy. Not only was politics now being contested through elections and in the parliament, outside the state an array of civil organizations and a newly liberated press emerged to submit politics to an unprecedented scrutiny. But there are some worrying features, not least being the apparent inability of President Wahid to construct a cohesive and effective government within the new democratic formula. Ministers come and go with startling rapidity in a political arena where confused pacts and deals are continuously forged and undone in the volatile labyrinth of Jakarta politics. Political parties show few signs that they are bound together by any ideological or policy coherence. Instead, as we shall see, they appear increasingly to be mechanisms for capturing and allocating the authority and resources of the state and, in turn, to be the captive of a rapidly evolving system of money politics.

Democracy also brought the promise of economic reform and an end to the predatory relations that provided the political cement of the old regime. Together with the IMF, reforming ministers under both Habibie and Wahid began to accelerate the pace of economic deregulation, to restructure debt and recapitalize banks, and to introduce accountability and transparency into those strategic gatekeeping institutions that were the conduits through which monopolies and contracts were allocated (Robison 2001).[6] Yet, the new government has been spectacularly unsuccessful in achieving institutional reform. It has experienced great difficulty in recapitalizing the country's debt-laden banks and bringing to heel the freewheeling corporate moguls refusing to hand over assets or to write down debt. With few exceptions it has proven unable to prosecute and convict any of the major corruptors from the Soeharto era. Indeed, many of these continue to play a central role in politics. In the end, Wahid's government was paralyzed in its capacity to deal with the economic problems but also politically by the growing determination of parliament to impeach him. In July 2001, his government was brought down.

Blaming it on Wahid

As explained earlier, transition theorists argued that successful democratic consolidation was highly dependent upon effective leadership and strategies. In particular, it was important to accommodate former élites and ease them from power without provoking a backlash, and to satisfy new supporters by allocating more effectively the political and economic resources of the state. Incompetence was an attractive explanation for the chaos and corruption that accompanied democratic consolidation in Indonesia's case, where President Wahid's apparent erratic behavior and his colorful personal idiosyncrasies, his lack of interest in economics, the qualities of his advisers and his failure to assemble broad alliances were so evident. Without doubt, Wahid has made the worst of a difficult task. As his former Attorney General, Marzuki Darusman, noted, Wahid had ideas but little notion of the political processes necessary to deliver them. In a system that required the negotiation of complex alliances, Wahid, the champion of democracy, showed little taste for the art of politics. He was unsuccessful in putting together a cohesive cabinet and regularly dismissed and replaced ministers as the primary means of getting his way. Unhappy with the advice of ministers and the bureaucracy, he established layers of "advisory" boards, particularly in the area of economic management, further adding to the confusion and lack of direction of the government.[7]

Yet, this seemingly erratic behavior and the failure to establish cohesive government also reflect the political realities of the new situation. At one level, the fragile alliance of reformers face a resentful "old guard" of apparatchiks entrenched within the apparatus of the state; its military and security forces, its profoundly corrupt judiciary and in the vast reaches of the civil bureaucracy. At the same time, it confronts the so-called "dark forces" operating outside the framework of the legitimate state and the legal process: the growing threat of extra-legal coercion imposed by gangs and militias in the service of political and business interests no longer able to call on the formal repressive organs of the state. Both are the legacies of the Janus face of the old regime. Wahid's attempt to undertake institutional reform attracted a deep hostility that extends beyond the question of his strategic capacities. Megawati Soekarnoputri recognized that no democratic government could rule without accommodating the old interests. The real questions are: what is the price of accommodation and how can institutional and legal reform be imposed where pervasive predatory interests colonize the new democratic institutions?

Caught in institutional pathways: dismantling the old state apparatus

Despite the fall of Soeharto, the vast and pervasive state apparatus built up over four decades has proven resilient. Most resilient has been a military that had carved for itself an arena of autonomous power and authority in political and economic life. Though with a powerful veto power, it had been reduced in the last decade of Soeharto's rule to the role of bodyguard of the regime. As the regime crumbled, the military struggled to maintain intact its position, often by manufacturing civil violence and unrest and raising nationalist and xenophobic fears. Humiliated and with its status demeaned in the wake of its brutal behavior in Jakarta in the last days of Soeharto, it was to play a resentful and obstructive role until the Wahid government began to collapse.

President Wahid showed a determination to subordinate military authority to civilian rule, seeking to negotiate ways out of crises in Aceh and

Irian that appeared to be heading for a bloody resolution under the heavy hand of the military. He was also successful in removing some of the leading military hard-liners, including General Wiranto, and replacing them with "progressives." Yet, without an efficient and loyal civil bureaucracy and police force at his command, Wahid had no way of dealing with the deepening spiral of unrest and instability spreading across the nation. As the contest between president and parliament intensified, the position of the military became critical. Wahid's elevation of the reformist general, Agus Wirahadikusumah, to command the Strategic Reserve (Kostrad), signaled the beginning of determined military resistance. While Wahid's leading political opponent Megawati Soekarnoputri began to build alliances with the military, the military itself declared its opposition to the state of emergency Wahid was planning to introduce to avoid impeachment by parliament. This was a strategic intervention. The refusal of Police Chief Bimantoro to accept his dismissal from office by the president in May 2001 finally signaled that the military was out of control (*Jakarta Post* June 2, 2001: 22 May 2001).

Wahid also chose to confront powerful interests embedded in state banks and other corporations as well as within economically strategic ministries such as public works, forestry and trade. Such strategic entities as the state banks, Pertamina (the state oil company), Bulog (the state agency for controlling pricing and distribution of basic commodities) and the state electricity company (PLN) have operated as virtual empires in themselves. On the one hand, they had provided officials and those political families of the Soeharto era with nonbudgetary funds for political and personal purposes.[8] On the other hand, they were the mechanisms for allocating monopolies, contracts and licenses to business interests, the channels that bound state power and private interest. It is no surprise that attempts to reform these institutions ground to a halt, partly because of determined opposition from state officials and vested interests in the corporate world whose influence reached into parliament. But democratic politicians, too, soon realized that these institutions were potential pots of gold in a systems of money politics where access to huge funds were essential to electoral victory (*Tempo* June 25, 2000: 26–31; July 16, 2000: 17–18; Adicondro 2000). Rather than seeking to eliminate them, money politics demanded that they be captured intact.

Nowhere has the struggle between the new democratic regime and the old state apparatus been more intense than in the judicial system and in the courts. Rather than being executors of a rule of law these had evolved as the instruments of rule by law within the Soeharto state. A *Jakarta Post* editorial (November 22, 1999) noted that "... subordination of the judiciary [under Soeharto] paved the way for total control by the state of every aspect of public life in Indonesia." The judiciary was characterized by Tim Lindsey as operating within a 'black state' outside the rule of law, where the real business of power and politics took place (Lindsey 2000: 288). The courts were to remain an obstacle in attempts to prosecute high-profile corruptors and to enforce bankruptcy proceedings on insolvent companies. The repeated acquittal of those charged with corruption, including Soeharto himself, and the seeming inability of creditors to obtain decisions against debtors confirmed the belief that the judiciary had to be cleared of its existing and highly corrupt corps of judges before it could be used as an effective weapon for reform (*Jakarta Post* March 11, 2000: 1; March 13, 2000: 4). The judges were not the only problem. Wahid also inherited, in Lindsey's view, a new set of commercial and competition laws designed in haste after the fall of Soeharto to be easily manipulated in favor of entrenched commercial interests in the less-predictable environment of a democratic Indonesia (Lindsey 2000: 283).

But dismantling or reforming these institutions and introducing "good governance" was no simple technical problem. Such institutions were embedded in a larger web of social power and interest; the officials dependent upon the authority and extra-budgetary funds generated within them and the business interests for whom access to the benefices of power were critical.

Confronting an uncivil society?

The fall of Soeharto brought to an end the system of exclusive corporatist power that provided no place for political organization and association outside the state. It created a new social space—civil society—within which liberals presumed individuals and institutional complexes would be enabled to develop their interests independent of state control (Berger 1992: 12). Indeed, as the regime faltered, students and other citizens took to the streets in increasing numbers, demanding democratic reform and an end to arbitrary and repressive rule. A vigorous and extensive media emerged, representing a vast range of ideologies and interests and highly critical of governments and politicians. At the same time, nongovernment organizations flourished. Human rights and legal aid organizations now jostled with corruption and corporate watchdogs to scrutinize the government. The forty-eight parties initially registered for the 1999 elections included populist and radical parties representing agendas and interests previously proscribed under the Soeharto regime.

But this apparent blossoming of civil society was to contradict the classical liberal view of civil society as comprising independent and self-reliant individuals who would demand rights and rules to guarantee their interests and to protect them from the arbitrary actions of the state. This romantic view overlooked the vast disparities in wealth and power and the intense conflicts that shape any society (Rodan 1996: 4). Reformist forces that take to the streets as regimes topple or who draw up the new constitutions seldom shape or dominate the new democratic systems. Just as the students who took to the streets in great numbers in 1965 and 1966 to support the new Soeharto government were shoved aside and excluded from power in the following decades, the same students and middle-class individuals who pressed home the pressure for his removal in 1998 would now watch the political entrepreneurs and former New Order businessmen and officials dominate the new parliament. As in Russia, the rapid unraveling of state power left reformers exposed to the full force of oligarchic power and gangsters—this was the sort of civil society unleashed in Indonesia.

Democratic reform in Indonesia left intact entrenched political institutions and power relationships, a pervasive state apparatus dominated by a Leninist core of politico-bureaucrat cadres increasingly integrated with the growing authority of powerful public and private oligarchies. This shifting and fluid coalition descended from the presidential palace in Jakarta to the regions and small towns, linking the coercive power of the military with the allocative authority of the bureaucracy and the wealth of corporate and commercial interest. The cement of economic life lay in relationships constructed upon the expropriation of and allocation of state resources and power by officials and political mandarins controlling the strategic gateways of economic life. It was within this framework that a new middle class and bourgeoisie had been nurtured. Their survival depended upon their access to the patronage and protection of the state and its officials rather than their capacity to organize politically in defense of their collective interests.

There is no doubt that the power of these entrenched élites has been seriously disturbed by the economic crisis. No longer are they able to impose control over markets and society through the use of extra-economic coercion and political repression exercised by a highly centralized authoritarian state. At the same time, massive levels of debt and a loss of international confidence has devastated their financial and corporate institutions. But though the old order is reeling, no coherent new ruling class or coalition of political and economic interests has emerged to drive the reform agenda in Indonesia. Rather, reformers are isolated "heroes" within the ministries and the government, heavily dependent on the leverage of the IMF in their assault on the apparatus of state capitalism and the links binding powerful predatory officials to corporate conglomerates. So successful had Soeharto been in destroying the forces of social radicalism and reactionary populism in the mid-1960s and in disorganizing civil society and co-opting middle classes and business over the ensuing three decades that no effective or autonomous political organizations existed outside the state. So powerful was the repressive apparatus of the state and so pervasive the ideology of corporatism that opposition in any effective form did not exist either as a reality or as a legitimate concept.

Among the politicians of the new parliament the *nomenklatura* of the old regime are to be found in abundance. The formerly dominant state party, Golkar, still attracted 21 per cent of the vote and won 120 seats in the new parliament (DPR). It reportedly brought a war chest of US$70 million into the 1999 elections and continued to attract the support of wealthy corporate interests. It was accused of misusing foreign aid earmarked to alleviate poverty for electoral purposes (*Far Eastern Economic Review* May 6, 1999: 26; *Jakarta Post* May 27, 1999; *Kompas* June 3, 1999). Prominent Golkar figures include one of the most consummate of Soeharto's state appa-ratchiks, Akbar Tanjung. He is now speaker of the DPR and has been a contender for president and vice-president. Other prominent members include Ginandjar Kartasasmita, former Minister of Mines and Energy and Economics Co-ordinating Minister under the Soeharto and Habibie govern-ments.

Even though parties formerly marginalized under Soeharto were now to hold the majority of seats, their character was to change under the new circumstances. Subjected to violent military-instigated attacks and forced to shed its leadership in 1996, the Indonesian Democratic Party (PDI) returned as the Indonesian Democratic Party-Struggle (PDI-P), to claim 34 per cent of the vote in 1999. Its leader, Megawati Soekarnoputri, became vice presi-dent and in July 2001, president. Though dependent on the support of urban poor and workers in the election, few of the new PDI-P members and none of its leadership were drawn from this constituency. Rather, the PDI-P leadership is focused around a corps of secular nationalist figures, including a range of recent defectors from Golkar and former generals whose agenda is difficult to distinguish from that of Golkar. PDI-P has also attracted the support of a number of businessmen formerly well connected in the Soeharto regime who have reportedly provided the party with the generous donations necessary to contest elections (*Republika* August 30, 1999; *Kompas* March 29, 1999). While economic liberals like Laksamana Sukardi and Kwik Kian Gie carry influence within the party, it also provides a place for those able to operate in the hurly-burly of predatory business politics. Most important of these is Arifin Panigoro, a business figure formerly close to the Soeharto family. Megawati's husband, Taufik Kiemas, is also well ensconsed and connected in the world of business (*Panji Masjaraka* August 30, 2000: 24–31; *Tajuk* March 2, 2000: 18–21).

While the number of players has expanded and the repressive apparatus of the state is no longer the main instrument of political control, the new democracy draws on political institutions well established under Soeharto. Money politics had been a fundamental part of the Soeharto regime. Whereas Soeharto simply required that private corporate cronies and state banks provide political funds through his notorious foundations (*yayasan*), today a range of parties and power centers compete for money. In just three short years, Indonesia's new democracy has been rocked by corruption scan-dals as parties and leaders scramble to attract business financiers and build war chests to contest elections. Wahid himself has been deeply implicated in such scandals (Adicondro 2000). Gangsters, thugs and militias had also been important instruments in enforcing the authority of the Soeharto regime. They have become even more important as parties and politicians are no longer able to call on the formal repressive apparatus of the state to enforce their will or defend their turf. Contending political groups now surround themselves with a vast and confusing range of gangs and militia. Such highly established gangs, for example the Pemuda Pancasila, Ansor and the PNI's Satgas (task force), operate together with numerous Muslim and right-wing nationalist organizations such as the infamous Timor militia, Laskar Merah Putih, and with local religious and criminal organizations.[9] The recent assassination of Sjafaiudin Kartasasmita, the judge who sentenced Tommy Soeharto to a prison term, is a sinister reminder of the growing influence of this aspect of politics.

With the rapid shift toward decentralization of government and administration in Indonesia, the same coalitions locked in struggle for power at the national level have developed their own systems of patronage down to the local level, competing intensely for control over provincial and subprovincial parliaments and government machineries. As the new political laws give regional legislatures more autonomy and authority, and as new fiscal arrangements promise a shift of resources to the provinces, these become important new prizes, especially in resource-rich regions. Thus the election of some mayors and *bupati* (regents) have been attended increasingly by allegations of widespread bribery (*Kompas* March 22, 2000; April 17, 2000; *Detikcom* July 17, 2000). At the same time, gangs, militia and informal security organizations are playing a greater role in the organization and enforcement of power here just as they are nationally.

The "contingent" bourgeoisie

In no small measure, Indonesia's political regimes have evolved in the way they did, not because its bourgeoisie or middle class has been weak (Liddle 1989), but because they have been able to survive and flourish, first under authoritarian rule and now under predatory democracy. The idea that at specific points in history a bourgeoisie may see its self-interest in authoritarian or predatory regimes rather than in liberal democracies is well developed. Explanations focus on its lack of hegemony—its need for the support of a strong state, or its need to maintain the protection from the cold wind of international markets afforded by mercantilist states (Bellin 2000). Indeed, there is much to be said for the proposition that the bourgeoisie, far from being champions of democracy, have always opposed democratic reforms that extend real power to the mass of the population (Therborn 1977)

Indonesia's bourgeoisie is not to be underestimated and has been an important element in the resistance to liberal political and market reforms in that country, and it now plays a pivotal role in shaping the new democracy. Throughout the Soeharto regime, Indonesia's corporate moguls flourished as the financiers of the regime and as partners in the metamorphosis of its political leaders into powerful business families. Authoritarian rule suited them for two reasons. First, the vulnerable social position of their dominant, ethnic Chinese groups in a sea of both reactionary and radical populism that swept through the 1960s and early 1970s required the sort of protection that could best be provided by an authoritarian regime. Hence, its relationship to the state could be seen in *Bonapartist* terms. But this explanation has its weaknesses. By the end of the 1960s, the Indonesian Communist Party had been destroyed and the Muslim parties, together with reactionary and xenophobic populism, had been marginalized. As the 1980s opened, Indonesia's largely ethnically Chinese bourgeoisie had entrenched themselves in large corporate conglomerates that operated across the region and embedded themselves in business alliances with powerful politico-business families (Robison 1997). Essentially, capitalism had made repressive authoritarianism redundant as the market imposed its own discipline and provided a "… unique political dispensation …", wherein, "… citizenship, civil liberties and rights can be separated from the distribution of social power" (Woods 1990: 61, 72).

Most important were the economic links built up over decades between business and the core of politico-bureaucrats within the state apparatus. Business benefited from economic monopolies, forestry concessions, discretionary state bank credit, trade and investment licenses and state contracts for public works and infrastructure. Incubated in a system where patronage and power constituted the cement of economic life, the Indonesian bourgeoisie played no active role in driving the democratic transition. Selective economic reforms introduced in the 1980s enabled Indonesia's private sector alliances to seize control of monopolies formerly in the hands of the state— the banks, public utilities and telecommunications being the most important. But this desire to deregulate did not extend to the political sphere. In the transition of public monopoly to private monopoly, authoritarian government still played a critical role (Robison 1997; Pincus and Ramli 1998).

In the post-Soeharto struggle to consolidate democratic reform most of Indonesia's large corporate moguls have been fully engaged in a last ditch attempt to resist government efforts to recapitalize banking systems and to write down private sector debt. Reformers initially made considerable headway as the authority of a range of state agencies to investigate corruption and audit state companies and banks was strengthened. Vast conspiracies in the state corporations, the banking and electricity industry, some involving members of the Soeharto family, have been documented and revealed by an eager press (Robison 2001: 124–128). Indonesia's corporate moguls sought to maintain opaque processes in corporate governance and to resist the operation of accountability and transparency inherent in a rule of law. With the bulk of their funds now overseas, these corporate interests have largely been successful in resisting efforts to force them to repay huge loans extended by the government to bail them out or to hand over assets to the reconstruction agency. In turn, IBRA now sits on a huge stockpile of corporate assets, struggling to sell these and realize the vast sums expended in bailing out the banks (Robison 2001: 120–124).

Like their Thai counterparts, the form of democracy that appears most functional for Indonesia's bourgeoisie is that defined by money politics, a parliament and party system that is an auction house for the wealthy and powerful. As Anderson pointed out in the case of Thailand, specific forms of democracy can be more useful to business than authoritarian rule: "As the financial backers of many MPs, the banks can exert direct, independent political influence in a way that would be very difficult under a centralized authoritarian military regime.... It can thus provisionally be concluded that most of the echelons of the bourgeoisie—from the millionaire bankers of Bangkok to the ambitious small entrepreneurs of the provincial towns—have decided that the parliamentary system is the system that suits them best; and that they now have the confidence to believe that they can maintain this system against all enemies" (Anderson 1990: 46).

As we have noted earlier, Indonesia's bourgeoisie too are adapting to the dispersal of authority among a broader range of power centers. Relationships between business and the new parliamentary and party politicians are becoming more pervasive. This is reflected in a growing wave of business scandals and claims of nepotism that are touching the new political leaders. Within the parties themselves, particularly in the PDI-P and Golkar, parliamentary members and local party apparatchiks and power brokers are drawn increasingly from regional entrepreneurs rather than from former officials and party stalwarts. In the struggle between reformers and what Co-ordinating former Minister for Economics, Finance and Industry, Kwik Kian Gie has termed the "dark forces" (*Tempo* March 26, 2000: 102, 103), Indonesia's courts and its parliament were to be important instruments in obstructing prosecution of bankrupts and the implementation of institutional reform of state companies and ministries.

The ambiguous relationship: markets, globalization and democracy

Is the sort of predatory democracy now emerging in Indonesia only a temporary phenomenon? Will the deepening entrenchment of Indonesia's economy in global markets sweep away the system of business state relations based on corruption, collusion and nepotism as expanding global markets demand predictability, transparency and accountability. The idea that third world economies would inexorably be subsumed within a system of capitalist markets or mode of production through processes of globalization is an idea well entrenched in both liberal and Marxist thought.[10] So too is the idea that democratic political institutions are a natural consequence of market capitalism. In the liberal view, free markets are the necessary basis for freedoms in other arenas, constituting a system in which economic and social power is dispersed thus requiring a political apparatus able to accommodate these numerous interests.[11] As neo-liberals gained ascendancy within the World Bank, the IMF and in the policy corridors of Western governments in the 1980s, it was assumed increasingly that the best way to encourage democratic reform was simply to develop markets. Hence, in the debate over sequencing of reform sparked by the transformations in Russia and China, neo-liberals like Overholt (1993) argue strongly for the Chinese strategy: market capitalism as a foundation for democracy rather than for the establishment of political reforms in the hope that this will lead to market reform.

In some ways the Indonesian experience appears to confirm that the globalization of markets undermine highly centralized authoritarian regimes and systems of government that are closed and opaque. As the IMF, the World Bank and other international financial institutions established influence over the policy options of a government besieged by the threat of financial crisis, they have focused on problems of weak institutional capacity, poor governance and the capture of government by predatory coalitions and vested interests. As far back as 1993 a whole section in the World Bank's Report on Indonesia (*Indonesia: Sustaining Development*: 135–164), was dedicated to the question of institutional reform, including reform of the commercial legal system, public enterprise reform, civil service reform, fiscal decentralization and environmental management. This pressure has continued and in successive letters of agreement with the Indonesian government, the IMF has embodied such reforms as conditions for its financial aid (Government of Indonesia 1997–2001).

But the association of markets with democracy or even with systems of regulation that are transparent and accountable is also contradicted by the globalization of markets in Indonesia. It should not be forgotten that globalization of financial and capital markets in the 1980s enabled the rapid growth of corporate conglomerates and consolidated the political authority of the Soeharto regime (Winters 1997). Short-term bank loans replaced oil money as the driving force of investment in the decade before the crisis. When the crisis struck it revealed a private sector in Indonesia with over US$82 billion in debts, most of them unhedged.

It must be remembered also that international investors flourished for decades in Indonesia under regimes that were inherently authoritarian, corrupt and predatory. International investors were fully aware of the "moral hazards" within which they operated. A pre-crisis survey showed that "[b]ureaucratic strings, corruption, insider trading and the weak financial system did not deter investors ... Almost all business players truly understood the weakness of the legal system, the lack of transparency in decision-making and the role of political forces.... But there were still no signs of hesitation on the part of investors" (*Kompas Online* December 22, 1998). Ironically, Western business was to express considerable admiration for certain aspects of authoritarian rule in East Asia before the recent crisis (Barro 1993: 6). They presented a model where wealth might be more effectively concentrated in the hands of investors free of constraints by labor unions, environmental groups and welfare lobbies (Robison 1996: 10–16).

Private investors have largely refused to re-enter Indonesia after the shock of 1997, despite the apparent bargains to be had. They cite, among other problems, social unrest, political instability and the unraveling of central power, uncontrolled land claims in the resource sector, growing industrial unrest and the disintegrating social situation (*Jakarta Post* August 18, 2000: 12; Morgan Stanley Indonesia 2001; Sadli 2000). There is an underlying nostalgia for the good old days of Soeharto when things were certain. Ironically, then, investors are not primarily concerned with whether there is democracy or not, or even whether there is corruption or not. What is paramount is a strong government, democratic or authoritarian, that provides predictability and keeps in check coalitions that might contest the terms under which they operate.

Globalization of markets, far from being an abstracted technical process is driven by a complex and fluid neo-liberal coalition whose central agenda is the constraint of the rent-seeking activities of powerful distributional coalitions and the removal of obstacles to market forces, notably, social democratic agendas. Within this public choice perspective, democratic politics offer such coalitions ideal opportunities to capture the political parties and policy-making organs of the state through organized lobbies and divert resources from efficient investment and growth (Olson 1982). Neo-liberalism is ambiguous in its view of democracy (Gourevitch 1993; Almond 1991). As Gourevitch states it, "Does economic growth require democracy (in order to prevent rent-seeking by those who control the state), or on the contrary, is democracy a threat to solid economic policy (because of populist raids on efficiency)?" (Gourevitch 1993: 1271). Globalization brings a new amalgam of market liberalism and political conservatism in which decision-making is transformed into a "technical" exercise based upon notions of efficiency. It is not the representative, democratic state that is the ideal political shell for neo-liberalism but the regulatory state that insulates its institutions; including central banks and policy making bodies, from capture by those vested interests that inhabit such institutions as parliaments (Jayasuriya 2000).

Where to now?

With the ascendance of Megawati Soekarnoputri to the presidency, the priority is to restore effective government and bring to a halt both political chaos and violence and the continuing economic hemorrhaging. Does this come at the cost of accommodation with powerful interests within the state that would constrain attempts by reformists to protect citizens from arbitrary rule and to impose accountability upon the state? For neo-liberals, the priority is an effective state able to regulate markets and to eliminate "social dysfunction" by improving the institutional capacity and ideological willingness of society to support the market economy.[12] Proliferating aid projects focused on building civil society and social sector capacity aimed at developing norms and values that favor markets and social networks that are dense and resilient: in other words citizens must be useful and functional. Liberal and social democrat reformers are failing to construct effective parties and win elections. At the moment they are caged within old parties dominated by various coalitions of predatory and nationalist interests. Organized labor has failed to expand its activities beyond strikes and demonstrations into the broader political sphere. Any alternative to predatory or regulatory democracy is predicated upon the political organization of these forces, and this is inescapably, as it was in Europe, a long and often violent process.

Notes

1   Lucien Pye proposed that: "All governments are put under pressure by the increasingly significant flows of international trade, finance and communications; by the effects of contemporary science and technology; and by all the other elements that make up what we imprecisely call modernization. But the authoritarian regimes are the most vulnerable and are therefore being seriously undermined" (1990: 6).
2   As O'Donnell *et al.* explain it: "This is not to deny that macro-structural factors are not there: world system, class etc. Short-term political calculations are only loosely influenced by such factors and cannot be deduced from or imputed to such structures. Instead, unexpected events, insufficient information, hurried and audacious choices, confusion about motives and interests, indefinition of political identities, talents of specific individuals are all decisive in determining outcomes" (1986: 5).
3   As Huntington had earlier noted (1984: 212), a controlled shift to democratic rule might be calculated as a mechanism that would prolong the rule of entrenched élites by pre-empting social unrest and a descent into mass democracy.
4   O'Donnell *et al.* had recognized that strategies of negotiation and compromise to achieve more democratic regimes came at the cost of leaving intact much of the social and economic power of the incumbent ruling classes. But they argued that: "… the consolidation of political democracy is a desirable goal. Is it worth deferring or forgoing opportunities for social justice and economic equality? … we all agreed that the establishment of certain rules of regular, formalized, political competition deserve priority attention by scholars and practitioners" (1986: 3).
5   The sources on changes to the political laws are extensive. See: MPR Decree No. XVIII 1998 and Law No. 2, 1999 on political parties; *Jakarta Post*, September 14, 1999; *Kompas* November 24, 1998; *Kompas* February 19, 1999; Hadiz 1999).
6   Among these strategic gateways are Bank Indonesia and the State Banks as well as the state oil company Pertamina, and a range of Ministries, including the Ministry of Plantations and Forestry.
7   Wahid began his turbulent economic management by sacking the Minister of Trade and Industry, Jusuf Kalla, and State Enterprises Minister, Laksamana Sukardi. Since then, no less than six individuals have been appointed to head the key banking restructuring agency IBRA, and other strategic institutions have fared little better. Wahid's lack of confidence in his economic advisers has been reflected in the establishment of several economic advisory councils with unclear powers and responsibilities and conflicting agendas (*Tempo*, March 26, 2000: 102–103; *Kontan Online*, 28/IV, April 10, 2000).

8 As late as July 2000, ministries and agencies reported the existence of around Rp.7.7 trillion (US$860 million in off-budget funds (Government of Indonesia, July 31, 2000: 8).

9 As an example, the recently formed "Anti-Communist Front," which has conducted book burnings and intimidation directed against progressive Indonesian politicians and NGOs, comprises a new alliance of fundamentalist Muslim organizations (Hizbullah, Front Pembela Islam and Ikhwutan Sunnah Waljamaah) with others close to the former regime and the Soeharto family (Pemuda Pancasila, FKPPI and Laskar Merah Putih).

10 In Marx's famous dictum the globalization of capital was the engine of change for the noncapitalist world: "The bourgeoisie ... compels all nations, on pain of extinction, to adopt the bourgeois mode of production ... to become bourgeois themselves. In one word, it creates a world after its own image" (Marx and Engels 1848).

11 See the discussion of Hayek's notion of the indivisibility of liberty in Laurence Whitehead (1993: 1252). That the classical liberal view linking markets and democracy remains a dominant force in the ideology of Western capitalism is evidenced by its pre-eminence in such publications and the *Wall Street Journal*. An article by Michael Novak of the American Enterprise Institute is a typical restatement of the classical liberal view in the op. ed. page of the *Asian Wall Street Journal* (December 28, 1994: 8): "Capitalism tends towards democracy as the free economy tends towards the free polity. In both cases the rule of law is crucial. In both, limited government is crucial. In both, the protection of the rights of individuals and minorities is crucial. While capitalism and democracy do not necessarily go together ... both their moving dynamism and their instincts for survival lead them towards a mutual embrace."

12 The idea of social capital reproduces the structural functional thesis that underpinned the Parsonian modernization theory of the 1960s and it is no surprise that many of the luminaries of this school are at the head of the new social capital thrust. See Coleman (1988).

References

Adicondro, G. (2000) *Post-Soeharto Multi-party Corruption in Indonesia: The Absence of Control Mechanisms*, draft paper for the proceedings of the CAPSTRANS conference, University of Wollongong, December, 2000.

Almond, G. A. (1991) "Capitalism and Democracy," *Political Science and Politics*, xxiv, 3, September: 467–474.

Anderson, B. (1988) "Cacique Democracy in the Philippines: Origins and Dreams," *New Left Review*, 169: 3–33.

—— (1990) "Murder and Progress in Modern Siam," *New Left Review*, 181: 33–47.

Barro, R. J. (1993) "Pushing Democracy is No Key to Prosperity," *Asian Wall Street Journal*, December 27: 6.

Becker, D. G. (1984) "Dependency, Development and Democracy in Latin America: A Post-imperialist View," *Third World Quarterly*, 6, 2: 411–431.

Bellin, E. (2000) "Contingent Democrats: Industrialists, Labor and Democratisation in Late-Developing Countries," *World Politics* 52, January: 175–205.

Berger, P. L. (1992) "The Uncertain Triumph of Democratic Capitalism," *Journal of Democracy*, 3, 3: 7–16.

Coleman, J. S. (1988) "Social Capital in the Creation of Human Capital," *American Journal of Sociology*, 94: 95–120.

Diamond, L. (1989) "Introduction: Persistence, Erosion, Breakdown and Renewal," in L. Diamond, J. J. Linz and S. M. Lipset (eds.), *Democracy in Developing Countries: Asia*, Boulder: Lynne Rienner.

—— (1993) "Introduction: Political Culture and Democracy", in L. Diamond (ed.), *Political Culture and Democracy in Developing Countries*, Boulder and London: Lynne Rienner.

Gomez, E. T. and Jomo, K. S. (1997) *Malaysia's Political Economy: Politics, Patronage and Profits*, Cambridge: Cambridge University Press. pp. 117–166.

Gourevitch, P. A. (1993) "Democracy and Economic Policy: Elective Affinities and Circumstantial Conjunctures," *World Development*, 21, 8: 1271–1280.

Government of Indonesia (1997–2001) *Letters of Intent and Memoranda of Economic and Financial Policies addressed to the International Monetary Fund*, http://www.imf.org/external/NP/LOI.

Hadiz, V. R. (1999) "Contesting Political Change After Soeharto," in A. Budiman, B. Hatley and D. Kingsbury (eds.), *Reformasi: Crisis and Change in Indonesia*, Clayton: Monash University, Centre of Southeast Asian Studies, pp. 105–126.

Haggard, S. and Kaufman, R. R. (1995) *The Political Economy of Democratic Transitions*, Princeton: Princeton University Press.

Handley, P. (1997) "More of the Same: Politics and Business 1987–96," in K. Hewison (ed.), *Political Change in Thailand: Democracy and Participation*, London: Routledge.

Harris, N. (1988) "New Bourgeoisies," *The Journal of Development Studies*, 24, 2: 247–249.

Hewison, K. (1993) "Of Regimes, States and Pluralities: Thai Politics Enters the 1990s," in K. Hewison, R. Robison and G. Rodan (eds.), *Southeast Asia in the 1990s: Authoritarianism, Democracy and Capitalism*, St. Leonards: Allen & Unwin, pp. 159–190.

Huntington, S. (1968) *Political Order in Changing Societies*, New Haven: Yale University Press.

—— (1984) "Will More Countries Become Democratic?", *Political Science Quarterly*, 99, 2: 193–218.

—— (1987) "The Goals of Development," in M. Weiner and S. P. Huntington (eds.), *Understanding Political Development*, Boston: Little Brown, pp. 3–32.

Jayasuriya, K. (2000) "Authoritarian Liberalism: Governance and the Emergence of the Regulatory State in Post-crisis Asia," in R. Robison *et al* (eds.), *Politics and Markets in the Wake of the Asian Crisis*, London: Routledge, pp. 315–330.

Jessop, B. (1983) "Capitalism and Democracy: The Best Possible Shell," in D. Held (ed.), *States and Societies*, New York and London: New York University Press, pp. 272–289.

Liddle, R. W, (1989) "Development or Democracy," *Far Eastern Economic Review*, November 9: 22, 23.

Lindsey, T. (2000) "Black Letter, Black Market and Black Faith," in C. Manning and P. Van Dierman (eds.), *Indonesia in Transition: Social Aspects of Reformasi and Crisis*, Singapore: Institute of Southeast Asian Studies.

Linz, J. J. (1997) "Some Thoughts on the Victory and Future of Democracy," in A. Hadenius (ed.), *Democracy's Victory and Crisis*, Cambridge: Cambridge University Press. pp. 404–426.

Marx, K. and. Engels, F. (1848) *Manifesto of the Communist Party*, http://www.marxists.org/archive/marx/works/1848/communist-manifesto/ch01.htm.

Morgan Stanley Indonesia (2001) "The Need to Sustain Growth" February 22, on-line.

O'Donnell, G., Schmitter, P. C. and Whitehead, L. (eds.) (1986) *Transitions From Authoritarian Rule: Prospects for Democracy*, Baltimore and London: Johns Hopkins University Press.

Olson, M. (1982) *The Rise and Decline of Nations*, New Haven: Yale University Press.

Overholt, W. H. (1993) *The Rise of China: How Economic Reform is Creating a New Superpower*, New York: Norton.

Pempel, T. J. (ed.) (1999) *Politics of the Asian Economic Crisis*, Ithaca and London: Cornell University Press.

Pincus, J. and Ramli, R. (1998) "Indonesia: From Showcase to Basket Case," *Cambridge Journal of Economics*, 22: 731.

Przeworski, A. (1986) "Some Problems in the Study of Transition to Democracy," in G. O'Donnell, P. C. Schmitter and L. Whitehead (eds.), *Transitions From Authoritarian Rule*, Baltimore and London: Johns Hopkins University Press.

Pye, L. (1990) "Political Science and the Crisis of Authoritarianism," *American Political Science Review*, 48, 1: 3–19.

Reeve, D. (1990) "The Corporatist State: The Case of Golkar," in A. Budiman (ed.), *State and Civil Society in Indonesia*, Clayton: Monash University, Centre of Southeast Asian Studies, Monograph No. 22.

Robison, R. (1986) *Indonesia: The Rise of Capital*, Sydney: Allen & Unwin.

—— (1993) "Indonesia: Tensions in State and Regime," in K. Hewison, R. Robison and G. Rodan (eds.), *Southeast Asia in the 1990s: Authoritarianism, Democracy and Capitalism*, St. Leonards: Allen & Unwin, pp. 39–74.

—— (1996) "The Politics of Asian Values," *Pacific Review*, 9, 3: 309–327.

—— (1997) "Politics and Markets in Indonesia's Post-Oil Era," in G. Rodan, K. Hewison and R. Robison (eds.), *The Political Economy of Southeast Asia: An Introduction*, Melbourne and Oxford: Oxford University Press, pp. 29–63.

—— (2001) "Indonesia: Crisis, Oligarchy and Reform," in G. Rodan, K. Hewison and R. Robison (eds.), *The Political Economy of Southeast Asia: Conflict, Crises and Change*, Melbourne: Oxford, pp. 104–137.

Robison, R. and Rosser A. (1998) "Contesting Reform: Indonesia's New Order and the IMF," *World Development* 26, 8: 1593–1609.

Robison, R., Beeson, M., Jayasuriya, K. and Hyuk Rae Kim (eds.) (2000) *Politics and Markets in the Wake of the Asian Crisis*, London: Routledge.

Rodan, G. (1993) "Preserving the One Party State in Contemporary Singapore," in K. Hewison, R. Robison and G. Rodan (eds.), *Southeast Asia in the 1990s: Authoritarianism, Democracy and Capitalism*, St. Leonards: Allen & Unwin, pp. 75–108.

—— (1996a) "The Internationalisation of Ideological Conflict," *Pacific Review*, 9, 3.

—— (1996b) "Theorising Political Opposition in East and Southeast Asia," in G. Rodan (ed.), *Political Oppositions in Industrialzsing Asia*, London: Routledge, pp. 1–39.

Sadli, M. (2000) "Restoring Investor Confidence," *Jakarta Post*, September 2: 4.

Therborn, G. (1997) "The Rule of Capital and the Rise of Democracy," *New Left Review*, 103.

Whitehead, L. (1993) "Introduction: Some Insights from Western Social Theory," *World Development*, 22, 8: 1245–1261.

Winters, J. (1997) "The Dark Side of the Tigers," *Asian Wall Street Journal*, December 12–13: 10.

Woods, E. M. (1990) "The Uses and Abuses of Civil Society," *Socialist Register*.

World Bank (1993) *Indonesia: Sustaining Development*, Jakarta, May 25, Washington, D.C.: World Bank.

7 Globalization, authoritarian regimes and political change
Vietnam and Laos

Kristina Jönsson

Change does not necessarily mean displacement. Instead it can represent new forms built upon old ones. Thus, there is both novelty and continuity, and the new and the old can be combined without total replacement (Holsti forthcoming). In the last few decades two sources of change have been particularly in focus—globalization and the end of the cold war. Globalization is widely discussed in public as well as in academic circles mainly because it is said to have effects on economic development that may eventually lead to democratization. The end of the cold war has had profound effects because two superpowers no longer have to guard their positions around the world—including in Asia. The fall of communism in Europe changed the global political map drastically, and many thought that it was only a matter of time until the rest of the communist world would follow in this latest wave of democratization.

This all makes sense—until you look at Asia. Four of the five remaining socialist states are Asian, namely China, North Korea, Vietnam and Laos (Cuba is the fifth). Vietnam and Laos, in focus here, have both opened up to the global market, allowing economic liberalization with economic development as a result. The end of the cold war directly affected Vietnam and Laos as the support from the Soviet Union ceased and new partners for collaboration had to be found. Nevertheless, and contrary to what one could expect, the regimes have managed to pursue their Marxist-Leninist doctrine not allowing for any major political reforms—especially not reforms aiming at democratization. How can that be explained? What makes Vietnam and Laos different from other socialist states? Or is it only a question of time until forces related to global processes will lead toward democratization in these countries as well?

The point of departure in this chapter is that Vietnam and Laos represent a puzzle allowing for alternative interpretations of the relationship between globalization and democratization. Both Vietnam and Laos are far from being democratic and are less integrated in global processes than most other countries. Nevertheless, something is happening in these societies, and below I will attempt to show how the liberalization process initiated by the regimes may in fact undermine their own power base—but not necessarily in favor of democracy as could be expected. Political change may go in an unexpected direction. The kind of direction this may take is, however, much dependent on how the regimes manage to handle the effects of accelerating globalization. The focus in this chapter is accordingly on the effects of globalization, within the framework of authoritarian regimes, in relation to liberalization processes.

The rest of the chapter is divided into three parts. First I discuss liberalization in relation to globalization in general terms. In the second part I briefly outline what kind of reforms have taken place in Vietnam and Laos up until now, and in the third part I discuss what could influence future developments. Finally I relate the situation in Vietnam and Laos to the dynamics of globalization and democratization in order to identify the main characteristics of change in Vietnam as well as in Laos.

Liberalization in a globalizing world

The literature on globalization is very diverse, both with regard to specific approaches adopted and to conclusions reached. Globalization can for example be seen as a diffusion of neo-liberal values and market principles. It can also be viewed as a higher level of internationalization or regionalization, alternatively as something completely unprecedented in the sense that there is no longer a clear distinction between foreign and domestic affairs (McGrew *et al.* 1998). Regardless of opinion, there is a focus on what is seen as an accelerating global trend, noticeable at both economic and cultural levels, with potentially major political consequences. Included in the notion of globalization is so-called time and space compression, in which the development of transport and communication plays a decisive role. The processes of economic integration and developments in communication technology are thought by many to give rise to increasing cultural interconnectedness and homogenization worldwide, as indicated earlier (Randall and Theobald 1998). The exact impact of these processes is hard to estimate, but it is indisputable that people (at least in the urban areas) are exposed to forces beyond national borders through the growth of the global economy, the revolution of information technology, and the diffusion of political and cultural ideas—though globalization is not necessarily linear or unidirectional. Instead of homogenization, a process of fragmentation may result. Some would argue that there is a process of homogenization in the economic and technological areas but not in the social relational area (Robertson 1994). From a development perspective it is even fair to say that globalization as a phenomenon is indeed very uneven, as many rural areas never, or only to very limited degrees, become affected by so-called global forces. Parts of rural Vietnam and Laos are good examples of this phenomenon.

In order to relieve various pressures and to obtain support without altering the power structure, one strategy for authoritarian regimes is to allow for some kind of liberalization (O'Donnell *et al.* 1993: 8). However, the liberalization process may also be the starting point for much more profound changes in society. For example, economic liberalization may lead to development, which could lead to higher rates of literacy, which in turn may make people more tolerant and hence open to democratization, and so on (the modernization argument). With this logic, the authoritarian regimes undermine their own power base by far-reaching economic reforms. However, the modernization approach is not always an accurate reflection of reality. Economic development can change or lead to the abandonment of political institutions without determining the political system that will replace them. Other factors—such as the underlying culture of the society (different classes and groups), the values of the élite and external influences—can be decisive in this respect. Dietrich Rueschemeyer, Evelyn Huber Stephens and John D. Stephens (1992) stress the importance of interaction between classes, and the fact that economic development changes the power structure within a country. Asian experiences show that economic development does not necessarily lead to democratic development, at least not in the short term. At the same time, democracy is no prerequisite for development, as demonstrated by examples such as Taiwan and South Korea. There is an important difference between liberalization and democratization however. Democratic reforms include deeper institutional changes supported by the public that make the process less likely to reverse, while there is a possibility that liberalization can be aborted relatively easily by a return to more repressive measures (Gainsborough 1997).

The role of the state and its autonomy are naturally central when discussing globalization, especially in connection to authoritarian regimes and their fear of losing control over society. For example, a civil society independent of the state may develop and challenge the regime—regardless of whether the civil society is seeking democracy. Here I merely refer to the state's ability to insulate itself from outside pressures, something of great concern for both Vietnam and Laos. It is clear that it is becoming more and more difficult for national governments to control the flow of information and ideas across national borders. For example, the Internet has proved to be not only a medium for communication, but also a vehicle for political change, as it has given an alternative medium for oppositions to voice their demands. In Vietnam an official newspaper has accused "anti-Vietnamese forces" of using the Internet "to slander the communist country, exaggerate conflicts and fan religions tensions" in order to increase political pressure on the Communist Party (*Reuters* February 19, 2001).

According to Vicky Randall and Robin Theobald (1998), the reduction of state autonomy is most striking in the economic sphere, but in the longer term it may effect the political domain as well. The inability to meet the demands of the people for employment, education and health, etc., at a time of budget cutbacks may undermine the legitimacy of the state and its government, whether the problems are caused or only reinforced by global processes. However, the development of information technology and communication could also have opposite effects, with a country's administration as well as its military and policy surveillance becoming more efficient. Also, economic liberalization requires an effective state and stable institutions for translating policies into action.

Some scholars challenge the view that globalization leads to the erosion of the state. They agree that control is lost, but not as much as is sometimes perceived. The reason for this perception can be found in the lag between new challenges and the state's ability to address them through policy. A good example of this problem is the privatization of the pharmaceutical sector in Laos and in Vietnam. The lack of regulations has, among other things, created chaos and resulted in extensive self-medication. This precarious situation eventually forced the governments to adopt national drug policies so that some order could be created in the pharmaceutical sector (Jönsson forthcoming). Another aspect concerning the autonomy of the state in relation to globalization is that governments for political reasons may overemphasize that they are victims of financial markets or other global forces (Lord 1998: 21–22), as has happened in relation to the Asian financial crisis.

Combining the arguments above leads to the conclusion that far-reaching liberalization as a means to relieve various pressures and to obtain support without altering the power structure is a tricky business in a globalizing world. The liberalization process itself may trigger more profound changes in society, and in combination with increased access to information and the diffusion of ideas, these changes could quickly accelerate. However, following the discussion above, it is not evident what direction these changes will take. The relationship between liberalization and democratization is complicated. Liberalization might lead to democratization through changes in the power structure and social forces outside the state apparatus. At the same time it could also create opportunities for groups who have strong commercial interest, who may wish to influence political development away from democracy. The liberalization process may even come to an abrupt end. Globalization does encourage liberalization, and vice versa, but it does not necessarily affect all segments of society and does not inevitably result in democratization. Below, this discussion will be applied to the situation in Vietnam and Laos.

Liberalization in Vietnam and Laos

Vietnam and Laos only recently opened up to the world economy and introduced market-oriented reforms including trade liberalization and privatization. In Laos, socialism was introduced as late as 1975, but the consequence was economic decline rather than prosperity. Therefore, an economic reform was initiated, the New Economic Mechanism (NEM), in the middle of the 1980s. Reform in Vietnam, *doi moi*, was initiated around the same time as a response to so-called fence breaking. This implies that discontent over the authoritarian nature of the party–state symbiosis led to spontaneous initiatives in the private sector at local and provincial levels in order to increase production. When the authorities saw the improvements they retrospectively approved the new way of doing things (Ljunggren 1992: 28).

Laos and Vietnam are both eager to develop economically—Vietnam even aspires to become the next Asian tiger—and the question is what consequences this will have for their political systems in the long run. Limited political reforms are being undertaken within the framework of the one-party state, and the idea is to strengthen the credibility of party and state as legitimate forces of change. The Vietnamese Communist Party has clung to the Leninist principle of "democratic centralism" and has resisted the establishment of conditions necessary for multipartism. However, the party has begun to recognize that profound changes in Vietnam's economic system are imperative if the country is to survive in the post-cold-war world. It has also hesitantly acknowledged that political change of some sort might not be far behind. Nevertheless, the scope and pace of change are disputed within the party. The question is whether Vietnam, and Laos for that matter, can achieve economic improvements in the absence of greater political openness. There are those who would say yes—but only in the short term (Brown 1996: 84).

The paradox is that the regime wants funds and modern technology from the outside world at the same time as it wants to be insulated from globalization (Quan Xuan Dinh 2000: 382). Still, economic development requires more involvement in the global, or at least the regional, markets. Dependency and economic development stand against independence and less economic development—and hence pose a threat to the regime's legitimacy. Popular awareness of what neighboring countries have, and what their own country does not have, is increasing. There is also a generation shift: half of the population was born after 1975, and the question is if the revolutionary ideals can match those of consumerism (Kerkvliet *et al.* 1999). Arguably the globalization processes will put more pressure on the regimes to act—maybe more so in Vietnam than in Laos due to its higher aspirations to economic development.

In conjunction with *doi moi* in Vietnam, limited political reforms were conducted. In 1992 the constitution was redrafted confirming the reforms that had already taken place since the middle of the 1980s under *doi moi*. The redraft was also an attempt to separate the state and the party and to enhance the rule of law. Another aim was to have nonparty members elected to the legislatures and to create a more open debate before decision making (Ljunggren 1992: 196; Tønnesson 1993: 35). The party remains in power, however, even if some of its functions have been reduced (Dang Phong and Beresford 1998: 88). Dang Phong and Beresford (1998: 104) call the political transformation taking place a process of "statisation." They argue that this process is a reflection of two tendencies at work within the Vietnamese state system. On the one hand, the society is getting stronger: people are materially better off, better educated and better organized. On the other hand, the legitimacy and prestige that the leadership gained from its early revolutionary successes can no longer be taken for granted. Today prestige has to be won and re-won. Also, there is a tendency toward regularization of the political processes. Internal secret party relations are replaced with public and formal ones, thus opening them to greater public scrutiny. According to Irene Nørlund and Melanie Beresford (1995: 10), the leaders in Vietnam act like the leaders in most other political systems in the sense that they build their power on coalitions of interests to support certain policies. The difference is that they do it within a one-party structure. The power balance is partially regulated by appointing candidates both from the reformist camp and the ruling communist party's old guard to top positions.

Some themes, which summarize the main views of the regime, can be distinguished in the Vietnamese rhetoric. According to the leaders, a number of factors can undo the progress made so far: the danger of lagging behind economically; deviation from the socialist orientation; red tape and corruption; and "peaceful evolution" (that is, "hostile forces operating under the guise of peace," which implies the erosion of communism due to influences of Western culture, ideology and trade) (Ljunggren 1997: 12). However, the reluctance to change in combination with the isolationist attitude has hampered the economy. The easy reforms have been made but not the tough ones, such as revamping the legal system and the debt-ridden state banks. Institutional or public administrative reform has stalled, and corruption and administrative power abuse are still serious problems (Quan Xuan Dinh 2000: 373). With regard to corruption, criticism has come not only from foreign companies but also from the Vietnamese themselves. The party has disciplined officials, even ministers, but the problems remain. The fear of deviation from the socialist orientation, or of unleashing political opposition, is pronounced. Warnings against Western influences have been issued, and even if the regime officially wants to appear fair and just, most unofficial reports tell another story. External interference of any kind is a sensitive issue—not only in combination with demands for democratization but for any kind of involvement in domestic affairs. Still, Vietnam is eager to be "friends with everyone," and diplomatic relationships have been established with the majority of the countries in the world (Biu Dinh Cham 2000).

Laos, too, wants to combine a one-party system with a market economy. In 1991 the first constitution since the communists came to power in 1975 was promulgated. This states that the Lao People's Revolutionary Party is the only party allowed, at the same time as the country should be a market economy with protection for private ownership. Like Vietnam, Laos tries to separate state and party, to enhance the rule of law, to have nonparty members elected to the legislatures, and to create a more open debate before decisions are taken (Ljunggren 1992: 196). Still, the government structures continue to be tightly intermeshed with, and controlled by, the party (Fredriksson and Falk 1998). The government has indicated concerns as to how liberalization will affect the political system, but it should be pointed out that political reform is very limited.

According to Grant Evans, a new process of legitimization is going on in Laos as well. For example, even if there cannot be a full-blown personal cult like that of the king in Thailand as it would go against the rationale of the revolution, a cult has been created around the deceased former president Kaysone. This should be viewed from the perspective that Laos never had a Ho Chi Minh as a self-evident national hero. Nevertheless, the Lao government has increasingly emphasized nationalism, and nationalism needs its heroic figures and myths. Rituals, traditions and national symbols can be seen as ways to cope with rapid changes, like those related to globalization. They can, in other words, act as a way to find something to hold on to. If the regime fails in regaining legitimacy through nationalistic myths and heroes, the country could fall apart, even if this is unlikely within the near future. One has to remember that only between 50 and 60 per cent of the population is ethnic Lao, and that the rest of the population is made up of diverse minorities. In addition, many ethnic Lao live in other countries, primarily in Thailand (Evans 1998; Fredriksson and Falk 1998). The regime has tried to increase ethnic pluralism in top positions in order to strengthen national identity and to avoid tension between different ethnic groups. There is a fear that if a multiparty system is allowed, the risk of ethnic conflicts will increase (Fredriksson and Falk 1998). Still, the biggest fear for some Laotian leaders is not so much Western influences but rather the "Thai-fication" of Lao culture and way of life—even though the Western and Thai styles may be related (Bourdet 1996). Thai television with its soap operas is extremely popular and so is Thai music. Here the similarities between the Lao and Thai languages naturally help to diffuse new ideas and impressions—including those of democratization. Thus, globalization has many faces and includes several different paths.

Evans (1998) characterizes Laos as a post-socialist society—socialism has come and gone. The regime has survived, but not socialism. According to Evans this is because Laos is an agrarian society, and because the government decided to liberalize the economy. The socialism that once was there was a Laotian version, a kind of indigenous socialism closer to nationalism than European socialism. When Laos got its first constitution after the revolution, That Luang, a *stupa* in the capital Vientiane, replaced the hammer and sickle as a symbol. This would indicate a shift from socialism to nationalism and a way to legitimize the regime in a time of change. However, at the time of the revolution socialism served as a uniting ideology in a society with many ethnic groups and borders drawn by colonial powers. The Marxist-Leninist rhetoric, still in use, is, according to Evans, a sign of Laos' close relationship to China and Vietnam in political matters. It is also a way to proclaim that the one-party state has no intention of allowing liberal democratic reforms. Besides, leaving out the Marxist-Leninist rhetoric would be to question the revolution itself.

Vietnam and Laos are both marked by colonial servitude followed by revolution, war and extensive domestic turmoil, and the past can in many ways explain the current regimes' mistrust of outsiders and their refusal to countenance any form of political competition. Though Vietnam was proclaimed an independent state in 1945, French rule did not end until 1954. The country was divided into two parts, North and South, and the division of the country lasted until 1976. After the reunification of the nation, the political intention was clear—to build a society emphasizing the collective over the individual (which proved to be difficult, especially in the South). The struggle against the French gave the Vietnamese Communist Party legitimacy, while the South Vietnamese rulers were seen as "American puppets." Colonialism left Vietnam with a very strong sense of patriotism (Brown 1996: 74–76). The French never emphasized the colonialization in Laos, as the real intention was to conquer Thailand (which they never did). The Lao élite could continue to rule, and nationalism did not evolve until the Second World War. The country was declared independent in 1953, but shortly afterward a civil war broke out, which lasted from 1954 to 1973. Two years later the communists came into power (Thalemann 1997).

The revolutionary past has been one of the main pillars for legitimizing both regimes. When socialism failed to fulfill its promises, the leaders had to find a new rationale to stay in power. The economic reforms were initiated in order to regain legitimacy, not to make the countries more democratic. The question is whether the effects of more distant historical and cultural differences will be more influential than the ideals of communism in a rapidly changing world. It is interesting to note that in Laos the socialist institutions only lasted for a very brief period of time, with few strong social interests attached to them as has been the case in Vietnam. Hardly a generation was socialized in school, and many of the old institutions in the villages, along with religion, remained intact (Evans 1995). Political institutions are in general not very developed, and Lao political culture still rests on interlinked family and regional/ethnic patronage networks that are both hierarchical and personal (Stuart-Fox 1998/99). In Vietnam the Communist Party and the People's army are relatively strong political institutions, but also in Vietnam personal relationships and patron–client relationships are the basis for political life. Below I will discuss some factors, or aspects, that I think are decisive for future political developments in Vietnam and Laos.

Domestic structures and agents of change

It is important to remember that despite economic progress, Vietnam and Laos are still among the poorest countries in the world. The urbanization rate is small in both countries, though people have started to move to the urban centers in order to find work. The majority of the labor force is engaged in the agricultural sector, and in the countryside, where most people live, not much has happened since the start of the reforms in the 1980s.

Many live in remote areas and have little contact with, or knowledge about, the rest of the nation—or the world for that matter. Though the school system in Vietnam is relatively well developed and the literacy rate is high, the quality of education does not meet international standards. In Laos the poor infrastructure prevents many children from going to school at all, and the lack of human resources is today one of the biggest obstacles to development. Both societies are extremely elitist, and the division between urban and rural, town people and peasants, is a major challenge for development (Bring *et al.* 1998). Economic development has favored corruption at all levels and business is risky. Foreign investors struggle, not only with corruption and red tape, but also with high costs. Vietnam has problems meeting its free-trade commitments, including those set out by the ASEAN, and it will take many years before the country can expect to move to the status of a fully industrialized nation. The last couple of years Laos has suffered severe problems with rapidly increasing inflation and a collapsing banking system. Bank loans often remain unpaid and large sums have been moved out of the country. Even if most of the economic problems in today's Laos and Vietnam can be found in domestic structures, the AFC exaggerated the situation. Capitalism is still more or less viewed with skepticism, and there have been official warnings about the consequences of capitalism in Vietnam as well as in Laos.

International organizations, donors and MNCs play an increasingly important role, both economically and politically, in the internal affairs of these countries. Vietnam and Laos are extremely aid-dependent and have been so for a long time (before the collapse of the Soviet Union the Eastern bloc was the main contributor). The American boycott of Vietnam has come to an end, and even if trade is still limited, it is a sign of an improved relationship with the biggest capitalist state in the world. In Laos the change in economic politics has also led to more contact with capitalist countries, especially Thailand. Moreover, distant provinces in Laos are engaged in economic activities with provinces in Thailand, China and Vietnam. Laos is surrounded by booming capitalist development, and regardless of what the central government decides to do, border trade is thriving. The increased wealth in certain regions, and concomitant increased power *vis-à-vis* the central government, may pose a threat to national unity (Evans 1995). In Vietnam it is perhaps the question of independence that poses the most difficult problem. Integration of the Vietnamese economy into the world market system increasingly threatens the ability of the Vietnamese state to direct the development process. Western multilateral institutions and investors continue to complain that government procedures are insufficient and difficult and that reforms will be necessary in order to attract foreign funds (Dang Phong and Beresford 1998: 105). It is interesting to note that at the same time as Vietnam became a member of the ASEAN and the relationship with United States became normalized, the conservatives renewed their emphasis on the competition between socialism and imperialism and expressed worries about the effects of openness and integration in the world economy on the one-party system (Thayer 1999: 10–11).

Brown (1996: 84) believes that though foreign actors may have some influence on the domestic political environment, institutional political change in Vietnam (and presumably in Laos as well) will most likely originate from within the Communist Party, probably from the younger cadres who are frustrated by the slowness of change in society. The army has warned the Vietnamese of "peaceful evolution," but how far the army would go to prevent external influences, which they think promote democratic values and practices, is hard to tell. The army plays a significant role in both countries. However, it seems that the army will support economic development because of its substantial commercial interests in the economy. In 1993 it was reported that 12 per cent of the Vietnamese army was employed full time in various commercial enterprises, and that the number of army-run commercial enterprises was more than 300, ranging from construction firms to garment factories, hotels and night-clubs, as well as joint ventures with foreign companies (Thayer 1994: 53). The Lao army has not yet been studied, and it is therefore hard to know about the situation in Laos. What is known, however, is that semi-military companies were given rights to logging and exporting timber, and there have been allegations of involvement in the drug trade (Evans 1995). Moreover, the army has good connections in the Lao communist party. For example, out of nine members of the Politburo seven have a military background. The current president and head of the party also has his background in the army (Stuart-Fox 1998/99).

The younger generation in general will without doubt push for change also (Brown 1996: 83). The generation educated in the former Soviet Union and Eastern bloc countries now has to retrain and learn English and Western ways of doing business, both in Vietnam and in Laos. Many feel they have wasted time learning Russian, Bulgarian, Hungarian, and so on. In addition, the skills they have acquired are often obsolete (Thalemann 1997). Due to low salaries and rigid structures many leave state employment to become entrepreneurs. In Laos, expensive new cars and palatial new houses are being built on the outskirts of the capital Vientiane, and the new economic policy has created a small newly-rich group, primarily consisting of businessmen but also party officials (often those with access to foreign currency). Robison and Goodman (1996: 6–7) label the new social strata as the "new rich." They are individuals with private control of investment capital and often large amounts of private disposable wealth. As a result a growing middle class based on educational qualification and expertise confronts old networks of patronage and loyalty. One could say that a new, though still very small, urban middle class is emerging in Laos consisting of not only businessmen but also mid-level civil servants, teachers, doctors, shopkeepers, industrial managers and entrepreneurs, most of whom received their education abroad. However, there is no sign of these kinds of group in the remote areas, and the benefits of the new world are still very unevenly distributed (Fredriksson and Falk 1998). Ten to fifteen years ago the dispari-ties were not there, and frustration is now mounting—albeit still below the surface. The increasing inequalities are becoming more and more visible, and the difference between living standards in urban and rural areas will most likely add to the growing social tension (Bourdet 1996; Evans 1995; Lintner and Crispin 2000).

Thus, the pressure for a more pluralistic political system may in fact be pressure for political supremacy of new interest groups, namely those bene-fiting from the market system (Beresford 1993: 234). James W. Morley (1997: 29) talks about a process of social differentiation in Vietnam caused by the economic renovation that includes the breaking of the state's domination of the economy and destruction of the party's monopoly of information. Older special interests, like the clergy, are reasserting themselves and new interest groups are forming. Further, access to computer networks, foreign newspa-pers and television is becoming more common. Though these are still mainly accessible to the élite (Brown 1996: 82), the increased flow of information will eventually influence the views of society in general and how it is orga-nized. An increasing number of tourists are visiting the until fairly recently closed countries at the same time as more and more students get their degrees in countries like Thailand, Australia and the United States. This interaction contributes to the spread of new ideas and ways of living—for better and for worse. However, a civil society separated from the state is hard to find in either Vietnam or Laos (Ljunggren 1994; Fredriksson and Falk 1998). Instead, most of the society is organized around various mass organi-zations linked to the communist parties. In Laos, as well as in Vietnam, there has been a religious revival during the last few years. A possible scenario is that religious groups will be an important part of a growing civil society due to the lack of other independent organizations. So far this is not the case in Laos, but in Vietnam religious groups already play a role politically.

At the same time as the political situations in Laos and Vietnam seem stable or, as in Laos, even close to inertia, there have been outbursts of opposition. For example, in conjunction with *doi moi* dozens of newspapers and magazines sprang up in the South. Veterans of the South expressed bitter resentment at Northern dominance challenging the authority of the party. The consequence was a backlash to *doi moi* as the party explicitly rejected the concept of political pluralism (Brown 1996: 77–78). In Laos the party temporarily encouraged discussions about democratization in 1990. However, this proved merely to be a way to expose those in favor of democ-ratization (so-called social democrats), and the most influential leaders were arrested and sentenced to long prison terms (Ivarsson *et al.* 1995; Fredriksson and Falk 1998; Stuart-Fox 1996).

Juan Linz makes the distinction between what is commonly referred to as loyal and disloyal opposition in liberal democracies, and opposition inside and outside the system in authoritarian regimes (in Rodan 1996: 11). In Vietnam and Laos very little opposition outside the system is allowed.

Criticism within the party has been permitted, but to voice discontent about the regime in public is not allowed—as noted above. Officially, there is no censorship, but the self-censorship is strong due to repeated imprisonment of journalists. The foreign media are extremely controlled as well, which limits alternative sources of information. Thus, any profound political debate is not allowed in the media, and demonstrations are in practice illegal. Needless to say, freedom of expression is clearly restricted (Marr 1998). However, recently a large settlement scheme in the central highlands sparked violent protests between the region's ethnic minorities and the army. This event has, surprisingly, been published by the tightly controlled state media (Quan Xuan Dinh 2000: 369, 379; *Agence France Press* April 27, 2001). Furthermore, many political prisoners have been released, but unfortunately religious leaders have been arrested instead. There is also an escalation of state executions, and Vietnam's human rights record still leaves much to be desired even if there have been improvements the last few years (Freedom House on Vietnam 2000–2001).

Recently there have also been reports about violent outbreaks in Laos. Army convoys have been ambushed and houses burnt down in northeast Laos. Who was behind the attacks is not clear as officially no one has accepted the blame. The regime accuses remnants of the Hmong guerrilla, supported by the CIA during the Vietnam war. A number of bombs have been thrown in restaurants and other public places in Vientiane (albeit without serious casualties), and unconfirmed rumors say that those responsible could be either "crazy individuals" or those wanting to legitimize authoritarian measures. Regardless, as a result of the attacks the government has tightened its control of intellectuals and students. However, the oft-forgotten Laos seldom gets severe criticism either from foreign governments or from international organizations, and government opponents cannot expect much support from abroad (*Economist* April 22, 2000, April 28, 2001). According to Lintner and Crispin (2000), the present development has led the Laotian government to partly turn away from their Western-oriented donors to their fraternal communist parties in Vietnam and China. China supports the political status quo in Laos, as China itself is facing the same sort of pressure for political change. Nevertheless, a process of change has been initiated and new groups with power potentials are becoming discernible in Vietnam as well as in Laos. The question is, of course, what impact these groups may have in directing future developments.

From what to where?

Officially Laos and Vietnam pursue a Marxist-Leninist ideology, but in reality both countries seem to move away from revolutionary ideals. Besides, the communist parties have shown a greater capacity to adopt and evolve than the former European communist regimes. Pragmatic concerns about national development and the legitimacy of the party have been more important than sacred socialist ideals (Ljunggren 1992: 200, 1994: 30). One has to remember though that the rationale for Vietnam's and Laos' political systems differs from the those of the former European socialist states in a few crucial aspects (besides the lack of simultaneous transition, both economic *and* political transition). The spread of communism in Europe was a result of Soviet expansionism, and the collapse of the Soviet Union ended Soviet supremacy. In Vietnam and Laos communism was primarily a lever to fight colonialism and achieve independence, and accordingly it contained a fair amount of nationalism. Thus, the logic that led to the upheaval in Europe does not apply to Vietnam and Laos. Moreover, the economic liberalization in Vietnam and Laos actually started before the collapse of communism, and consequently the reason for economic reforms has to be found elsewhere, though the lack of funding from the Soviet Union certainly reinforced the need for economic reforms. The surrounding booming Asian economies most probably made a strong impression on the regimes, not the least since they were the enemies and could pose a security threat, and news about the problems in Eastern Europe and the Soviet Union were already spreading. However, according to Evans (1995) the most important difference between the communist regimes in Asia and their counterparts in Eastern Europe—the difference which led to collapse in the latter but not in the former—is the social and economic structure. The European countries were industrialized with highly urbanized and educated populations, and the Stalinist system of economic management increasingly contradicted the structure it had created. Eventually these contradictions led to its collapse. In communist Asia the economic reforms took place in an agrarian setting less vulnerable to social and political discontent.

Assessments of future scenarios seem to be fairly united—even if predictions should be treated with caution: the authoritarian regimes will remain in Vietnam and Laos albeit in a softer version. Hence, democratization, or even the collapse of the present systems, is not an immediate option (see for example Ivarsson *et al.* 1995; Tønnesson 1993; Scalapino 1997; Ljunggren 1994). The crucial question is what these "new" authoritarian systems will look like, and how long it will take them to get there. Economic liberalization may lead to political liberalization, but it could also lead to even greater unity and discipline within the communist party in order to ensure that long-term aims are pursued (Evans 1995: 183). Lately a large number of people have joined the Vietnamese Communist Party, most of them with higher education, which may be a sign of increasing control by the Party. But as Tønnesson (1993: 63) points out, an authoritarian state can very well practice various sorts of popular participation at the local level. In Vietnam a decree known as the "People Know, People Discuss, People Execute and People Supervise" (Decree No. 29/CP of May 1998) allows direct elections at the commune level (Quan Xuan Dinh 2000: 379). In Laos the acceptance of participatory, bottom-up community development and the formation of community development institutions could be seen as a step toward local democracy (Fredriksson and Falk 1998: 7). Also, there are attempts being made to separate the party and the government, at least in Vietnam. But even if some tentative steps have been taken toward allowing broader participation in the shaping, or debating, of issues concerning the people's fundamental well-being, democracy in any liberal sense is not an issue (Brown 1996: 75). A more likely scenario would be an authoritarian pluralist system under which political restrictions will remain, but some kind of civil society separated from the state will be allowed. Taiwan and South Korea had this system for decades, and Singapore still has it (Scalapino 1997: 62).

At the moment the Vietnamese government can maintain control. The masses, the students, the middle class and the educated are not organized, and enough reform is happening to satisfy most people. In Laos the state is weaker albeit still controlling the people, but at the same time pressure for change is less than in Vietnam and opposition is practically nonexistent. What is true for both countries though, is that the regimes will continue to legitimize their policies and authoritarian measures by blaming unrest and other problems on "hostile forces" including external influences such as "social evils" and "US-based exile groups." The Asian crisis also strengthened the position of the hard-liners and military figures adverse to economic reform.

Vietnam and Laos suffer to a great extent from the same kind of problems, but in relation to globalization processes the outcome may still vary between the two countries. For example, there is a difference between Vietnam and Laos in regard to state–market relations. In Vietnam the state is relatively strong even if the role of the market is increasing, while in Laos neither the state nor the market is strong. Consequently, the effect of globalization processes may differ between the two countries. The tension between state and market in Vietnam could be more intense but possible to control due to the relatively strong state. In Laos the state may be challenged even after minor changes in society due to the lack of resources in combination with a decentralized administrative structure and a large number of ethnic groups. Thus, the liberalization process is by no means automatically unidirectional, and with the increasing flow of information and diffusion of ideas anything could happen.

Conclusion

There are two processes of change at work in Vietnam and Laos: one process based on the legacy of colonialism, domestic turmoil and the legitimacy of socialist rule; and one process connected to more recent global forces affecting economic and societal development at large. Naturally these processes do not work independently of each other, but so far the former has overruled the latter by keeping Vietnam and Laos socialist. My point is that globalization today reinforces existing processes, processes partially running parallel to globalization, and the outcome of these processes is unpredictable due to the ambivalent effects of globalization. Globalization may lead to democratization, but the result may also be a shift in power to groups in society that are not interested in democratic reforms. But regardless of what kind of political system is in place, globalization puts additional pressure on the leaders as they have to give up some of their room to maneuver when their economies become more integrated in world trade and finance. At the same time, the new openness and information flows make them increasingly accountable for their actions, and they cannot get away with things in the way to which they have been accustomed. New groups, or classes, are emerging based on economic success, threatening old power structures. This may in turn release other forces based on national or ethnic origin that could lead to fragmentation, especially in Laos where the state is relatively weak and decentralized. With regard to information flows within the countries, and from urban to rural areas, the picture differs. The regimes still control the media, which prevents a broader discussion about economic and political affairs. In addition, many people who live in remote areas are secluded from the transformation taking place in other parts of society. For these people, the information technology revolution has had limited impact so far. Thus, there is a tension between the increased openness and the regimes' urge to control.

Our theoretical point of departure influences how we perceive the present situation as well as future scenarios. If one compares Vietnam with the former Eastern Europe, for example, not much is happening. But if one compares today's Vietnam with its own past, the changes appear more visible. So-called peaceful evolution and values associated with liberal democracy are feared by the regime, but at the same time some kind of grass-roots democracy is allowed, and there are attempts at greater openness and scrutiny of the leadership. Eventually Vietnam will probably develop toward some kind of soft authoritarianism, with possible and temporary backlashes. Laos will be one step behind Vietnam, and consequently changes there will take more time and perhaps be less pronounced—unless globalization processes speed up and reinforce the change. The Lao leadership tries to tighten its ties to Vietnam and China, but among the people ties are stronger to Thailand—which could influence development in the long run. The argument is thus that the transitions will take place within the framework of liberalization, in the economic as well as in the political sphere, yet will not necessarily lead to democratization and liberal democracy. But then again, who could predict the political changes in the former Eastern Europe and the Soviet Union?

Globalization, from the leaders' point of view, is on the one hand perceived as something evil as it threatens the power of the regime, while on the other hand it is crucial in order to develop economically and satisfy the people. However, the problems of too little transparency, too much corruption and too little real reform remain, and in an era of rapid change the outcome of the ongoing liberalization process is hard to predict. The pace and the direction is much dependent on how the regimes handle the effects of accelerating globalization.

References

Agence France Press (2001) Vietnam Settling Soldiers, Militiamen in Restive Central Highlands, April 27.

Beresford, M. (1993) "The Political Economy of Dismantling the Bureaucratic Centralism and Subsidy System in Vietnam," in K. Hewison, R. Robison and G. Rodan (eds.), *Southeast Asia in the 1990s. Authoritarianism, Democracy and Capitalism*, St. Leonards: Allen & Unwin.

Biu Dinh Cham (2000) *Vietnam's Foreign Policy in Transition and Vietnam–US Relations*, paper presented at the Annual Meeting of International Studies Association, Los Angeles, March 14–18.

Bourdet, Y. (1996) "Laos in 1995. Reform Policy, Out of Breath?", *Asian Survey*, XXXVI, 1: 89–94.

Bring, O., Gunnarsson, C. and Mellbourn, A. (1998) *Vietnam. Demokrati och mänskliga rättigheter*, Stockholm: The Swedish Institute of International Affairs, Research Report 30.

Brown, F. Z. (1996) "Vietnam's Tentative Transformation," *Journal of Democracy*, 7, 4: 73–87.

Dang Phong and Beresford, M. (1998) *Authority Relations and Economic Decision-Making in Vietnam. A Historical Perspective*, Copenhagen: NIAS Publications.

The Economist (2000) "Old War, New Campaign," April 22: 58–59.

—— (2001) "No Dissent," April 28: 64.

Evans, G. (1995) *Lao Peasants under Socialism and Post-Socialism*, Thailand: Silkworm Books.

—— (1998) *The Politics of Ritual and Remembrance. Laos since 1975*, Thailand: Silkworm Books.

Fredriksson, G. and Falk, H. (1998) *Step by Step. A Study of the State of Democracy and Human Rights in the Lao People's Democratic Republic*, Stockholm: Sida. Studies in Democracy and Human Rights, Laos.

Freedom House on Vietnam 2000–2001.

Gainsborough, M. (1997) "Political Change in Vietnam," in D. Potter, D. Goldblatt and M. Kilon (eds.), *Democratization*, Cambridge: Polity Press in association with The Open University.

Holsti, K. J. (forthcoming) "The Problem of Change in International Relations Theory," in Y. H. Ferguson and R. J. B. Jones (eds.), *Political Space: The New Frontier of Global Politics*, New York: State University of New York Press.

Ivarsson, S., Svensson T. and Tønnesson, S. (1995) *The Quest for Balance in a Changing Laos. A Political Analysis*, Copenhagen: NIAS Report No. 25.

Jönsson, K. (forthcoming) *Translating Foreign Ideas into Domestic Practices: Pharmaceutical Policies in Laos and Vietnam*, Lund University: Lund Political Studies.

Kervliet, B. J. T., Chan, A. and Unger J. (1999) "Comparing Vietnam and China: An Introduction," in A. Chan (eds.), *Transforming Asian Socialism. China and Vietnam Compared*, St Leonards, NSW: Allen & Unwin Australian Pty Ltd,

Lintner, B. and Crispin, S. W. (2000) "Brothers in Arms," *Far Eastern Economic Review*, 11 May.

Ljunggren, B. (1992) *Market Economies under Communist Regimes: Reform in Vietnam, Laos and Cambodia*, revised and updated version of HIID Development Discussion Paper No. 394 as PhD Dissertation, Southern Illinois University.

—— (1994) "Beyond Reform: On the Dynamics between Economic and Political Change in Vietnam," presented at a conference on Democracy and Democratization in Asia, University of Louvin, Center for Asian Studies, May 30–June 2.

—— (1997) "Vietnam's Second Decade under Doi Moi. Emerging Contradictions in the Reform Process?", in B. Beckman and L. Román (eds.), *Vietnam Reform and Transformation*, Stockholm: Center for Pacific Asia Studies.

Lord, K. M. (1998) *The Globalization Scare: Are States Losing Control of Their Economies?*, paper presented to the Annual Meeting of International Studies Association, Minneapolis, March 20.

Marr, D. (ed.) (1998) *The Mass Media in Vietnam*, Political and Social Change Monograph No. 25, Canberra: Australia National University.

McGrew, A., Eatwell, J., Jelin, E., McGrew, J. and Roseneau, J. (eds.) (1998) "Globalization: Conceptualization a Moving Target," in *Understanding Globalization*, Stockholm: Almquist & Wiksell International.

Morley, J. W. (1997) "Politics in Transition," in J. W. Morley and M. Nishihava (eds.), *Vietnam Joins the World*, New York: ME Sharpe.

Nørlund, I. and Beresford, M. (1995) *Democracy and Power in a Transitional One-Party State*, paper presented at the conference Democracy in Asia, NIAS, Copenhagen, October 26–29.

O'Donnell, G., Schmitter, P. C. and Whitehead, L. (1993) *Transitions from Authoritarian Rule. Tentative Conclusions about Uncertain Democracies*, Baltimore and London: Johns Hopkins University Press.

Quan Xuan Dinh (2000) "The Political Economy of Vietnam's Transformation Process," *Contemporary Southeast Asia*, 22, 22: 360–388.

Randall, V. and Theobald, R. (1998) *Political Change and Underdevelopment*, Basingstoke: Macmillan Press Ltd., 2nd edn.

Reuters (2001) "Paper Says Anti-Vietnamese Forces Using Internet," February 19.

Robertson, R. (1994) *Globalization. Social Theory and Global Culture*, London: Sage Publications.

Robison, R. and Goodman, D. S. G. (1996) "The New Rich in Asia. Economic Development, Social Status and Political Consciousness," in Robison and Goodman (eds.), *The New Rich in Asia. Mobile Phones, McDonald's and Middle-Class Revolution*, London and New York: Routledge.

Rodan, G. (1996) "Theorising Political Opposition in East and Southeast Asia," in Rodan (ed.), *Political Opposition in Industrialising Asia*, London: Routledge.

Rueschemeyer, D., Stephens, H. E. and Stephens, J. D. (1992) *Capitalist Development and Democracy*, Chicago: University of Chicago Press.

Scalapino, R. A. (1997) "East Asia: Peace and Prosperity, and Some Democracy," in *Freedom House, Freedom in the World: 1996/1997. The Annual Survey of Political Rights and Civil Liberties*, USA: Freedom House, pp. 59–70.

Stuart-Fox, M. (1996) *Buddhist Kingdom Marxist State, The Making of Modern Laos*, Studies in Asian History No. 2, Bangkok: White Lotus.

—— (1998/1999) "After the Sixth Party Congress," *Lao Study Review*, 3, http:/www.global.lao.net/laostudy/6congress.htm.

Thalemann, A. (1997) "Laos: Between Battlefield and Marketplace," *Journal of Contemporary Asia*, 27, 1: 85–105.

Thayer, C. A. (1994) *The Vietnam People's Army under Doi Moi*, Singapore: Institute of Southeast Asian Studies (Pacific Strategic Papers).

—— (1999) "Vietnamese Foreign Policy: Multilateralism and the Threat of Peaceful Evolution", in C. A. Thayer and R. Amer (eds.), *Vietnamese Foreign Policy in Transition*, Singapore: Institute of Southeast Asian Studies.

Tønnesson, S. (1993) *Democracy in Vietnam?*, Copenhagen: NIAS Report No. 16.

8 Social movements, civil society and democracy in Japan

Hugo Dobson

The received wisdom today is that Japan faces a number of crises. Its economy continues to stagnate after the decade-long "Heisei" recession and refuses to respond to a series of stimulation packages which have had the unintended result of making the Japanese government the most indebted in world history. Since 1992, over ¥117,000 billion has been spent in pump-priming measures resulting in government debt reaching an estimated 130 per cent of GDP at minimum (*Financial Times* September 19, 2000). The organization of Japanese postwar society, once held up as an example of how a nation could modernize rapidly without the associated social dislocation and still maintain a strong national identity and sense of mission, has been blamed for a number of social ills from the Aum Shinrikyō's (Supreme Truth Cult) sarin gas attack on the Tokyo subway in March 1995, to an increase of cases involving both child killers and children being killed, to an increase in teenage prostitution. Politically, the nation is seen to be mired in scandal among politicians (traditionally tolerated) and bureaucrats (a new and more worrying development). Added to this is voter disillusionment with all the political parties, but especially with the LDP, which has maintained its position as the natural party of government since its creation in 1955 either alone or in coalition, except for a brief period from August 1993 to June 1994. In March 2001, on the eve of his resignation, the approval rating for Prime Minister Mori Yoshirō plummeted to the lowest levels since the Second World War (*Daily Yomiuri* May 1, 2001). Concomitant with this is a declining voting rate signaling general disillusionment with the political process. As a result, the Japanese public sector, and in particular the bureaucracy, has experienced a decline in prestige from the status of infallibility to one of impotency, and there is consensus that the only solution for these chronic problems is overdue and radical restructuring. This assessment of the Japanese malaise stands in contrast to the predictions being made only a decade or so previously about Japan as a new superpower (Horsley and Buckley 1990), that of an economic and social model from which the West could learn (Vogel 1979), and the dawn of an era of *Pax Nipponica* (Leaver 1989).

This chapter intends to cut through the once celebratory and recently *schadenfreude*-tinged characterizations of Japan in the Western literature in order to assess the state of democracy in Japan today with regard to its historical development and to evaluate the impact of globalization. It will examine whether it is accurate to talk of a Japanese tradition of democracy, gauge the importance of and the role played by cultural and behavioral norms, highlight the relationship between democracy and the pursuit of economic development in postwar Japan, and analyze the changing relationship between state and society in Japan as a result of globalization in light of the rising profile of Japanese nonstate actors.

Democratic traditions?

In order to understand the current state of democracy in Japan it is necessary to examine its introduction and development just over 100 years ago. Traditional liberal definitions of democracy have stressed an open and accountable government which is assured through free and fair elections and which guarantees civil and political rights within a developed civil society. With this definition in mind, looking back at Japan's recent history gives the impression that Japan has never experienced a revolution of its own design that has embedded a democratic tradition. Certainly it has experienced two salient periods of great change—the Meiji Restoration of 1868 and the American Occupation of 1945–1952—but as these were both essentially top-down phenomena, it is questionable as to whether they constitute a democratic tradition. Some have gone so far as to assert that: "there are no important features of the indigenous and traditional political culture of Japan which could be plausibly characterized either as 'democratic' in their own right or as serving to lay a foundation for ideas which would later be realized and identified as 'democratic'." (Marriage 1990: 229). In contrast, *kanson minpi* (literally, respect the bureaucrats and humble the people) is the phrase which encapsulates the historical relationship between the Japanese government and its people and the overbearing, preponderant power of the former. In elevating the bureaucracy to the chief political actor, Chalmers Johnson has judged the Japanese political process to be one of "soft authoritarianism" (Johnson 1982).

Meiji—restoration not revolution

The first of these historical turning-points, the Meiji Restoration, was essentially an exercise in crisis-management hastened by the arrival of Commodore Perry's Black Ships in Tokyo Bay and aimed at retaining power among a small number of Meiji oligarchs. Prior to this, the Tokugawa period (1603–1867) was characterized by the presence of an emperor who reigned but did not rule, with political power lying with the shōgun and the emperor providing legitimacy (the origins of the norm of veiling the source of political power can be traced to this point and will be adumbrated later). The social structure was tightly defined into samurai, farmers, artisans and merchants, but as Japan was secluded from the outside world and at peace for most of this period, the warrior class was no longer needed and the samurai moved into regional bureaucratic roles. This hastened the development of a highly motivated, disciplined administrator who paid great attention to local conditions and tried to garner as much support as possible from the respective region (again the origins of Japanese-style pork-barrel politics can be traced to this period). It was these bureaucrats of samurai origin who instigated and guided the restoration of the imperial institution in order to deal with the arrival of the West, the opening of Japan, and its rapid development into a great imperial power.

The Meiji Restoration lacked any of the traditional defining factors of a revolution. There was no radical ideology as in France, Russia, or the United States: rather, it was a nationalist plan to preserve Japan's sovereignty. It was not as violent and bloody as the French and Russian revolutions despite a short-lived civil war; there was no flight of Japanese loyal to the shōgun; and there was no execution of the shōgun unlike the Western revolutions. Nevertheless, the Meiji oligarchs did set Japan on a radically different course, with the goals of modernization and catching-up with the West. However, democracy was relegated to a cosmetic means to these ends, rather than to an end in itself. If the promulgation of a constitution (1889) or the establishment of an elected assembly (1890) were the hallmarks of a developed, Western nation-state, then the Meiji leadership were keen to introduce them but only insofar as they accelerated its developmentalist agenda and reinforced their power base. Thus, the Constitution, political and education reforms, wholesale import of Western technology, even the architecture (Coaldrake 1996) which constituted the Meiji Restoration, were motivated by the desire to gain the respect of the European great powers of the day and at the same time place the emperor as the symbolic head of state to gain the Japanese people's loyalty with the objective of stressing social harmony and avoiding the disruption that democracy would bring about. Thus, despite the veneer of Western democracy, the restoration aimed at ensuring the Meiji leaders' political position behind the veil of the imperial institution.

The flip-side of the "enlightenment" of the period (*meiji kaika*) was strict censorship (newspapers were forced to register with the government and the Home Minister could ban any article that attacked the government), a Peace Preservation Law of 1887 which allowed the police to arrest anybody simply suspected of plotting in the new capital of Tokyo, and a limited franchise until universal male suffrage in 1925. The bicameral Diet was limited in its powers. It could overrule a new budget but the previous year's budget would then be used. The House of Peers was populated by nobles who tended to support the Meiji leadership and was able to negate the power of the elected House of Representatives through a veto. The cabinet was not responsible to the Diet. The emperor was able to sanction laws, decide the length of Diet sessions (usually only three months), and dissolve the House of Representatives and call elections (in which only about 1 per cent of people could vote). Any further constitutional reform had to be approved by the emperor. Despite the apparent powers conferred upon the emperor, in 1888 the Privy Council was established to act as an advisory body to the emperor separate from the cabinet. It could advise but could not initiate action and provided a means of influencing and controlling the powers and rights of the emperor. The emperor was there to preside over Japan's development—a modern monarch for modern times—giving legitimacy to the Meiji government officials who actually directed Japan's growth.

The occupation period—a gift from the gods?

The primary objectives of the occupation were to ensure that Japan could not again become a menace to the peace and security of the world, by becoming a responsible and peaceful member of the family of nations, through the twin processes of demilitarization and democratization. Enthused by the anthropological work of Ruth Benedict, the occupiers saw the social structure of Japan as to blame for the militarization of Japan and consequent war, and in order to achieve this "revolution," Japan was forced into accepting Western (rather, blatantly American) democratic norms of behavior. However, this initial enthusiasm was replaced by *realpolitik* and the strategic concerns of the cold war with the American desire to use Japan as a base of operations for its "hub and spoke" security system in East Asia.

The demilitarization of Japan was carried out through the demobilization of Japan's war-making capabilities, the Tokyo War Trials, and the rewritten constitution of 1947, which included the controversial Peace Clause, Article IX, and embedded the norm of anti-militarism in Japanese society (see below). The democratization process was chiefly concerned with dealing with the position of the emperor. Calls for his trial and execution as a war criminal were rejected and the imperial institution was retained with the aim of making Japan governable. In the new constitution, the emperor was described as "the symbol of the state and of the unity of the people, deriving his position from the will of the people in whom resides sovereign power," renouncing his divinity and providing a starting point for a new constitutional monarchy.

As regards governing Japan, the Diet was to remain bicameral but with both houses elected and it was made the highest organ of state power. The Lower House of Representatives took precedence over the Upper House of Councilors. The Lower House elected the prime minister who had to be civilian and a member of the Diet (Article 66 of the Constitution). Prime minister and cabinet were responsible to the Diet, not to the emperor, and universal adult suffrage was introduced from the age of twenty. Labor relations improved so that Japanese workers gained the right to form unions and strike. By the end of 1948 around 34,000 unions had been formed with seven million members. Furthermore, freedom of speech for the media was protected. Anybody suspected of being unsympathetic to the new order was purged from government, media and education positions, a move which affected in total 200,000 people. In contrast, those who had opposed the wartime government were freed. In government, one of the first prime ministers from October 1945 to May 1946 was Shidehara Kijūrō, a noted liberal and internationalist of the pre-war period.

MacArthur claimed that Japan had undergone a "spiritual revolution" that "tore asunder a theory and practice of life built upon 2000 years of history and tradition and legend" (Dower 1996: 169). However, by the late 1940s the international context changed with the onset of the cold war and the American taxpayer was unwilling to support the status quo demanding instead that Japan do something to defend itself; but also within Japan the reverse course was an effort by conservative politicians to undo many of the Occupation reforms. Examples of the Reverse Course can be seen in Prime Minister Yoshida Shigeru's attempts to reintroduce the teaching of ethics in 1951 which, though halted by public opinion, were hastened by Prime Minister Hatoyama Ichirō's Local Education Law of 1956 which weakened the powers of local education boards and gave the Ministry of Education the right to guide the contents of textbooks, a uniform curriculum, and then in 1959 the teaching of ethics. In addition, by 1949 the purge was redirected to apply to communists and socialists. This led to a "red purge" of 22,000 left-wingers from public and private sectors. Unions were weakened and in 1948 civil servants were banned from striking. The previous purge of militarists was reviewed allowing various conservatives to reappear in government and business. Kishi Nobusuke became prime minister in 1957 having been vice minister in the departments of Commerce and Industry and of Munitions during the war.

Both the Meiji Restoration and American Occupation were essentially top-down solutions to national crises—an attempt to impose a political system on the Japanese people in the face of an overwhelming crisis. Even the so-called Taishō Democracy (1912–1926), which was sandwiched by these two events, is a misnomer as the period was far from democratic—the vote was only extended to men over twenty-five; women were not allowed to vote; and the Peace Preservation Law in 1925 expanded police powers in putting down dissent. Thereafter Japan descended into its own form of militarist totalitarianism as the country turned away from gaining the acceptance of the status quo Western powers and allied itself instead with the revisionist powers of Germany and Italy with the objective of creating its own sphere of influence in East Asia. Thus, it can be argued that Japan has never had a solid tradition of democracy and has never experienced a true revolution that worked from the bottom up. It has been asserted that "if Japan had not experienced the defeat [in WWII], it would not have gained democracy. Herein lies the tragedy of Japan's contemporary history. In a sense, the tragedy is that we did not win our freedom and democracy; we were beaten and received it" (Nakamura 1994: 76). The result has been the creation of "undemocratic idiosyncrasies and tendencies" within the Japanese political system (Asai 1990: 4). It is to these idiosyncrasies and tendencies within Japan's political structures and culture that this chapter now turns.

The "1955 system"

Building upon both the fully-fledged reforms and policy U-turns of the occupation, the "1955 system" was instrumental in guiding the postwar recovery and economic development of Japan. Through this process it also served to create and shape a set of behavioral norms that defined Japan's political culture. However, more recently the system has been cited as the cause of the current malaise the Japanese government and its people find themselves in with the end of the cold war and the onset of a globalizing world. Attempts to reform this system of governance and the rise of the activities of nongovernmental actors and citizens' movements have been the most salient development of recent years—issues which will be discussed later in light of the prevalent "1955 system" and the norms it engendered.

Eleven years ago the Japanese political landscape (which by definition meant the "1955 system") was described in the following terms:

> Reduced to caricature, the situation is this. One party, the LDP, has been in power now for thirty-five years. Insofar as it has any policies at all they are a commitment to endless economic growth and a nativism which is sometimes menacing but more often banal. Furthermore, this party is not simply prey to factions: it is *constituted* out of factions, and in the general din of horse trading the voice of the public interest is scarcely to be heard at all. The opposition, split by intransigent sectarian difference and tactically inept, is an opposition in name only. Thus the LDP shares government not in alternation with other parties but in complicity with other interest groups. Chief among these, of course, are the huge corporations which dominate the economic life of Japan, speaking either through their official associations and organs of policy or through channels of a more informal and covert kind. The remaining major element in the *real* machinery of governance in Japan (as opposed to what is merely constitutionally inscribed) is a large and arrogant bureaucracy, deeply involved with the other two power centres but out of touch with the mass of ordinary people
>
> (Marriage 1990: 231).

At the dawn of the new millennium cynics would say that little has changed despite the blip in the mid-1990s in the LDP's long-term grip on power. However, this characterization of the Japanese system of governance, which is more commonly known as the iron triangle of the LDP, bureaucracy and big business, is not wholly accurate today. The policy-making process in Japan impacted by globalization is open to a number of influences so that Japan is far from being a nation "run by a small compact of interlocking elites acting upon a docile mass who periodically ratify the whole arrangement at the ballot box" (Marriage 1990: 231). Yet, for the most part, the postwar period can be characterized as having been dominated by a ruling iron triangle which mutually reinforced itself through old school ties (especially the Law Faculty at the University of Tokyo) and the exchange of personnel between the three poles (the practice of *amakudari*, literally, "descending from heaven"), in addition to the championing of a political agenda dubbed the Yoshida Doctrine after Japan's most influential postwar prime minister, Yoshida Shigeru. This "doctrine" privileged economic recovery "to rebuild Japan as a trading economy with only limited armaments, a system squarely within the confines of liberal democratic politics and the international trade regime that characterized *Pax Americana*" (Nakamura 1994: 74). Thus, Yoshida willingly sacrificed Japan's independence and sovereignty in foreign affairs, and much of its own domestic affairs, by tying its fortune to that of the United States.

The "1955 system" essentially set Japan on the road to economic recovery but equally diluted the Japanese people's interest and sense of stake holding in the political process with the promise of the benefits of economic development, as exemplified by the income-doubling plan of Prime Minister Ikeda Hayato. The Japanese people were willing to entrust the ruling iron triangle, and specifically the bureaucratic élite, with the task of managing the country in return for economic benefits and rising living standards. Also, the system clearly shaped, encouraged and appealed to a number of norms of Japanese political behavior which will be discussed next.

Norms of political behavior

The way in which politicians, bureaucrats and people "do" politics is important to understanding the dynamics of any political system, and in the case of Japan a number of behavioral norms and processes, rooted in the above historical experience, can be discerned. Arthur Stockwin in *Governing Japan* has demonstrated through a number of anecdotal vignettes the prevailing norms which shape, limit and encourage Japanese political behavior (Stockwin 1999: 23–35). These stories include Japanese Diet members playing a highly visible, avuncular role in his/her constituency and/or hometown; a blissfully uninformed electorate voting for friends rather than on policy issues; intra-ministerial friction manifested in spying and mistrust; and Q&A sessions held by politicians often becoming nothing more than a rehearsal of prepared answers.

We can extrapolate a number of aspects of the cultural context of Japanese politics from these examples and Japan's historical experience: the importance of personal ties and links with the local constituency and/or hometown; building up connections and obligations between the politician and electorate; the distance felt by Japanese citizenry from the decision-making process so that personality takes precedence over policy content; a single-minded bureaucracy which runs Japan—highly disciplined and motivated and engaging in internecine rivalry and battles over jurisdiction. These all suggest the importance of the hierarchical, locally based, group-oriented nature of Japanese society and the role played by factions whether they be based on politic affiliation, personal affiliation or the old school tie. In addition, a preference exists for political decisions to be pre-arranged, decided behind the scenes and then play acted in public without fear of anything untoward or unexpected happening. Thus, the idea of *kagemusha* (shadow general or power behind the throne) mentioned above and the importance of blurring the decision-making process through consensus building are aspects of the political process in Japan.

In addition to these behavioral traits, a number of other historically contingent norms are worth highlighting: namely, anti-militarism, economism, developmentalism, and bilateralism. First, Japan's experience of imperialism, the Second World War, the nuclear bombings of Hiroshima and Nagasaki, and the fire bombings of Tokyo have created a strong sense of resistance to both subtle and overt militarist posturing and a preference for nonmilitary, often economic, solutions to human problems. This has been manifested in the Preamble and Article IX of the 1947 Constitution, the Three Non-Nuclear Principles, the restrictions placed upon the limited participation of Japan's Self-Defense Forces in UN peacekeeping operations. Second, and connected to the first, is the norm of economism. As a result of the norm of anti-militarism and the way in which it limits policy options, the Japanese government and its people have privileged economic above political and military activity. This has often been dubbed as GNP-ism and the ruthless pursuit of profit devoid of any humanitarian responsibility. With the end of the cold war, this has led to criticism of Japan's role in the world as nothing more than "checkbook diplomacy." Third, the norm of developmentalism has run throughout Japan's recent history as Japan has sought to "catch-up" with the West either in terms of imperial reach, economic power or living standards, whether it be as a result of the Meiji Restoration or the American Occupation. Finally, bilateralism has been the overriding norm shaping Japan's relations with the outside world and has demanded a close relationship with the great power of the day, whether it be Britain, Germany or the United States. The sum of these parts can be dubbed the Yoshida Doctrine, ruthlessly pursued by the ruling iron triangle for most of the cold war period. However, with the end of the cold war and the advent of a rapidly and progressively globalizing world, these norms have been seen to increase and decrease in influence.

Even this brief portrait of the chief norms of Japanese political behavior raise important questions in an increasingly globalizing world as to how democratic Japan is, whether the "1955 system" and the political culture allow corruption to flourish, and who "does" politics and for whose benefit? How these norms have metamorphosed and shaped Japan's political structures and behavior at the end of the cold war will provide the focus of the following section.

Impact of and responses to globalization

This crisis of Japanese "democracy," or more correctly, the "1955 system," highlighted in the introduction has been compounded by the necessity of responding to the impact of globalization. In the simplest terms, globalization can be defined as "the intensification of worldwide social relations which link distant localities in such a way that local happenings are shaped by events occurring many miles away and vice versa ... Local transformation is as much a part of globalization as the lateral extension of social connections across time and space" (Giddens 1990: 64). As a result, both time and space have been reduced and this transnational aspect of globalization has both placed the shortcomings of the "1955 system" in stark relief and impacted on an ever-expanding civil society in Japan. Over recent years there has been a huge growth in the number of NGOs and NPOs dealing with environmental issues, development issues, human rights issues, ever-broadening security issues, women's issues, and so on, on both a local and transnational basis. Though modest compared to the United States, the number of NPOs in Japan is reported to be about 21,000. Thus, globalization has led to an increase in NGOs and NPOs playing an active role as part of, and serving to define, an oft-overlooked civil society in Japan.

"Civil society" competes with globalization for the dubious accolade of the most commonly used but undertheorized phrase in political science. What is meant here are organizations beyond the control of the state. These organizations are not formally part of the state, though they may have links with the state, and in a great many cases (though there are several notable exceptions) they do not wish to assume the reins of political power. These organizations are equally not part of the market. Rather, they are noncommercial and non-profit-making (Scholte 1999: 2–3). Civil society groups often have links with similar groups abroad through direct contact facilitated by information technology. This contact is direct and avoids government channels whereas once it was dependent on the mediation of the state. This has led to the growth of a global civil society, often epitomized and organized into NGOs such as Greenpeace and Amnesty International. However, civil society is broader than that and not always so positive. Right-wing extremist groups are equally part of the broader definition of civil society.

A comprehensive overview of the recent history and future direction of a number of civic movements in Japan stressing consumers' (*seikatsu*) groups, workers' collectives, environmentalist and women's issues has argued against the "accepted wisdom" and has posited a healthy and buoyant civil society in Japan (Bouissou 2000). The reasons for the growth of this civil society can been seen in the failure of traditional forms of governance as epitomized by the scandal-ridden ruling iron triangle, and in the inability of local governments to respond to local issues for "fear of retaliation by ministries with discretion over funds ... Local elites, especially conservatives, believed that deference toward the centre and avoidance of conflict were both proper and practical behaviour, in the best interests of the community" (McKean 1981: 24). Faced with the lack of activism on the part of local governments, citizens' movements shouldered the burden of improving the lot of Japanese people and challenging the norms of political behavior.

Japan's citizens' movements are usually divided into *jūmin undō* (residents' movements) and *shimin undō* (citizens' movements)—the latter tend to be more organized and experienced in contrast to the concerns of the more parochial former movements. One commentator has gone so far as to point to Japan's civic movements as demonstrating "the vitality of the Japanese citizenry as a political actor" (Bouissou 2000: 336). What is more, there is evidence that the concept of civil society in Japan has a longer history than previously thought despite complications in translation into and definition of the term in Japanese (Takabatake 2001). In contrast, traditional cultural interpretations have posited an impassive civil society in Japan due to traditional Confucian ideals of respect for authority. However, over recent years there has been a noticeable increase in the number of social movements, NGOs and NPOs attempting to plug the holes of governance engendered by globalization and the crisis in the traditional forms of governance, especially in the fields of security, and environmental and gender issues. These first two of these three constituted some of the most pressing political and developmental issues faced by the Japanese state and its people. With the end of the cold war the third has risen in prominence. The following section will give an overview of these organizations and make a prognosis as to the health of civil society in Japan.

Security issues

In postwar Japan, the problem of how democracy could be maintained without lapsing into pre-war militarism provided a focus for debate among Japanese intellectuals such as Maruyama Masao, Ōtsuka Hisao and Hirata Kiyoaki, and private organizations of citizens free of association with the government were seen as key elements of a civil society (Takabatake 2001: 6–7). *Heiwa mondai danwakai* (Peace Problems Symposium) provided an exemplary forum for this where Tokyo and Kyoto intellectuals could discuss peace issues and declare famously that "atomic war teaches the paradoxical truth that to be realistic, we must be idealistic" (Nakamura 1994: 72). Thereafter, the 1960 *Anpo* demonstrations against the revised US–Japan Security Treaty were one of the first calls to action for Japan's civil society.

This constituted a large-scale protest against the security milieu of the cold war, increasing Japanese militarism, and disrespect for parliamentary procedures in the Japanese Diet. Two organizations, the Citizens' Federation for Peace in Vietnam (*beheiren*) and the Association of Voiceless People (*koe naki koe no kai*), provided examples of anti-militarist, anti-American citizens' movements created as a result of the 1960 demonstrations. Every day for the month of June 300,000 union members protested outside the Diet building with the result that President Dwight Eisenhower's visit was cancelled.

However, during this period of Japan's high-speed economic growth, support for these organizations was marginal, with the majority of people instead buying into the benefits that would accrue from Japan's economic development. This did not mean the end of civil society groups, but rather a change in their focus in line with the norms of economism and developmentalism toward consumer and environmental problems, resulting in the rise in importance of the *seikatsu* clubs (discussed below).

With the end of the cold war and the broadening of the definition of security, Japanese NGOs have most noticeably campaigned for a reduction in the American military presence in Okinawa and a strategy to combat landmines. The former can be seen in a number of citizens' movements in Okinawa over the years, but most recently in the Red Card movement which organized a human chain of over 27,000 Okinawans during the G8 summit of July 2000 to protest at the continued presence of American military bases (Yonetani 2001: 86–87). The latter can be seen in the work of the Japanese Campaign to Ban Landmines (JCBL) and Association for Aid and Relief, Japan (AAR) which cooperated with the Ministry of Foreign Affairs (MOFA) in conducting research on landmine disposal and placing pressure on the Japanese government to sign the 1997 Ottawa Landmine Ban Treaty.

Environmental issues

The Japanese state has been dubbed an environmental bogeyman in the postwar period as it entered its period of high economic growth and pursued its developmentalist agenda (Holliman 1990: 284). As a result, the Japanese people have had to contend with some of the most publicized cases of environmental degradation during the postwar period—Minamata disease caused by organic mercury poisoning, *itai itai* disease caused by cadmium poisoning in Toyama prefecture, to name but two. Even before these infamous postwar cases which gave birth to "the largest and most significant social movement in Japan's modern history" (McKean 1981: 1), protests were organized as Japan modernized during the Meiji period—at the turn of the nineteenth century industrial pollution caused by the Ashio copper mine provided the focus for environmentally minded protest. More recently, during the bubble period, opposition to the construction and subsequent expansion of Narita international airport provided the impetus for social protest at governmental disrespect for the environment. Though having been characterized as impotent and "politically marginalized, more underfunded than most, and almost unrecognized by the general public" (Mason 1999: 187), there is cause for believing that the environmental NGO movement in Japan is in a healthy state, is responding to recent environmental disasters, and fulfills the conditions of civil society as outlined above by Scholte.

The impact of a series of environmental disasters—the 1995 Kobe earthquake, oil spills near Yokohama and Toyama in 1997, accidents at the Tōkai nuclear fuel reprocessing plant in 1997 and 1999—ensured that pollution issues were paid attention to but also highlighted the impotence of government responses and the flexibility of social movements (it has been argued that before these high-profile cases, environmental grass-roots organizations have been "the true motivating force" behind any reforms of environmental policy (Ui 1989: 109)). According to the Japanese Environment Agency, there are 4,500 environmental NGOs in Japan working mostly on a local, rather than a national, basis (Mason 1999: 193). In addition to being effective on a local level, some NGOs have employed transnational techniques to promote their cause. Victims of Minamata disease appeared at the 1972 Stockholm Conference on the Environment. Japan's Save the Ozone Network took out a full-page advertisement in the *New York Times* in order to highlight the Kyoto convention on climate change and exert pressure on the Japanese government to fulfill its obligations in limiting CFCs (Mason 1999: 201–202). Japan's Global Network for Anti-Golf Course Action has worked to prevent the development of golf courses in Japan, East Asia, Australia and North America (Yamada 1990). Encouragement has come from other governments, and Thomas Foley, the former American Ambassador to Japan, has sought to promote the spirit of volunteerism in addition to the Common Agenda program between the United States and Japan in collaboration with NGOs and NPOs to tackle environmental, health and social problems in various parts of the world. The program was established by President Bill Clinton and Prime Minister Miyazawa Kiichi in 1993.

The government has come to recognize the appeal and abilities of these NGOs and has worked with them. At the 1994 UN World Conference on Population and Development in Cairo, NGO representatives were included for the first time as part of Japan's official representation (Mason 1999: 204). This trend tends toward NGOs being co-opted by the government and nothing more than token recognition being paid and minimal influence being exerted. MOFA commissioned a private-sector research institute to begin investigations into how the United States, Canada and European nations have encouraged and fostered NGOs. Japanese NGOs also played an important role in providing assistance through medical teams and makeshift housing to Taiwan after it was hit by an earthquake in September 1999. The Japanese government channeled ¥62 million to organizations with these objectives (*Kyodo News* December 10, 1999). In addition, Prime Minister Obuchi also earmarked ¥10 billion to help establish a foundation, with the assistance of NGOs and the *zaikai* (business world), to encourage forestation projects in China (*Kyodo News* July 5, 1999).

This level of active cooperation between the government and Japanese people stands very much in contrast to the government's former policy of excluding Japan's environmental movements from the political process, as happened at the Tokyo Conference on the Global Environment and Human Response Toward Sustainable Development, September 11–13, 1989 which forced Japan's environmental groups to create their own parallel meeting named the International People's Forum on Japan and the Global Environment (Holliman 1990: 288).

Gender issues

During the Occupation Period, women's groups such as the Japanese League of Women Voters and the Women's Democratic Club managed to exert influence upon American occupiers, often bypassing the male-dominated Japanese government during the enactment of legislation protecting women's rights and equality, and mobilized popular support for the new constitution which guaranteed these rights (Pharr 1987; Ogai 1999).

However, women's political participation has been dominated by two organizations—the Housewives' Alliance (*Shufurengōkai*, abbreviated to and commonly known as *Shufuren*) and the Tokyo Seikatsusha Network. Shufuren was essentially a corporatist organization established in 1948 with government backing. Its objectives were related to household management, raising families, ensuring fair prices and encouraging a people-centered capitalism. It managed to influence the political process through participation in government advisory councils, building up a body of specialized knowledge on various issues and members standing for election to the Diet (Ogai 1999). Though pressing for similar issues as Shufuren, the Tokyo Seikatsusha Network was created during Japan's postwar period of high growth in the 1960s to be less corporatist than Shufuren and has attempted to influence the political process from the bottom up through participation in local, rather than national, politics. It has remained "an urban network of concerned citizens, autonomous from the informal negotiations with the government that were so important to Shufuren's political successes" (Ogai 1999: 73). Both organizations demonstrate the influence of the housewife extending from the private into the public sphere. What is more, the majority of women involved in the environmental groups mentioned above are housewives: "in Japan the kind of person most apt to represent an environmental concern on a television program or in the printed media is a middle-aged woman who calls herself a housewife" (Goebel Noguchi 1992: 339).

With an increasingly globalized economy, the movement of immigrant workers has increased and has led to related human rights issues and unstable employment conditions, both generally and specifically in regard to the female labor market. This provided the impetus for both the creation of a number of gender-related NGOs in Japan and the Fourth World Conference on Women in Beijing. The Beijing JAC (the Beijing Japan Accountability Caucus) is a network of NGOs created as a direct outcome of lobbying the Japanese government at the Beijing Conference. The Women's Policies Information Network is concerned with educating women about women's issues in the Diet by providing information by facsimile to women throughout Japan. The East Asian Women's Forum was established to discuss female workers' issues and holds a forum biennially (Japan in 1994, South Korea in 1996, Ulan Bator in 1998 and Taiwan in 2000). Most of the NGOs which were established after the Beijing Conference, are "network type organizations, in which individual members are expected to be the core of activities ... [working] on the basis of equal partnership through horizontal, not vertical, line[s] of organization" (Japan NGO Report Preparatory Committee 1999). The Japanese government's response to these organizations was the Plan for Gender Equality 2000: National Plan of Action, and the Basic Law Designed to Promote a Gender-Equal Society passed by the Japanese Diet in 1999. Both aim to "achieve gender equality in the workplace, family and community; [create] a society where the human rights of women are promoted and protected; and [contribute] to 'equality, development and peace' in the global community" (Japan NGO Report Preparatory Committee 1999). The Plan for Gender Equality 2000 was drawn up after the government dialogued with a variety of NGOs through opinion-gathering fora and a nationwide public opinion survey. However, one of the biggest drawbacks of these projects is the monitoring process, which lacks both explicit time limits and realistic targets other than an optimistic goal of attaining 20 per cent female members of the Diet by 2000. As of December 2001 there were 34 female and 446 male members of the Lower House, and 39 female and 208 male members of the Upper House in the Japanese Diet.

Even more recently, a number of NGOs from across Japan and East Asia came together to create the Women's International War Crimes Tribunal on Japan's Military Sexual Slavery (more commonly known as the Tokyo Tribunal) which held a mock trial from December 8–12, 2000 in Tokyo. On the one hand, the mock trial was a clear rejection of the Japanese government's 1995 initiative establishing the Asian Women's Fund to provide financial compensation. And on the other hand, it was intended to raise global consciousness and mobilize networks of women's movements on the issue of the sexual violence committed against the so-called comfort women, an issue ignored by the International Military Tribunal for the Far East.

Government responses

All these citizens' movements demonstrate that the top-down authoritarian model of Japanese democracy is not a wholly accurate reflection of the political process and that bottom-up activity on a number of issues demands revision of the recent Japanese democratic tradition and lends weight to Bouissou's claims for a healthy and buoyant civil society.

As already seen above, the government's response to these developments has been to bandwagon on NGO activities and encourage these organizations through the passing of the NPO Law. In the aftermath of the Kobe earthquake and the swift response of Japanese volunteers, the government began the legislative process which culminated on March 19, 1998, when the Law to Promote Specified Non-Profit Activities (the NPO Law) was passed in the Japanese Diet with the objective of simplifying the system for voluntary organizations to gain recognition as corporate status. Due to this catalyst "people saw the importance of having institutions like NPOs which helped out very quickly, while the government reaction was slow" (Greene 1999: 4). The law recognizes the legal status of voluntary organizations in fields such as health and medical care, disaster relief, women's and human rights, international cooperation, education, culture, the arts and sports. Conferring this status facilitates the right to own property, open bank accounts, and accords official recognition in addition to allowing NPOs a greater role and voice in the formulation of public policy. Previously, recognition had only been accorded to organizations created under the jurisdiction of a particular government ministry. Director of the NPO Centre in Tokyo, Yamaoka Yoshinori, described the position of NPOs in Japanese society prior to the law in the following terms: "NPOs were regarded as exotic, unique, different, strange and bizarre entities" (Greene 1999: 1). Post-enactment of the NPO Law, the government was keen to contract NPOs in providing social and economic services to the Japanese public, as epitomized by the creation of a Parliamentary League to Support NGOs in 1999 which now numbers over 200 members (Greene 1999: 3).

The Japanese government has also realized the importance of NGOs and joint consultative panels have been institutionalized in order to facilitate a dialog. Former Foreign Minister Kōno Yōhei has stressed the role NGOs can play in addressing global challenges such as refugees, poverty, cross-border crime and environmental problems. To this professed end of instrumentalizing NGOs as "important actors in conflict prevention," the Japanese government has established a Small Arms Fund within the UN to tackle the proliferation of small arms and light weapons and contributing around $2 million (*Kyodo News* July 17, 2000). Japan's own norm of anti-militarism has infused this policy as it has been framed within the language of Japan's Three Non-Nuclear Principles that Japan does not export these weapons. Especially with 2001 having been designated the year of international volunteers, MOFA has sought to increase its aid to Japanese NGOs.

Equally, an evolving East Asian identity and norm that Japan should assist the development of its East Asian neighbors are in evidence as Japan has sought to promote the Small Arms Fund policy initiative in Cambodia—an ongoing conflict in which Japan has traditionally played an active role. Moreover, the 1999 crisis in East Timor has also provided the Japanese government, as the largest aid donor to Indonesia, with a problematic issue of whether to support its bilateral relations with Jakarta or to seize the humanitarian opportunity to interface with NGOs and provide assistance. The Free East Timor Coalition of thirteen Japanese NGOs dispatched volunteers to oversee the referendum of August 30, 1999. It was a Japanese NGO, the Network for Indonesian Democracy, which invited independence campaigners from East Timor to conduct speaking tours in Japan during September and October 1999 in an attempt to raise consciousness and influence government policy—a policy which had been dubbed "malicious, hypocritical and totally selfish" by the Nobel Peace Prize winning East Timor independence leader Jose Ramos-Horta: "if I was in government, not one yen would I welcome from the Japanese government" (*Kyodo News* August 17, 1998).

The other development has been the increase in the government's use of referenda to gauge the will of the Japanese people. In 1996, two local referendums were held with regard to specific problems: American military bases in Okinawa prefecture and the building of a new nuclear power plant at the town of Maki in Niigata prefecture. Thereafter referenda have been held over the construction of a waste disposal facility in Gifu prefecture in June 1997 and the expansion of a quarry in Nagasaki prefecture in July 1999. Voter turnout was in all these cases surprisingly high, perhaps indicative of Japanese people's desire to have their collective voice heard. As one Japanese newspaper editorialized: "Instead of ignoring direct appeals, mayors and municipal assemblies should incorporate local referenda as a means of judging the people's will and this should also invigorate debate in the assemblies. Ways to increase local referenda should be sought" (*Asahi Shinbun* January 26, 2000).

Conclusions

This chapter has demonstrated that though the democratic tradition in Japan has been both recent and of a top-down nature, over recent years and with the growth of a civil society induced by an ever-globalizing world and represented by a number of active citizens' movements, new processes of governance and standards of government accountability are beginning to take root in Japan. This attitude has been summarized by Wakahara Yasuyuki of Asahi Mutual Life Insurance Company: "Globalization brings to Japan, as everywhere else, a revolution in attitudes against the social codes of the past. Over the next century, Japanese society will be formed by citizens, for their needs. That recognition has started to penetrate government sectors" (Chanin 1998).

As described above, these changes challenge Japan's political marketplace and the norms which have shaped it. Whereas once upon a time Japanese people entrusted the role of governance to highly trained bureaucrats and local politicians expected to protect their regional interests, a more audible civil society is beginning to make itself heard. Whereas an opaque decision-making process resting on behind-the-scenes "fixing" and the role of the *kagemusha* were once acceptable, now open and transparent processes which meet global standards of accountability are demanded. Thus, as claimed by Hoshino Shinyasu of the National Institute for Research Advancement, "over the past four or five years, citizens are gaining a sense of their importance in society. Government has not been able to fulfil all its responsibilities, so people are judging for themselves and then acting" (Chanin 1998). However, if the Japanese people are to judge for themselves, then some fear that this will lead to unbridled, rampant individualism and the collapse of the traditionally hierarchical structure by which Japanese people have conducted their political and social relationships. Some, like Yamaoka, have argued that "NGOs are needed to focus individual interest and initiative. Without this institutional focus, the unrestrained growth of individuality will cause chaos in Japan" (Chanin 1998). Thus, though NGOs not only challenge the traditional way of doing politics in Japan, they also provide a safety net against too radical a change.

The norms which have traditionally informed Japan's political behavior and culture in the postwar period have retained and even increased in relevance with the collapse of cold war structures and the advent of a globalizing world. Japan's anti-militarist and economist norms fit neatly with an ever-expanding, nonmilitary security agenda. Bilateralism could be seen to have waned over the years with the United States now regarded as a threat, rather than a guarantor, of Japan's security. In its place, a renewed enthusiasm for the East Asian region has risen in relevance. However, to portray this as a simple zero-sum game would be inaccurate as the Japanese government and its people have tended to respond to both of these norms— supplementalism is probably a fairer description. As seen above, globalization, the actions of civil society, NGOs and the Japanese government have encouraged these shifts in norm relevance.

However, the extent of these shifts should not be reified. The degree to which government will take NGOs into account is still unclear and the question remains for further research as to whether these organizations monitor and expedite the work of the government. In fact, it could be argued that the reverse has been more prevalent, and that many NGOs and citizens' movements in Japan have been subject to approval from and supervised by government, and as a result are beholden to and suffer from the same symptoms of fatigue and rigidity as traditional structures of government in responding to the demands of globalization.

References

Asai, M. (1990) "Democracy, An Unintended Victim," *Japan Quarterly*, 37, 1:4–13.

Bouissou, J. (2000) "Ambiguous Revival: A Study of Some 'New Civic Movements' in Japan," *Pacific Review*, 13, 3: 335–366.

Chanin, C. (1998) "Voices of the People: The Development of NGOs in Japan," paper presented at the Japan–America Society of Washington, D.C. Conference,

Civil Society in Japan and America: A Comparative View. Found at http://www.us-japan.org/dc/civil/cspaper.chanin, visited on May 8, 2001.

Coaldrake, W. H. (1996) *Architecture and Authority in Japan*, London: Routledge.

Dower, J. (1996) *Japan in War and Peace: Essays on Culture, History and Race*, London: Fontana.

Giddens, A. (1990) *The Consequences of Modernity*, Cambridge: Polity Press.

Goebel Noguchi, M. (1992) "The Rise of the Housewife Activist," *Japan Quarterly*, 39, 3: 339–352.

Greene, S. G. (1999) "Activists on the Move in Japan," *The Chronicle of Philanthropy*, December 2, 1999.

Holliman, J. (1990) "Environmentalism with a Global Scope,"*Japan Quarterly*, 37, 3: 284–290.

Horsley, W. and Buckley, R. (1990) *Nippon: New Superpower: Japan since 1945*, London: BBC Books.

Japan NGO Report Preparatory Committee (1999) *Women 2000, Japan NGO Alternative Report*, visited on May 12, 2001 at: http://www.jca.ax.apc.org/fem/bpfa/NGOreport/0_en_Overview.html

Johnson, C. (1982) *MITI and the Japanese Miracle: The Growth of Industrial Policy, 1925–1975*, Stanford: Stanford University Press.

Leaver, R. (1989) *Restructuring in the Global Economy: From Pax Americana to Pax Nipponica*, Canberra: Peace Research Centre, Australian National University.

Marriage, A. (1990) "Japanese Democracy: Another Clever Imitation?", *Pacific Affairs*, 63, 2: 228–233.

Mason, R. J. (1999) "Whither Japan's Environmental Movement? An Assessment of Problems and Prospects at the National Level," *Pacific Affairs*, 72, 2: 187–207.

McKean, M. A. (1981) *Environmental Protest and Citizen Politics in Japan*, Berkeley: University of California Press.

Nakamura, M. (1994) "Democratization, Peace, and Economic Development in Occupied Japan, 1945–1952," in E. Friedman (ed.), *The Politics of Democratization: Generalizing East Asian Experiences*, Boulder: Westview.

Pharr, S. J. (1987) "The Politics of Women's Rights," in R. Ward and Sakamoto Yoshikazu (eds.), *Democratizing Japan*, Hawaii: Hawaii University Press.

Ogai, T. (1999) "The Political Activities of Japanese Housewives: From 'Invisible' to 'Visible' Political Participation," *Journal of Pacific Asia*, 5: 59–97.

Scholte, J. A. (1999) *Global Civil Society: Changing the World?*, University of Warwick, Coventry: Centre for the Study of Globalisation and Regionalisation Working Paper No. 31/99.

Stockwin, J. A. A. (1999) *Governing Japan*, Oxford: Blackwell.

Takabatake, M. (2001) "'Shimin Shakai' Mondai: Nihon ni okeru Bunmyaku" (The Problem of Civil Society in the Context of Japan), *Shisō*, May: 4–23.

Ui, J. (1989) "Anti-Pollution Movements and Other Grass-roots Organizations," in S. Tsuru and H. Weidner (eds.), *Environmental Policy in Japan*, Berlin: Edition Sigma.

Vogel, E. F. (1979) *Japan as Number One: Lessons for America*, Cambridge: Harvard University Press.

Yamada, K. (1990) "The Triple Evils of Golf Courses," *Japan Quarterly*, 37, 3: 291–297.

Yonetani, J. (2001) "Playing Base Politics in a Global Strategic Theater: Futenma Relocation, the G8 Summit, and Okinawa," *Critical Asian Studies*, 33, 1: 70–95.

9 Globalization, democratization and civil society in Southeast Asia

Observations from Malaysia and Thailand[1]

Anders Uhlin

Processes of globalization have had a significant impact on the fast-growing Southeast Asian economies. To various degrees the leaders of these countries have embraced a neo-liberal version of economic globalization. This has resulted in impressive economic growth rates, but the more open economies were also among those hardest hit by the 1997–1998 economic crisis. Political and cultural aspects of globalization have also influenced these societies. Since the 1980s there has been a marked increase in civil society activism and the global wave of formal democratization has reached Southeast Asia, manifested in the "people power" uprising against Ferdinand Marcos in the Philippines in 1986, the Thai democratization process following the May 1992 killing of protestors, the fall of Soeharto in Indonesia in May 1998, and the emergence of a reform movement in Malaysia in 1998. Parts of civil society have been crucial in the pressure for democracy. Meanwhile, processes of globalization have made civil societies less limited by geographical boundaries. There is evidence of the emergence of a transnational civil society in Southeast Asia.

The aim of this chapter is to analyze the relationship between these processes of globalization, democratization, and the development of civil society, in the Southeast Asian context. Two broad questions guide the analysis: How can we understand the changing relations between state and society as a result of globalization? How is the emergence of civil society groups related to processes of globalization and democratization? Dealing with Southeast Asia in general, the specific focus is on Malaysia and Thailand, two countries that have been very open to the impact of globalization, but which have different political regimes. Through a comparative analysis I hope to be able to show some significant trends and dynamics. Empirically the analysis is built on fieldwork carried out in 1997, 1998 and 1999. Interviews were conducted with civil society activists engaged in transnational activities and written material about their organizations and networks was collected.[2]

In this chapter I first discuss the relationship between globalization and democratization, on a theoretical level and with empirical illustrations from Malaysia and Thailand. In the next section I focus on the role of civil society in the process of democratization—again starting on a conceptual and theoretical level and continuing with an empirical overview. In the third section I analyze the development of a transnational civil society in Southeast Asia, focusing on transnational political opportunities and constraints. Theoretical arguments are supported by empirical examples of civil society groups based mainly in Malaysia and Thailand.

Globalization and democratization

Globalization is first and foremost a process of de-territorialization, indicating emerging supra-territorial and transborder social spaces (Scholte 2000: 3). This process has generated changes within economic, political and cultural spheres. Proponents as well as critics of the capitalist world economy tend to emphasize economic aspects of globalization, often equalizing globalization with the spread of neo-liberal values and practices. The multidimensional conceptualization of globalization that I adhere to notwithstanding, I will pay most attention to the economic dimensions as they have been most observed and debated in the Southeast Asian context, not least as a result of the 1997–1998 crisis. It should be stressed that globalization does not necessarily mean the end of the role of the state. On the contrary states are still important centers of power. Some states play the role of promoters of economic globalization whereas others try to redefine or resist the present form of globalization (Shari 2000). In the same way sections of civil society, as we will see, may embrace or resist globalization or try to promote an alternative form of globalization.

Like globalization, the other main concept to be discussed here—democratization—is a highly contested concept. In much of the literature on democratization definitions tend to converge around some procedural aspects of liberal democracy, typically equalizing democracy with the existence of free and fair elections combined with a minimum of civil and political liberties (see for example Huntington 1991). With the focus on regime transitions—that is, the transition from one set of rules and principles of state governance to another—most attention has been paid to the democratization of formal political institutions. However, if a broader definition of democracy is applied, the analysis of democratization processes becomes quite different. Democratization can for example be seen as "the creation, extension and practice of social citizenship throughout a particular national territory" (Grugel 1999: 11). The concept of citizenship implies a power struggle concerning who is entitled to take part in decision making. The main advantage of this definition is that it introduces a power perspective and a focus on social relationships. According to this view, the existence of formally democratic institutions, while necessary, is not enough for democracy to exist. Democracy also requires "popular consent, popular participation, accountability and a practice of rights, tolerance and pluralism" (Grugel 1999: 11–12). Democratization involves not only the

elimination of authoritarian institutions, but also the elimination of authoritarian social practices. In this study I focus on both formal institutional
democratization, as analyzed in most mainstream democratization studies,
and the form of societal democratization discussed above. These two aspects
of the democratization process are treated as analytically distinct. Formal
institutional and societal democratization may accompany and strengthen
each other, but they may also conflict.

How are processes of globalization related to democratization? Two
extreme positions can be identified in the public discourse, and to some
extent are also reflected in the academic discourse. First, those who celebrate
contemporary economic globalization claim that the economic liberalization
that is associated with globalization paves the way for political liberalization
and finally democratization. As authoritarian regimes open up for global
economic forces they also undermine their political authority, and sooner or
later they are swept away in the global wave of democratization. Second,
from a critical perspective, global forces are mainly negative for democratization, particularly its broader societal aspects. Neo-liberal economic
policies promoted by the dominant institutions in the world economy create
social and economic misery, increase inequality and undermine democratically elected governments. Massive military and economic aid strengthens
an authoritarian state apparatus and alters the balance of class forces, thus
creating obstacles to democratization.[3]

Malaysia is a most interesting case concerning attitudes and policies
related to globalization. Despite Prime Minister Mahathir's anti-Western
rhetoric, Malaysia has embraced most aspects of contemporary globalization. The use of modern information technology, in particular, has been
vigorously promoted. This includes the abolishment of taxes on personal
computers and the promotion of computer literacy in all schools. Expansion
of the use of English should also be seen in this light. The result has been
the emergence of a Western consumer culture among the growing middle
classes (Rajamoorthy 1999: 92–93; Welsh 1999). When the currency crisis hit
Malaysia in 1997, the deputy Prime Minister and Finance Minister Anwar
Ibrahim seemed inclined to cooperate with the IMF, but Mahathir chose
another direction. In September 1998 Anwar was sacked and arrested.
Malaysia rejected the involvement of the IMF and implemented nationalistic economic policies. Based on widespread anger over the treatment of
Anwar and inspired by the Indonesian popular protests against "corruption,
collusion and nepotism" that brought down Soeharto, a broad reform movement gained strength. Nevertheless, the political system served Mahathir
well. In the snap elections in November 1999 the government coalition
retained its two-thirds majority in parliament though more voters than ever
before voted for the opposition. Despite some measures of real electoral
contestation, the 1999 elections were neither free nor fair. Many first-time
voters were excluded from the rolls as the election commission claimed it
could not process the new registrants in time for the elections. The existence

of "phantom voters," that is, people paid to vote in the name of deceased or fictious voters, threats and other irregularities must have had some impact on the result. The ruling coalition made strong use of its superior economic resources, control over media and the government machinery (Weiss 2000). Despite the substantial loss of Malay votes—mainly to the Parti Islam se-Malaysia (PAS)—Mahathir seems to have strengthened his grip on Malaysian politics. Unlike Indonesia, the economic crisis did not trigger a regime transition, though it gave birth to a reform movement in Malaysian society.

Whereas the handling of the economic crisis in Malaysia did not improve the already highly limited and restricted democracy in the country, the nationalist economic policies—including selective capital control, the official fixing of the currency (the ringgit) to the US dollar, and measures to elimi-nate international trade in the ringgit—seem to have reduced the social impact of the crisis. Policies dictated by the IMF worsened the social impact of the crisis in Indonesia and Thailand. Malaysia, whose government refused to involve the IMF, seems to have fared better in this respect (Shari 2000: 973). In fact, three years after the beginning of the crisis, Malaysia was the only Southeast Asian country whose economy appeared to have recov-ered (Case 2001: 43). In terms of societal democratization, Malaysia can even be said to have registered a better performance than Thailand.

Thailand has been open to global economic and political forces since the nineteenth century. The Thai economy is characterized by an extremely high level of structural integration in the global economy (Hamilton-Hart 1999). This has not led to any stable democratic development. A series of military coups—the latest in 1991—have ended civilian rule. Following the popular uprising and dramatic killings of demonstrators in May 1992, the military withdrew to the barracks. What was perceived as less corrupt political parties under the leadership of Chuan Leekpai formed a new government and a process of democratization had clearly begun. A new constitution was adopted in 1997, and in the late 1990s there were signs that a more demo-cratic regime might be consolidated.

Thailand was the first country to suffer from the so-called "Asian finan-cial crisis." Unlike Malaysia, the economic crisis led to a change of government, but not a regime transition as in Indonesia. Popular dissatisfac-tion with the handling of the currency crisis brought about the resignation of General Chavalit's government. The peaceful transfer of power to a more reform-oriented coalition government under the leadership of Chuan Leekpai might be seen as an indication of a strengthening of Thai democ-racy. The adoption of a new constitution was a further step in a democratic direction. Nevertheless severe problems of corruption remain and marginal-ized groups in society still lack meaningful political influence (cf. Bello *et al.* 1998). The Chuan government has done all it could to satisfy the IMF despite popular opposition to what is considered élitist economic policies that make the poor pay for an economic crisis they did not create (cf.

Hewison 2000: 206–8). Focusing on societal democratization, the economic crisis had a negative impact on Thailand.

In conclusion, there is no uniform relationship between globalization and democratization. The impact of globalization on national political systems is mediated by domestic structures. In Malaysia globalization has served the semi-authoritarian regime well. Thailand's openness to global economic forces has prevailed under both authoritarian and more democratic regimes. Malaysia and Thailand have been open to global economic forces for a long time, but there is no evidence that this has supported a process of democratization. Thus, there is little support for neo-liberal claims about the positive impact of economic globalization on the state of democracy, especially if we also consider the broader societal aspect of democratization.

Democratization and the role of civil society

Processes of democratization cannot be understood only in relation to global economic factors. Civil society is another domain that has received much attention in efforts at understanding and explaining processes of democratization. In liberal theory civil society is typically defined as a public space between the state and the individual citizen, comprised of voluntary associations autonomous of the state. Whereas the state is associated with repression, civil society is seen as the realm of freedom (Diamond 1994). However, state and civil society are highly interconnected. The state provides the legal framework for civil society and civil society groups may seek democratization of civil society through the state. Civil society groups are also often incorporated or co-opted into the state structure (Rodan 1997: 161). As demonstrated in the introductory chapter, the rather romantic view of civil society in liberal theory is also a problem. Empirically it is obvious that there are significant inequalities based on class, gender, ethnicity, etc., within civil society. It should be noted, however, that not only liberal theories, but also poststructuralist and postmodernist studies of new social movements tend to see civil society as the morally "good" whereas the state is considered to be repressive (Rodan 1997: 159–160). If civil society is defined as those associations that support liberal democracy and other independent groups are described as "vested interests" or "uncivil" forces and are thus excluded from the definition of civil society, it is obvious that civil society supports liberal democracy. But this is a circular reasoning that severely weakens much of liberal theorizing on civil society (Beckman 1997: 2). This criticism against a liberal understanding of civil society may result in what might be called a post-Marxist approach to civil society. Post-Marxists and critical theorists, following Gramsci, see civil society as a network of institutions between economic structures and the state through which groups in society represent themselves. State and civil society are interconnected. Civil society is a sphere of indirect domination and democratization is needed not only of the state but also of civil society (cf. Cohen and Arato 1992).

Politically active civil society groups strive to reorganize state–society relations. This often involves both the demand for more autonomy in relation to the state and the demand for more participation in decision making within the state. In this way the activities of civil society groups have important implications for democratization. But we cannot assume that the strengthening of civil society automatically leads to more democracy. Rather, we should see civil society as an arena for political struggles—struggles that might be for or against democracy and that are related to the formal political sphere as well as civil society itself.

In Malaysia, political space in civil society has been systematically limited by the state. Politics in Malaysia is characterized by a mix of democratic procedures and authoritarian practices (Jesudason 1996; Crouch 1996; Case 2001). Formal democratic institutions and elections have been in place since independence, but the opposition has never had a real chance to defeat the ruling National Front dominated by the United Malay National Organization (UMNO). In this pseudodemocracy the ruling élite has powerful resources, including control of state finances, a subservient media and anti-subversion laws. The government also manipulates ethnic divisions in order to fragment the opposition (Jesudason 1996). There has been a pattern of systematic harassments against civil society activists, which ensured that civil society in Malaysia remained weaker and less developed than in Thailand. Violent repression of the kind that civil society activists in Soeharto's Indonesia could suffer has, however, been rare. Malaysian civil society groups have mostly been based in the middle classes, have had a non-Malay majority, relied on a few key figures and been dependent on external funds (Jesudason 1996: 151). Interviewed activists claim that very few real grass-roots groups have been able to develop in Malaysia. Some groups of urban squatters, plantation workers and indigenous people have managed to exist, but they have been under very tight surveillance and activists have often been arrested (interview March 7, 1997). In 1987 more than 100 activists and opposition leaders were arrested under the Internal Security Act (ISA). This weakened civil society even more though some new groups emerged after the crackdown.

For oppositional groups within civil society the economic and political crisis that began in 1997 presented an opportunity to mobilize popular support, but state repression also increased. Following the arrest of Anwar Ibrahim, political space for opposition has been even more limited. Demonstrations were brutally crushed with beatings, tear gas and water cannons. Media attacks and legal harassment against the more radical NGOs intensified, but the split within the political élite created new opportunities for civil society groups too. Opposition against Prime Minister Mahathir and his ruling party grew. The new opposition party—the National Justice Party—led by Wan Azizah, the wife of Anwar Ibrahim, included several prominent NGO leaders. The economic crisis led to an increased polarization between the ruling élite that turned even more authoritarian and an opposition that managed to mobilize within both civil society and political society to an extent never seen before. The new reform movement is highly heterogeneous. It includes the political parties in the oppositional Barisan Alternatif as well as a wide range of NGOs focusing on different issues and the small part of the media that is not government controlled (Weiss 1999).

The openness of the Thai political system has varied dramatically over time. Civilian rule, 1973–1976, provided a wide political space and there was a dramatic growth in the number of civil society organizations. The 1976 coup led to a crackdown on civil society and many activists were forced underground. Class-based social movements in the 1970s gradually fragmented and were replaced by a wide range of issue-specific NGOs when the political space widened in the 1980s (Clarke 1998: 27). The 1991 military coup was not simply against the civilian government but also aimed at limiting the political space for civil society. The popular uprising in May 1992, in which civil society activists were instrumental, forced the military back to the barracks. Parts of civil society played a significant role in this struggle for democracy and new opportunities for civil society groups were created. Pro-democracy groups within civil society have influenced a number of constitutional amendments in a democratic direction (Quigley 1996: 269). Sections of civil society took an active part in drafting the new 1997 constitution, which is more democratic than earlier constitutions in Thailand (Suchit 1999).

A "Directory of Non-Governmental Organizations" published by the Thai Development Support Committee (TDSC) in 1997 listed 465 Thai NGOs. Different groups have been brought together in the NGO Coordinating Committee (NGO-CORD). This network received support from the National Economic and Social Development Board, probably in an effort by state officials to co-opt civil society groups (Bello *et al.* 1998: 244). Civil society groups with a moderate program can often find élite allies within the formal political sphere. It is not unusual that NGOs participate in government committees and share information with state authorities. More radical civil society groups do not meet the same response from élite actors. Corruption and "money politics" are obstacles to more long-term élite alignments. NGOs with a clear political agenda tend to get little coverage in the government-controlled media. They face bureaucratic harassments when they try to register and they may have problems with the security forces, but outright repression is rare (cf. Quigley 1996: 279).

Within civil society in Thailand there is a clear division between élite–urban and popular–rural groups. Grass-roots NGOs to some extent serve as a link between the two (Naruemon 1998). In recent years the emergence of the Forum of the Poor has been important for overcoming the rural–urban cleavage as well as the class division of Thai civil society. The Forum of the Poor is a coalition of grass-roots NGOs and villagers from all over Thailand. It emerged in late 1995 as a protest movement against the

Pak Moon dam construction in the northeast of Thailand, but soon broadened its focus to other problems affecting the poor and disadvantaged people. The Forum has helped create a public space for citizens' participation in Thai civil society. It has been in a position to advance the struggle and to press the state to take account of local concerns when planning policy. In this way it has assisted in the people's empowerment and struggle for participatory democracy (Naruemon 1998: 45). Thus, the Forum has been important in the process of democratization in Thailand, especially concerning the broader societal dimension of democratization. It may even be argued that the emergence of the Forum of the Poor indicates a democratization of Thai civil society.

In concluding this section it is obvious that Malaysia and Thailand show different patterns of state control of civil society. Whereas state restrictions in Malaysia have been relatively stable over time, the political space for civil society in Thailand has fluctuated more. Under military regimes there has been a high level of repression against more radical sections of civil society, but under democratic regimes—particularly since the early 1990s—there have been political opportunities for civil society to expand. Today Thailand has a large number of NGOs, many of which are politically active and have been able to influence policies. The number of NGOs in Malaysia is less and their political impact is more limited due to state restrictions. In both countries certain actors within civil society have been in the forefront of the struggle for democracy. Political space in civil society is used in order to press for formal democratic reform as well as a democratization of civil society itself. Civil society groups focusing on issues of inequality and using emancipatory tactics contribute to a process of societal democratization. It remains to be analyzed how processes of globalization influence such developments within civil society. The remaining part of this chapter examines the emergence of a transnational civil society in the context of contemporary globalization.

Toward a transnational civil society in Southeast Asia

A transnational civil society is a public sphere across state boundaries in which different kinds of actors find space to act in relative (but far from absolute) autonomy in relation to forces in other social spheres, including state and market forces. Whereas states are territorially bounded, civil societies are not, and this spatial flexibility is a major potential resource of civil society groups. Transnational civil society challenges the arbitrary boundaries of nation-states (He 1999). It consists of different actors that are transnational in different ways and to various degrees. This public sphere that provides an arena for political activism across state borders includes transnational organizations and movements (like Greenpeace and Amnesty International). But also NGOs and social movements whose membership and organizational and mobilizational structures are limited to one single country may be part of a transnational civil society if they focus on transnational issues (like migration, environmental problems, etc.) and/or are engaged in communication, networking and cooperation with like-minded groups in other countries. In this way local and national civil society groups become players in a "multi-level game" (della Porta and Kriesi 1999: 6). Groups based on some kind of transnational solidarity (for example, with independence movements in other countries) are also transnational civil society groups.

There is a growing literature on this phenomenon, but so far relatively little has been written about the Southeast Asian context.[4] The same kind of criticism directed against liberal notions of civil society in the previous section also applies to most studies of transnational civil society. The distinction between state and civil society tends to be too sharp and power relations and inequalities within transnational civil society, though not completely ignored, are insufficiently analyzed. Further, the emergence of transnational civil society groups has not been systematically and thoroughly analyzed. In this respect the political opportunities approach seems most fruitful. By analyzing transnational opportunities and constraints I seek to demonstrate how processes of globalization have a fundamental impact on civil society. Further, I discuss how this is related to processes of democratization.

Transnational political opportunities and constraints

Some theories of social movements have emphasized the political context of movements, including their relationship to the state and formal political institutions. For this purpose the concept of political opportunities has been applied (McAdam 1996). This conceptualization, however, does not pay attention to the transnational dimension. In order to understand the emergence and activities of transnational civil society groups we need to explore political opportunities not only on the national, but also on the transnational, level. Globalization is redefining the parameters for political activity. Civil society to some extent transcends the state and thus emerges as a "major site of contestation where diverse groups seek to restructure politics" (Mittelman 1999: 77). Processes of globalization create new forms of political opportunities and constraints for political activism within civil society. I will discuss eight aspects of transnational political opportunities that might contribute to an understanding of the emergence of transnational civil society groups.[5]

First, much activism within civil society is a reaction to what is perceived as negative aspects of globalization (cf. Bello *et al.* 1998: 246)—social and environmental damage connected to the global capitalist system provokes activism within civil society. There are basically two different approaches to challenges by what is perceived as negative aspects of globalization. On the one hand, civil society groups may choose global or transnational strategies, countering élitist globalization with an alternative globalization from below. On the other hand, civil society groups may reject globalization altogether and emphasize "localism." This cleavage is particularly evident in Thailand where, in the wake of the 1997–1998 economic crisis, "localism" has become a popular discourse. While "localism" offers a moral argument against neo-liberal globalization, Hewison (2000) is right in concluding that it fails to develop a politically and economically viable alternative model. Like other forms of populism it is reactionary, romantic, anti-urban and chauvinistic. All Thai NGOs, however, are not opposed to all aspects of globalization. On the contrary, a large part of Thai civil society seems to support a more democratic form of globalization. Many Thai NGOs and social movements are involved in transnational networking in the Southeast Asian region and beyond. Unlike in Thailand, the "localism" discourse is not prominent in Malaysia. On the contrary, Malaysian civil society groups tend to be very active on a transnational level, dealing with different problems of globalization.

The actual movement of people across state boundaries is an aspect of globalization that is an obvious background condition to the development of a transnational civil society. Thus, it is not surprising that we find intense transnational activism in support of migrants. In response to the suffering of increasing numbers of migrant workers, NGOs were set up in different Asian countries in the 1980s. Labor migration is an important issue in both Malaysia and Thailand. Until the economic crisis in 1997, Malaysia was Asia's major importer of foreign workers and Thailand was both a significant exporter and importer. Working on issues related to migrant labor it is natural, not to say necessary, to cooperate with organizations from other countries. Given the fact that most foreign workers in Malaysia come from Indonesia, one of the most active NGOs in this field—the women's organization Tenaganita—cooperates with like-minded Indonesian organizations (interview March 13, 1997). Migrant workers often have more trust in their own nationals. Language and cultural barriers can be overcome if activists from their country of origin are involved in the process. When an Indonesian activist stayed in Malaysia for six months, it was easier to get access to Indonesian migrant communities (interview July 8, 1999).

Not only the transnational character of problems related to migration, but also the perceived incapacity of governments to adequately protect the rights of migrants can explain civil society activity in this field. CARAM Asia—a transnational civil society group that presents itself as a nonexclusive, open network of NGOs in South and Southeast Asia concerned with problems of HIV/AIDS, especially in relation to migrants—gives priority to cross-border migrants because national health programs usually do not target foreigners (interview July 8, 1999). The lack of adequate state responses to problems related to globalization is thus met with transnational civil society activities.

A second aspect of transnational political opportunities is a transnational solidarity that may develop in a world where geographical distance is becoming less important and the legitimacy of state boundaries are increasingly questioned. For example, solidarity with the East Timorese people suffering under Indonesian occupation led to the establishment of a transnational solidarity movement. Asian human rights NGOs formed the Asia-Pacific Coalition on East Timor, which—as part of a more global civil society network—played an important role in putting East Timor on the international agenda and preparing the ground for the referendum and foreign intervention leading to the independence of East Timor. Civil society activists from Malaysia and Thailand also have made important contributions to this struggle.

Third, a lack of domestic political opportunities may stimulate transnational networking. The relative closeness of the political system, harassment from state authorities, and the absence of élite allies indicate a need for transnational networking to compensate for the lack of domestic political opportunities for civil society groups in Malaysia. In Thailand, where the domestic political system is more open, there is still a lack of serious élite allies for many civil society groups, especially for grass-roots organizations.

Fourth, civil society groups may find both targets and élite allies within international organizations or foreign states. A typical example is the efforts of a movement of small-scale fishermen in southern Thailand to involve transnational organizations like Greenpeace and the Gaia Foundation in its struggle against the large-scale fishing industry and Thai authorities (interview October 23, 1999). When there is a lack of local civil society groups, transnational networks may find that the only possibility is to work together with state authorities. This is, for example, the case of Thai NGOs working on issues of trafficking. With few NGOs in many of Thailand's neighbor states they tend to develop a close relationship with state institutions in these countries, though cooperation typically seems to depend on personal links to individual staff in state authorities (interview July 1, 1999).

Fifth, the development of new and cheaper communication technology creates opportunities for more intense and extensive transnational contacts. The introduction of less-expensive international phone calls, fax machines, and not least email and the Internet, has meant a revolution for certain civil society activities as it has made instant communication on a daily basis possible. Cheaper air flights also enable activists from different parts of the globe to meet face to face at international meetings and workshops. While constituting a basic precondition for the emergence of a transnational civil society, the development of new communication technology does not lead to increased equality. Access to modern communication technology is still the privilege of a relatively small minority of well-educated and wealthy people. The Internet does provide a new medium for civil society groups and other forces opposing authoritarian rule. However, as pointed out by Abbott (2001), the emancipatory potential of the Net is offset by the digital divide between the North and the South as well as within specific countries. Nevertheless, the Internet has been an important vehicle for political opposition within civil society in more or less authoritarian states. Civil society groups in Malaysia in particular have been able to capitalize on the government's policy of promoting the use of electronic communication as part of Malaysia's development strategy. Whereas printed media, radio and television are to a large extent controlled by the government, the opposition has found an uncensored public space on the Net.

Sixth, the availability of transnational funding provides necessary economic resources. Like the existence of modern communication technology, this is a necessary precondition for the emergence of a transnational civil society, but it also creates and strengthens resource inequality within civil society. In all cases examined for this study, funding agencies in "Northern" countries provided the necessary financial resources for transnational activities in the Southeast Asian region. Many activists see these agencies as important allies and welcome their support, but others are concerned about foreign influences on the agenda of civil society groups.

Seventh, international regimes and conventions as well as multilateral agreements and global discourses can be used as points of reference for civil society groups targeting specific governments. Thai civil society groups have been especially successful in linking their activities to broader regional and global discourses on good governance and democracy. Concern about Thailand's international image has been emphasized in relation to authoritarian tendencies such as the 1991 coup and the May 1992 violence (Lizee 2000). Another example is the importance of a global discourse on human rights, manifested in the UN declaration for example. Civil society activists often refer to this international human rights regime in campaigns against specific states. The reframing of women's rights as human rights has been essential for the transnational women's movement (Piper 2001). Such transnational opportunities, however, have different strength depending on the national political context. Activism in relation to migrant workers' rights is more constrained in Malaysia than in many other countries because—in the context of the anti-Western "Asian values" rhetoric—references to international standards and norms concerning the treatment of migrant workers make activists subject to government accusations of being pawns of the West (Gurowitz 2000).

Eighth, already existing transnational networks enhance the establishment of new networks. The Asia-Pacific Coalition on East Timor, for instance, has its roots in the 1992 Bangkok NGO meeting of the People's Plan for the Twenty-First Century (PP 21) (Miclat 1995). In Thailand the ACFOD has been instrumental in facilitating the transnational networking of the Forum of the Poor as well as small-scale fishermen. In this process the organization has been able to draw on its transnational NGO links.

We can conclude that civil society groups in both Malaysia and Thailand have been able to make use of transnational political opportunities. This has been particularly important for Malaysian NGOs, which have more limited opportunities on the domestic level. What is perceived as negative aspects of globalization—and the incapacity of states to deal with these problems as well as a sense of transnational solidarity—stimulate civil society activism on a transnational level. The lack of domestic political opportunities is also a driving force behind the transnationalization of civil society groups. Allies and targets are increasingly found in other countries or within international organizations. The development of new communication technology—a prioritized issue in both Malaysia and Thailand—and the availability of transnational funding, provide necessary conditions for the development of a transnational civil society. Activists are able to make use of international regimes and discourses as well as multilateral agreements in their campaigns. There is a cumulative effect as the existence of transnational networks may stimulate the emergence of new networks on related issues. However, it is important to note that processes of globalization not only create opportunities for transnational activism, but also constraints and obstacles. National differences in political culture might be an obstacle. Transnational civil society—like any other social sphere—is stratified based on gender, class and ethnic divisions. Such cleavages constitute obstacles for successful transnational cooperation. Given the high cost of transnational activities, processes of transnationalization tend to increase resource inequality within civil society. The lack of political opportunities within specific countries is also an obstacle to transnational civil society networking. This is typically related to processes of democratization.

Transnational civil society and democratization

On the one hand, processes of democratization tend to create more space for civil society, including its transnational dimension. Most transnational civil society groups in Southeast Asia have their roots in countries with less authoritarian regimes, especially the Philippines and Thailand. The highly repressive Burmese state does not provide conditions for the emergence of a national—let alone—transnational civil society. On the other hand, the development of a transnational civil society creates new political space for pro-democracy actors in countries ruled by authoritarian leaders. Transnational civil society offers new channels for popular participation, consultation, debate, representation and pressures for democratic governance (Scholte 1999: 22). Thus, democratization on the national level and the development of a transnational civil society might be seen as mutually supportive processes. The emergence of a transnational civil society also raises questions about the possibility of some kind of transnational democracy. Held (1995: 237, 281) acknowledges that transnational grass-roots movements are creating political space for the development of what he calls "cosmopolitan democracy." However, he also warns that such grass-roots movements are not inherently "good" and democratic (Held 1995: 286).

According to Scholte (1999) transnational civil society can strengthen democracy, for instance by civic education, by giving voice to politically weak and marginalized actors, by fueling debate, by increasing transparency and accountability, and by providing legitimacy for suprastate governance. However, transnational civil society groups can also—intentionally or unintentionally—work against democracy. Just like within the state and the market sector there may be undemocratic practices within civil society. Inadequate representation can reproduce or even enlarge structural inequalities based on class, gender, nationality, race, religion, etc. (Scholte 1999: 30).

Concerning formal procedural democratization, transnational civil society groups have played an important role, for instance, in election monitoring. Election watchdogs like Namfrell in the Philippines and Pollwatch in Thailand inspired and supported the establishment of the Independent Election Monitoring Committee (KIPP) in Indonesia (Uhlin 1997: 205). Activists from Thailand and other Southeast Asian countries went to Indonesia to monitor the June 1999 elections. They also sent observers to East Timor for the referendum in August the same year (interview July 1, 1999). Many transnational civil society groups in the region, however, seem to be more concerned with broader societal aspects of democratization. Through support for disadvantaged groups like migrant workers and people being trafficked, urban poor, peasants and small-scale fishermen, transnational civil society activists try to empower the lower classes and increase the political participation of resource-poor people.

The most fundamental consequence of the development of a transnational civil society in Southeast Asia for prospects for democracy in the region is that it constitutes a new arena for political contestation. This means more political space for democratic struggles. On the regional level civil society groups with a pro-democracy agenda have made use of the new arena offered by the APEC. In connection with meetings on the élite level, transnational civil society networks have organized "People's Forums," challenging official APEC policies and putting forward a more egalitarian and democratic agenda (Price 1998). However, it is important not to see transnational civil society groups as inherently "good" forces struggling against authoritarian states. As noted above, there is much inequality within transnational civil society and the internal democracy of many transnational civil society groups can be questioned. The problem of how transnational activism can be anchored democratically is not resolved. This, however, requires further research that goes beyond the framework of the present study.

Concluding remarks

There is certainly not any clear causal link between processes of globalization and democratization. Globalization—in its various aspects—has a different impact in different countries depending on the specific national context. The political leadership in both Malaysia and Thailand has embraced contemporary economic globalization, though Malaysia rejected some neo-liberal policies linked to the IMF following the 1997–1998 economic crisis. Despite globalization the semi-authoritarian state in Malaysia has been able to keep its restrictions on civil society. The economic and political crisis gave rise to a reform movement, but for the time being the political regime is intact. Thailand has a long history of openness to global forces. There has been an alteration between military and more democratic civilian regimes, but this cannot be related to any changes in the impact of globalization. The present democratic regime is beginning to consolidate, but it is a rather limited form of élite democracy. The economic crisis and the policies to handle it have had a negative impact on societal democratization.

The most fundamental impact of globalization on civil society is that it creates new arenas for political struggles and thus widens political space. The emergence of a transnational civil society is a result of efforts by civil society activists to take advantage of transnational political opportunities when national opportunities are limited or nonexistent. Much transnational civil society activism is directed at what is perceived as negative aspects of globalization. Transnational problems require transnational cooperation. But globalization and the development of a transnational civil society also pose dangers for civil society activism. The reliance on transnational funding for civil society activities create new dependencies and may even reinforce inequalities within local civil societies. There is also a risk that local mobilization decreases as more activists turn to the transnational arena.

Formal democratization has created more space for civil society activism, including transnational networking. Meanwhile activists within civil society—national as well as transnational—have been crucial actors in the struggle for democracy, both in its formal procedural and broader societal forms. Nevertheless the relationship between the emergence of a transnational civil society and problems of democratization is complicated. Like in other social spheres, there are democratic shortcomings within transnational civil society. Processes of globalization and the related transnationalization of civil society also raises serious questions about the future of democracy in a globalizing world where the link between democracy and a territorially defined state is not obvious.

Notes

1   I am grateful for constructive comments on earlier drafts from the editors and Nicola Piper. Funding for research journeys has been received from SAREC, the Magnus Bergwall Foundation and the Nordic Institute of Asian Studies.
2   Interviews referred to in the text are listed in the reference section. For a more elaborate presentation of the different cases of transnational civil society activities see Uhlin (2001, 2002).

164   *Anders Uhlin*

3   In the academic literature the first position is represented by liberal theorists (e.g.
    Fukuyama 1992) whereas the second position is connected to critical theory (e.g.
    Gill 1996). See also the introductory chapter in this book.
4   Many studies do not explicitly refer to a transnational civil society but examine
    "transnational social movements" (Smith *et al.* 1997) or "transnational advocacy
    networks" (Keck and Sikkink 1998). Empirical studies focusing on Southeast
    Asia include Lizee (2000), Price (1998), and Uhlin (2001, 2002).
5   A first attempt at distinguishing between different aspects of transnational polit-
    ical opportunities can be found in Piper and Uhlin (2001).

References

Abbott, J. P. (2001) "Democracy@internet.asia? The Challenges to the Emancipa-
    tory Potential of the Net: Lessons from China and Malaysia," *Third World
    Quarterly* 22, 1: 99–114.
Beckman, B. (1997) "Explaining Democratization: Notes on the Concept of Civil
    Society," in E. Özdalga and S. Persson (eds.), *Civil Society, Democracy and the
    Muslim World,* Swedish Research Institute in Istanbul, Transactions Vol. 7.
Bello, W., Cunningham, S. and Li Khang Poh (1998) *A Siamese Tragedy. Develop-
    ment and Disintegration in Modern Thailand,* London: Zed Books.
Case, W. (2001) "Malaysia's Resilient Pseudodemocracy," *Journal of Democracy,* 12,
    1: 43–57.
Clarke, G. (1998) *The Politics of NGOs in South-East Asia. Participation and Protest
    in the Philippines,* London: Routledge.
Cohen, J. L. and Arato, A. (1992) *Civil Society and Political Theory,* Cambridge and
    London: MIT Press.
Crouch, H. (1996) *Government and Society in Malaysia,* St. Leonards: Allen &
    Unwin.
Diamond, L. (1994) "Toward Democratic Consolidation," *Journal of Democracy,* 5,
    3: 4–17.
Fukuyama, F. (1992) *The End of History and the Last Man,* London: Hamish
    Hamilton.
Gill, S. (1996) "Globalization, Democratization, and the Politics of Indifference," in
    J. H. Mittelman (ed.), *Globalization: Critical Reflections,* London and Boulder:
    Lynne Rienner.
Grugel, J. (1999) "Contextualizing Democratization: The Changing Significance of
    Transnational Factors and Non-State Actors," in J. Grugel (ed.), *Democracy
    Without Borders. Transnationalization and Conditionality in New Democracies,*
    London: Routledge.
Gurowitz, A. (2000) "Migrant Rights and Activism in Malaysia: Opportunities and
    Constraints," *Journal of Asian Studies,* 59, 4: 863–888.
Hamilton-Hart, N. (1999) "Thailand and Globalization," *Asian Perspective,* 23, 4:
    287–313.
He, B. (1999) "The Role of Civil Society in Defining the Boundary of a Political
    Community: The Cases of South Korea and Taiwan," *Asian Studies Review,* 23, 1:
    27–48.
Held, D. (1995) *Democracy and the Global Order. From the Modern State to
    Cosmopolitan Governance,* Cambridge: Polity Press.
Hewison, K. (2000) "Resisting Globalization: A Study of Localism in Thailand,"
    Pacific Review, 13, 2: 279–296.

Huntington, S. P. (1991) *The Third Wave. Democratization in the Late Twentieth Century*, Norman and London: University of Oklahoma Press.

Jesudason, J. V. (1996) "The Syncretic State and the Structuring of Oppositional Politics in Malaysia," in G. Rodan (ed.), *Political Oppositions in Industrialising Asia*. London: Routledge.

Keck, M. E. and Sikkink, K. (1998) *Activists Beyond Borders. Advocacy Networks in International Politics*, Ithaca and London: Cornell University Press.

Lizee, P. P. (2000) "Civil Society and Regional Security: Tensions and Potentials in Post-Crisis Southeast Asia," *Contemporary Southeast Asia*, 22, 3: 550–569.

McAdam, D. (1996) "Conceptual Origins, Current Problems, Future Directions," in D. McAdam and J. D. McCarthy (eds.), *Comparative Perspectives on Social Movements. Political Opportunities, Mobilizing Structures, and Cultural Framings*, Cambridge: Cambridge University Press.

Miclat, G. (1995) *Breaking the Silence. The Story behind APCET*, Quezon City: Asia-Pacific Coalition for East Timor.

Mittelman, J. H. (1999) "Resisting Globalisation: Environmental Politics in Eastern Asia," in K. Olds, P. Dicken, P. F. Kelly, L. Long and H. Wai-chung Yeung (eds.), *Globalization and the Asia-Pacific*, London: Routledge.

Naruemon Thabchumpon (1998) "Grassroots NGOs and Political Reform in Thailand: Democracy behind Civil Society," *Copenhagen Journal of Asian Studies*, 13: 31–59.

Piper, N. (2001) "Transnational Women's Activism in Japan and Korea: The Unresolved Issue of Military Sexual Slavery," *Global Networks* 1, 2: 155–170.

Piper, N. and Uhlin, A. (2001) "Transnational Advocacy Networks and the Issue of Trafficking and Labour Migration in East and Southeast Asia," paper presented at the 51st Political Studies Association Conference, April 10–12, 2001, Manchester, UK.

della Porta, D. and Kriesi, H. (1999) "Social Movements in a Globalizing World: An Introduction," in D. della Porta and H. Kriesi (eds.), *Social Movements in a Globalizing World*, London: Macmillan.

Price, J. (1998) "Shadowing APEC: Nongovernmental Organizations Build Regional Alliances," *Asian Perspective*, 22, 2: 21–50.

Quigley, K. F. F. (1996) "Towards Consolidating Democracy: The Paradoxical Role of Democracy Groups in Thailand," *Democratization*, 3, 3: 264–286.

Rajamoorthy, T. (1999) "Globalization and Citizenship in Malaysia," in A. Davidson and K. Weekley (eds.), *Globalization and Citizenship in the Asia-Pacific*, London: Macmillan.

Rodan, G. (1997) "Civil Society and Other Political Possibilities in Southeast Asia," *Journal of Contemporary Asia*, 27, 2: 156–178.

Scholte, J. A. (1999) *Global Civil Society: Changing the World?*, University of Warwick, Coventry: Centre for the Study of Globalisation and Regionalisation Working Paper No. 31/99.

—— (2000) *Globalization. A Critical Introduction*, London: Macmillan and New York: St. Martin's Press.

Shari, I. (2000) "Globalization and Economic Disparities in East and Southeast Asia: New Dilemmas," *Third World Quarterly*, 21, 6: 963–975.

Smith, J., Chatfield, C. and Pagnucco, R. (eds.) (1997) *Transnational Social Movements and Global Politics. Solidarity Beyond the State*, New York: Syracuse University Press.

Suchit Bunbongkarn (1999) "Thailand's Successful Reforms," *Journal of Democracy*, 10, 4: 54–68.

Thai Development Support Committee (1997) *Directory of Non-Governmental Organizations*, Bangkok: TDSC.

Uhlin, A. (1997) *Indonesia and the "Third Wave" of Democratization. The Indonesian Pro-Democracy Movement in a Changing World*, Richmond, Surrey: Curzon Press and New York: St. Martin's Press.

—— (2001) "The Transnational Dimension of Civil Society. Migration and Independence Movements in Southeast Asia," in B. Beckman *et al.* (eds.), *Civil Society and Authoritarianism in the Third World*, Stockholm: PODSU/Stockholm University.

—— (2002) "Regionalism from Below. Transnational Civil Society Links in Southeast Asia," in E. Palmujoki (ed.), *Southeast Asian Regionalism from Above and from Below*, (forthcoming).

Weiss, M. L. (1999) "What Will Become of *Reformasi*? Ethnicity and Changing Political Norms in Malaysia," *Contemporary Southeast Asia*, 21, 3: 424–450.

—— (2000) "The 1999 Malaysian General Elections. Issues, Insults, and Irregularities," *Asian Survey*, 40, 3: 413–435.

Welsh, B. (1999) "Malaysia and Globalization: Contradictory Currents," *Asian Perspective*, 23, 4: 261–286.

Interviews

Coordinator CARAM–Asia Project, Tenaganita, Kuala Lumpur, July 8, 1999.

Grass-roots activist, facilitator for fishermen's movement, Bangkok, October 23, 1999.

Human rights activist, Asian Forum for Human Rights and Development, Forum-Asia, Bangkok, July 1, 1999.

Human rights activist, SUARAM (Voice of the Malaysian People), Kuala Lumpur, March 7, 1997.

NGO activist, Centre for the Protection of Children's Rights Foundation (CPCR), Bangkok, July 1, 1999.

Women activist, Tenaganita, Kuala Lumpur, March 13, 1997.

Women activist, Tenaganita, Kuala Lumpur, July 8, 1999.

Part IV
Identity and citizenship in a glocalized Asia

10 Democratic citizenship and minority rights

A view from India

Bishnu N. Mohapatra

The theme of equal citizenship has a troubling presence within the narrative and practice of democracy in many societies today. This can be for several reasons, of which two stand out as salient. First, there is a growing realization that the values entailed by equal citizenship are not properly or inadequately realized within many existing democratic societies. Immigrants, minorities and aboriginal people living in several democracies over the years have drawn our attention to the dissonance between their formal, legalistic status as citizens and their real lives that are so full of discrimination and neglect. They also point out the ways in which their cultural/ethnic/religious identities remain invisible within the polities in which they live. This is much more than a mere empirical point. Underlying such perceived dissonance lies, they argue, a particular conception of citizenship that is hopelessly inadequate and exclusive. Second, the link between the notion of citizenship and the idea of "political community" is seen as deeply problematic. It is arguable that the idea of political community, at least in this century, has often taken on a nationalist hue. Yet, nationalist identity, as famously argued by Anderson (1983), is not only an imagined construct but also a deeply contentious project. The relationship between the idea of citizenship and national identity is not necessarily an intractable problem. However, when the national identity is defined in an exclusivist way and it tries to make the idea of citizenship subservient to it, then minority groups feel less equal, less at home within such a political community. They also feel that this itself undermines the project of universal citizenship. How do the ascriptive identities of the people and the idea of universal citizenship frame each other? Does the recognition of ascriptive identities of the people within the public sphere of a society necessarily undermine the project of universal citizenship? Or does it, on the contrary, lead to a better realization of equal citizenship by the members of the minority groups? In this chapter I argue that the recognition of ascriptive identities of the people in a substantive sense contributes to a better realization of equal citizenship and increases people's sense of belonging to the political community in which they live. I have tried to argue the above points by explicating the discourses on minority rights in contemporary India. There is no doubt that a real tension exists between the project of universal citizenship and the demands for specific rights for minority groups in a democratic society. Yet, this chapter tries to suggest that it is possible to bring about a creative and political reconciliation between the two. The possible reconciliation between the two, though this is bound to be influenced by specificities of circumstances, cannot be a matter of pure contingencies. Hence it is appropriate to view the relationship between the two in a larger theoretical context.

Minority rights and democratic citizenship: a contextual theorization

The last two decades have witnessed a remarkable upsurge of community mobilizations all around the world. The greater theoretical awareness of "pluralities" or "diversities" in the context of inequality and hegemony in several societies has been constitutive of a particular kind of collective mobilization that Charles Taylor (1994) evocatively called the "politics of recognition." There are three fundamental ways in which contemporary politics of recognition tends to draw our attention. First, it manifests as a negation. Often it interrogates the notion of a monolithic nation-state and puts forward a critique against the process of homogenization in a society. It also unmasks the unequal relationship among various cultural/religious/ethnic groups. Second, the politics of recognition is not only about dignity; it is also about entitlements, substantive rights and freedom. It is this that has brought the politics of multiculturalism directly into the domain of democracy. Finally, the recognition of ascriptive diversities has raised serious questions regarding the liberal definition of "rights," "community," citizenship, and so on. A detailed discussion of the "multiculturalism" debate is not attempted here. However, I will try to bring out the key theoretical issues raised by this debate that have a direct bearing on our discussion on minority rights and its problematic link with the idea of equal citizenship.

The presence of contesting Christian sects centuries ago raised the issue of majority and minority in the West. In order to avoid religious persecution and violence, it was necessary to articulate the idea of toleration. The pragmatic defense of tolerance was subjected to abuse. The principled defense of minority rights was yet to come. The initial defense of the existence of internal minorities within a nation-state, quite paradoxically, came through the articulation of individual rights. Gradually this gave rise to the liberal-individualist position. The liberal-individualist response is in principle against discrimination. Through a network of procedures, arrived at lawfully, society makes the varied cultural world of the people remain outside the domain of the public sphere. This stance of "neutrality" is often defended by invoking the principle of "equality." The idea is that when public/political institutions are based on the multiple, often incommensurable, culture-world of the people, then it would somehow result in a compromise with the idea of equality. It is not true that liberals usually overlook pluralism in societies. Indeed, "the fact of pluralism" (Rawls 1993) is recognized by liberals as an inescapable or an antecedent condition of modern societies, characterized by the presence of divergent and irreconcilable "comprehensive doctrines." The insistence on neutrality and anti-perfectionism tends to keep the politics of difference at bay.

The idea of a universal citizen is often employed by the liberal individualists as a counter-idea to that of a culturally rooted individual. According to this view, citizens are supposed to be culturally invisible, at least in the public sphere. During the last three centuries this idea of a "citizen-man" has been used by the democrats to undermine the privileges of the wealthy and the aristocrats in Europe and to pull down the barriers that existed between the people and the process of democratic governance. This ideal of citizenship, however, pushed to the background the earlier conception of citizenship, such as the civic-republican ideal, in which solidarity was of more value than individuality. The consequences of moving away from these latter traditions of citizenship implied that the citizen of the liberal-individualist tradition was completely severed from all cultural attachments and the gap between individual freedom and community-belonging, between the imperatives of democracy and the demands of diversity, could not be bridged.

The liberal ambivalence toward cultural/ethnic diversity has been subjected to scrutiny in recent times. The argument is that the individual-right framework, though important, is not enough for the protection of minority cultures and identities in a multicultural society. Ethnocultural and religious minorities in several societies are demanding special forms of recognition, often in the idiom of "group rights." The conventional liberal suspicion toward these communitarian demands is found to be unjustified. The defenders of group rights often argue that the emphasis of the liberal-individualist on the disembodied citizen-self and on the difference-blind stance of the public institutions, particularly in the context of entrenched inequalities in a society, promotes neither equality nor freedom. They also suggest that the neutrality of the state *vis-à-vis* cultural or religious groups in fact legitimizes the dominant culture and values in a society. On this view, the cultural world to which individuals belong shapes their choices and makes their life-plans more meaningful and purposive (Kymlicka 1995). Defenders of minority rights are often critical of the individualist bias of liberalism and see no objection in supporting special provisions for the minority groups in a society. They also believe that recognition of diversities can make a democratic state more legitimate and responsive. Finally, the relationship between individual well-being and the prosperity of the cultural group to which they belong is viewed as complementary (Kymlicka 1989; Tamir 1993; Raz 1994). One can see in these theoretical exercises attempts to reconcile the demands of unity and diversity between the citizenship values and the import of cultural membership (Taylor 1991; Parekh 1999).

It is within these contending claims for unity and separateness that the relationship between democratic citizenship and "minority rights" is framed in the multicultural societies in the West as well as in India. In concrete terms, "minority rights" encompasses several heterogeneous claims. Two types of claim are quite familiar. First a minority group demands rights against the larger society, to protect itself against the majoritarian tendencies of the society. In some cases a minority culture wants rights against its own members, who in the name of individual rights can challenge certain collective practices. There are occasions in which a minority group wants autonomy as the best way of protecting their collective existence. In other circumstances they need special and exclusive provisions in order to survive as a community. In exceptional circumstances they can demand the right to self-determination as the only option for protecting their culture and way of life in the world. Normatively speaking, what rights are morally justified to grant to the minority groups depends upon specific circumstances and other contingent factors in a given society. It is quite possible that a minority group can start with the demand for special provisions but due to specific circumstances can find self-determination as the only option to counter the forces of majoritarianism. Yet one can see that all such demands tend to share some crucial features. They go beyond an abstract conception of citizenship of liberal democracy; and they make the recognition and protection of cultural differences central to the project of democratization.

How is this debate between the liberals and communitarians played out in India? What do the votaries of an abstract conception of citizenship respond to the proliferation of caste and community mobilizations in recent decades in India? To what extent can the citizenship argument explain the specific anxieties of the Muslims in the aftermath of the demolition of Babri Masjid on December 6, 1992 in Ayodhaya? A detailed discussion on this is not possible within the limited space of this chapter. However, let me point out, albeit briefly, some of the ways in which the "citizenship argument" is mobilized in India and the manners in which they are contested and challenged. More often than not, in the social science literature in India, the idea of citizenship was and still is overlaid with "people's rights discourse" and "national identity narratives." Similarly, in political discourse, both high and low, it is the term "people" (*janata*) that has overtaken or stood for the term "citizen" (*nagarik*). Is it because the term "people" is more inclusive and less technical than the term "citizen"? This may explain partly the popularity of the term "people." However, it is the ability of the term to go beyond the legal and constitutional level to that of a moral one that constitutes the unending appeal of the term "people" among the social activists and scholars. It is also possible to argue that in numerous social movements in India, whether involving lower castes, tribals and displaced people, and so on, the "citizenship argument" remains submerged within the discourse on "social justice," which goes far beyond the definition of justice offered by the formal structures of the state.

It is not surprising that most social movements in India articulate their demands in terms of "people's rights" rather than "citizens' rights." However, within the civil rights discourse in the country, the idea of citizen is valorized. There is no doubt that, as in the West, the idea of an "unmarked citizen" is also used in India as a weapon to combat the authoritarian power of the state. The fight against the National Emergency

(1975–1977) in India was waged in the name of protecting citizens' civil and political rights. However, in recent decades the dissatisfaction with an abstract conception of citizenship is clearly visible within the sphere of mobilizational politics in the country. A major source of the critique has come from the "dalits" (Ilaiha 1998; Nigam 2000; *Seminar* 1998), "feminists" (Menon 1998; Jayal 1999), tribal communities and minorities. The nature of their critique, of course, varies across as well within these groups. A large majority of them are not offering an outright rejection of the idea of universal citizenship. Instead, they are critical of the process that forces them to abandon their specific identities in order to achieve citizenship status. They also highlight the fact that a large majority of them, because of their weak statuses, are not able to access even the minimum set of rights awarded to them by the constitution. It is through their critiques that one can see the underside of the citizen-making process in the country. The demands for recognition of their sectional interests on the part of the dalits or minorities in India point clearly to a strong link between the existence of certain minimal conditions of well-being and the effective enjoyment of citizenship rights. In order to see how this link is forged in the minority rights discourse in contemporary India, we have to turn to the next section.

Minority rights and citizenship: the postcolonial predicament

In a constitutional democracy, minority rights are best understood when they are seen alongside a broader regime of rights. Special minority rights are meant to protect the identity and interest of minorities. What makes the minority rights special is that they, in contrast to general rights, are group-differentiated or community-specific. Some of these rights are collectively exercised by the group and others by the individuals belonging to the group to whom the rights are awarded. In a democracy, both general as well as group-specific rights are provided in the law of the land. India is no exception to this.

Part III of the Constitution of independent India provides a set of "fundamental rights" for all its citizens. It too contains rights that are meant to be enjoyed only by specific groups. Take for instance the Right to Equality (Articles 14–18), Right to Freedom (Articles 19–22), Right to Freedom of Religion (Articles 25–28), which are the fundamental rights meant for all the citizens of the country. Their justiciability makes sure that any infringement with these rights can be contested in the judiciary of the country and the state has to provide adequate constitutional grounds for its suppression. Some of the key rights in the Fundamental Rights Chapter of the Indian Constitution embody the principle of nondiscrimination. Article 15 (1) reads thus: "The State shall not discriminate against any citizen on grounds only of religion, race, caste, sex, place of birth or any of them" (The Constitution of India: 7). And Article 16 suggests that "no citizen shall, on grounds only of religion, race, caste, sex, descent, place of birth, residence or any of them be ineligible for, of discriminated against in respect of, any employment or office under the state" (ibid.). Another area to which the Indian Constitution has extended the principle of nondiscrimination is that of education. Clause 2 of Article 29 provides that "no citizen shall be denied admission into any educational institution maintained by the state or receiving aid out of state funds on grounds only of religion, race, caste, language or any of them" (ibid.: 14).

Nondiscrimination, and the equal treatment of citizens by the state are inevitably related. These two principles together have laid down the foundation of equal citizenship in India. However, the Constitution provides exceptions to the principles of nondiscrimination and equality. For instance, it can make special provisions for the welfare of women and children. The state through special provisions can also legislate to improve the conditions of citizens belonging to socially and educationally backward classes or to the Scheduled castes and tribes. The adoption of universal suffrage by rejecting the communal electorate (Article 325) also reflects the constitutional commitment to the principle of equal citizenship. It is true that the individual remains at the core of the equal citizenship principle, enshrined in the Constitution. However, one can see clearly in Articles 15 and 16 a productive combination of rights meant to be enjoyed by individual citizens as citizens and the obligation of the state toward citizens belonging to specific communities. The awareness of individual and community in their relationship remains central to the Indian constitutional discourse since 1950. Even though the right to equality, as a fundamental right of the Constitution, applies to all the citizens of the country, it has special significance for minorities, and particularly those disadvantaged. In a strict sense, these rights are not minority rights; but its significance for the minority community is relatively more significant. There are numerous instances where the weaker communities have used the principle of nondiscrimination to highlight the persistence of discrimination in different spheres of society. Particularly in recent years, the stories of discrimination toward the dalit communities in India have been widely reported in the print as well as in the electronic media of the country.

The principle of nondiscrimination, though important, is not enough however. Similarly, the presence of universal rights alone is not sufficient to address the claims of the minorities. Article 29 (1) of the Constitution states: "Any section of the citizens residing in the territory of India or any part thereof having a distinct language, script or culture of its own shall have the right to conserve the same" (ibid.). Language is fundamentally social and a right to preserve one's own language is inescapably a collective right. This, the Supreme Court declared, includes even the citizens' "right to agitate for its protection."[1] According to this judgment, this right is more or less "absolute," "unqualified" and "positive" (Wadhwa 1975: 98). According to Article 30 (1), "all minorities, whether based on religion or language, shall have the right to establish and administer educational institutions of their choice" (The Constitution of India: 14). It further provides in Article 30 (2) that: "the State shall not, in granting aid to educational institutions, discriminate, against any educational institution on the ground that it is under the management of a minority, whether based on religion, or language" (ibid.: 15). The first part of the article protects the right of the minorities to have their own educational institutions. The second involves a limited obligation on the part of the state toward these institutions. One of the objectives of this article is clearly to do with the protection of the distinctive identities of the linguistic and religious minorities of the country. In a famous judgment connected with Article 30, the Supreme Court declared that, "[T]he minorities, quite understandably, regard it as essential that the education of their children should be in accordance with the teachings of their religion and they hold, quite honestly, that such an education cannot be obtained in ordinary schools designed for all the members of the public, but can only be versed in the trends of their religion and in the tradition of their culture."[2]

The relationship between the state and the minority educational institutions has raised many issues concerning the state of minority rights in India. It has been made clear through judicial pronouncements that the state can lay down some restrictions in the matters dealing with syllabi for examinations, conditions of employment of teachers, and health and hygiene of students, but it cannot force a minority educational institution to teach in a particular language.[3] The state can also prescribe reasonable conditions while giving grant-in-aid to the educational institutions administered by a minority community. The nature of state intervention in the minority-governed educational institutions in the country still remains a sensitive issue. In this, the role of the Supreme Court has been of great significance.

Besides the above-mentioned articles, the Constitution of India also contains special provisions for the education of the linguistic minorities. The issue of linguistic minorities is indeed quite old. The early stirrings of the linguistic groups in India can be traced to the early part of the twentieth century. It is within the larger provinces of the British Empire that several language groups perceived themselves as minorities, and demand for reorganization of provinces on linguistic lines was often raised by them. As early as the 1920s, the National Congress recognized the identity claims of the language groups. The recognition of their distinctness, and the redrawing of the provincial boundaries, were the main strategies through which linguistic minorities were made into majorities within the provincial arenas. In spite of the Congress's early promise, reorganization of provinces was not an easy affair in the post-independent India. Even the reorganization of provinces did not resolve the problem of linguistic minorities in the country.

Article 347 of the Constitution states: "[On] a demand being made in that behalf the President may, if he is satisfied that a substantial proportion of the population of a State desire the use of any language spoken by them to be recognized by that State, direct that such language shall also be officially recognized throughout that State or any part thereof for such purpose as he may specify" (ibid.: 212). A sizeable and vocal linguistic minority can take advantage of this provision in order to get their language recognized by the state. The Constitution allows persons to submit their petitions for the redress of grievances to the state in any language (Article: 350), and provides for education in the mother tongue to children of linguistic minorities (Article: 350 A). In the wake of the State Reorganization Commission's recommendations, a special officer for linguistic minorities was created (Article: 350B), whose function was to look into the implementation, or lack of it, of the safeguards for the linguistic minorities in the provinces. The unresolved problems of linguistic minorities in India have created tensions among groups in the provinces. It is arguable whether the Indian state is better endowed to handle the territorially concentrated linguistic minorities in comparison to the religious ones.

The adoption of secularism as an ideology by the Indian state right from the time of independence can be seen as a response to its religious diversities. Though the term secular was inserted in the preamble of the Constitution by the forty-second amendment in 1976, the principle was integral to the ideology of the Congress and to the constitutional discourse as it evolved during the course of the anti-colonial struggle. On July 8, 1948, Nehru in a letter to the Nawab of Bhopal, clearly asserted the secularity of the Indian state:

> I believe in India being a secular state with complete freedom for religious cultures and for cooperation between them. I believe that India can only become great if she preserves that composite culture which she had developed through the ages. I confess however that doubts sometimes assail me whether this is going to happen or not. ... I am anxious therefore that the Muslims in India as well as other religious groups should have the fullest freedom and opportunity to develop themselves. I am entirely hostile to Hindu or any other communalism in India.[4]

Secularism was one among the key values with which the postcolonial state in India started its journey in 1947, and the question is how the secularity of the Indian state has affected the exercise of minority rights. In the context of the Partition and the large-scale violence that followed it, acceptance of secularism by the Congress was itself a matter of forging a political choice, an exercise in asserting a collective political agency. In a minimal sense, it was part of a political consensus that was supposed to inform the structure of governance in the country. The drafters of the Constitution agreed to embody the key principles of secularism such as the religious freedom of the communities, equal treatment by the state of all the religious communities, and dissociation of the state from religion and so on, in the political institutions of the country.

By the early 1980s, the early consensus showed signs of fracture and dissensions. Against this backdrop, the liberals see the period of Nehru as the golden era of Indian secularism. For some, in spite of Nehru's modernist ideological predilection, his rule did not witness the deepening of secular vision in India (Bilgrami 1998). There are scholars who argue that the doctrine of secularism itself, rooted in the historical experience of the West, is responsible for its limited appeal in India (Madan 1998). To others, the doctrine of secularism, being a feature of a statist modernity, neither addresses the issue of faith nor the inter-religious tension well. On this view, secularism sanctions the "imposition of an imported language of politics on a traditional society that has an open polity" (Nandy 1998). Even the defenders of secularism find problems, not with the doctrine itself but with the manner in which it was being constructed and justified. Bilgrami makes this point by drawing a distinction between the terms "archimedean" and "substantive" secularism (Bilgrami 1998). During the last two decades or so, the debate on secularism has become polarized in India. Without any agreed definition or shared understanding, the term has come to mean different things to different people. The Hindu right brands its opponents as pseudosecular and views itself as the defender of true or genuine secularism in this country. They also allege that in the past the Congress, in the name of secularism, had appeased the minorities. In this context, attempts are being made by political theorists to explicate the meaning of secularism and its significance in a plural society like India (Bhargava 1998).

India's constitution provides for religious liberty to all its citizens as individuals as well as as members of religious groups to which they belong as stated in Article 25 (1) and Article 26 of the Indian Constitution (p. 13). Both these articles, however, are subject to several limitations, including that of public order, morality and health. The state can also limit the freedom on the ground of bringing about reforms within the religious communities and also on the plea of welfare and other relevant secular considerations. The Right to Equality, embodied in Articles 14, 15 and 16, gives the equal citizenship status to all. Article 325, which deals with universal franchise, states that: "no person shall be ineligible for inclusion in any such roll or claim to be included in any special electoral roll for any such constituency on grounds only of religion, race, caste, sex or any of them" (ibid.: 198). The separation of the state from religion is enshrined in Articles 27 and 28 (1) of the Constitution. According to these, no one can be compelled to pay taxes for the promotion or maintenance of any particular religion, and no religious instruction is to be provided in those schools wholly funded by the state.

The current debates on secularism draw attention to the problematic relationship between its constituent values and the state and their cumulative impact on the secularity of the Indian state. There are scholars who argue that the Indian constitution, though it does not follow strictly the American model, is still modern and embodies the core values of secularism. In other words, just because a thoroughgoing separation of state and religion does not exist in India, as it arguably does in the United States, does not mean that the Indian secularism is in any way less secular or an inferior brand of secularism. As a matter of fact, a strong argument exists that considers the intervention of the Indian state in the domain of religion, a differentiated conception of citizenship, and the presence of robust minority rights, as perfectly compatible with the main ideals of secularism (Bhargava 2000).

The tenuous relationship between secularism and other substantive values such as equality, impartiality and liberty is best seen in the context of the Indian state's intervention in the realm of religious practices. In the early years after independence, the Indian state had to bring about several reforms in the realm of religious practices. The Acts abolishing untouchability or allowing the dalits to enter Hindu temples or reforming the Hindu personal law necessarily took the Indian state into the realm of religious practices of several communities. In most cases, the Indian courts (see Galanter 1998) had to intervene to settle the disputes between the concerned religious establishment and the state. The intervention of the state in the affairs of the religious communities created several problems in India. That was not due to intervention per se but to the use of such interventions for political ends. The glaring example in recent times is the intervention of the Indian Parliament in the Shah Bano affairs. The legislation that subverted the verdict of the Supreme Court was seen by many as a product of political calculation, of electoral arithmetic of the ruling party at the Center. The declining legitimacy of the state and of the political regimes has played a crucial role in undermining the secular fabric of India in recent decades.

From the vantage point of "minority rights," the establishment of a secular Constitution in 1950 was a significant moment. It is clear that throughout Nehru had understood the importance of a secular state for a plural society like India. Though he felt the necessity of secularizing civil society in India, it was the construction of a secular state that received most of his attention. It is within this context that one has to examine the Nehruvian project of the 1950s and 1960s. There was a downward trend in communal violence from 1954–1960 (Hasan 1997: 161). The attempts of the Hindu communal organizations to spread their exclusivist ideology were strongly resisted by the Congress. After the assassination of Mahatma Gandhi, the RSS (Rashtriya Swayamsevak Sangh) was very much on the defensive and the Hindu Mahasabha found it difficult to increase its popular base beyond the newly arrived refugees from Pakistan. Their attempts to mobilize people against cow-slaughter in Uttar Pradesh and other provinces of north India did not gather the expected momentum. In 1954, the anti-cow slaughter bill was defeated in the Delhi Assembly, and attempts to bring it to the Parliament were also strongly resisted by the Congress. During the early years after independence, most minority communities (including the Muslims) saw their collective well-being as inextricably linked to the secularity of the Indian state. On the political/electoral front, by and large they supported the secular parties of which the Congress was the main beneficiary. In the first two Lok Sabha elections, the Congress got the maximum support from the minority communities in the country. Following this, electoral support of the minority communities toward the Congress gradually dwindled. Sensing the growing disenchantment of the minorities, the Congress had instituted a subcommittee to look into the "problem" in 1957. After long deliberation, the committee highlighted three areas of concern for the minorities in India. First, it highlighted the feeling of discontent prevalent among the minority groups due to their poor representation in the service sector, at the Center as well as in the provinces. The Committee also felt the necessity of giving adequate representation to the minorities, particularly in the lower-ranking jobs in the military, the railways, and so on (Kabir 1968). Second, it noted that the minority groups felt discriminated against in connection with the distribution of state-resources for trade, industry and commerce. Finally, the subcommittee drew attention to the feeling of the minorities that they were not being adequately represented in various representative bodies of the state.

The feeling of alienation was not confined to the Muslims alone. The attack on Christian missionary activities by the Hindu communal groups naturally created a strong resentment among the Christian communities in the late 1950s. In 1956 Niyogi Committee's report, looking into the activities of the foreign Christian missionaries, was published. The Christian community felt as if the entire community was on trial. The findings of the Committee by and large threw a negative light on the activities of the church missions. In the wake of the publication of the Committee's report, there were several incidents of violence against the Christians and church property and the campaign of the Hindu religious organizations intensified particularly among the Scheduled tribes (Smith 1963; Beaglehole 1967). The freedom to propagate their religion and to run their educational institutions were the twin issues which structured the relationship between the Christian communities and the Hindu nationalists. In case of conflict between the two, the Indian courts played a vital role at least in putting a brake on the majoritarian designs of the Hindu communalists.

The decline of Muslim support for the Congress was quite visible in the Parliament election of 1967. In some sense, the electoral behavior of the majority of the Muslims in 1967 followed the all-India pattern. Yet, it is arguable that the Congress's inability to contain the alienation and reflect the interest of the Muslims prompted them to look for alternative political platforms. As this process gained momentum, the importance of the Muslims as a "vote-bank" was becoming a part of the electoral arithmetic of the Congress and the other contending parties. Growing incidents of communal violence in the 1960s in several provinces brought the issue of physical security to the heart of the minority discourse articulated by the majority of the Muslims. The temporary communal peace achieved during the reign of Nehru appeared to have come to an end.

The reactions of the Muslim minority groups to the changed political and communal scenario since the 1960s were, undoubtedly, not uniform or of a homogeneous cast. The number of districts affected by communal riots increased from 61 in 1961 to 250 in 1986–1987 out of a total 350 districts in the country (Hasan 1988). There was a corresponding growth of communal organizations in the country: from 12 in 1951 to over 500 in 1987–1988 with a membership totaling over a few millions (ibid.: 2469). As the shared space between communities shrank as a result of sectarian violence, it created conditions for the revival and growth of "fundamentalist" forces among the majority as well as among the minority groups. Though in pockets, the communal organizations became the only vehicles through which the Muslims started expressing their identitarian voices. The relative decline of the Congress and the Muslims' growing disenchantment with it gave these voices a new sense of urgency. The increasing influence of the Muslim League in Kerala, the rise of the Ittehadul Musilmeen (Alam 1993, 2000) in Hyderabad, and the growing political influence of Jamat-I-Islami in Kashmir, all conservative ideologically, need to be seen against the changing political backdrop of the 1970s and 1980s. Within the discursive space provided by these conservative forces, the issue of minority rights became synonymous with the preservation of the community's separate space within a particular framework of Islam. The presence of a separate Personal Law and polygamy, on this line of thinking, became essential for the "preservation of a separate Muslim culture in India."[5]

The conservative reactions and the reactive anxieties, however powerful, could not fully colonize the minority rights discourse in post-1960s India. The articulation of community concerns did not necessarily follow a single, exclusivist trajectory. The formation of the All India Muslim Convention and the Majli-I Mushawarat belonged to a different genre of political interventions. There were attempts to carve out an independent political space, outside the orbit of the Congress, for the Muslims in Uttar Pradesh and Bihar. Though these initiatives did not succeed in creating a separate political agency for the Muslims (Khalidi 1993), they did break the old habit of looking toward the Congress as a natural ally of the community. The liberal and left intellectuals belonging to the Muslim community reiterated their faith in the secular constitution from time to time, and expressed their concerns at the growing menace of communalism in the country (Hasan 1997: 269–270). The question of political representation for the religious minorities has remained since colonial days a contentious issue. A cursory look at the data pertaining to the Muslim representation in Lok Sabha during the first forty years of democracy is quite revealing. The percentage of Muslim members[6] in the Lok Sabha during this period varied from 4.45 per cent to 9.04 per cent. The percentage point of the Muslim legislators was the lowest (4.45 per cent) in the 1962 election and the highest (9.04 per cent) in the election of 1980. Without the system of proportional representation or reservation of seats for them in the legislatures, their only hope to gain a voice within the legislatures lay in establishing strategic alliances with different political parties or political formations.

By the early 1970s, the limitations of the parliamentary democracy, as far as the representation of the minority communities was concerned, were quite visible. The general political ambience both at the regional and national level played a vital role in this. Any mainstream secular political party found it difficult to champion the cause of the minorities beyond a point for fear that it might alienate voters belonging to the majority community. Representation of the Muslims in the decision-making bodies of the main political parties was equally dismal (Razzack and Gumber 2000: 14). The competitive and formal democracy's capacity to respond to the demands of the minorities was also evidently limited. On the other hand, the élites of the minority groups made the contestation of views and strategies difficult to emerge. At any rate, the desire to change their status from objects of electoral politics (vote-banks) to subjects of political change is gradually occupying a central place within minority discourse in the country. To view these political sensibilities as a pure reflection of an undifferentiated minority community is mistaken. At the same time, to treat them as pleas for "separateness"/divisiveness is unfair and does not do justice to the democratic potential of such communitarian concerns.

The communitarian concerns of the minorities, however, were not merely confined to the sphere of politics and culture. The theme of backwardness and relative deprivation was, and still is, a vital part of the minority rights discourse in India. The discussion on economic and educational backwardness of the minority groups in general and the Muslims in particular in India has a long history. During the colonial period, the claims of the minority groups for special provisions and safeguards were inextricably linked to their economic and educational backwardness. As pointed out earlier, the theme of backwardness is still one of the crucial components of minority rights discourse in the postcolonial period. In the past, and so also today, Muslim groups often use the theme of economic and educational backwardness to show their relative status *vis-à-vis* other communities in the country. More than half of the Muslim urban population live below poverty line, compared to about 35 per cent of Hindus. In urban areas a majority of Muslims are self-employed (53.4 per cent) in comparison to 36 per cent amongst Hindus. The self-employed category for the Muslims included, by and large, low-status occupations such as cobbler, rickshaw-puller, small artisan, and so on (Razzack and Gumber 2000: 11). According to a recent report on India, 43 per cent of the Muslims and 27 per cent of Christians live below the poverty line in comparison to 39 per cent of Hindus (Shariff 1999: 44).

The economic backwardness of Muslims, since the colonial period, had had a constitutive link with their educational backwardness. In its report on the minorities in 1983, the Gopal Singh Committee drew attention, among other things, to the educational backwardness of Muslims. On the basis of a survey, it highlighted the excessive dropout rate of Muslim children at the primary school level and their under-representation in the domains of higher and technical education.[7] In this respect, according to this report, the situation of other minorities such as Christians and Sikhs was relatively better. By the turn of the twentieth century, the male illiteracy for the Muslims in the rural and urban areas was 58 per cent and 59 per cent, respectively. Female illiteracy was far worse, at 76 per cent and 42 per cent in the rural and urban areas respectively (Razzack and Gumber 2000: 5).

The position of the Muslims with regard to employment was and still is, the mirror image of their relative backwardness in education. According to the Gopal Singh Committee Report, the employment of Muslims[8] in the government offices at the Center as well as in the provinces varied from 5 per cent to 6 per cent of total employees. In this regard Muslims are even relatively worse off in comparison to other minorities such as the Christians and Sikhs, their representation in Class I and II services varying between 3 and 4.5 per cent. For instance, as of January 1, 1983 the number of Muslims in the Indian Administrative Service (Hasan 1988: 2471) numbered only 90 (2.14 per cent) out of a total of 4,195. Around the same time, Muslim representation in the Indian Police Service (ibid.) was a meager 3 per cent (67) of the total (2,222). In the private sector of the Indian economy, the presence of Muslims in the executive, as well as in supervisory cadres, was equally derisory.

How does the fact of educational and economic backwardness feature in minority right discourse in postcolonial India? There is no doubt that considerable regional and class variations exist as far as the economic status of Muslims is concerned. For instance, a large number of Muslims in Uttar Pradesh and Bihar, in comparison to other states, are poor. The situation of Muslims in Kerala, for instance, is not the same as that in Rajasthan. Even within one province, the economic condition of Muslim wage-laborers is not the same as that of the professional class. Yet, the theme of backwardness is incorporated in the minority rights discourse as a generalized state of affairs, as a marker of the community as a whole, and of its collective predicament.

In contemporary minority discourse, welfare concerns and identity issues are often blended together. Though analytically separate, in reality, they overlap with one another. The issue concerning the Urdu language clearly demonstrates the point we are making. The decline of Urdu in North India has had a negative impact on the Muslim ability to gain employment. The demand of Muslims to give Urdu a proper status in select provinces was and still is directly related to real economic benefits. This is also related to the identity concerns of the community. The neglect of Urdu thus becomes a sign of the community's powerlessness and the reflection of a majority community's politics of "mis-recognition." In a sense, the concern about Urdu language for the Muslims embodies simultaneously the issue of economic welfare and that of identity. Likewise, the demand for the protection of educational institutions managed by Muslims and Christians clearly involves the simultaneous presence of economic and identity concerns.

Since the process of "mandalisation" has unfolded in the 1990s, the framing of welfare issues within the minority discourse has undergone some significant changes. V. P. Singh's decision to implement the recommendations of the Mandal Commission quickened the process, particularly in north India, of making a political bloc composed of Other Backward Castes (OBCs). The already existing contradiction between this bloc and the upper caste thus became sharper. The reservation of jobs for OBCs, no doubt, was the immediate issue against which violent protests broke out in many places in the country. However, its impact on provincial and national politics was quite significant. The growing assertion of Hindutva forces and the decline of the Congress helped create the formation of a new space for political mobilization comprised of deprived communities such as dalits, OBCs, and so on. This new context too created new political possibilities for Muslim groups in India. The

OBCs among the Muslims, like their counterparts among the Hindus, got the benefit of reservation of government jobs. While in the realm of electoral politics, political parties tried to forge a coalition among different deprived groups such as dalits, OBCs, and Muslims, and so on. The process still continues today.

With such sectional mobilization, it was difficult to sustain the concept of an undifferentiated, deprived Muslim community fighting for its due share in the polity. The element of caste within the Muslim communities was always there. But in the post-Mandal times, it acquired a new salience and the lower-caste identities among them made their presence felt. The articulations of dalit-Christian and of lower-caste Muslims surely have opened up new possibilities in the realm of inter-community relationship and of electoral politics. As discussed above, the fact of economic and educational backwardness of Muslims was invariably used as a cementing force for the symbolic construction of the community. However, with the growing awareness of caste-identity, the theme of backwardness is now used by the low-caste groups within the Muslim community to undermine their old leadership, and to forge new linkages with similar groups belonging to other religions. The debate on reservation of jobs for Muslims in recent years brings this dimension to the fore (Wright 1997).

The demolition of Babri Masjid in December 1992 was a turning point in the history of secularism in India. The communal violence that followed the tragic event increased the sense of vulnerability among the Muslims. Similarly, repeated attacks on Christian missionaries and the destruction of churches raised insecurities among the Christians to a new height.[9] Nearly two decades ago, the violence against the Sikhs after the assassination of Indira Gandhi caused an acute sense of alienation and helplessness in that group. The point I am trying to make is that the experience of vulnerability and of discrimination is not new to the minority groups in India. Whether it is the question of honor or dignity, or economic well-being of the minorities, the institutional response to these concerns have been woefully inadequate in India. Though important, minority rights, one can argue, cannot be protected only by entrenching them in the domain of competitive politics. For the effective protection of minority rights, institutional mechanisms are of the utmost importance. In this regard, the role of the judiciary has been and continues to be of great importance. The justiciable character of the "fundamental rights," as provided in Part III of the Indian Constitution, ensures that their violations can be challenged in the courts. At least in principle, these rights, some of which are specially relevant for minorities, tend to lay several obligations upon the state and also to act against its majoritarian impulse. But the mere existence of rights is not enough. Similarly, a society without discrimination on the basis of religion, caste, race, and so on, cannot be willed into existence just by enacting a democratic constitution.

On January 12, 1978, the Janata Government at the Center notified a resolution with an objective of setting up a Minorities Commission in the country.

Despite the safeguards provided in the Constitution and the laws in force there persists among the Minorities a feeling of inequality and discrimination. In order to preserve secular traditions and to promote national integration the Government of India attaches the highest importance to the enforcement of the safeguards provided for the Minorities and is of the firm view that *effective institutional arrangements are urgently required for the enforcement and implementation of all the safeguards provided for the Minorities* in the Constitution, in the Central and state laws and in Government policies and administrative schemes enunciated from time to time. The Government of India has, therefore, resolved to set up a Minorities Commission to safeguard the interests of the Minorities whether based on religion or language.[10]

The first Commission was formed on February 22, 1978. Until 1992, when the National Commission for Minorities received the statutory status, the Commission had functioned under the guidance of four chairpersons. Very early on, the need for providing a constitutional basis to the Commission was voiced in the Parliament.[11] On May 4, 1992, the Welfare Minister, Sitaram Kesri, introduced the National Commission for Minorities Bill in the Lok Sabha. The defenders of the Bill offered broadly two reasons for conferring the minority commission with a statutory status. First was an argument for greater efficacy. They argued that armed with statutory power, the Minorities Commission would be an effective instrument for protection of minority rights. The implication was that in its first incarnation, it was a mere advisory institution without much power at its command. The second was a legitimacy argument. The Bill, Sitaram Kesri pointed out, would "instill confidence in the minorities."[12] This in turn would increase the legitimacy of the argument.

The supporters of the Bill, mostly belonging to the Congress and other non-BJP parties, grounded their arguments on the principle of secularism. Their starting assumption was that the Indian constitution embodied several provisions exclusively for the minorities. The existence as well as the protection of minority rights remained central to their understanding of secularism. In their arguments, a minority community appears as one that is vulnerable, at least potentially threatened and inadequately represented in various spheres of society. It was also assumed in their discourse that without an effective watchdog it would be impossible to check the acts of discrimination against the minorities. The notion of minority rights that ran through the arguments of the defenders of the Bill was broad and contained both the positive as well as its negative elements. They highlighted the ways in which minorities suffer from discrimination and indignities in the society.

On the other hand, the opponents of the Bill, mostly belonging to the BJP, described it as "divisive" and "retrograde." Some even described the introduction of the Bill as a ploy by the Congress to win Muslim votes. In the Lok Sabha, L. K. Advani spearheaded the BJP's opposition to the Bill. In a long speech on May 11, 1992, he argued that the Bill would create separateness and division in the country. He even went further and suggested that it was against the spirit of the Constitution as conceived by its founding fathers. To Advani, even enacting a commission for the minorities would be an unjustified concession to them. The lack of precise definition of "minority" also came in for a lot of criticism from the opponents of the Bill. Advani feared that the power given to the Central government by the Bill to decide who is a minority could be used for partisan ends. He also argued that, contrary to the objectives of the Bill, the Muslims would be the prime beneficiaries of the Commission. This fitted quite well with the "appeasement of Muslim thesis" propagated by the Hindutva forces in general and Advani's BJP party in particular. It was also pointed out that a National Integration-cum-Human Rights Commission could act as a proper watchdog for minority rights. The terms of the debate, as far as opponents of the Bill were concerned, were not something new. In fact, suspicion of the Hindu right toward any special provision for minorities had a long history. However, in a new context the old argument took on a new meaning. The position of the Congress and others, from the point of view of the Hindu right, appeared as an abandonment of the principle of neutrality of the state toward different religious groups in the country.

For the defenders of the Bill, the forces of majoritarianism could only be countered by instituting proper safeguards. Attempts were also made on the floor of the House to ground the proposed National Commission on a shared but minimal understanding of rights of minorities at all levels of society. The argument is that once a minority is defined in relation to the jurisdiction of a particular law, one group may be a majority within the sphere of a state but can very well be a minority within a district within that particular state. Similarly, a religious group may be in a majority if one takes the national level into account but a minority within the context of a province or other such levels. The minority problem, as P. M. Sayeed said in the House, "is not therefore just a Muslim problem. It is a political problem and a national problem."[13] By keeping this in view, some even argued for creating parity between the National Minorities Commission and the National Commission for Scheduled Castes and Tribes.[14]

The National Commission for Minorities Bill was finally passed on May 17, 1992 and came into effect a year later. The new Commission, while discharging its duty of protecting minority rights, was empowered to exercise the power of a civil court trying a suit. The point of discussing the debate is to demonstrate the contestatory terrain of minority rights in India. Any special provision for the religious minorities immediately becomes a matter of contention. Those who oppose it accuse the supporters of political manipulation as well as appeasement of minorities. A minimal consensus on this has yet to be achieved by the contending political parties in India. This is one of the reasons why the theme of minority rights, in terms of providing special provisions, creates so much controversy both in legislatures as well as in civil society. One can also argue that the lack of a minimal consensus tends to undermine the efficacy of the institutions meant to protect the rights of minorities in the country.

The functioning of the National Commission for Minorities is a case in point. There is no doubt that during the period 1978 to 1992 the Minorities Commission received a large number of complaints concerning the discrimination of minorities from different parts of the country. During the first two years of its existence, it received 441 complaints both from individuals and organizations.[15] In the year 1989–1990, the Commission received 381 representations, of which 243 came from individuals belonging to minority communities and 138 from several minority organizations.[16] Right from its inception in 1992, one of the important functions of the National Minorities Commission has been to act as a storehouse of grievances pertaining to the minorities in the country. After checking the nature of grievances, the Commission usually took up the case and advised the concerned authorities for its redressal. From time to time, the Commission sent its committee to look into the incidents of communal violence and gave recommendations to the concerned government as to how to combat such incidents in the future.

There are three areas in which the advisory role of the Commission was clearly evident. The first area dealt with the security concern of the minorities in different parts of the country. The second theme on which it spent a lot of its institutional energy was the incidents of discrimination (related to both individuals and groups) faced by the minorities. Many times minority communities drew the Commission's attention to the government interference with their educational institutions. The third area in which the Commission took a lot of interest was the economic and educational backwardness of the minority groups in the country. It generated and compiled data on the theme, produced reports, and from time to time made the state and central governments aware of their duties toward the welfare of the minorities. It is possible to argue that the National Commission has succeeded in raising the problems of the minorities and aggregating them for the purpose of policy making. At this point it is worth remembering that aggregating the problems of minorities is one thing while persuading the state to devise and implement the solutions is quite another. In the latter respect, the role of the Commission has been quite limited. Since 1992, not a single annual report submitted by the Commission to the central government has been discussed in the Parliament. Often the concerned authorities did not take the Commission's recommendations seriously. According to one of its former chairpersons, even his letters of recommendations to the central as well as state governments were often not even acknowledged (Mahmood 2001). From the vantage point of efficacy, it is obvious that the National Minorities Commission has not done that well. As an institution it has not taken roots. However, from the minority rights point of view, it is clear that through its practices, the Commission has helped vitalize a discourse that tries to blend the security concerns of the minorities with that of their dignity, and that links their economic well-being with their collective identity. It has also highlighted the point that the protection of minority rights needs a responsive democratic state and can act as a genuine ground for the enjoyment of equal citizenship.

Conclusion

Any discussion on the relationship between democratic citizenship and minority rights cannot ignore the problematic link between "majority" and "minority" in a society. According to some scholars, the best way to defend the ideals of democratic citizenship is to take it outside the limiting domain of "majority" and "minority." They point out that allowing minorities to have specific rights not only isolates them from the rest of society, it also valorizes their particularistic identities over the citizenship identity. In recent times in India, the argument for the priority of the citizenship identity over the particularistic identities of the minority groups has taken on two dominant forms. In the hands of the Hindu right, the priority argument is essentially "nationalistic." Too much emphasis on minority rights, they argue, has created tension between the majority and minority communities and has placed obstacles on the path of creating a homogenized national identity in India. The other argument is made from the vantage point of liberalism. Recognition of separate identities of the minority groups, in this view, can only be supported to the extent they are compatible with the principles of citizenship. The presence of particularistic identities with a sense of strong boundary, according to this argument, inevitably undermines the citizenship ethos in a society (Gupta 1999).

The argument of the Hindu right for equal citizenship defined in terms of uniform treatment of religious or cultural groups (including the minorities) is itself part of a larger majoritarian discourse. The presence of intense inequalities among the groups makes this commitment to the principle of equality facile and vacuous. However, the point raised from the vantage point of liberal and universal citizenship is serious; namely that differentiated citizenship rights for the minority groups do not necessarily compromise the norms of universal citizenship. As a matter of fact, in specific situations these rights contribute toward a better realization of these norms.

It is also argued that minority rights encourage people to stick to their exclusivist identities. Following this logic one can say that "minority" and "majority" identities are nothing but exclusive identities that are not conducive to creating a democratic society. Who belongs to the majority and who to the minority, even within the context of a territorial state, is not always clear. In the case of India, the status of a group varies as it moves from one level to the other. Yet it is politically futile to abandon these categories altogether. There are scholars who suggest that to view a society in terms of majority and minority is to view it as being composed of bounded, culturally or linguistically or racially unified communities. Over the years, anti-essentialism has become central to many works on identity politics and on multiculturalism. Against the idea that identities have fixed essence, these works have shown that identities are primarily differentiated, hybrid and multilayered. Broadly speaking, anti-essentialism as a methodological strategy has made it possible to interrogate the claims of the leaders who present their community as a homogeneous entity. It has also helped unmask the ways in which identity politics tends to paper over contradictions inherent within a community such as class, caste and so on. No doubt these are clear-cut advantages. But the question is how far can we push the logic of anti-essentialism? If a minority community has no coherent ontological dimension, does it mean that the community simply does not exist? Let us take a concrete example. Against the people who argue that the Muslim community has a fixed and undifferentiated essence, scholars have pointed out that it is divided within in terms of class, caste, and other affiliations. In the same way the claims of the Hindu right that the Hindus form a homogeneous entity is found to be erroneous. From this can we conclude that the idea of a Muslim community is simply a fiction? If community as an entity cannot exist, then how do the categories of majority and minority make sense? Are they fictitious also?

This chapter is informed by the basic conviction that it is possible to talk of communities and collective identities without being essentialistic. One should not adopt an extreme anti-essentialism that makes collective identity and agency impossible. It is not surprising then that several marginalized groups today find such radical anti-essentialism as politically disempowering or debilitating. Some of them, feminists for instance, even take recourse to "strategic essentialism" as a way out. It is possible to speak of minority or majority community without suggesting that it is either undifferentiated or completely hybrid.

If one were to look at past events, it is quite evident that majority–minority relations in India have not always been conceived within the "rights discourse." Gandhi's discourse on inter-community relations, even in the tragic days of Partition, was based on fellowship and mutual identification. Talk of rights was never admitted into it for, according to him, that was simply centered on claims and counter-claims. The language of "fellowship," "*bhaichara*" (brotherhood), survives even today. The utility of this language need not be jettisoned. However, since independence, inter-community relations and minority rights have been and still are framed within rights discourse. It is presupposed within a constitutional democratic order where minority communities enjoy certain rights that are not dependent on the majority community's goodwill or fellowship. In principle, a democratic state, along with its institutions, is portrayed as the protector of minority rights. The protection of minority rights in India, as this chapter argues, needs not only a responsive state but also a vigilant civil society.

No doubt the Indian Constitution contains several provisions that are meant to protect the distinct cultural or linguistic or religious identity of the minority communities. It also provides for the functioning and sustenance of institutions created by them. The desire of the makers of the Constitution to create a secular state was also essentially a response to India's pluralist social order. However, in spite of all this, five decades after the Constitutional Republic was inaugurated, the minorities in India have expressed their feeling of alienation. Even the track record of the Indian state's responsibility for protecting the lives of the minorities is, to put it mildly, not satisfactory. The increasing amount of communal violence in the last decades in India in which the minority groups suffer the most cannot be explained away in terms of the rise of general violence in the country. It is not surprising that the security-concern has remained and continues to be at the top of the agenda of the religious minorities in India. Can this be explained in terms of the gaps that exist between constitutional theory and its practice? Some try to explain the issue by showing the growing decline of certain foundational values, including secularism, in the Indian polity. For others, if secularism, on which rests the notion of "minority rights," has become a highly contested doctrine, then one should look for another foundation. The principle of "substantive equality," as some scholars suggest, can be one such alternative foundation. We do not have to be a deconstructionist or a postmodernist to believe that in politics no foundation, even a desirable principle like substantive equality, can ever be fully secure. Nor can it provide the ultimate resting place for "minority rights." For instance, special provisions for minorities can be justified on the ground that it addresses the problems of inequality in society. For some it amounts to mere appeasement of minorities and thus violates the principle of equality. No doubt both positions are based on two different conceptions of equality. Can these contending views be reconciled? In fact, some argue that the crisis of Indian secularism lies not in the doctrine itself but in its non-negotiated character. Can one say the same thing with regard to minority rights?

During the days of the Constituent Assembly debates, the issue of minority rights for religious minorities was subjected to much debate and controversy. By the end of the debate, except for granting political safe-guards to the religious minorities, other rights meant to protect their identity and prevent discrimination against them were put in place. However, the discussion on religious minorities was filled with anxieties. This was not entirely caused by the Partition. This, to a large extent, was prompted by an excessive preoccupation of the leaders with the idea of "nation-building." There was an underlying fear that too much recognition of the religious minorities would disrupt the project of Indian nationhood. Even the well-meaning liberals belonging to the Congress shared this view. Many who believed in the liberal utopia and the rationality of modernity believed that the project of development would eventually blunt the rough edges of iden-tity politics in India. This did not happen, and the power of majoritarianism kept the idea of an exclusive nation alive. Unless the ideology of majoritari-anism in its different forms is tackled squarely, the regime of minority rights in India will remain painfully fragile. To the extent that special provision for minorities is viewed as "appeasement," it would undermine the basis of minority rights. A minimal consensus among different political parties on this is an absolute necessity.

Contemporary discourse on minority rights and its relationship with democratic citizenship contains two important issues. The first issue is articulated in the demands for physical security and nondiscrimination. The second highlights the economic status of the minority groups in the country. The economic and educational backwardness of the minorities remains important. Whether it is the plight of the dalit-Christians or of the plebian Muslims, the issue of deprivation is at the forefront. Honor and dignity, an overarching theme in recent decades, is often seen in connection with these two issues. I have argued that the identity question and concerns for economic prosperity, though analytically separable, continue to overlap within the minority rights discourse.

A significant focus of minority rights discourse in India has been, and continues to be, on the nature of the state and related institutions. The allegation of "discrimination" and a sense of alienation among minorities can be seen with reference to the functioning of the state. Underlying the demands put forward by minority groups, for example recruiting more of their numbers into the police force, preventing discrimination in different sectors of the economy, making public institutions impartial, is the belief that better protection of minority rights is possible only when the state and other institutions behave impartially and democratically. Any discussion on minority rights today inevitably confronts us with several related and broader issues. First, it is important to realize that reimagining the principles of political association can be a step toward resolving the majority–minority conundrum in India. The democratic perspective on minority rights suggests that demands for rights can never be arrested arbitrarily; it goes all the way down and sideways and so on. Hence there is a need to protect the individual and others' rights within a minority community. Second, without the establishment of adequate institutions, protection of minority rights can never be strengthened. Without the effective functioning of institutions, minority rights can never be fully realized in India. The idea of democratic citizenship is persuading the communities to base their political demands not solely on reasons internal to their communities but on the reasons that can be accessible to a larger body of citizens. Similarly, the minority rights perspective is making the state and public institutions see the point that a non-negotiated transcendent political position in a society can mask a great deal of inequalities and discrimination. In an uneven sort of way, the dialogue still continues. This, we hope, will play a considerable role in the ongoing process of democratization in India.

Notes

1 The judgment of the Supreme Court in the case *Jagat Singh* vs. *Pratap Singh*, quoted in Wadhwa (1975: 98).
2 The case of Kerala Education Bill 1957, quoted in Massey (1999: 42).

3 The judgment of Justice M. Hidayatullah in *State of Kerala* vs. *Rev. Mother Provincial*, quoted in Massey (1999: 45). Also see the judgment in *D. A. V. College* vs. *State of Punjab*, quoted in Mahajan (1998: 99).
4 Letter from J. Nehru to the Nawab of Bhopal, quoted in Hasan (1997: 135–136).
5 The statement of Jamaat-I-Islami, quoted in Hasan (1988: 2474).
6 From M. K. Siddiqui (ed.) *Muslim in Free India*, quoted in Razzack and Gumber (2000: 13).
7 *The Gopal Singh Panel Report on Minorities*, 1983, Chapter IV.
8 *The Gopal Singh Panel Report on Minorities*: 48.
9 Regarding the issues confronted by the Christian groups in India, see Massey (1999: Chapter 3).
10 Government of India Resolution, Home Ministry Notification, No. II-160/2/2/77-NID, January 12, 1978, quoted in Mahmood (2001: 25), emphasis added.
11 *Lok Sabha Debates*, February 22, 1978, March 28, 1978, April 5 and 11, 1978, May 10, 1978, July 26, 1978 and August 2, 1978.
12 *Lok Sabha Debate*, May 11, 1992: 91.
13 *Lok Sabha Debate*, May 11, 1992: 200.
14 *Lok Sabha Debate*, May 11, 1992: 201–202.
15 The division of the complaints was as follows: Muslims – 294, Christians–48, Sikhs–23, Buddhists–15, Parsis–3, Linguistic Minorities–58. *Third Annual Report of the Minorities Commission* (for the year ending December 31, 1980), Annexure X.
16 *Twelfth Annual Report of The Minorities Commission*, 1–4–1989 to 31–3–1990, Chapter VII: 90.

References

Alam, J. (1993) "The Majlis-e-Ittehad-ul-Muslimeen and the Muslims of Hyderabad," in G. Pandey (ed.), *Hindus and Others: The Question of Identity in India Today*, Delhi: Viking.
—— (2000) "A Minority Moves into Another Millennium," in R. Thapar (ed.), *India's Another Millennium*, Delhi: Viking.
Anderson, B. (1983) *Imagined Communities: Reflections on the Origins and Spread of Nationalism*, London: Verso, 1991.
Annual Reports of the Minorities Commission, 1978–1991.
Beaglehole, J. H. (1967) "The Indian Christians – A Study of a Minority," *Modern Asian Studies*, 1, 1.
Bhargava, R. (ed.) (1998) *Secularism and its Critics*, Delhi: Oxford University Press.
—— (2000) "Democratic Vision of a New Republic: India, 1950," in F. R. Frankel, Z. Hasan, R. Bhargava and B. Arora (eds.), *Transforming India. Social and Political Dynamics of Democracy*, Delhi: Oxford.
Bilgrami, A. (1998) "Secularism, Nationalism, and Modernity," in R. Bhargava (ed.), *Secularism and its Critics*, Delhi: Oxford University Press.
The Constitution of India (as modified up to January 1, 1995), Delhi: Lok Sabha Secretariat.
Galanter, M. (1998) "Hinduism, Secularism, and the Indian Judiciary," in R. Bhargava (ed.), *Secularism and its Critics*, Delhi: Oxford University Press.
Gopal Singh Committee (1983) *The Gopal Singh Panel Report on Minorities*, June 14.
Gupta, D. (1999) Survivors or Survivals: Reconciling Citizenship and Cultural Particularism, *Economic and Political Weekly*, August 14.

Hasan, M. (1988) "In Search of Integration and Identity: Indian Muslims Since Independence," *Economic and Political Weekly*, Special Issue.

—— (1997) *Legacy of a Divided Nation: India's Muslims since Independence*, Delhi: Oxford University Press.

Ilaih, K. (1998) "Towards the Dalitization of the Nation," in P. Chatterjee (ed.), *Wages of Freedom: Fifty Years of the Indian Nation-State*, Delhi: Oxford University Press.

Jayal, N. G. (1999) *Democracy and the State: Welfare, Secularism and Development in Contemporary India*, Delhi: Oxford University Press.

Kabir, H. (1968) *Minorities in a Democracy*, Calcutta: Firma K. L. Mukhopadhyay.

Khalidi, O. (1993) "Muslims in the Indian Political Process: Group Goals and Alternative Strategies," *Economic and Political Weekly*, January 2–9.

Kymlicka, W. (1989) *Liberalism, Community and Culture*, Oxford: Oxford University Press.

—— (1995) *Multicultural Citizenship: A Liberal Theory of Minority Rights*, Oxford: Clarendon Press.

Lok Sabha Debates (relevant years).

Madan, T. N. (1998) "Secularism in its Place", in R. Bhargava (ed.), *Secularism and its Critics*, Delhi: Oxford University Press.

Mahajan, G. (1998) *Identities and Rights: Aspects of Liberal Democracy in India*, Delhi: Oxford University Press.

Mahmood, T. (2001) *Minorities Commission: Minor Role in Major Affairs*, Delhi: Pharos Media & Publishing (P) Ltd.

Massey, J. (1999) *Minorities in a Democracy: The Indian Experience*, Delhi: Manohar.

Menon, N. (1998) "Women and Citizenship," in P. Chatterjee (ed.), *Wages of Freedom: Fifty Years of the Indian Nation-State*, Delhi: Oxford University Press.

Nandy, A. (1998) "The Politics of Secularism and the Recovery of Religious Tolerance," in R. Bhargava (ed.), *Secularism and its Critics*, Delhi: Oxford University Press.

Nigam, A. (2000) "Secularism, Modernity, Nation: Epistemology of the Dalit Critique," *Economic and Political Weekly*, November 25–December 1.

Parekh, B. (1999) "Balancing Unity and Diversity in Multicultural Societies, " in D. Avon and A. de-Shalit (eds.), London: Routledge.

Rawls, J. (1993) *Political Liberalism*, New York: Columbia University Press.

Raz, J. (1994) *Ethics in the Public Domain*, Oxford: Clarendon Press.

Razzack, A. and Gumber, A. (2000) "Differentials in Human Development: A Case for the Empowerment of Muslims in India," in M. K. Siddiqui (ed.), *Muslims in Free India*, Delhi: National Council of Applied Economic Research Publication.

Seminar, No. 471, November 1998, Special Issue on Dalit.

Shariff, A. (1999)*India Human Development Report*, Delhi: Oxford University Press.

Smith, D. E. (1963) *India as a Secular State*, Princeton: Princeton University Press.

Tamir, Y. (1993) *Liberal Nationalism*, Princeton: Princeton University Press.

Taylor, C. (1991) "Shared and Divergent Values," in R. L. Watts and D. M. Brown (eds.), *Options for a New Canada*, Toronto: Toronto University Press.

—— (1994) "The Politics of Recognition," in D. T. Goldberg (ed.), *Multiculturalism: A Critical Reader*, Oxford: Blackwell.

Wadhwa, K. K. (1975) *Minority Safeguards in India*, Delhi: Thompson Press (India) Ltd.

Wright, T. Jr. (1997) "A New Demand for Muslim Reservations in India," *Asian Survey*, xxxvii, 9.

11 Globalization and democratic developments in Southeast Asia

Articulation and social responses

Shamsul A. B.

In this chapter I wish to take a look at the big picture as well as the little portraits, or to put it another way, at "the abstract" and "the empirical," of not only "globalization" but also of "development." Viewed from a historical perspective, these are indeed two closely intertwined phenomena. "Development" here refers to the modernization project that came with decolonization soon after the Second World War and that continued with increasing speed during the cold war. Recent discourse on globalization seems to be too contemporary and/or ahistorical as it ignores the fact that many countries around the world, especially in Southeast Asia, are still in the embrace, or throes, of the "modernization-development" project. Indeed "development" and "globalization" co-exist, and each has had different effects in different sectors of the society (Roberts and Hite 2000). For example, in Malaysia we still have, on the one hand, hunters-and-gatherers living off the endangered tropical forest and, on the other hand, "head-hunters" of the corporate kind surviving in the postmodern polluted concrete jungle of Kuala Lumpur. Some sectors of this astonishing variety of societal forms in Malaysia have now been impacted by globalization while others are still struggling to become modern.

I mention also that democracy did not come to Asia, or Southeast Asia, with globalization. Ideas related to or about democracy have been in Asia since the arrival of modernity on its shores along with European colonialism. Indeed, the whole process of nation-formation that began to take shape during the colonial period has sown the seeds of democracy in various forms, including through nationalist movements (Haynes 1997). The arrival of the modernization-development project and, subsequently, globalization changed the form of democracy and the internal configuration of its various components, ritual and practices, but not really its essence (Featherstone 1991; Preston 1997). Therefore, the task of examining "globalization and democratic developments in Asia" before us is an exercise which is both historical and contemporary in nature, as well as abstract and empirical.

I shall begin this endeavor with a survey of the evolution from "development project" to "postdevelopmentalism" to "globalization project" that has taken place in Southeast Asia, and in some sense in the rest of the world also, at least in the last five decades. The second part of the chapter examines the articulation of democratic developments, both during the development project and the globalization project periods, through the people's social responses to both projects, mainly through the formation of new social movements around major social concerns such as "environmentalism" and "fundamentalism."

I shall try to draw as many examples as possible from the experiences of the different Southeast Asian countries and communities within them. However, the examples that I know best are those from Malaysia. I should mention also that most of the social concerns I wish to raise and discuss are not only relevant or affect only the people of Southeast Asia—they affect everyone around the world.

From "development" to "postdevelopmentalism" to "globalization": the abstract and the empirical

Western secular and religious crusades in the forms of administration, education, and missionary efforts accompanied colonial rule to stimulate progress along the European path in the colonized world, for example in Southeast Asia. The problem of course was that the ruling Europeans were unable to see the dynamics of the non-European cultures (Davies 1996). Another problem was that Europeans ignored the paradox of bringing progress to those colonized peoples whose sovereignty they systematically denied—a paradox experienced daily by non-Europeans—and best exemplified in the form of "elections without democracy" or "electocracy" before "democracy" (Shamsul 2000).

This paradox generated anti-colonial movements seeking to wrest independence from Western occupiers. But independence would occur in a changed world, a postcolonial world. In that world, non-European cultures had either been destroyed or irrevocably changed through the colonial impact and its particular form of "colonial knowledge," which had totally deconstructed indigenous knowledge systems (Cohn 1996). Newly independent states emerged within a framework defined by the European conception of development. The adoption of the European model across the formerly colonial world was the underpinning of the post-Second World War development project. The founding assumptions and practices of the development project represented "historical choices" rather than an inevitable unfolding of human destiny. It was an strategy organized to overcome the legacies of colonialism (Preston 1994).

Global economic integration played a substantial role in the development project. From the beginning, when the Bretton Woods system was formed, the postwar world order rested on two pillars. One was the nation-state, the arena in which development was to be pursued, and the other was the international institutional structure, including the Bretton Woods agencies (the

World Bank and the IMF), and the development establishment, such as the Ford and Rockefeller Foundations, the USAID, and the traditional agricultural institutions, such as the IRRI. These institutions shared common assumptions and procedures with regard to development (Flemming 1961; Block 1977; Wood 1986).

The development project had offered a "universal" blueprint for national economic development. Technologies and infrastructure programs were universal hardware. Modernization was a universal ideal. The nation-state was to be the vehicle of these shared goals in the postwar era. It was the logical political unit with which to mobilize populations around the ideal of modernization—not only because national independence and material advancement were high on the agenda, but also because states themselves constituted power centers that were able to coordinate such mobilization. Membership in a system of states, in which sovereignty concerns were paramount, oriented states toward multilateral and bilateral programs of assistance. In this way, national and international development initiatives were intertwined (Shamsul 1999a).

The debt crisis of the 1980s shifted the terms of development from a national to a global concern. States still pursue development goals, but these goals are less and less managed nationally. Certainly, some specific assistance projects are cast in terms of national developmentalism, often at the subnational level, but the infrastructure of economic development largely has been shifted to the level and goals of the globalization project.

The globalization project combines several strands: (1) an emerging consensus among policy makers favoring market-based rather than state-managed development strategies; (2) centralized management of global market rules by the G7 states; (3) implementation of these rules by the multilateral agencies, such as the World Bank, the IMF and the WTO; (4) concentration of market power in the hands of transnational corporations and financial power in the hands of transnational banks; (5) subordination of former second and third world states to these global institutional forces; and (6) the subordination of first world states, or parts of the societies, to the same global institutional forces (Sklair 1989; Mittleman 1998, 1999).

The goals of the project involve the development of a world market in which states expect to share benefits. The development project has shed its national characteristics and is now undergoing reformulation as the globalization project, conducted within the framework of global managerialism that has its roots in the Bretton Woods system and cold war organization. This framework has coordinated the process for managing national economies.

But the global managers emerging on the scene in the 1980s made explicit claims about managing global economy, and they included the development establishment in the Bretton Woods institutions, individual state governments reformed by the monetarists and debt-rescheduling, transnational corporate and political élites across the world (Chomsky 1994). However, despite the fact that the process of global economic management has begun, our frame of reference still lags behind. For instance, our present systems of economic accounting are nationally framed, that is, production, finance, and trade statistics are collected, recorded, and represented as national data. Such a contradiction is only one of the many signs of postdevelopmentalism, especially, in the once third world countries.

Postdevelopmentalism here refers to the demise of the project in which states pursued nationally managed economic growth. In this project, development dovetailed with nation-building in the postcolonial world. It had a definite political arena: the national territory. This initiative is now disintegrating. Key indicators are the current fragmentation of some nation-states into ethno-regional segments and the universal dismantling of public support for populations, especially the underprivileged sectors. These signs suggest that a new project is under way. It no longer simply addresses the postcolonial world. It is universal, and it concerns the attempt to build a global economy under global management. All states are involved, even those of the second world, now that the Soviet bloc has unraveled and China, Vietnam, North Korea and Cuba are entering the world market (Mittleman 1998).

Inevitably, as a result of these developments, states are exploring new ways of governing. Decentralization and centralization, as political processes, are occurring simultaneously in the developed, developing and underdeveloped countries. For instance, the formation of macro-regional groupings, such as APEC, in which member states agree to establish certain economic rules about trade and investment, is an example of the process of centralization power among states. Everywhere, states are renegotiating their reach, often along bureaucratic lines beyond the control of their citizenry (Preston 1997). It could be argued that, at present, there is no single state spared the effects of the postdevelopmentalism phase, in which elements of both the "development project" and "globalization project" co-exist. Why, one may ask, is that the case?

The development project was an ideal that some see as an illusion because the world economy has always rested on an exploited base—the periphery— while others say it has been a success because it was never intended to be absolute. Whatever the case, it is clear that the development project was a project wherein states attempted to manage national economic integration, but the integration was often incomplete. This was because the process of development often spread benefits unequally. It was also because segments of the domestic economy were either absorbed into, or marginalized by, the growing global reach of the new commodity chains. In either case, states often exploited weaker communities in their hinterlands, justifying this action in the name of national development. Global financiers and firms funded this activity. In short, large social segments of the third world remained on the margins or experienced dislocation as the development project took hold (Sklair 1995).

The advent of the globalization project does not much change the position of the marginalized because they are still trapped in the development project paradigm and its activities, while those in the mainstream have begun to enjoy the fruits of the globalization project, or for some to suffer from it. The situation is best described as such: if there existed a national integration trend under the development project, there appears to be a disintegrating trend at the national level under the globalization project, because of an integrating trend at the global level. However, this is not necessarily an homogeneous integration. It may be true that more people around the world now consume standardized products. It is also true that the people who produce these products do so under quite diverse, some indeed under adverse, labor conditions. In other words, any integrating trends in the composition of labor, during current forms of national capitalism, are reversing as economic globalization deepens. It would be fair to conclude that the world markets standardize consumption but differentiate production and disorganize producing communities.

Indeed, the globalization project is also a utopia, like its predecessor, the development project. Further social and national disintegration will occur under globalization as a result of two major trends. First, neither nation-states nor world community is composed only of market-oriented individuals: there are class, gender, and ethnic relations that divide people. There is an historical context in which some regions are more equal than others. And there are powerful institutional forces that actually organize and reorganize markets, with profits rather than social welfare in mind.

Second, there are social movements in the world, of various ideological persuasions, and state organizations that actively resist and/or accept the globalization project. Many of these movements reject the belief in the self-regulating global market as the most logical principle of social organization. Some movements aim to protect their communities by re-regulating the market; others see withdrawing from the market as the most satisfactory form of resistance.

Whatever the alternatives, the globalization project is only one way, albeit the most powerful we have seen, of reorganizing the world. It is so in part because it has not had to confront its contradictory effects in any fundamental way, except in the recent Asian Financial Crisis due to the fragility of the world monetary system. It is indeed an attempt to fashion the world around a central principle through powerful political and financial institutions. Because the principle is framed in the liberal discourse of rights and freedom, its power ultimately depends on consent.

Most governments around the world do feel the pressure to observe and abide by the new global rules. But their citizens may think otherwise. And where globalization weakens the nation-states, citizens have fresh opportunities to renew the political process. It is useful therefore to survey some of the social responses of these citizens groups, exploring their origins and goals and highlighting the range of opposition, particularly in Southeast Asia.

Examining each movement offers a particular perspective and angle on the dilemmas associated with both the development project and the emerging globalization project. It is through these social responses that we can observe the development of democratic trends at the local levels. Interestingly, though the various "democratic-oriented" opposition movements have emerged in different ways and places and at different overlapping times, there is a sense in which they converge, thus expressing a common condition around the world (Whitehead 1997). For instance, there seems to be an increased tension between the global–universal and the local–particular as the globalization project slowly swallows the development project.

Of the many social movements that have emerged, I wish to examine two major kinds that seem to have been informed by some versions of democratic-oriented trends or activities: namely, environmentalism and fundamentalism. I chose these in particular because each occupies its own unique space in the making of social life in the Southeast Asian region, and elsewhere too. Environmentalism highlights the critical symbiotic relationship between the people and their physical surroundings, the destruction of one resulting almost automatically in the destruction of the other. Fundamentalism focuses on the relationship between the present and the past, of tradition-making, of norm-creation and value-orientation, within and between societies in the region and beyond.

Democratic developments: "new" social movements and responses

NGO is a term widely known and accepted today, almost naturalized into our everyday lives, especially known to the poor and the disadvantaged. To the powers that be it has often been perceived as a negative term, but this is not necessarily the case for the general public. To the latter it is synonymous with social struggle of sorts, irrespective of the concern, cause or issue. To the former it has been associated with opposition of all kinds, including political party opposition. In other words, the NGOs, particularly from the 1970s onward, have become the all-important conduit through which social responses have, to a large extent, been successfully integrated in reaction to both of the grand projects, development and globalization. It usually adopts a populist approach spiced with democratic orientations, at least in its pronouncement.

NGOs could be considered "new" forms of social movements. If the "old" ones were established and legitimized by institutional structures of the state with the primary aim of supporting well-organized state-sponsored activities of various kinds, the "new" social movements often emerged to articulate differences, plurality and dissent. It could be perceived as a nation-wide or worldwide, a movement engaging in the politics of resistance, struggling for social justice, freedom of speech and democracy, articulated through all sorts of issues and causes. In other words, new social movements can be seen as an attempt to transform "civil society" into "democratic civility" (Marcussen 1996).

The so-called new social movements, such as the green, feminism and grass-roots politics, share criticism of the development project. Where the development project advocated state economic management, the new movements tend to reject centralism and stress community empowerment instead. Where the development project emphasized industrialism and material abundance, the new movements tend to seek post- or pre-industrial values of decentralization, flexibility, and simplicity. And where the development project championed state and the market institutions, the new movements seek grass-roots autonomy and the reassertion of cultural values over those of the market.

In short, the new social movements are distinguished, for want of a better term, by their "expressive politics," and their challenge to economism and instrumental politics of the "developed society" model. They have grown up in states where institutions that cater, for example, for the welfare of the proletariat or the disadvantaged, have receded. Hence they have contributed, directly or indirectly, to the declining legitimacy of the development project and to the continuous "interrogation" of the general appropriateness and social relevance of the globalization project (Eldridge 1996). Let us now examine some empirical examples articulated through concerns such as environmentalism and fundamentalism.

Environmentalism

Globally, environmentalism as a social movement involves questioning modern assumptions that nature and its bounty are infinite. It has two main strands; the first emerged in the West, the second in the third world.

The first grew from the awareness, inspired partly by Carson's *Silent Spring* (1994 [orig. 1962]), that documented the disruption of the earth's ecosystem that was being caused by modern economic practices such as the use of agricultural chemicals. More importantly, the book emphasized the shortcomings of Western rationalism's perception of nature as "external" to society that led to the belief that nature is an infinitely exploitable domain. The "green" movements in the West mushroomed as the simple truths revealed by Carson gained an audience. The battle was to fight a rather middle-class cause, that is, to maintain a "natural aesthetic" to complement the consumer lifestyle through the preservation of human health, on the one hand, and through enhancing leisure activities, on the other hand. It was indeed Eurocentric middle class, which can be exemplified by the fact that the tragic ecological disaster inflicted by the Americans upon the social life of millions of peoples in Indo-China during the Vietnam war was never part of the "green" discourse in the West (Lewallen 1971), while, ironically, the destruction of Vietnam's tropical forest in post-Vietnam war was (Lang 1996).

The second strand of environmentalism appears in active movements to protect particular ecological regions from environmentally damaging practices, especially in the third world. In the third world human communities depend greatly on the viability of regional ecologies for their livelihood. Such movements are therefore often distinguished by their attempts to protect existing cultural practices. In contrast to the "middle-class" oriented first world environmentalism, which attempts to regulate the environmental implications of the market economy, in third world regions environmentalism questions the benefits of unregulated market forces. This is especially true where states and firms seek to "monetize" and harvest natural resources on which human communities depend (Guha 1989).

In the past decade, however, a more dynamic approach to environmentalism has appeared, one that sees a serious threat to essential natural elements such as atmosphere, climates, and biodiversity. Trees may be renewable through replanting schemes, but the atmospheric conditions that nurture them may not be so easily replenished. There is also concern about the survival of the human species as pollution and environmental degradation has led to public health epidemics, such as the emergence of new strains of cancer, lead poisoning, immune suppression by ultraviolet radiation and so on (Abramovitz 1991).

What is also interesting is the fact that there has been various grass-roots movements focusing attention on the growing conflict on the margins between local cultures and the global market. The pressure on natural resources for the rural poor has also intensified. This pressure stems from the long-term impoverishment of rural populations forced to overwork their land and their fuel resources in order to eke out subsistence. As land and forest were increasingly devoted to export production in the 1980s, millions of rural poor were pushed into occupying marginal tropical forest ecosystem, resulting in environmental degradation (Broad with Cavanagh 1993; Cooke 1999).

The various developments mentioned above have awakened peoples and communities, both within and outside the governments around the world, to take steps to try and find solutions to resolve the ever-increasing environmental problems. The actions and reactions could be broadly divided into two: one is the authority-defined type; the other the everyday-defined one. The former is one that is authoritatively defined by people who are part of the dominant power structure. The latter is that experienced by people in the course of their everyday life.

The authority-defined approach to solving environmental problems has largely been informed by the 1987 Brundtland Report, entitled *Our Common Future*. The concept of "sustainable development" gained currency as a result of the report, and is defined as meeting the need of the present without compromising the ability of future generations to meet their needs. How to achieve this remains a gigantic puzzle. The 1992 UNCED organized a conference to review the progress of the Brundtland Report at Rio de

Janeiro, popularly referred to as the "Earth Summit," that produced a document called *Agenda 21*, that details a global program for the twenty-first century.

On the whole, the program, instead of linking environmental concerns to issues of social justice and resource distribution, has converged on four priorities: (1) reducing greenhouse emissions, primarily from cars and burning forests; (2) protecting biodiversity, mainly in tropical forests; (3) reducing pollution in international waters; and (4) curbing ozone-layer depletion. The World Bank through its Global Environment Facility (GEF) channeled monies into global environmental projects, especially in the four areas mentioned above. In the end the management of the world's environment would be in the hands of a group of technical and bureaucratic élite accountable to no one.

The governments of Malaysia, Indonesia and Thailand have been actively involved in promoting ideas from *Agenda 21*, most of which have been integrated into their respective development plans. Whatever they promulgate as policies, in the end they seemed to have successfully served only commercial interest. Very rarely indeed do these programs benefit or fulfill the social needs of the communities affected by the various types of environmental problems found in the countries mentioned (Cooke 1999).

The everyday-defined approach is best exemplified by environmental resistance movements. Let us take an example from Indonesia and Malaysia. The Forestry Department in Indonesia controls 74 per cent of the national territory, and it claims (in 1990) that the forest belongs to the state and not to the people and that therefore the people has no right to receive compensation when their habitats fall to logging concessions (Peluso 1992). Similarly, when the Malaysian government decided to embark upon a gigantic project to construct the Bakun dam, costing about US$4 billion, which would flood about 700 hectares of tropical forests and displace about 5,000 native people in the area, the people received little compensation because the land they had been living off for generations was legally defined as state land (Cooke 1999: 82–83).

As a result of such situations, grass-roots environment movements have proliferated. They come in two forms: first, active resistance, which seeks to curb invasion of habitats by states and markets; and, second, adaptation to environmental depredation, which exemplifies the centuries-old practice of renewing habitats in the face of environmental deterioration. The Penan Association of Sarawak is the Malaysian version of the active resistance environmental movements and Sahabat Alam Malaysia (SAM) represents the adaptive type. There is the Buddhist group in Thailand that promotes eucalyptus plantations to save large numbers of forest dwellers in Northeast Thailand from being displaced. On the island of Mindanao, indigenous communities have reclaimed state and pastoral lands for subsistence farming, organizing themselves democratically along the Chipko movement's approach found in the Central Himalayan region of India.

The challenge for grass-roots environmental movements in the third world is twofold: first, to create alternatives to the global MNC-initiated capital and energy-intensive forms of specialized agriculture and agro-forestry that are appropriate to the goal of restoring and sustaining local ecologies; and, second, to build alternative models to the bureaucratic, top-down development plans that have typically subordinated natural resources to commercial rather than social ends. These challenges are both environmental and political in nature. They underlie the growing conflict between local and global forces.

What is more significant in the Southeast Asian context is how environmental protection, or environmentalism, has emerged as an important focus of state–society conflict, and how in that process the involvement of transnational groups, both NGOs and rich groups of companies, has become more pronounced. A desire to protect the natural environment has often become a factor in wider demands for political and economic reforms in the region, not without moral and financial support from groups and governments outside the region. It is not surprising therefore to find environmental groups in Southeast Asia challenging both governmental and corporate practices, while advocating sustainable development strategies.

However, environmental campaigns, in general, can only succeed under certain conditions. The evidence from Southeast Asia seems to point to the following factors. First, there must be democratic and legal avenues to pursue environmental goals. Second, it is crucial to build a broad network or coalition of environmental and non-environmental groups that can take on the state and its allies. The coalition, too, must be of a sufficient size and tenaciousness in order to be effective. Third, in order for the above-mentioned conditions to nurture healthy environmentalism-oriented activism, the emergence of a stronger civil society is almost the single most important prerequisite.

Fundamentalism

Usually, fundamentalism is explained as the expression of a desire to return to the simplicity and security of "traditional" codes of behavior. However, this apparent simplicity hides a rather complex frame of action, process, and consequence. Who decides what is "traditional?" There may be sacred texts, but these are open to interpretation, thus fundamentalist movements are usually factionalized based on how each interprets and defines the "tradition," the "traditional," or the "primordial." What are the conditions that would lead to the emergence of fundamentalism and subsequently its domination of the public and private spheres? These conditions are likely to shape the leadership and the interpretation of the "tradition."

In uncertain times, fundamentalism often moves people to gravitate around it for protection and security. We have seen a variant of this in the rising use of ethnic politics as competition for jobs grows while the economy shrinks. One may argue that nothing is absolute or definite about the content of fundamentalism or about the elevation of ethnic identity as a way to draw boundaries between people. However, in an increasingly confused and uncertain globalized world, the presumed essentialism of ethnic identity either comforts people or allows them to identify scapegoats. In whatever form, fundamentalist politics, either in the developed, developing or underdeveloped world, has become a powerful weapon for mobilization. As the political and class coalitions expand in the context of the crumbling development project era and the rise and the decentering effects of the globalization project, people feel increasingly dislocated.

Globally, there are two major forms of fundamentalism that have expressed themselves forcefully: religious and ethnic. Religious fundamentalism, such as that of Islam, could be understood as a response to the development project that, in many circumstances, has intensified materialistic inequality and cultural divisions within indigenous communities around the world. There are two main faces of Islamic fundamentalism: one a status-quo and modernist face; the other, a radical, and sometimes rather militant, one. We find both forms in Southeast Asia (Camilleri and Chandra 1998; Hefner 2000; Hefner and Horvatich 1997).

The status-quo, modernist Islamic face dominates sociopolitical movements in Indonesia and Malaysia. These seem to be based on democratic-oriented participatory modern electoral politics. The movement's main concern in the last two decades, for instance, has been to bring Islam into the mainstream, for example through "Islamic economics" and the like (Shamsul 1999b). We have also heard of a push for "Buddhist economics" in Thailand (Putasen 1999).

This does not mean that radical fundamentalist/militant Islamic groups, such as those in Southern Thailand, Southern Philippines and Indonesia, have disappeared or been disbanded. They still exist but on the periphery, sometimes grabbing world headlines through their daring money-motivated kidnappings of tourists, such as the ones in Sabah, Malaysia and also in Sulu, the Philippines. A few of these groups are still conducting secessionist struggles (Hefner and Horvatich 1997), receiving external support (cash, weapons and training) from abroad, mainly from their exiled members, within a framework of what Ben Anderson calls a "long distance nationalism" (Anderson 1998). It is however the local expression or articulation of such movements that seems more exciting to examine, such as the one in Acheh, in Southern Philippines and Southern Thailand. The odd case is that of Malaysia, where the "radical Islamists" have instead become the source of the much-needed catalyst for the rise of the new politics in the country, especially in the last three decades (Shamsul 1997).

The emerging pattern seems to be that the rise of the Islamist groups in Southeast Asia is related to two rather contradictory trends. On the one hand, it is related to the condition of economic hardship, unemployment, a lack of democracy, fears of both secularization and Westernization, thus attracting mostly the young and alienated, such as in Indonesia, Southern Thailand and Southern Philippines. On the other hand, it was brought about by a condition of economic stability and prosperity, lack of democracy, the perceived need to contain secularization and Westernization, as well as the emergence of civil society, thus attracting mostly the young, educated middle-class Muslims, as in Malaysia and Singapore. In both cases, the influence of "global political Islam" is significant in the sense it has helped to initiate and sustain the religious conscientization process experienced by Muslims in the region, mostly centered around the concept of *ummah*, or brotherhood (Esposito and Voll 1996).

The other type of fundamentalism, namely the ethnic kind and its variants, existed long before globalization. Imperialism, colonialism and nationalism are social phenomena steeped in some form of ethnic fundamentalism—eurocentrism, orientalism, racism, apartheid and so on. In fact, based on colonial records, it has been argued that ethnic groups as a social category is a colonial construction (Hirschman 1986, 1987). However, during the decolonized development project era, for instance, such fundamentalism took the form of an ethnic-based "affirmative action" policy. In Southeast Asia, Malaysia has been the main proponent of such policies (Jesudason 1990). Many sections of Malaysian society were not happy with such policies and they have organized activities meant to build public support to oppose them through democratic means, including using the ballot box. With the advent of the globalization project such policies have been under threat. For instance, if Malaysia were to accept the IMF package to help it resolve the recent economic crisis, it would have to jettison its ethnic-based pro-affirmative action policy. In Indonesia, on the other hand, the Chinese minority became the violent target of sections of the economically unhappy indigenous groups. Suggestions are aplenty now, from within Indonesia, that they should adopt the Malaysian style of having a pro-indigenous affirmative action policy to "re-correct" the ethnic imbalances in economic ownership and distribution.

The interesting response from the Chinese community in Southeast Asia to the developments in Malaysia and Indonesia has indeed engendered another version of ethnic fundamentalism—the Chinese type. For example, in Malaysia, sections of the Chinese community, especially those involved in Chinese school-based organizations, such as teachers, parents, and members of the Chinese business guilds, have felt rather strongly that the Chinese culture and language is under threat as a result of the official adoption of Malay language and culture as the basis of "national culture." They have taken numerous steps to counter this threat, including conducting a nationwide campaign with the theme "Save the Chinese language and culture." With the support of the Chinese-based political parties and organizations, the Chinese in Malaysia, through peaceful and democratic means, requested that the Malaysian government amend the Education Act, in 1996, without affecting the position of Chinese education (Kua Kia Soong 1998). The request was granted. Here is an example of what could be termed as "ethnic minority fundamentalism."

Another interesting dimension to this ethnic Chinese "minority fundamentalism" presents itself as a new form of imagination called "cosmopolitan localism" (Sachs 1992: 112), the assertion of diverse localism as a universal right, which as a result questions the assumption of uniformity in the global project. This is indeed a protective response, insofar as communities seek to avoid the marginalization, or disruption, associated with unpredictable global markets. Such a trend asserts also the need to respect alternative cultural traditions as a matter of global survival. More importantly, it is related to the question of preserving or asserting human and democratic rights within the broader context, whether a world community or individual national arenas. Under the guise of cosmopolitan localism the minority fundamentalism of the ethnic Chinese finds a new social platform.

The Chinese case in Southeast Asia is an interesting one to consider. In her recent published studies, Ong, Aihwa, a Malaysian-born anthropologist and a professor of anthropology at UC Berkeley, elaborates on how intensified travel, communications, and mass media have created a transnational Chinese public (Ong Aihwa with Nonini 1997; Ong Aihwa 1999). She argues that political upheavals and global markets have induced Asian investors, particularly the Chinese, to blend strategies of migration and of capital accumulation, and discusses how these transnational subjects have come to symbolize both the fluidity of capital and the tension between national and personal identities. Refuting claims about the end of the nation-state and the clash of civilizations, Ong presents a clear and impressive account of the cultural logics of globalization by examining the rise of Chinese transnationality across the Asia-Pacific, and especially in Southeast Asia, as a version of cosmopolitan localism and linking it directly to global social change.

Unlike the Chiapas version of cosmopolitan localism observed in Mexico, the Chinese demand for the "renewal of citizenship" does not address issues such as the need for free and fair elections or market reforms. The Chinese "citizenship politics" in Southeast Asia is about social entitlement articulated in the form of associative politics, connecting various social causes, conducted in various national locations, using both party politics, or realpolitik, and the politics of business.

In sum, the fundamentalist movements springing up around the world, including those in Southeast Asia, have three main features. First, they articulate the uncertainties and distress brought about by the social decay that populations experience as a result of the limits of developmentalism and the increasing selectivity of globalization. Second, they often take the form of a nationalist resurgence against perceived threats to their culture. The combination frequently involves contesting the assumptions of global development, presenting alternative ways of organizing social life on a national or local level. Third, it also encourages transnational ethnic interaction, networking and bonding, for economic as well as political survival reasons.

In the end one may ask, does fundamentalism engender democratic practices and promote democratic solutions? In Southeast Asia this is a moot question.

Conclusion

We have observed and narrated how social movements respond to the failures of developmentalism and the further disorganizing impact of globalism, using some examples from Southeast Asia. There are many similar examples that could be drawn from other parts of the world.

The observed responses range from withdrawal into alternative projects to attempts to reframe development as a question of rights and fundamental social protection. All these responses express the uncertainties of social arrangements under globalizing tendencies. Many express a strong desire to break free of the homogenizing and disempowering dynamics of globalization and to establish a sustainable form of social life based on new forms of associative politics. It seems as if the opportunity of political renewal lies, paradoxically, in the weakening of the nation-state by globalization. The opportunity arises as states shed their public largesse and patronage politics loses its financial foundation. The developmentalist state loses its salience, resulting in austerity policies that force public scrutiny by the economically disenfranchised.

As we have observed repeatedly, globalization involves states surrendering leverage to more powerful private global and public authorities over domestic policy and institutions. The downsizing of the labor unions is but one of many consequences of such a development. However it has given rise to new labor internationalism, which often forms links or coalitions with consumers, environmentalists and others opposing state–MNC business coalitions.

Another significant trend that we cannot ignore in relation to globalization is the increase of transnationalism or the strengthening of transnational collectives. I am referring here to the case of Chinese diasporic transnationalism, which provides an excellent example of global connectivity between national, regional and global levels. As a result of such connectivity and, of course, because of their materialistic prowess, the Chinese have been able to negotiate with existing states over the terms of local and/or cultural sustenance, thus breathing new life into "politics." Their efforts transcend the centralizing thrust of the developmentalist states of the postwar era. The success story of the Chinese is perhaps the only one of its kind in Southeast Asia.

The overriding question remains: how will new political and social movements (that is, local, national, transnational and global) become articulated within states and will they, in a longer perspective, replenish nation-states? Many of the people and communities left behind by the development and globalization projects look to NGOs, rather than to states or international agencies, to represent them and to meet their needs. Being "NGOized" is not the same as being "developed" or "globalized." It demonstrates only the fact that national governments and international institutions have lost much of their legitimacy.

We are also quite certain that the globalization project is not just a successor to the development project. Its prescriptions are double edged because its conception of the future erases the past, a past created by various sociopolitical activities and movements for social protection. As the development project has subsided a general reversal of thinking has emerged. The present is no longer the logical development of the past, rather it is increasingly the hostage of the future.

The puzzle remains how we, in the first instance, could ever suggest that "globalization" would bring "democratic developments?"

References

Abramovitz, J. N. (1991) *Investing in Biological Diversity: United States Research and Conservation Efforts in Developing Countries*, Washington, DC: World Resource Institute.

Anderson, B. (1998) *Spectres of Comparison: Nationalism, Southeast Asia and the World*, London: Verso.

Block, F. L. (1977) *The Origins of International Economic Disorder: A Study of United States International Monetary Policy from World War II to the Present*, Berkeley: University of California Press.

Broad, R. and Cavanagh, J. (1993) *Plundering Paradise: The Struggle for Environment in the Philippines*, Berkeley: University of California Press.

Camilleri, J. and Chandra, M. (eds.) (1998) *Globalisation: The Perspectives and Experiences of the Religious Traditions of Asia Pacific*, Petaling Jaya: International Movement for a Just World.

Carson, R. L. (1994) (orig. 1962) *Silent Spring*, New York: Houghton Mifflin.

Chomsky, N. (1994) *World Orders Old and New*, New York: Columbia University Press.

Cohn, B. (1996) *Colonialism and its Forms of Knowledge: The British Rule in India*, Princeton: Princeton University Press.

Cooke, F. M. (1999) *The Challenge of Sustainable Forests: Forest Resource Policy in Malaysia, 1970–1995*, Sydney: Allen & Unwin.

Davies, N. (1996) *Europe: A History*, London: Pimlico.

Eldridge, P. (1996) *Non-Government Organisations and Democratic Participation in Indonesia*, Kuala Lumpur: Oxford University Press.

Esposito, J. and Voll, J. (1996) *Islam and Democracy*, New York: Oxford University Press.

Featherstone, M. (ed.) (1991) *Global Culture: Nationalism, Globalization and Modernity*, London: Sage Publications.

Flemming, D. F. (1961) *The Cold War and its Origins*, New York: Doubleday.

Gray, J. (1998) *False Dawn: The Delusions of Global Capitalism*, London: Granta.

Guha, R. (1989) "Radical American Environmentalism and Wilderness Preservation: A Third World Critque," *Environmental Ethics*, 11, 1: 71–83.

Haynes, J. (1997) *Democracy and Civil Society in the Third World: Politics and New Political Movements*, Cambridge: Polity Press.

Hefner, R. (2000) *Civil Islam: Muslims and Democratization in Indonesia*, Princeton and Oxford: Princeton University Press.

Hefner R. and Horvatich, P. (eds.) (1997) *Islam in an Era of Nation-States: Politics and Religious Renewal in Muslim Southeast Asia*, Honolulu: University of Hawaii Press.

Hirschman, C. (1986) "The Making of Race in Colonial Malaya: Political Economy and Racial Category," *Sociological Forum*, Spring: 330–361.

—— (1987) "The Meaning and Measurement of Ethnicity in Malaysia: An Analysis of Census Classification," *Journal of Asian Studies*, 46, 3: 555–582.

Jesudason, J. V. (1990) *Ethnicity and the Economy: The State, Chinese Business and Multinationals in Malaysia*, Singapore: Oxford University Press.

Kua Kia Soong (ed.) (1998) *Mother Tongue Education of Malaysian Ethnic Minorities*, Kajang: Dong Jiao Zong Higher Learning Centre.

Lang, C. R. (1996) "Problems in the Making: A Critique of Vietnam's Tropical Forestry Action Plan," in M. J. G. Parnwell and R. J. Bryant (eds), *Environmental Change in Southeast Asia*, London: Routledge.

Lewallen, J. (1971) *Ecology of Devastation: Indochina*, Baltimore: Penguin.

Marcussen, H. (1996) "NGOs, The State and Civil Society," *Review of African Political Economy*, 33, 69: 405–423.

Mittleman, J. (1998) *Peace and Globalisation*, Bangi: Penerbit Universiti Kebangsaan Malaysia.

—— (1999) *The Future of Globalisation*, Bangi: Penerbit Universiti Kebangsaan Malaysia.

Ong, Aihwa (1999) *Flexible Citizenship: The Cultural Logics of Transnationality*, Durham and London: Duke University Press.

Ong, Aihwa and Nonini, D. (1997) *Ungrounded Empires: The Cultural Politics of Modern Chinese Transnationalism*, New York: Routledge.

Peluso, N. (1992) *Rich Forests, Poor People: Resource Control and Resistance in Java*, Berkeley: University of California Press.

Preston, P. (1994) *Discourses of Development*, Aldershot: Avebury.

—— (1997) *Political/Cultural Identity: Citizens and Nations in a Global Era*, London: Sage Publications.

Putasen, A. (1999) "The Asian Economic Crisis and the Crisis of Analysis: A Critical Analysis through Buddhist Economics," in M. C. Hoadley (ed.), *Southeast Asian-Centred Economies or Economics?*, Copenhagen: Nordic Institute of Asian Studies.

Roberts, J. T. and Hite, A (eds.) (2000) *From Modernization to Globalization: Perspectives on Development and Social Change*, Oxford: Blackwell.

Sachs, W. (eds.) (1992) *The Development Dictionary*, London: Zed Books.

Shamsul, A.B. (1997) "Identity Construction, Nation Formation and Islamic Revivalism in Malaysia," in R. Hefner and P. Horvatich (eds.), *Islam in an Era of Nation-States: Politics and Religious Renewal in Muslim Southeast Asia*, Honolulu: University of Hawaii Press.

—— (1999a) "Social Trends and Issues in East Asia: A Scholarly and Policy Interest Viewpoint," in Ng Chee Yuen and C. Griffy-Brown (eds.), *Trends and Issues in*

East Asia 1999, Tokyo: Foundation for Advanced Studies on International Development (FASID).

—— (1999b) "Consuming Islam and Containing the Crisis: Religion, Ethnicity, and the Economy in Malaysia," in M. C. Hoadley (ed.), *Southeast Asian-Centred Economies or Economics?*, Copenhagen: Nordic Institute of Asian Studies.

—— (2000) "Development and Democracy in Malaysia," in H. Antlov and Tak-Wing Ngo (eds.), *The Cultural Construction of Politics in Asia*, London: Curzon Press.

Sklair, L. (1989) *The Sociology of the Global System*, Baltimore: John Hopkins University Press.

—— (1995) *Sociology of the Global System*, Hemel Hempstead: Harvester Wheat-sheaf, 2nd edn.

Whitehead, L. (1997) "The Vexed Issue of the Meaning of Democracy," *Journal of Political Ideologies*, 2, 2: 121–136.

Wood, R.E. (1986) *From Marshall Plan to Debt Crisis: Foreign Aid and Development Choices in the World Economy*, Berkeley: University of California Press.

12 Global imaginings, the state's quest for hegemony, and the pursuit of phantom freedom in China

From Heshang to Falun Gong

Vivienne Shue

Globalization may give us our daily new hybridities, but it leads us not into homogenization. However sweeping the trends and processes we associate with globalization may be, they are neither straightforward in the social effects they engender nor linear in their unfolding. The forces of globalization do not reveal themselves in the self-same manner everywhere or at once. Ideals and practices emanating from the globalized imaginary are, rather, subject to forming unpremeditated patterns of refraction as they pass through the differing prisms of existing local contexts. Thus the essays collected here, highlighting the dynamics at play in several different Asian contexts, are designed in part to illustrate and analyze just how norms, values, techniques, and aesthetics drawn from the global arena may both penetrate and yet themselves be bent, sometimes to unexpected purposes, by the social structures and cultural problematics, as well as by the economic processes and the political struggles that are already active on the ground, animating human affairs in specific states and social communities.

In the master narrative of globalization theory, the assorted bending and skewing effects that can occur in local contexts are generally pushed to the periphery of our vision, so that we may better focus on the main motifs of technological and social change that are supposed to be about to engulf us all. One such key motif posits the waning of the power of individual nation-states and of national governments. The technologies of globalized communications, the accelerating forces of economic integration, the normatively highly charged activities of multilateral organizations and border-crossing NGOs, along with the cascading effects of transnational modes of cultural production and distribution, are all seen as eroding the significance of national governments, depleting their sovereign authority, and undermining their capacity to define and pursue their own ends. Not only is the concept of national sovereignty at risk, the very salience of national governments and of state authorities is thought to be in decline.

It is with this particular corollary of globalization theory that we grapple here, arguing against the grain as it were, by examining the Chinese case and observing both how determined and how resilient nation-state authorities have been in striving to shape and direct the prevailing discourses about politics and culture within their borders and beyond. As we consider more generally the prospects for democratization in different local contexts now evolving under the undeniably powerful influences we associate with global-ization, we must bear in mind that eroding a state's authority is not tantamount to vanquishing authoritarianism. A popularly held perception that a state may be weakening, in fact, has sometimes been known to provoke even more relentlessly hard-line political responses.

All modern states seek to influence the interplay of cultural forces and to impress their preferred systems of symbols, ideals, and values upon their people, to one degree or another. And for some states, such as the party-state in China, the effort to maintain the appearance of its own broad hegemony in cultural affairs is an especially crucial component in what are taken to be the basic, ordinary routines of governance. No state however, and certainly not the contemporary Chinese state, ever actually achieves total hegemony in cultural life. The attempts of states, like the attempts of various other organized social forces, to project and enforce their systems of meaning over others are almost always contested, as we know—either openly in public discourse or by more indirect means of disguised and subterranean resistance. Nevertheless, state interventions aimed at remolding or at sanitizing the cultural discourse can still have compelling consequences. As we will see in the case of China, such state interventions, though they may rarely, if ever, achieve the totalizing effects intended, may yet powerfully alter the course of local, and sometimes even global, history.

Preview of the argument

Twice in the period of a little over two decades, party-state leaders in China intervened deliberately to change the basic terms of the prevailing local political and cultural discourse, in order to protect and enhance the ruling coalition's own legitimacy, and to better secure the official cultural hege-mony. The first time, just a little before the opening of the 1980s, they shifted the main discursive motifs firmly away from the old Maoist maxims of "revolution" and "class struggle," on instead to the ideals of "modern-ization." The second time, at the onset of the 1990s (though they did not by any means abandon all talk of "modernizing" as such), the party-state leaders shifted their broad discursive emphasis to themes of cultural nationalism, Chineseness, and the recovery of the glory of the great Chinese tradition. In each episode, the discursive shift in official circles and in official propaganda empowered certain groups within society who had been (and who had felt) relatively marginalized or excluded from public affairs up until then. Pursuing combined public and personal agendas of their own then, certain sub-elements within these newly empowered groups pressed the prevailing rhetoric (first of modernization, then of cultural nationalism) in directions and to extremes that the party-state itself was to find threatening and would not tolerate. The first episode ended in the suppression of the student-led and élite intellectual-inspired demonstrations in Tiananmen Square in 1989. The second episode ended in the suppression of the popular-mystical Falun Gong spiritual movement, thousands of whose members staged demonstrations at Zhongnanhai, adjacent to Tiananmen Square in 1999. Both movements entailed direct demands made against the state for greater freedom. Both movements were condemned as dangerous and extremist by the state. In both episodes the complex interplay of political ideas was intense, featuring a blending of concepts and convictions drawn from the global imaginary on the one hand, with potent attitudes arising out of more indigenous political struggles and localized cultural discourses, on the other. In both cases the state reacted in shocked and brutal horror at the social forces its own discursive shifts had unexpectedly unleashed. And in both cases the global community offered a floodlit arena in which international alarm and outrage at Chinese state repression were ostentatiously expressed. In neither of these episodes does it seem that the cause of democracy and freedom in China has been substantially advanced.

Modernization as Westernization: the post-Mao intelligentsia's early gambit

In the very late 1970s and early 1980s, just as Deng Xiaoping embarked upon the policy of reform and "opening" to the outside world, China's party-state leadership made a concerted effort to redefine the national-political and cultural project from one of revolutionary "class struggle" to one of "modernization." Reacting then to what they could only have comprehended as ominous trends in global political economy—trends that had passed China by during the years of Maoist autarky—the new cohort of Chinese state leaders expressed with resolute urgency their aspiration to catch up with the modern world. The rise of Japan to undisputed economic and technological dominance in Asia, the galling challenges posed by Taiwan and the other surging, export-led developing East Asian "tiger" economies, the ever-more sophisticated high-tech demands involved in maintaining military credibility in the late cold war era, all contributed to the consensus in Beijing around a set of new policy initiatives aimed at overcoming Chinese "backwardness." Thus "modernization" became the official mantra of the 1980s, and this sudden paradigm shift in the state's own discourse had immediate and profound effects in recalibrating the state's demeanor *vis-à-vis* the Chinese public—the working classes and, especially, "the poor peasant masses." Whereas these very social groups had before been celebrated by the party-state as the bearers of authentic political virtue, standing militantly at the head of the revolutionary vanguard on the road to communism, they came now to be conceived instead as the embarrassingly still-backward and less-civilized subjects of the state's obligatory disciplining and modernizing pedagogy.[1]

The discursive shift to the ideals of modernization also implied important reconceptions of the potential contributions of the Chinese intelligentsia to the national project even as it reset the appropriate terms for cultural debate among the intellectual élite.[2] Visions of modernization conjured up expectations of more elevated roles for an educated élite of experts and technocrats. Among the earliest actually to enjoy first-hand the benefits of more open access to the global arena of knowledge and ideas were the more trusted academics and scientists who were promptly permitted to travel and study abroad, and the better-educated, relatively sophisticated urban élites who, though they still could not go abroad, nonetheless rapidly became hungry consumers of the smorgasbord of new translations of Japanese and Western scholarly and technical, literary and philosophical, artistic and critical publications and of the plays, films, operas, radio discussions and other foreign productions that suddenly, in the 1980s, broke the deadening intellectual isolation of the Mao years.

Chinese intellectuals had long been excoriated and silenced under Mao. Newly empowered now as a uniquely treasured social stratum in the modernist-reformist imaginary of the 1980s, and awash in the flood of unedited and only half-comprehended ideas, values, and aesthetics floating in from abroad, Chinese academics, scientists, and cultural luminaries responded with pent-up eagerness to the novel opportunity to express themselves more freely and authoritatively. But in their articulation of an urgent post-Mao social agenda, it was impossible not to discern—as if they had been freeze-dried in place in the collective memory of the Chinese intelligentsia—a host of abiding concerns, assumptions, and styles of action held over from the pre-communist past. Not all of China's leading intellectuals were swept up by the thrill of venting their long-suppressed yearnings for a thorough cultural renovation. Some did keep their feet, remaining circumspect and gradualist in the types of reform they recommended. But many others, the most outspoken intellectuals and scientists of the 1980s, seemed to pick up the discussion of reform and modernization in just the same holistic terms in which it had been left off by the May 4th cultural iconoclasts and social activists who had wished so hard to thoroughly transform China and the Chinese soul more than two generations earlier (Wan 1991). For them, as for their May 4th antecedents, the "modernization" of the still-peasant China they found so repugnant meant nothing short of total cultural overhaul. It meant rejection of the Chinese past and the triumph of science and cosmopolitanism. It meant, in the words of the incautious astrophysicist Fang Lizhi, who enjoyed giving perilously provocative lectures to audiences of adoring students in the mid-1980s, nothing less than "wholesale Westernization" (Kraus 1989: 303).[3]

The Westernizing modernist intellectuals' gambit of the 1980s reached one of its more ghastly, if poignant, pinnacles in the creation of the 1988 TV series *Heshang* (River Elegy), which credulously and lavishly lauded all things Western while it denigrated and reviled China's traditional culture.

This powerful six-part series, visually deploying many of the sacred images of Chinese tradition such as the Great Wall and the dragon, painted the "yellow" culture of China as turgid, despotic, hierarchical, endlessly agrarian, bound in poverty, corrupt, and closed while it held up an idealized vision of the West's "azure blue" culture as energetic, creative, high-tech industrial, free, expansive, powerful, and above all wealthy.[4] The series was applauded by many fascinated urban TV viewers even as it scandalized countless party-state officials and set off a storm of cultural and political controversy.

Some groups within the intelligentsia had clearly taken the state's own discourse on modernization into dangerous territory and put it to purposes well beyond any the regime could countenance (X. Chen 1995: 28). Intended originally to legitimate the Communist Party's new ruling coalition, its economic reform plans, and its policy of gradual "opening" to the world economy, the discourse on modernization had been pressed into service for a profoundly different, much more iconoclastic, anti-party agenda of "whole-sale Westernization." And with these calls for "wholesale Westernization" there sometimes came, usually as something of an afterthought, an ambivalent and very vaguely defined wish for greater "democratization" as well.

When the student-led demonstrations broke out in the spring of 1989, central party and military leaders dithered for weeks, unsure how to react under the unaccustomed and unrelenting glare of worldwide satellite coverage of events in the Square. In the end, the new national porousness and the heightened transparency of Chinese political affairs brought on by globalized communications systems would serve to stiffen, rather than soften, their responses to the protests. Chinese commentators living abroad and sympathetic with the demonstrators appeared on nightly news programs in the United States, Europe, Canada, Australia, and Japan. Fax machines relayed accounts of the latest events even from the country's interior. The students made a blundering bid for Western sympathy and support by raising their all-too-plainly American-inspired statue of the "Goddess of Liberty" in the Square. When the violent crackdown finally came, the photographs and frightened voices beamed frantically out of Beijing wrenched hearts around the world.

State-sponsored cultural nationalism: civilized and subaltern

Chinese party-state leaders, and especially the military officer corps, were sharply stung by the worldwide bad publicity they received and all the international condemnations that followed the June 4th debacle. They reacted yet again to what they saw as ominously hostile trends in the global arena. Sullen, angry, and perceiving themselves somehow to have been the most victimized of all by events, they began straightaway to grope their way toward a new regime-legitimating discourse, one that not so surprisingly in the circumstances dwelt mordantly, and often morbidly, on China's past victimizations at the hands of foreign intruders. In the profuse efforts of party-state propagandists to restore social discipline and to salvage, in particular, the heavily tarnished image of the People's Liberation Army, Chinese television, magazines, and other media were swiftly pressed into service and saturated with melodramatic narratives, depictions of old battles against foreign enemies, and of the agonizing deaths of innocent civilians and military martyrs. No old wound to the nation was allowed to be forgotten. Patriotic ardor and the transcendental value of personal sacrifice for the nation received immoderate public celebration. Striking back at enemies and maintaining national pride and dignity were held up to China's youth as the highest of all the ideals one might pursue. A very edgy, embittered and assertive official discourse of nationalistic anti-foreignism began to take coherent shape in the immediate aftermath of June 4th and on into the early 1990s.[5] By the middle of the decade, xenophobic diatribes such as the 1996 bestseller *China Can Say No* were being snapped up by Chinese readers and going into extra editions.[6]

The party-state's deliberately crafted new discourse on nationalism, however, like the old discourse on modernization, was to prove itself multifaceted and capable of being taken to unlooked-for extremes. It offered different appeals for various audiences and new opportunities for social critics of rather different stripes in China. For some it offered a platform upon which to issue calls for the recovery of China's grand "tradition," the brilliant accomplishments, the national glories, and the cultural riches of the Han Chinese past. Unlike the modernist iconoclasts of the 1980s who were so repelled by Chinese "backwardness" and wished out loud for complete Westernization, these other voices from within the intelligentsia hailed the modern-day validity of "Asian values" and promoted the sort of Confucian revival that implicitly or explicitly invoked the Singapore model and fitted very well with the neo-authoritarian political philosophy always favored by Deng Xiaoping.

Meanwhile, a younger generation of writers and critics was approaching the discussion of cultural nationalism not at all from a straight "traditionalist" standpoint, but armed (in a delicious turn of irony) instead with the theoretical apparatuses of "postmodernism" and "postcolonialism," modes of deconstructionist discourse and analysis acquired during their years of study in universities abroad or by their exposure, through globalized means of communication and debate, to intellectual trends of criticism current in the West. According to one very penetrating analysis, what emerged "from this prima facie unlikely union of Western theories and Chinese concerns" was "a unique sort of nativist cultural theory.... mix[ing] xenophobia, polemical rhetoric, and nationalist sentiment into a defiant third-world or postcolonial stance confronting Western cultural hegemony" (Xu 1998: 204). The result of this particular strain of élite cultural criticism has been to produce a "particularly pernicious and aggressive form of *national culturalism* ..." holding out the "dream of a China-centered rim of Chinese culture," a "dangerous dream of a new cultural hegemony ... disguised as a struggle for cultural independence and counteraction against the old Western hegemony" (Xu 1998: 220).[7]

This time around the lively intellectual debates—between the "traditional culturalists" on the one hand and the "postmodern nativists" on the other, all of them reacting sharply against the global community's negative assessment of Chinese political culture and building on the state's own officially encouraged discourse of nationalism—helped to create an atmosphere in the 1990s not only of renewed critical élite activism, but also of popular cultural revival. A rehabilitation of oriental philosophies and values, a search for the genuine essence of "Chineseness," and a recovery of the authentic native past, were all explicitly authorized by the new nationalist discourse, even as the marketizing and privatizing effects of China's crypto-capitalist economic reforms were destabilizing nearly all the familiar routines of social life. As it would turn out, much to the chagrin of most of the Chinese political and intellectual élite, the recovery and celebration of what it means to be "Chinese" could not be confined to a few Confucian homilies about loyalty, hard work, and obedience. "Chineseness" itself had become a contested domain. The reinvention and revival of various practices drawn from Chinese popular cultural traditions, for example, were also given added validation by the prevailing discourse. Thus, popular cultural expressions such as the playing of mahjong, the restoration and reconsecration of temples to local folk religious deities, and the practice of *qigong* meditation and exercise, which had all enjoyed an initial tentative renaissance in the 1980s, turned into veritable cultural "crazes" during the 1990s.[8]

Popular culture as popular protest

The term *"qigong"* is quite a recent invention (Xu 1999: 973), but the practices grouped under that heading inside China today combine elements of popular Daoism and Chinese medicine that spring from genuinely ancient lineages. The study and practice of *qigong* in post-Mao China has tended to organize itself into different schools with different masters, some of them charismatic judging from the types of followings they have been able to draw, and some of them incorporating elements of popular Buddhism into their philosophies as well. Many of these masters claim to have cultivated supernormal powers of clairvoyance and an ability to concentrate and project their own spiritual energy into the bodies of others for purposes of healing. Most of them recommend specific regimens of meditation and slow-moving exercise for those who wish to study and gain the benefits of *qigong*. Some of them also sell various teas, cookies, audio-tapes and the like to their followers to aid in healing. And some conduct lectures and public demonstrations of their seemingly magical arts.

The public fascination with and professed faith in the powers of *qigong* and of numerous *qigong* masters reached enormous proportions in China in the 1990s. It seemed that followers and practitioners could be attracted from almost every segment of society. And thus it was that some of these very popular faith healers and *qigong* masters came to be regarded nervously and with even more than the usual ambivalence by the party-state. Some *qigong* performers, who were thought to be cheating the public, were prosecuted as charlatans and frauds. But many others retained their connections to study groups and to associations officially registered with the state.

One of these officially authorized associations spawned a meditation group, known as Falun Gong, whose practitioners follow the teachings of Master Li Hongzhi. But Falun Gong had its official state registration withdrawn and its recognition as a legal social group denied in the mid-1990s because it was claimed by other *qigong* masters and aficionados that Master Li had taken the practice to extremes, that he was using it to attempt to deify himself and to denigrate the value of many other worthy schools of *qigong* practice. Li left China sometime after that, touring several countries, lecturing and making public appearances, and finally settling down to live in New York City. But his followers in China did not disband, nor did they desist in practicing his teachings. When, in early 1999, Falun Gong practitioners found their continued unauthorized activities under attack by various intellectuals close to the party-state as well as other critics, they began fighting back and demanding that the public criticisms of their beliefs be withdrawn and that official recognition of their right to teach and practice be restored. It was this goal of regaining minimal state recognition and approval to practice their beliefs peacefully, evidently, which prompted them to stage a strangely quietistic mass demonstration of some 10,000 people near Tiananmen Square in April 1999.

State leaders, taken wholly by surprise (just as they had been surprised by the student demonstrations a decade earlier), cleared out the demonstrators but did not take hostile action against the movement immediately. Some weeks and months of investigation and deliberation ensued, during which more demonstrations occurred, before the movement was officially declared a "heretical and evil cult" and was banned. The crackdown on Falun Gong that followed was nationwide and reportedly often violent. Many members were arrested. Some were put on trial and sentenced to long terms in prison. But fully one year later, despite the trials, the mistreatment of Falun Gong prisoners and the concerted barrage of state propaganda castigating Li and demanding that his followers give up their allegiance to his teachings, the suppression of the movement was not complete. In April 2000 the official *Xinhua News Agency* made what the *New York Times* called the "stunning admission" that continued Falun Gong protests had "been near-daily events, sometimes very large" all during the year since the initial demonstrations.[9] And by the spring of the following year, there were still sporadic press reports of Falun Gong protests despite the fact that the state's propaganda effort to thwart the movement remained in high gear.

Meanwhile, Li Hongzhi and other Falun Gong organizers abroad took to the Internet to appeal for support from the global community. Their numerous Web sites published in Chinese, English, and other languages Li's lectures, writings, and other sundry comments (which could all be downloaded for free), as well as testimony from hundreds of practitioners around the world who hailed the benefits of the practice for their health and general well-being. On the Internet, Falun Gong spoke back to the powers in Beijing, denying point for point the truth of the allegations made by the government against them, denying that the movement had any political, commercial, or other untoward motives, and calling for the release of Falun Gong prisoners. Li Hongzhi, it was rumored, though he was still living abroad, was made to fear for his life and was compelled to go into hiding. But Falun Gong activists were working overtime in the global public sphere, with sources of funding that were far from clear, in their overt bid for vindication in the court of world opinion. Hundreds, perhaps thousands of letters were sent to Western academics in the aftermath of the official crackdown, for example, calling for "unbiased research" on the Falun Gong phenomenon. Still more letters were sent to academics, civic leaders, and other prominent people in the West requesting that they consider nominating Li Hongzhi for the Nobel Peace Prize. The effort to suppress the movement inside China was intense. But Falun Gong had been able to flee the precincts of the nation for foreign lands and for cyberspace. And there, in the ongoing global discourse about freedom inside China, it remained a major thorn in the side of the government.

Thus it was that two deliberate discursive shifts—shifts calculatedly made by the party-state leadership to help mediate the nation's interactions with the global community while at the same time shore up their own legitimacy and capacity to rule at home—misfired very badly. In attempting to better secure its own cultural hegemony, the state inadvertently empowered different social groups among which were to be found certain fringe elements—first a group of radical Westernizing intellectuals, then a group of popular mystical religionists—whose new-found voices were heard as counterhegemonic and whose protest actions were understood by all as deeply threatening to the state itself.

Since the student demonstrators of 1989 had appropriated from the global political imaginary some of the rhetoric of rights, of representation, and even of democracy, outside observers had little difficulty understanding how their demands might indeed pose a direct threat to the authoritarian party-state and to the legitimacy of the ruling coalition in Beijing. How the meditative sit-ins staged by a group of popular religious mystics like Falun Gong, on the other hand, could have been construed by China's leaders as constituting a political threat of similar, or even greater, magnitude requires perhaps some further explanation.

The key here is to be found in the vital importance still attached by Chinese rulers to the party-state's maintenance of a monopoly on moral truth. It is a fact that many of the old "truths" once associated with Maoist political ideology have been drastically, often quite deliberately, undermined by expanded market relations in society as well as by the actions and statements of Chinese party-state officials themselves in recent years (Dutton 1998). And of course, by all reports, expressions of political skepticism, anti-idealism, and moral cynicism are to be found widely in China today among ordinary citizens and party-state officials alike. Commentators abroad thus frequently suggest that the present regime is tolerated by its people only because of the startling economic growth that has been achieved in China of late, or only because there is as yet to be found on the political scene any other force capable of taking and keeping control. Nevertheless, it also remains the case that the current government's claims to political legitimacy have *never* been permitted to rest merely on its economic successes; nor has it sought to buttress its legitimacy *only* by playing on popular fears of the social chaos that might ensue should it fall. The present government lays claim to the authority to rule, rather, primarily on the basis of its still-superior commitment to personal and social morality as well as its singular ability to discover and to promote throughout society that which is true and good. Amid all the other confusions of the present postsocialist moment, Chinese state leaders have never deviated from their determination to seek to justify their rule, in very large part and at every opportunity, by proclaiming and promoting the moral hegemony of their cause.

The teachings of someone like Master Li, seen in this light then, may indeed constitute a genuinely fundamental challenge to state authority. The party-state's own assertion that it both knows and has a sacred obligation to promote what is moral and what is true makes it difficult to be flexible. The claims of others in society to know another moral truth, and any organized actions they may take to promote that other truth, must inevitably be interpreted by state leaders as oppositional—as challenges too serious to be brushed aside, too fundamental to be tolerated. It is for nothing less than seeking to undermine the moral authority of the state, then, that Falun Gong ran afoul of the regime. For the teachings of Master Li Hongzhi, undeniably, do delineate a different kind of truth and an alternate moral universe from the one encompassed in the state's philosophy. And in Master Li's moral universe, the values proclaimed by the state can hardly even compete, much less command.

Falun Gong philosophy: the teachings of Master Li

Let us look briefly at what Li actually teaches.[10] Mankind, he tells his followers, now lives in a deplorably degraded state. Once, millions and millions of years ago perhaps, when human beings lived closer to their primordial essence, they were relatively pure and powerful, powerful enough to travel effortlessly in different time–space dimensions. Powers to heal, to levitate the body, and powers of clairvoyance that are considered "supernormal" today were universal then. But there have been no less than eighty-one near annihilations of humanity and civilization that have taken place in our unrecorded pre-history. After each of these catastrophes, only a few diminished human beings survived. By a process of progressive degradation, then, what we refer to today as humanity has become but the "dross" or the "scum" of what it once meant to be a human being. Human beings today are heavily contaminated with the "black substance" that is bad karma. They have many base desires and distorted values. By cultivating their minds and wills, however, people can cleanse themselves and replace the black with a "white substance." The white substance is *De*, or virtue. Virtue can be attained through suffering, enduring setbacks, and doing good deeds. Virtue is lost and the black karma grows again when one commits sins or wrongs others. The virtues to be cultivated are *Zhen–Shan–Ren*—*Zhen* can be translated as truthfulness; *Shan* as kindness (or benevolence and compassion); and *Ren* as forbearance (or tolerance).

It is only by cultivating the mind and the will that the Dao, the true way, and a kind of salvation can be obtained. This must be done while simultaneously abandoning various ordinary human "attachments" and desires. The desire for wealth, material comforts, and pleasures must be let go. The desire for fame, worldly achievement, influence, and power must be let go. Even sentimental attachments to other people must gradually be relinquished. Li tells his followers that they may marry and have families. They do not need to go to the extreme of entering a monastery to avoid worldly temptation. But as their level of enlightenment rises, their desires for sex and human love will become less and less important to them. One of the laws of the universe, Li stresses repeatedly in his lectures, is "No loss, no gain." True enlightenment and virtue come only through the sacrifice of what are regarded as ordinary human goals and desires. Even today there are present in the universe many great enlightened higher beings who have already attained supernormal powers and understanding. They frequently pass among us, observing the ordinary human world, and sometimes selecting persons they judge capable of cleansing themselves and attaining greater enlightenment.

Enlightened *qigong* masters like himself, Li teaches, can assist their followers in the cultivation of their minds and wills. They can impart directly to their practitioners a *Gong*, a cultivation energy, that helps them develop their own energy. The master's *Gong* transforms the virtue outside the practitioners' bodies and helps them to upgrade their own minds and wills. Master Li's own *Gong* is to install a small wheel, which is the Falun, into the lower abdomens of his followers. The Falun (or wheel of the Law) is a miniature of the universe that rotates constantly and forever in the practitioner's body. When it rotates clockwise, it absorbs energy from the universe; and when it rotates counter-clockwise, it emits energy and releases waste which is dispersed around the body. When energy is emitted, it can be released quite a distance, and it will bring energy back again. The energy Falun Gong practitioners emit in this way can benefit the people around them. As in the Buddha's teachings, Falun Gong practitioners seek not only self-cultivation but also the salvation of others.

Master Li can also help his followers acquire a "Third Eye" which, though it does not necessarily have to be just there, will usually be located in the middle of their foreheads, just between the eyebrows. Though modern science has discovered something called the pineal gland in the human brain, and it is known that this gland has a light-sensitive portion where melatonin is produced, and though this is sometimes referred to by scientists as a vestigial eye, scientists cannot yet explain how the Third Eye can actually be opened and made to see. But many who have attained higher levels of cultivation have had this experience and through this eye they are able to see through the time–space dimension we inhabit and into other dimensions. They may see through walls and look through human bodies. And they can see many other scenes of our universe that ordinary people cannot.

In his lectures, Li frequently compares his own teachings and his cultivation methods with those of other *qigong* masters. He warns his followers not to be overawed by the displays of supernormal powers other *qigong* teachers can mount. Most of them are but sham *qigong* masters who have not themselves attained any real enlightenment. It is not that difficult, after all, to study and acquire a few minor supernormal abilities. Most of us retain some remnants of our original primordial powers and with some cultivation we can recover them. But the sham *qigong* masters who do magic tricks for the public today have failed to abandon their attachments to worldly values or their desires for fame and money. As only partly enlightened people, they thus easily fall prey to spirit possession by animals such as foxes, snakes, and yellow weasels. It is a law of the universe that animals cannot practice cultivation or attain enlightenment—only humans can. And yet, since animals are closer than humans to their own primordial instincts and endowments, they do have great power and energy. Demons, ghosts, and animal spirits seek to acquire some of the essence of a human body so that they can move on to cultivate a human form and thereby attain the ability to reach enlightenment. They therefore enter into and prey upon the bodies of *qigong* masters who imagine they can utilize the additional energy of the animal spirit possessing them to vie even more successfully for fame and fortune in the world. But each time they emit some of the animal's energy to their followers, the animal spirit takes back a piece of their own essence. And thus they are gradually diminished and lose all chance of reaching high enlightenment. The same applies to the followers of these sham teachers who seem, on the surface, to be receiving energy from their masters but who are actually giving up a piece of their own essence to the demon inside the master.[11]

We are all living now in a time of great confusion and havoc. The standards for judging what is good and what is bad are all distorted. It is at times as depraved and despicable as these, when people all around seek only to use one another, committing acts of selfish venality every day, that great catastrophes have come in the past. Another catastrophe is surely in the offing. Not everyone, Master Li says, not even everyone who follows him, can attain the Dao. But the Falun he can give to his true practitioners will safeguard them.

There is much more to Li's philosophy than can be summarized here. But perhaps this much is enough to allow a few general observations. Li's teachings present an eclectic blend of themes and metaphors drawn from Daoism, Buddhism, Chinese folk myths, Chinese medicine, *qigong* practice, pop science and even science fiction.[12] Though Li sometimes appropriates the language of modern science, as when he alludes to time–space dimensions and to glands in the human brain, he does this, as he explains, only to make his own higher understanding more comprehensible to the ordinary people of today. His knowledge, it is understood, transcends what it is currently within the power of the language of modern science to explain.[13] In its evident rejection of science, rationalism and other Western enlightenment values, and in its claim to transcend those modes of understanding, Li's teachings may aptly be thought of as a kind of "post-modernism for the people" (Vermander 1999: 20). Though Falun Gong shares much in common with certain strands of Chinese philosophy that trace their origins back to ancient times, and with any number of traditional popular religious movements that may first have appeared in China centuries ago, Li's teachings are no mere recapitulation of older beliefs. The inclusion in his lectures and interviews of so many references to modern-day science and pseudo-science, as well as the deployment of various other New Age and postmodern elements, mark Li's highly synthetic philosophy as quite current (Ter Haar 1999). Li's teachings also, we can hardly fail to notice, contain within them strong expressions of repugnance at and a latent critique of emergent capitalist relations in China's contemporary, postsocialist, society. Li deplores the cutthroat competitiveness, the instrumentalism, the commercialism, and the materialism of present-day life in China. These phenomena are figured in his vision as vices which have recently reached new levels in abasing human society under current state policies of "reform and opening" (Li 1998: 354–355). He warns his followers against all materialist yearnings, and especially against the kind of get-rich-quick psychology that so many observers have noted is now broadly characteristic of the Chinese social scene. Li's oft-repeated slogan "No loss, no gain," a principle he asserts to be a veritable law of the universe, stands in direct denial of what must be the fondest hope of all entrepreneurial and venture capitalists—through cunning investment to make a huge fortune out of practically nothing at all.

Li castigates the commodification of all social relations, but especially the commodification of relations in the social organization of spiritual life. His denunciations of *qigong* masters who, seeking fame and fortune, are the victims of animal spirit possession, are sharply reminiscent of folk beliefs found in other societies undergoing processes of rapid capitalist transformation and the commodification of labor. Michael Taussig's classic study of the devil myths and rituals of South American peasant farmers forced to leave the land and turn themselves into wage laborers on Colombian sugar plantations and in the tin mines of Bolivia cannot help but come to mind when reading Li Hongzhi on the terrors of spirit possession. The peasants Taussig studied, confronting for the first time commodified relations of production, experienced themselves not as low-paid wage earners in the world capitalist system, but in terms more mystical and yet more familiar to them, as individual Christian believers making a pact with the devil so as to earn cash money. In return for the cash he delivered to them, the devil these poor laborers both feared and worshipped was expected, sooner or later, to claim back the physical health and strength of the workers themselves and to blight with natural disaster and disease whatever farm holdings they and their families had managed to retain. "These peasants represent[ed] as vividly unnatural, even as evil, practices that most of us in commodity-based societies have come to accept as natural in the everyday workings of our economy, and therefore of the world in general" (Taussig 1980: 3). Li Hongzhi's animal spirit-possessed *qigong* masters are figured similarly in his discourses as having made a pact with evil while striving for success in China's newly commoditized economy.[14] It is not difficult to see the appeal that Li's teachings could have for many in those segments of Chinese society today who are confronting capitalist relations of production and exchange for the first time and who are not faring well in the "great transformation." It should not surprise us to learn, as different observers have reported, that a disproportionately large number of China's Falun Gong practitioners seem to be older people. Raised in their early lives on the morality of Maoist egalitarianism and an abhorrence of market exploitation, and now no longer young, it is middle-aged and older people in China today who are among the least equipped to compete and to adapt to the new mentalities of nascent capitalism.

The state's quest for hegemony renewed

The party-state project in contemporary China presupposes a disenchanted universe. Magical belief is understood by China's political leaders as mere "superstition" and "false science." Thus popular practices based on such beliefs are heresies by definition—they challenge (to the point of negating) the official construction of the world. In ruling such practices and beliefs entirely out of all socially acceptable bounds, the state itself probably contributes to their capacity to serve as a "potent means of expressing counterhegemony, a subaltern conception of the world, or system of value" (Anagnost 1987: 58). The teachings of Li Hongzhi clearly amount to such a counterhegemonic system of values. Li designs, and invites his followers to inhabit, an alternate cosmos to the one upon which the state insists. As one student of the anthropology of urban *qigong* meditation groups noted quite early on: "While *qigong* practitioners are visibly situated in public parks, their alternative states of consciousness imply a withdrawal from the confines of city *and the state*" (N. Chen 1995: 361, emphasis added). And as others who have closely studied mystic cults in post-Mao China argue, networks of popular religious ritual and practice may best be regarded as forming "disruptive communities": what they disrupt is "the nation and its narration(s)" (Dean 1997: 178).[15] Religious practice in contemporary China "creates spaces and occasions to voice discontent with acts of government" (Feuchtwang 2000: 174). "To its participants, religious knowledge is true in a cosmological sense. It is by the cosmological scope of their claims to truth that religious practices are distinguished from other cultural practices. Religious culture links personal to collective truths which are large in potential scale, beyond the limits of a generational or a group identity or a particular period of a history, a government, regime or state. Such a large and authoritative stamp can challenge the practices of a state" (Feuchtwang 2000: 162–163).

A popular religious movement such as Falun Gong may appear to the state to be all the more of a challenge precisely because, as it quietly proselytizes its corrosively critical counterhegemonic system of value and its alternative transcendental cosmology, it affects an utterly nonpolitical agenda and pretends to seek from the state only forbearance (or tolerance)—*Ren*. It asks, or so it would seem, only for the recognition it needs to exist. And yet it is the very existence of such truth-claiming competitive systems of meaning that Chinese rulers must regard as dangerous and intolerable. For the state in China, now as ever before, still strives to legitimate its governance and enhance its authority by demonstrating the potency of its own moral force. In spite of the onrushing influences of globalization and pluralism, the state in China today "continues to assert the right and responsibility to shape its citizens' worldviews" (Lynch 1999: 223).

Thus, in addition to making arrests and conducting trials of Falun Gong activists, state leaders unleashed their propaganda apparatus, launching a typical barrage of didactic news coverage and other media assaults designed to warn the public away from Falun Gong and to make it clear why the movement had to be banned. Falun Gong philosophy was officially labeled mere "feudal superstitious claptrap";[16] official resolutions were passed condemning it as a "heretical and evil cult";[17] the leaders of officially tolerated religious organizations were trotted out to condemn Falun Gong as a fraud;[18] modernist intellectuals, siding once again with the state, ridiculed Li Hongzhi for being but a half-educated buffoon who expresses himself poorly in writing and suffers from delusions of grandeur;[19] the state's own official *qigong* association leaders and experts on Chinese medicine condemned Li as a fraud[20]—he was said to have lied about his own personal background and to be living a life of luxury in New York at the expense of his benighted followers;[21] dire warnings about the seductive dangers of mystical practice were printed in magazines directed at China's youth; former practitioners reportedly "recovering"—as if they had been opium addicts—warned off others with lurid stories of how their lives were nearly ruined once they fell into the clutches of Falun Gong teachings;[22] and stories were circulated of practitioners so besotted with Falun Gong that they refused to consult regular doctors for their illnesses and thus died, or were even driven to suicide.[23]

Above all, the state's multipronged offensive against the movement insisted that it was incompatible with science and that it preyed upon the weak and vulnerable in society. And the Chinese state joined the battle in cyberspace as well, using its own Web sites to counter the threat. Meanwhile, importuned no doubt by well-meaning citizens intent on protecting freedom of religion against the dark forces of authoritarianism in China, the cities of Chicago and Baltimore approved with proclamations the celebration of a day set aside as "Master Li Hongzhi Day," while the city of Houston named Li "an honorary citizen and goodwill ambassador," and the state assembly of New Jersey passed a resolution praising Li for his "selfless and tireless efforts to benefit others by conveying the practice of Falun Dafa from China to more than thirty countries throughout the world."[24] In the global house of mirrors we all now inhabit, no image—whether of ourselves or of the "other"—ever strikes the eye directly, or without manifold distortions.

Fighting demons and despots in the mirror of global imaginings

In the complex interplay now going on between global and local processes all across Asia, the discursive strategies adopted by specific states and their rulers constitute important intervening variables that shape the ways by which freedom can and cannot be pursued (both locally and globally), and thus skew the possible and probable political outcomes. As the discussion here is meant to illustrate using the case of China, where the state's interest in maintaining its hegemony in cultural affairs is very pronounced, so too can be the effects of its discursive interventions. Though these interventions do not, by any means, produce the hegemonic condition state leaders would prefer, neither do they allow for much cumulative development in a more democratic direction.

In the Chinese case, we see plainly how the state has struggled to adjust its course so as to steer between the paradigmatic extremes of modernism, on the one hand—which it finds ineradicably contaminated by Western ideals and values—and of nativism, on the other hand—which it finds ineradicably contaminated by popular mysticism and magic. By all the requisites of traditional and contemporary Chinese statecraft, state power must be projected and perceived by its subjects as infused with morality and truth. The cultural sphere, therefore, can never be conceded to any real or even potential counterhegemony. State leaders in China thus must remain forever poised to stamp out heresies, either of their bourgeois "liberal" élite or of their uncivilized "irrational" subaltern. Meanwhile, as reflected in the mirror world of global imaginings, the face of what is "liberal" and the face of what is "irrational" can so eerily be reversed.

There are no doubt many who still hope that the onrushing processes of global integration will somehow help, on balance, to isolate and snuff out the world's remaining local despotisms. But as others have already acutely observed, there may exist still many vicious dangers ahead as well, as more and more countries are constrained to conduct a portion of their local politics long-distance, as it were, and with the moral images all reversed in globalized reflections of reality (Anderson 1998). What the Chinese experience suggests so far is that the interactions of the global and the local can take many unexpected turns. The processes of social change entailed are profoundly confused and sharply contested. And they may lead first to more violence and oppression, before they ever give us freedom.

Acknowledgment

I am grateful to three young scholars for the help they have given me in thinking through the issues addressed in this paper: to Peter Gries for sharing his thoughts on Chinese nationalism and his Ph.D. dissertation with me; to Paul Festa for a number of good conversations and relevant source references; and to Zhang Wu for expert assistance with the research. My appreciation goes also to Benedict Anderson, Marc Blecher, Mary Katzenstein, Sidney Tarrow, and Keith Taylor for their thoughtful comments, and to the members of the New England China Seminar for their spirited reactions and probing questions when some parts of the argument here were presented at Harvard University in the winter of 2000. All remaining errors of fact and judgment are mine alone, of course.

Notes

1 Here I follow the insightful analysis developed in Anagnost (1997).
2 On the intellectual debates of the 1980s, see Wang (1996) Chapters 2 and 3, Kraus (1989), and Lee (1990).
3 Fang himself, of course, would later find it possible to seek asylum in the United States embassy to avoid arrest after June 4, 1989 when many students and others who had been galvanized by his words would be gunned down in the streets of Beijing.
4 Thoughtful analyses of the TV series can be found in Gunn (1993), Wang (1996), Lee (1990), and X. Chen (1995: Chapter 1).
5 See Xu (1998) for a thoughtful discussion of the shift toward a new nationalist discourse.
6 On Chinese nationalism in the 1990s, see Gries (1999). And for more on the tone this nationalist discourse can take internationally see Lu (1999a and 1999b), and the response by Friedman (1999).
7 See also Barmé (2000) and Tang (1993).
8 On mahjong, see Festa (1999); on local religious sects, Dean (1997); and on the practice of *qigong*, Xu (1999).
9 See the report by Elisabeth Rosenthal, "China Admits Banned Sect Is Continuing Its Protests," *New York Times*, April 21, 2000, p. A9. The respected dissident writer Liu Binyan, publishing in a New York based human rights journal, also commented on the state's failure to suppress the movement, saying that: "The scale on which the CCP mobilized the propaganda apparatus across the country to attack and slander Falungong was comparable to the 'great struggle sessions' of the Cultural Revolution. And the threats, detentions and criminal prosecutions directed toward Falungong members were also not much

different to the persecution in the Cultural Revolution. It is fair to say that the full panoply of psychological and physical weapons is being used against them. But Falungong has not surrendered, becoming the first social organization that the Party dictatorship has been unable to crush in 50 years. This has far-reaching significance, and will have a variety of social and political consequences" (Liu 1999: 19–20).

10 The summary that follows is based on my own reading of the nine lectures contained in Li (1998).

11 Master Li assures his followers that once he has installed the Falun in their bodies, they will be protected from going wrong in these and other ways. The Falun will make them appear younger, and they will be physically healthier, though they should not seek it for its health benefits alone. As long as they genuinely work to cultivate their minds and wills, the Falun will protect them because it comes from Master Li and he himself is rooted in the universal truth. Master Li represents himself as having many divine powers and many *fashen*, or spiritual bodies. He can be in many places at once and his *fashen* know all. If some of his followers cease genuinely to seek enlightenment and are misled into other pursuits, such as advertising their supernormal abilities or selling their knowledge of the higher arts for money, Li will know of it; and he will alter the Falun in their abdomens so that it will no longer work for them. Their bodies will then be returned to their original states.

12 See the interesting report by Vermander (1999), especially p. 16 where he quotes part of a *Time* magazine interview Li gave in which he responded to questions about "aliens" and seemed to hint that he himself might be classified as one.

13 For an extended discussion and analysis of the tension between science and *qigong* in contemporary China, see Xu (1999).

14 See further, however, Weller (1999: 83–93), who makes an important distinction between individualizing religious and moralizing religious responses to what he argues is a "split market culture." If Master Li's "sham *qigong* masters" represent the individualizing, ghost worshipping response to the expanding market economy, then Falun Gong (quite unlike Taussig's devil worshippers) might best be categorized as of the moralizing type, i.e. "an attempt to retrieve communal values in an era that has lost them" (Weller 1999: 92). More careful study of the Falun Gong phenomenon will need to be done before we can confidently place it in a sophisticated typology of contemporary popular religions.

15 On popular religious practice as counterhegemony and resistance, see also Gates and Weller (1987).

16 "Preposterous Heretical Teaching …" ("Huangdan de Xieshuo …"), *Renmin Ribao*, August 18, 1999.

17 The official resolution of the Chinese Ministry of Civil Affairs banning the Falun Dafa Research Institute was released on July 22, 1999. A resolution of the CCP Central Committee forbidding Party members from practicing Falun Gong was issued on July 19, 1999. The Ministry of Personnel also issued a resolution forbidding civil servants from practicing Falun Gong (Xinhua News Agency, Beijing, July 23, 1999) and on the same day the Communist Youth League did the same. Falun Gong publications were banned and, interestingly, the same office that is in charge of eradicating pornography was given the task of eliminating Falun Gong books and tapes (see "News Publishers …" ("Xinwen Chuban …"), *Renmin Ribao*, July 27, 1999).

18 See for example the report on the statements of several leading religious figures in Beijing, "Eradicate the Evil Teaching …" ("Chanchu Xiejiao …"), *Renmin Ribao*, November 11, 1999.

19 See for example "Li Hongzhi's So-Called Science …" ("Li Hongzhi de 'kexue cengci' …"), *Keji Ribao* (Science and Technology Daily), July 26, 1999. And also

228 *Vivienne Shue*

"Li Hongzhi is a Quack ..." ("Li Hongzhi shi pianzi ..."), *Renmin Ribao*,
November 13, 1999.
20 "Falun Gong is Without ... Virtue" ("Falun Gong wu ... de ...") *Huanan
Xinwen*, July 30, 1999. Also, "State Sports Commission Martial Arts Movement
Management Center Chairman ..." ("Guojia tiyu zongju wushu yundong guanli
zhongxin zhuren ..."), *Keji Ribao* (Science and Technology Daily), November 11,
1999.
21 See the report prepared by the research office of the Public Security Ministry,
"The Life and Times of Li Hongzhi", ("Li Hongzhi qi ren qi shi"), *Zhongxinshe*
(Chinanews.com, www.chinanews.com.cn), December 5, 1999. People who were
acquainted with Li in earlier times claim not to have noticed any supernormal
abilities in him in "Li Hongzhi's Old Colleagues Say ..." ("Li Hongzhi yuan
danwei tongshi shuo ..."), *Renmin Ribao*, July 29, 1999, and in "Still the Same
Old Face ..." ("Hai qi benlai mianmu ..."), *Renmin Ribao*, July 29, 1999.
22 See for example the long self-narrative report of a Qinghua University student,
"A Doctoral Student Breaks with Falun Gong" ("Yige boshisheng yu falun gong
de juelie"), *Renmin Ribao*, January 4, 2000.
23 "Falun Gong is a Typical Heretical Cult" ("Falun Gong shi didi daodao de
xiejiao"), *Renmin Ribao*, November 3, 1999. Also "Irrational Heresies
Propagated by Li Hongzhi", ("Li Hongzhi xuanyang de waili xieshuo"), *People's
Daily Online* (www.peopledaily.com.cn/item/lhz/t12.html).
24 These quotations and notations are taken from a promotional Falun Dafa
mailing emanating from Rochester, New York, dated November 24, 1999.

Bibliography

Anagnost, A. (1987) "Politics and Magic in Contemporary China," *Modern China*,
13, 1: 41–61.
—— (1997) *National Past-Times: Narrative, Representation, and Power in Modern
China*, Durham: Duke University Press.
Anderson, B. (1998) *The Spectre of Comparisons: Nationalism, Southeast Asia, and
the World*, London: Verso.
Barmé, G. R. (2000) "The Revolution of Resistance," in E. Perry and M. Selden
(eds.), *Chinese Society: Change, Conflict and Resistance*, London: Routledge.
Chen, N. (1995) "Urban Spaces and Experiences of Qigong," in D. Davis, R. Kraus,
B. Naughton and E. Perry (eds.), *Urban Spaces in Contemporary China*, New
York: Cambridge University Press, pp. 347–361.
Chen, X. (1995) *Occidentalism: A Theory of Counterdiscourse in Post-Mao China*,
Oxford: Oxford University Press.
Dean, K. (1997) "Ritual and Space," in T. Brook and B. M. Frolic (eds.), *Civil
Society in China*, Armonk: M.E. Sharpe, pp. 172–192.
Dutton, M. (1998) *Streetlife China*, Cambridge: Cambridge University Press.
Festa, P. (1999) "Mahjong Politics in Contemporary China: Civility, Chineseness,
and Mass Culture," unpublished manuscript.
Feuchtwang, S. (2000) "Religion as Resistance," in E. Perry and M. Selden (eds.),
Chinese Society: Change, Conflict, and Resistance, London: Routledge, pp.
161–177.
Friedman, E. (1999) "Comment on 'Nationalistic Feelings and Sports,'" *Journal of
Contemporary China*, 8, 22: 535–538.
Gates, H. and Weller, R. P. (1987) "Hegemony and Chinese Folk Ideologies: An
Introduction," *Modern China*, 13, 1: 3–16.

Gries, P. (1999) "Face Nationalism: Power and Passion in Chinese Anti-Foreignism," unpublished Ph.D. Dissertation, University of California, Berkeley.

Gunn, E. (1993) "The Rhetoric of River Elegy: From Cultural Criticism to Social Act," in R. Des Forges, N. Luo and Y. B. Wu (eds.), *Chinese Democracy and the Crisis of 1989*, Albany: State University of New York Press, pp. 247–261.

Kraus, R.C. (1989) "The Lament of Astrophysicist Fang Lizhi: China's Intellectuals in a Global Context," in A. Dirlik and M. Meisner (eds.), *Marxism and the Chinese Experience*, Armonk: M.E. Sharpe, pp. 294–315.

Lee, L.O. (1990) "The Crisis of Culture," in A. J. Kane (ed.), *China Briefing*, Boulder: Westview, pp. 83–105.

Li, H. (1998) *Zhuan Falun*, New York: Universe Publishing Co., 2nd edn., English version.

Liu, B. (1999) "Falungong: Unprecedented Courage in the Face of Cultural Revolution-Style Persecution," *China Rights Forum*, Winter: 18–20.

Lu, S. (1999a) "Nationalistic Feelings and Sports: The Incident of the Overseas Chinese Protest against NBC's Coverage of the Centennial Olympic Games," *Journal of Contemporary China*, 8, 22: 517–533.

—— (1999b) "A Response to Friedman's Comment," *Journal of Contemporary China*, 8, 22: 539–542.

Lynch, D. C. (1999) *After the Propaganda State: Media, Politics, and "Thought Work" in Reformed China*, Stanford: Stanford University Press.

Tang, X. (1993) "The Function of New Theory: What Does It Mean to Talk about Postmodernism in China?", in L. Kang and X. Tang (eds.), *Politics, Ideology, and Literary Discourse in Modern China*, Durham: Duke University Press, pp. 278–299.

Taussig, M. T. (1980) *The Devil and Commodity Fetishism in South America*, Chapel Hill: University of North Carolina Press.

Ter Haar, B. (1999) "Falun Gong: Evaluation and Further References," http://sun.sino.uni-heidelberg.de/staff/bth/falun.htm.

Vermander, B. (1999) "The Law and the Wheel," *China Perspectives*, 24: 14–21.

Wan, P. P. (1991) "A Second Wave of Enlightenment? Or an Illusory Nirvana? Heshang and the Intellectual Movements of the 1980s," in X. Su and L. Wang (eds.), *Deathsong of the River: A Reader's Guide to the Chinese TV Series Heshang*, trans. R. W. Bodman and P. P. Wan, Ithaca: East Asia Program, Cornell University, pp. 63–89.

Wang, J. (1996) *High Culture Fever: Politics, Aesthetics, and Ideology in Deng's China*, Berkeley: University of California Press.

Weller, R. P. (1999) *Alternate Civilities: Democracy and Culture in China and Taiwan*, Boulder: Westview.

Xu, B. (1998) "'From Modernity to Chineseness:' The Rise of Nativist Cultural Theory in Post-1989 China," *positions*, 6, 1: 202–237.

Xu, J. (1999) "Body, Discourse, and the Cultural Politics of Contemporary Chinese Qigong," *Journal of Asian Studies*, 58, 4: 961–991.

13 Appropriating the global within the local

Identity formation among the Minahasa in contemporary Indonesia

Michael Jacobsen

According to the French philosopher Edgar Morin, economic globalization demonstrated a capacity for unleashing unprecedented destructive forces during the 1997–1999 economic crisis in East and Southeast Asia. As a concomitant aspect, fear has been expressed that this crisis might spill over into an accelerated development of individualism, social anomie, and a standardization of cultures, homogenizing otherwise specific identities, threatening the different societal constellations in the region during the process. Despite these disturbing scenarios Edgar Morin maintains that the same developments offer a unique opportunity for expanding communication and understanding between the different people(s) and cultures thus emphasizing the contradictory nature of globalization (*Politiken* May 1998).

To go beyond these generalized statements, it is important to stress that all experience so far shows that cultures are not being standardized and people are not being acculturated and turned into anonymous agents of a monolithic global culture, as first envisaged by Marshall McLuhan[1]—in fact quite the opposite has happened. There seems to be certain trends within globalization that lead toward an assertive resurgence of local identities embedded in cultural idioms in many parts of the world, producing increasingly diversity at the subnational level.

What then are the mechanisms behind the current (re-)construction of local identities? Stuart Hall writes that to be English is to know oneself in relation to the hot-blooded Mediterraneans and the passionate, traumatized Russian soul. When you know what everybody else is then you are what they are not. Arguably, identity is a structured representation, which only achieves its positive through the stringent judgment of the negative. It has to go through the eye of the needle of the other before it can construct itself (Hall 1997: 21).

Hall's message is that "the other" is a precondition for identity formation, an insight, I would argue, that is not confined to contemporary societies given that cultures throughout history have always used "the other" as a mirror when constructing their own particularity. What is new, however, is our perception of culture as not constituting a monolithic or primordial entity unaffected by the passing of time. Culture then is constantly molded into a form that is capable of incorporating the past in the present in order to prepare for the future.

This chapter suggests envisaging identity as being formed out of culturally influenced conceptions of what constitute the relationship between "modern" and "traditional" experiences. By their nature, such perceptions are in a constant state of flux. Culture and tradition, then, are relatively contemporary constructions that are constantly more or less consciously invented and reinvented. They are the outcome of conflicting perceptions of what constitutes "authentic" culture. Taking such an approach provides us with a hint of how ethnic groups use their culture and history in a contemporary context, and how they relate their cultural inheritance to a national ideology and an ever-entrenching global consumer culture.

This chapter also emphasizes that to understand the relationship between ethnicity and the nation-state it is important to focus on the processes of globalization and how they influence this relationship. Ethnic groups like the Minahasa in eastern Indonesia do not perceive themselves as victims of globalization, that is, as acculturated beings in a unicultural world. On the contrary, they actively utilize the various instruments forwarded to them through processes of globalization as vehicles for promoting their own agenda *vis-à-vis* the state by merging new forms of communication, international norms and values together with a politicized (re-)interpretation of their past.

In the following it is shown how processes of globalization indirectly influence contemporary identity formation among the Minahasa in North Sulawesi Province in eastern Indonesia when it comes to engaging with the current transformation of the Indonesian state and nation. As an overall framework, the chapter commences by critically outlining how to ground theories of globalization. In particular, the question of how processes of globalization can be manifested at the local level is discussed. This is then connected to a general discussion of how ethnicity relates to state sovereignty and nation-making. Narrowing down the discussion, the Minahasa, and especially their aspirations for influencing the current national policy of economic decentralization and regional autonomy, are selected as a case study. The chapter argues that given the combination of greater possibilities for voicing ethnic aspiration at the international level and the fact that the Indonesian state is under international pressure for reforming its political and economic set-up, ethnic groups like the Minahasa have a good chance of influencing the ongoing transformation of Indonesian society. The chapter closes with some general remarks on the role of the state in local-cum-global interactions.

On the question of the global in the local

In trying to ground theories of globalization, Jonathan Friedman defines in economic terms globalization as referring primarily to the decentralization of capital accumulation. The unification of the world in terms of

technology is a process that is financed by decentralizing capital investment, not by some autonomous cultural or even technological process.
While it certainly generates a global perspective for those who travel along
the upper edges of the system, there are other processes that are equally
global in terms of their systematicity, but which are exceedingly
local–national– ethnic–indigenous in terms of their construction. This,
according to Friedman, is the crux of the problem: the current situation is
one that produces both globalized and localized identities. In sociological
terms, both of these phenomena are in fact local. Globalization is thus a
process of local transformation, the packing of global events, products and
frameworks into the local. It is not about de-localizing the local, but about
changing its content, not least in terms of identity (Friedman 1998: 6).

Arguing along similar lines Stuart Hall maintains that for capital to
maintain its global position it has to incorporate and partly reflect the social
and cultural differences it is trying to overcome. He continues:

> Is this the ever-rolling march of the old form of commodification, the
> old form of globalization, fully in the keeping of capital, fully in the
> keeping of the West, which is simply able to absorb everybody else
> within its drive? Or is there something important about the fact that, at
> a certain point, globalization cannot proceed without learning to live
> with and working through differences?
>
> (Hall 1997: 30–33)

Ulf Hannerz tries to answer this question by identifying two tendencies in
the long-term reconstruction of peripheral cultures within the global ecumene,
the saturation and maturation tendency. In relation to the first, he suggests
that as the different transnational manifestations influence peripheral cultures
the latter will step by step assimilate more and more of the imported meanings
and forms, thereby gradually becoming indistinguishable from the center.
What is considered local culture is more or less penetrated by the transnational, which changes it compared to what it was before, though the contrast
between the local and the transnational can still be drawn and is still regarded
as significant, at least by the local cultures themselves. Thus the cultural differences celebrated and recommended for safeguarding may now only be a pale
reflection of what once existed, and will sooner or later be gone as well,
replaced by other forms of hybridization (Hannerz 1997: 122–123).

The tendency of maturation reflects processes of recontextualizations of
global influences into a localized frame of understanding in order to use
them in local socio-political discourses. Hannerz writes that culturally
defined frameworks of life also possess the power to colonize the market
framework. The periphery takes its time reshaping metropolitan culture to
its own specifications. It is in this phase that the metropolitan forms in the
periphery are most marked by their purity, but on closer scrutiny they turn
out fairly ineffective and vulnerable in their relative isolation. In the second

phase, and in innumerable phases thereafter, as they are made to interact with whatever else exists in their new setting the metropolitan forms are no longer so easily recognizable—they themselves have become hybridized. Local entrepreneurs have gradually learned to master the alien cultural forms, which reach them through the transnational commodity flow, to such a degree that the resulting new forms are more responsive to, and in part outgrowths of, local everyday life (ibid.: 123–124).

The three authors, Friedman, Hall, and Hannerz have been included in this discussion as they counter the criticism against the aloofness of theories of globalization by relating these high-level theories to grounded theory. By doing this they agree with Kirsten Hastrup, who writes that there are no human beings in these theories. There are only "decisions" that are being taken in New York which have consequences in Kuala Lumpur or which perhaps provoke a fall at the London stock exchange with dire impacts in New Zealand. Perceived in this way, globalization can provocatively be defined as a primitivization of the Orientalism that Edward Said once criticized, not only because of its neo-colonial attitude toward "the other," but also because of its exterior relation to the empirical. According to Hastrup, this leads to a profound ahistorical perception of current world affairs. For her there exist no social actions or cultural events without some kind of imagined localized framework within which they unfold. She maintains that as an anthropologist she and her fellow anthropologists have a comparative task and a theoretical project that is global in the sense that it spans over differences in experience, but does not blur or erase them in the process (Hastrup 1998: 26–27, 31, 33).

Trying to be faithful toward the perspective of grounded theory in relation to theories of globalization, thereby taking Kirsten Hastrup's criticism into account, the following discussion focuses on how the local, defined within the framework of ethnicity, is capable of influencing nation-building processes.

Ethnicity and the sustainability of the nation-state

Taking my point of departure in the global exchange of culture and identities as delineated by Hall and Hannerz, I agree with Rita Smith Kipp, who defines ethnicity as something that cannot be determined by simply noting the differences between people. Instead one has to concentrate on what differences matter to people and how these differences become culturally embedded (Kipp 1993: 17–24). Employing this broad definition of ethnic identity, I furthermore concur with Benedict Anderson that politics of ethnicity have their roots in modern times, not in ancient history, no matter how they are ideologized (Anderson: 1987: 10).

Ethnicity then can be conceived of as an imaginative framework that encompasses a variety of related identities. This framework is understood as the products of ascription and self-ascription and is based generally on ideologies of common descent. Following Katherine Verdery, ethnicity can furthermore be conceived of as constituting a cultural matrix for a given social organization. The point of departure for analyzing ethnicity, according to her and others, is thus not culture per se, but rather the potential aspect of social or political manipulation of identities and thus their "situational" character (Verdery 1994: 34–35; see also Barth 1994: 12–13). The cultural matrix then, besides being an important aspect of the local socialization process, thus constitutes a reservoir of identity markers that a given social organization relates to when expressing itself in terms of ethnicity.

As can be seen, linking ethnicity to social organization makes it contemporary, not primordial, meaning that an ethnic identity is not based on some "objective" cultural features. Ethnicity and affiliated identities are thus situational and fluid in content, and as such are highly potent politically. Frederik Barth writes that leaders who pursue their own political agenda affect the mobilization of ethnic groups in collective action, but do not necessarily express their group's cultural ideology or represent a popular will (Barth 1994: 12–13). I concur with this and shall later on, when discussing ethnicity in Minahasa, maintain that a revival of cultural identity can also be interpreted as a local aspiration toward (re-)creating Minahasa as a political community.

Because of the fluidity and thus the political potential of ethnicity many states perceive ethnic groups as a threat to national unity (Brown 1994: 2). Depending on the organization of the state the ideological aspect of it can be made fit to accommodate the various alternative identities found within the national hinterland. The Indonesian national motto, "*Bhinneka Tunggal Ika*" or "Unity in Diversity" is a case in point. This is in recognition of the state's limited ability to control the development of ethnic identities and the latter's resilience toward attempts to transform or contain them. What is not up for discussion, however, is the state's perception of having the exclusive or sovereign right to manipulate those ideologies and to enforce its interpretation with power if need be. In this sense, the claim to sovereignty is of utmost importance for the state.

What is meant by "sovereignty"? In 1990 Robert Jackson wrote that sovereignty is a legal, absolute, and unitary condition. Legal in that a sovereign state is not subordinate to another sovereign but is necessarily equal to it in international law—though not necessarily in international fact. Absolute in that sovereignty is either present or absent. When a country is sovereign it is independent categorically: there is no intermediate condition. Unitary in that a sovereign state is a supreme authority within its own jurisdiction. This is the case whether or not a state has a unitary or a federal constitution, because in either case it is a sole authority in its external relations with other states (Jackson 1990: 32).

The question is whether this perception of state sovereignty still holds today, over ten years after Jackson wrote the above in what can be interpreted as adhering to the Realist School in International Relation Theory. This "school" portrays the state as an almost absolutist and total sovereign entity. The international community, however, has in the meantime become much more complex.

For example, to become a successful player on the contemporary global scene there appear to be certain rules that have to be followed, especially those that stress economic transparency and good governance in a country's internal affairs. Furthermore, to be a serious global player also implies a willingness to relinquish aspects of national sovereignty to the international community by, for example, allowing institutions such as the IMF, WTO, ILO, and the UN to intervene in national political and economic policies— especially in times of crises.

Paradoxically, these international forces empower, so to speak, the various ethnic and religious groups within the individual national hinter-lands, thereby enabling them to mount pressure on the state to grant them political autonomy and cultural recognition (Friedman 1998: 1–19; Brown 1995: 54–68; Smith 1990: 171–191). The process of empowerment has in many cases in Southeast Asia led to the creation of resistance movements that have tried to mobilize "the people" in order to further their claims. Various Muslim groups in Malaysia and in the southern part of the Philippines are a case in point. In Indonesia we have seen the re-emerging of a whole range of ethnic and religious groups, which have become more vocal since the collapse of the New Order regime in May 1998. The empowerment of these groups has not created secessionist movements. Instead, in post-Soeharto Indonesia, they are concerned with cultural recognition and political positioning. I shall return to this later.

These developments have had certain implications for the conventional perception of citizenship, namely that it is the exclusive privilege of the state to bestow certain rights upon a person, thereby making him or her a citizen, that is, a national. In the case of Indonesia, under former president Soeharto, it was the state that through the national ideology of *Pancasila* defined what Indonesian citizenship consisted of and to whom it should be granted. After the fall of Soeharto in May 1998, many groups throughout the Indonesian archipelago have contested this exclusive right to define and bestow. Today Indonesian citizenship has become a complex issue in itself because of the uncertainty as to what an Indonesian identity consists of, how to relate ethnic identities to national identity, and where to deposit one's loyalty? To go further into this discussion I shall discuss the contempo-rary restructuring Indonesian state and nation with special emphasis on the ongoing processes of decentralization. I use as a case study the Minahasa, a Christian ethnic minority group from the province of North Sulawesi.

On the question of identity in contemporary Indonesia

One of the most important developments since the fall of Soeharto in May 1998 has been the introduction of economic decentralization and regional autonomy. This process was initiated by the interim president Habibie, and has been given further impetus through the election of the presidential duo of President Abdurrahman Wahid and Vice President Megawati Soekarnoputri on October 20, 1999. Generally this national restructuring has been received positively both nationally and internationally as it is conceived as one of the most important tools for changing the authoritative societal structure inherited from Soeharto's New Order regime. There are, however, some groups that are sounding warning notes. Many Indonesians within academia and the political establishment have argued that if this process is not carefully implemented then the unity of Indonesia is at stake (see Jacobsen 1999). The World Bank echoes this. It has publicly stated that decentralization can make or break Indonesia: "It is a strong political imperative for the country, and makes good economic sense, since Indonesia is unusually centralized for a country of its size and diversity."[2] Due to the latest political developments in Indonesia further doubts, however, about the future entrenchment of the decentralization process can be raised after Megawati Soekarnoputri on July 27, 2001 became the fifth president of Indonesia. She is known to be a strong nationalist and will go to great lengths to keep Indonesia within the confines of a unitary state form. The main question is whether she is ready for a more flat societal structure in which an increasing critical Outer Indonesia demands having a greater say in the running of the nation?

Unfortunately, Indonesia has not become a more stable nation since it began implementing decentralization and regional autonomy in January 2001. Besides unleashing a huge politicization of various groups throughout the nation the political élite in Jakarta is engaged in a fierce battle among themselves over how to position itself as powerfully as possible in the new Indonesia that will eventually arise out of the ashes of the New Order society. This infighting has had a destabilizing effect on Indonesian society as it leaves the economy, state apparatus and army in a power vacuum, thereby undermining their ability to guide and stabilize Indonesia toward a new societal framework that has been called for since the early days of *reformasi* in 1998. As a result, democratization, decentralization, and human rights have become hollow political catchwords without any reference to the current Indonesian reality.

Returning to the development from an authoritarian society toward a decentralized democracy it is clear that regardless of how rudimentary this process might have been, it is having a great impact on how many ordinary Indonesians imagine themselves. This is especially true in the outer regions of Indonesia, where many movements based on a combination of ethnic and religious affiliation have openly begun to reflect on their cultural background besides that of being Indonesian. This has unleashed a variety of ethnic and religious turbulence throughout Indonesia. These developments have not yet reached Minahasa, but people there are interested intensively in what happens in Maluku and in other parts of Indonesia and how it might affect them.

Individuals in Minahasa, with whom I have recently been talking, are generally very critical toward the former New Order regime, especially with regard to its gradual Javanization of Outer Indonesia and the suppression of ethnic sentiments. This stand has to be seen against the historical position of the Minahasa during the Dutch colonial period and during the early years of nation-making in Indonesia. In the Dutch East Indies the Minahasa occupied a rather privileged position due to a strong attachment to Protestantism and Western norms and values compared to other ethnic groups in North Sulawesi. As a consequence they held many important positions within the colonial administration and educational system. They furthermore joined the Dutch colonial army in large numbers and fought in various wars throughout colonial Indonesia. After the proclamation of independence on August 17, 1945 by Sukarno and Hatta, and after gaining full independence from the Dutch in 1949, the newly established Indonesian nation under new president Sukarno strived to set up a unitary state. This led in 1957 to a rebellion in, especially, North Sumatra and Sulawesi against the nationalist government in Jakarta, as they felt Outer Indonesia was being exploited by the Javanese-dominated government. The rebellion, called *Permesta*, culminated in Minahasa district as the Minahasa people found that a federal Indonesia was more just than the unitary state form preferred by Jakarta. This led to an invasion of Minahasa by Javanese forces in 1957 that gradually developed into a guerrilla war that lasted until 1962 when the Minahasa fighters finally had to give in. Since then Minahasa, and North Sulawesi in general, has become a political and economic backwater in Indonesia, completely co-opted by and integrated in the New Order society. The changes that have taken place in Indonesia since May 1998 have made the Minahasa reconsider their present perception of identity.

Let us take a closer look at contemporary Minahasa identity.[3] According to informants, it consists of a number of ascribed and locally perceived characteristics. Which one to become activated when discussing identity depends on the context in which the discussion happens to take place. Minahasa identity is therefore not monolithic in substance, dependent on cultural history and language for definition. It is much more fluid, consists of several layers of explanation, and changes in content according to time and place. When studying the relationship between identity, time, and place it is important to stress that this relationship changes its terms of references according to who is defining what Minahasa identity is, where, and when. Minahasa might thus refer to different matters that transcend, for example, language borders or local perceptions of culture and traditions when defining what they find constitutes Minahasa identity. Identity can therefore mean different things to Minahasa in different parts of the district, that is, *Kabupaten* Minahasa, but all Minahasa, regardless of differences in perception of identity, are united by the umbrella concept of Minahasa ethnicity. This fits perfectly with the discussion earlier in this chapter, namely that culture and traditions are relatively modern constructions, ones that are more or less consciously invented and reinvented over time. There is thus no "authentic" Minahasa culture but a whole range of perceptions that are constantly being contested in relation to a given context.

The main reason for the contemporary re-evaluation of Minahasa identity stems from the Soeharto era. Here it was maintained that all people(s) who lived in North Sulawesi province were regarded as citizens of this region regardless of origin. This included various ethnic groups, Muslims, Christians, Chinese, and individuals from other parts of Indonesia. The previous governor of North Sulawesi Province, E. E. Mangindaan, promoted the acronym "BOHUSAMI," which covers all four *Kabupaten* in the province. namely: *Bo*laang-Mongondou, *Hu*lontalo or Gorontalo, *Sa*ngir/Talaud, and *Mi*nahasa. The idea behind lumping all the different people(s) together was to promote the idea of a "trans-ethnic" regional identity, as the category privileged by the New Order was region instead of ethnic group. In this way the Minahasa as a distinct ethnic group was co-opted by New Order ideology. Today Minahasa ethnicity is perceived more exclusively as it is closely related to a variety of cultural-specific factors, identity markers so to speak, which distinguish the Minahasa from other ethnic groups in North Sulawesi. Informants mentioned a variety of variables that each represented an aspect of Minahasa identity, for example and in order of local priority: land, genealogies, Christianity, education, Westernization, language, food, and cultural history. These factors might be either grouped or referred to individually when discussing Minahasa identity. Having this variety of identity markers to draw on when defining Minahasa ethnicity actually lifts it out of a specific place and time period, thereby making it adaptable to the contemporary sociopolitical changes in *Kabupaten* Minahasa in particular and in North Sulawesi province and Indonesia as a whole.

In order to invigorate a post-Soeharto Minahasa identity attempts to revive aspects of the pre-colonial cultures and substantiate current interpretations of identity are presently taking place. These attempts can be divided into three categories: those initiated by NGOs, by churches, and by individuals within the arts. Among the NGO community, emphasis is placed on what is perceived as pre-colonial norms and values, namely openness, generosity, braveness and adaptability. These are seen as a counter to Western individualism and moral decadence and are to be framed in traditional forms of organization, *Mapalus*, which are based on reciprocity and cooperation. Basically, the NGOs promote a kind of localism in which cultural roots, personal relationships, and sustainable development are the key words. In relation to the churches it is especially the Christian Evangelical Church in Minahasa that is engaged in the cultural revival movement. This group incorporates various rituals to make people relate to a Christianity that is capable of peacefully coexisting with pre-colonial beliefs. For example, to lend a Minahasa aspect to baptism they have selected an old rite in which people ritually cleansed themselves by going to a mountain stream to pour water over their bodies while beseeching their ancestors and deities to relieve them of their misdeeds. The only thing the ministers have changed in this ritual is the reference to the traditional deities, replacing their names with the Christian God. In this way they combine baptism with a traditional Minahasa form of ritual cleansing. Finally, sculptors, painters, and poets are also engaged in the cultural revival movements. The two former are making carvings and paintings with symbolic references to pre-colonial mythology together with references to a close relationship between man and nature thought to prevail during those times. Poets are very critical toward Western norms and are trying through their work to reintroduce the pre-colonial norms and values mentioned above. Occasionally all three representatives of the arts arrange joint happenings, exhibitions, and public meetings to get their message across. Judging from people's reaction to these attempts to revive what is thought of to be authentic Minahasa culture, there is a huge interest in at least discussing the idea. Whether such attempts are succeeding in penetrating the Westernized facade is another matter, one still pending further research.

There are, however, two factors that make it difficult for the Minahasa to probe their identity. These constitute a kind of a double blindfold that prevents a clear and critical insight into how a revived Minahasa identity can be made fit to accommodate a transforming Indonesia. The first is Christianity. During the last two centuries missionaries have been quite effective in transforming most aspects of pre-colonial value systems, replacing a traditional Minahasa perception of cultural specificity with that of Christian ethical values. During this period missionaries have managed to create a negative image of the pre-colonial societies, which have been stigmatized as unacceptable to a righteous Christian, that is, Western way of life. Under such conditions, the remnants of the pre-colonial societies have gradually been transformed into mythological stories, curious animistic rituals, and colorful performances for use on official occasions. This religious blindfolding has continued undisputed up to today, effectively pre-empting whatever might be left of pride in rediscovering remnants of pre-colonial culture and societies.

The second factor making the Minahasa apprehensive toward pre-colonial cultures stems from the indoctrinated New Order's nationalist ideology. According to this ideological framework, indigenous cultures are important as they underline the national motto of "Unity in Diversity." However, care was taken to ensure that it was only the performative aspects of a local culture that were allowed, not those that could jeopardize the inculcation of the *Pancasila* ideals (Foulcher 1990: 301–303). To further underpin this integrative ideology, the complementary ideological concept of *Pembangunan* (developmentalism) allied with a more tangible administrative and military command structure was introduced during the same period. Confronted with this nationalistic ideological and administrative set-up, Minahasa identity as well as any other ethnic identity in New Order Indonesia had no choice but to follow suit. In the case of Minahasa ethnicity, this did not pose a great problem as the church had already paved the way by redefining the "dangerous" aspects of pre-colonial Minahasa culture(s). It is against this background that current aspiration from many parts of Minahasa society to reinvent or reintroduce various aspects of the pre-colonial cultures into an otherwise elusive contemporary Minahasa identity has to be seen.

In this chapter one of the main theses has been that ethnicity can be perceived as a dynamic, organizing construct that superimposes its framework on a social organization, thereby coordinating interaction within that organization. As such ethnicity entails a consciousness of difference. Vermeulen and Govers have made a distinction between "low" and "high" degrees of a consciousness of difference. When the first condition prevails, cultural differences tend to be marked and inter-ethnic relations are relatively stable: people accept differences as given, they hardly take time to reflect on them and there is no pronounced ethnic ideology, let alone an ethnic movement. During a period of a high degree of consciousness of difference, however, interaction increases and people lose or fear they will lose their cultural distinctiveness. In the process they become more aware of their culture, and may start to "repair" or reinvent aspects of it, demanding cultural and political rights from the state as a result of that development (Vermeulen and Govers 1994: 4).

The Minahasa too have traveled along such a continuum—a journey initiated by a transforming nation and further accelerated by a variety of more or less direct influences from processes of globalization. The Minahasa have now entered a phase in which they are reorganizing their perception of culture in order to formulate a policy of cultural rights. What we observe in Minahasa right now is a unique historical state in which an elusive identity, dominated as it is by Christianity and New Order ideology, is gradually being replaced by a clearer perception of cultural specificity. We are thus witnessing a rare coinciding of several factors that facilitate this situation: the New Order society is gradually being dismantled, democratization, economic decentralization and regional autonomy are on their way, creating room for enhanced ethnic consciousness and for new types of NGOs which, together, are struggling nationwide to strengthen an emerging civil society.

Combined, these developments help to extrapolate the basic elements behind a more explicit and politically sensitive Minahasa identity based on a coalescence of re-emerging pre-colonial cultural values, Christian values, and a modern Minahasa reading of Indonesia in an era of globalization. The question is how such an invigorated identity will be used in a local political context? Will it become radicalized in relation to Muslims, making them wonder whether this is the beginning of a forced exodus for them as non-Minahasa, thereby creating a potential for inter-ethnic cum religious tensions and possible clashes like those in Maluku and elsewhere in Outer Indonesia?

Arguably, this revitalization process is closely linked to provincial politics taking the distribution of political power in the province into account. Minahasa constitute a minority in the province of North Sulawesi but a majority in *Kabupaten* Minahasa. This is important to recognize as Minahasa have had, and continue to have, a dominant political influence in provincial affairs, a position they no doubt will fight to maintain and even boost if possible.

Why is this development taking place now? Besides being possible only here in the post-Soeharto era, a culturally reinforced Minahasa identity is a perfect political platform for Minahasa politicians to utilize in mobilizing an otherwise heavily de-politicized population. What is at stake is thus the creation of Minahasa as a political community. If Minahasa can keep or further co-opt political power in the province then they are in a position to control the use and allocation of economic assets in most of North Sulawesi Province. This becomes all the more important when economic decentralization, initiated on January 1, 2001 throughout Indonesia, becomes more entrenched as this scheme inaugurates a whole new economic set-up that is designed to back up the rejuvenated political power in each autonomous region.

Toward an ethnification of the state and nation

Leaving North Sulawesi and turning toward the national scene and especially to the present restructuring of the Indonesian state and nation, I shall point toward some aspects in the relationship between the state and ethnic groups in Outer Indonesia that have the potential for influencing the emerging new societal set-up together with the formation of a new national vision for Indonesia. I begin by briefly recapitulating how processes of globalization have the capability of influencing perceptions of ethnic identity at the local level, thus demonstrating how ethnic groups become major players in the national political power game. Arguably, various processes of globalization are leading toward an empowerment and thus assertive resurgence of local identities, generating an increasing social and political awareness during the process. Furthermore, globalization facilitated the development of a budding supranational moral construct in which human rights and democracy play a major role.

Put together, these effects of globalization constitute the beginning and end in an interrelated movement. This is what Friedman (1998) termed the "packing in" of global events, products and frameworks into the local. For example, the budding supranational morality within the international community has created room for NGOs and ethnic groups to push through issues to an international level and thus garner support in their fight for cultural recognition and political autonomy with local state institutions and national ideologies. In this way globalization has, through processes of empowerment, indirectly endowed ethnic and religious groups with commanding tools for initiating qualitatively different shifts in the conditions of people's lives at local level (see also Holm and Sørensen 1995: 5).

Globally interconnected means of communication and transportation have also, however, caused great concern among, for example, ethnic groups. Some are worried that their identity is being watered down and creolized beyond recognition by participating in the global exchange of different cultural practices, alternative patterns of consumption and lifestyles, together with international perceptions of moral values. In recognition of this, people attach themselves more closely to what they perceive as their culture of origin in order to maintain their awareness of identity. Not in the sense of returning to a dogmatic reading of actual cultural history, but rather by using aspects of their culture as a filter through which to domesticate external influences. This is what Hannerz (1997) termed the "maturation" aspect of globalization.

An interesting consequence of the connection between local identities and international normative patterns is that they tend to reinforce each other, leaving the state and its perception of supremacy on the sidelines. As we have seen several times in Indonesia, the state cannot legitimately force ethnic groups into submission by referring the matter to a question of national security without immediately having to defend itself from international criticism. The reason is that having an ethnic identity as well as a national one is quite legitimate according to the Human Rights Bill that Indonesia ratified in 1999 (*Jakarta Post* September 9, 1999). Moreover as human rights constitutes part of the IMF's humanitarian platform the Indonesian government is forced to initiate policies that guarantee the rights of ethnic groups to participate in the current transformation of the Indonesian state and nation. This holds for the organizational, political, ideological and economic aspects of nation-making.[4] Ethnic groups are thus secured, at least theoretically, international support in their jockeying for cultural recognition and political and economic influence. On the basis of this, the perception of sovereignty as put forward by Jackson has been permeated by sociopolitical developments, a process initiated by the ongoing forces of globalization, disempowering the state in the process.

A factor that has a real possibility of reinforcing the political maneuverability of ethnic groups is that many of the natural resources that are of vital importance for the Indonesian economy lies in those areas where some of the most vocal ethnic groups have their heartlands. I am here in particular talking about parts of Sumatra, Kalimantan and Papua, where timber, gas, oil, minerals, and many other important natural resources are found in abundant quantities. They were once the sources on which the New Order's power structures rested and thus depended. Given a higher degree of political and economic autonomy many ethnic groups, who are the original title-holders of these natural resources, suddenly find themselves having some very powerful cards in their hands when dealing with the Indonesian authorities.

Indonesia is still undergoing profound processes of societal transformation, so talking about a new national ideology to replace New Order nationalism is perhaps a bit premature. What is important to pinpoint at this moment is that the nationalist project does not belong anymore to the state and the persons managing the various power apparatuses. Creating a new national vision for Indonesia has become a nationwide project in which representatives of the state, the emerging civil society, and different ethnic groups within the national hinterland work together, backed by the international contacts that each entertains. Nationalism is thus gradually becoming a genuine multicultural and a multidimensional project that is embedded in a nationwide cum international context.

Disempowered states and a global politicization of ethnicity

From being subordinate components in the previous authoritarian Indonesian New Order society, various ethnic and religious groups throughout the national hinterland have moved to the center stage where political power and economic assets are being distributed. This fundamental shift in Indonesian nation-making has not been initiated because of political consent, but rather because the overall preconditions for nation-making have changed. It is interesting to note that these changes have not only occurred because of institutional changes, but also because previously low-key groups such as ethnic groups have been empowered by new developments within the global system that not only promote interdependence between different nation-states, but also imputes new energy into subnational regions and the various groups living there.

When taking a closer look at the "glue" that keeps the various groups together, ethnicity emerges as an overall imaginative paradigm for constructing related identities. The latter can thus be perceived as constituting a structured representation of the former. Taking on such a perspective, culture per se does not constitute an obligatory primordial foundation for organizing ethnic groups, but rather a reservoir of identity markers to be drawn upon when a social organization expresses itself in terms of ethnic identity. This relationship between ethnicity, ethnic identity, and culture underlines its situational or fluid character, drawing on the past to deal with the present in order to prepare for the future.

We are thus confronted with social systems in a constant state of flux. The real challenge, then, is to relate this fluidity to contemporary processes of globalization. I think it is important analytically to distinguish between the two in terms of "output." The approach used here is a "bottom-up" perspective so as to be able to catch the motivation behind ethnic groups' social and political strategies when dealing with either local or national political and economic issues. Here Hannerz's maturation and saturation distinction is very useful as it also replaces a primordial perspective on identity with a dynamic one, launching identity as a political tool to be used in social and political strategies.

The "output" created when the global co-opts the local is usually economic distress, widespread fear of losing cultural specificity, and societal marginalization. On the other hand, the "output" created when the local co-opts the global is invigorated social and political strategies directed toward self-preservation and societal positioning. This is especially so where the global creates new room in which the local can maneuver in relation to the state. This has been illustrated by the attempts the Minahasa are making in order to position themselves in anticipation of greater political and economic autonomy of the state through processes of democratization and decentraliza-tion—a development that was also initiated by global economic imperatives.

What affects do these processes have on the constitution of the state? This chapter has argued that the movements of the state as well as its perception of sovereignty have been curtailed by recent developments within the inter-national community. The state can thus be characterized as being "sandwiched" between international demands to honor internationally agreed conventions, and demands from ethnic and religious groups to have a say in the current nation-making process.

Has the classical form of the state thus reached its climax, historically speaking? David Jacobson writes that new transnational, international and regional entities, from international human rights institutions to the EU are both constraining the state in some respects and enhancing its role in others. He continues that today we are witnessing the disaggregation of the nation-state. The political, communal, and territorial components of the nation-state, once thought so intertwined as to be unremarkable, are being unbundled. Territory no longer constitutes identity in that a territory and a people are no longer viewed as being "inextricably" linked. Diasporas and transnational identities are increasingly common. He stresses, however, that the state is not in a decline—on the contrary, its bureaucratic role is enhanced. It is the marriage between nation and state that is in question (Jacobson 1998: 444).

In the case of Indonesia the authoritarian state has certainly outplayed its role. At present it is undergoing a profound transformation that at least according to plans should result in the creation of a transparent and more democratic state. The question is whether the Indonesian nation-state is becoming disaggregated in the sense of Jacobson. There are developments that point in that direction. The twenty-seventh province in Soeharto's Indonesia, East Timor, has left post-Soeharto Indonesia, and other provinces in Sumatra and Papua are threatening to follow suit. Furthermore, in terms of identity, having an Indonesian identity is now being sidelined by ethnic identities, making the overall picture of Indonesia in terms of identity much more complex. As such, there is an ongoing displacement between state and nation during the present transformation of Indonesia. As this displacement can be seen as the result of a power struggle between the constituting parts of the state and the ethnic and religious groups in the national hinterland, it remains to be seen whether the present state can keep its unitary structure or will be forced to adopt a more federal-like one in order to accommodate the otherwise fractural societal forces.

Whatever the result of this power struggle, the state is no longer the only player in this field. The question is, what role does the state have in a future Indonesia? Perhaps the "sandwiched" position of the existing state provides us with a hint. Being in an intermittent position between the local and the global, the right role for the state, not only in Indonesia but also in many other countries, is perhaps as a bureaucratic organizer and problem solver between the local and the global. Such a state would represent a type of "custodian state," coordinating among other things relations between the different groupings that make up the nation. As to the question of identity—this is a matter that will be dealt with through various ethnic-inspired diaspora networks that get their substance from oscillating between the local and the global.

Notes

1   See especially his "The Global Village" (reprint, New York, 1989) and "The Medium is the Message: An Inventory of Effects" (New York, 1967). For more literature on McLuhan see http://www.mala.bc.ca/~mcneil/cit/citlcmcluhan .htm
2   Quoted in "Indonesia. Strategic Framework for a Danish Pilot Development Programme," Final Report, January 17, 2001, p. 16.
3   For a detailed description of Minahasa identity, see Jacobsen (2000). The following information is collected during a fieldwork in October and November 1999 and again in June 2000.
4   For a case study in this connection, see Jacobsen 2000.

References

Anderson, B. R. O'G. (1987) "The State and Minorities in Indonesia," in Cultural Survival Report No. 22: 73–81, *Southeast Asian Tribal Groups and Ethnic Minorities. Prospects for the Eighties and Beyond*, Cambridge: Transcript Printing Company.

Barth, F. (1994) "Enduring and Emerging Issues in the Analysis of Ethnicity," in H. Vermeulen and C. Govers (eds.), *The Anthropology of Ethnicity*, Amsterdam: Het Spinhuis, pp. 11–32.

Brown, D. (1994) *The State and Ethic Politics in Southeast Asia*, London and New York: Routledge.

Brown, Robin (1995) "Globalisation and the End of the National Project," in J. Macmillan and A. Linklater (eds.), *Boundaries in Question: New Directions in International Relations*, London: Pinter and New York: St. Martins Press, pp. 54–68.

Foulcher, K. (1990) "The Construction of an Indonesian National Culture: Patterns of Hegemony and Resistance," in Arief Budiman (ed.), *State and Civil Society in Indonesia*, Clayton: Monash University, Centre of Southeast Asian Studies, Monograph No. 22, pp. 301–320.

Friedman, J. (1998) "Indigenes, Cosmopolitans and the Discreet Charm of the Bourgeoisie," in Udvalgte oplæg fra årsmøde i 1998. Dansk Ethnografisk Forening, *Grænser for Globalisering*, Aarhus and Copenhagen: University of Aarhus, pp. 1–20.

Hall, S. (1997) "The Local and the Global: Globalisation and Ethnicity," in A. D. King (ed.), *Culture, Globalization and the World-System. Contemporary Conditions for the Representation of Identity*, London: Macmillan, pp. 19–40.

Hannerz, U. (1997) "Scenarios for Peripheral Cultures," in A. D. King (ed.), *Culture, Globalization and the World-System. Contemporary Conditions for the Representation of Identity*, London: Macmillan Education Ltd., pp. 122–124.

Hastrup, K. (1998) "Det Antropologiske Objekt: Målestok og Metode," in Udvalgte oplæg fra årsmøde i 1998. Dansk Ethnografisk Forening, *Grænser for Globalisering*, Aarhus and Copenhagen: University of Aarhus, pp. 1–20.

Holm, H. and Sørensen, G. (1995) *Whose World Order? Uneven Globalisation and the End of the Cold War*, Oxford: Westview.

Jackson, R. K. (1990) *Quasi–States: Sovereignty, International Relations, and the Third World*, Cambridge: Cambridge University Press.

Jacobsen, M. (1999) "Indonesian Nationalism Reconsidered. Scenarios from a Restructuring Society," paper for a workshop on "Nationalism and Particularism in Present-day Southeast Asia", held at the Royal Institute of Linguistics and Anthropology in Leiden, the Netherlands, December 13–16, pp. 1–27.

—— (2000) "On the Question of Contemporary Identity in Minahasa, North Sulawesi, Indonesia," first presented at a seminar at the Kring der Leidse Urbanisten (KLU) in Leiden, the Netherlands, February 9, (mimeographed), pp. 1– 29.

Jacobson, D. (1998) "New Border Customs: Migration and the Changing Role of the State," *Journal of International Law and Foreign Affairs*, 3, 2: 443–462.

Kipp, R. Smith (1993) *Dissociated Identities. Ethnicity, Religion and Class in an Indonesian Society*, Ann Arbor: University of Michigan Press.

Smith, A. D. (1990) "Towards a Global Culture?," in M. Featherstone (ed.), *Global Culture: Nationalism, Globalisation and Modernity*, A Theory, Culture and Society, Special Issue. London: Sage Publications, pp. 171–191.

Verdery, K. (1994) "Ethnicity, Nationalism and State-Making," in H. Vermeulen and C. Govers (eds.), *The Anthropology of Ethnicity*, Amsterdam: Het Spinhuis, pp. 34–35.

Vermeulen, H. and Govers, C. (1994) "Introduction," in Vermeulen and Govers (eds.), *The Anthropology of Ethnicity*, Amsterdam: Het Spinhuis, p. 4.

Part V
Conclusion

14 The global–local nexus revisited

Constructing Asia in times of globalization

Catarina Kinnvall and Kristina Jönsson

Interpreting globalization in Asia

Globalization as conventionally understood is not a new phenomenon, but it does involve a number of novel dimensions as a result of its unprecedented scale and speed. Increased awareness of events occurring in a different geographical and political context has affected the way in which we study both our own and other people's political and social reality. This is at the core of the global–local nexus as a process through which global events, values and ideas are localized in interpretation and outcome. It is within this process that it becomes necessary to introduce the "missing link" of the cultural construction of identity, as without such a link we are left with simplistic binary representations of Asia in times of globalization. By using identity as the prism of local context it becomes possible to use Asia to understand globalization as a contextual phenomenon, at the same time as we can use the concept of globalization to understand Asia. Moving beyond binaries and toward a more complex picture of Asia, we are also able to say something about the indigenization and interpretation of democracy and civil society in different contexts, while also providing an enhanced understanding of how culture becomes cemented and institutionalized through economic, political, and social relations.

The chapters in this volume all draw attention to this observation as they emphasize history, culture and context as essential ingredients for understanding the "glocalization" cake. This is quite different from much literature on globalization, which has been careful to make a clear distinction between globalization on the one hand, and theories of modernization and colonialism on the other hand, thus searching for a break with a value-laden past. In large part this has meant a discussion of globalization and globalization theory as something defined negatively: it is not just a process of economic reductionism or determinism as much traditional modernization theory has suggested, neither can it be reduced to the logic of capitalism as suggested by Marxist accounts, such as world systems theory. Instead globalization is said to be something far less rigid, something that goes beyond the traditional preoccupation with the state.

But in trying to find such a niche or breach with the past, there is a risk that globalization, as a theoretical approach, may prove too eager to leave behind not only the state as an analytical concept, but also theories of modernity and Marxist theoretical approaches. This is not to argue that realist state-centric approaches are desirable or even believable, but merely to acknowledge that the state, as both an idea and an institution, remains powerful in many respects despite its weakening role in domestic and international affairs. Similarly, as long as the idea of modernization, as related to its theoretical underpinnings, remains a real instrument in world affairs in reinforcing unequal structural relationships between and within countries, we cannot close our eyes to the fact that modernization and unequal capitalist relations (resembling world systems arguments) must be part of any approach to globalization. In other words, rather than seeing "modernity as inherently globalizing" (Giddens 1990: 63, 177), modernity must be considered an important dimension of globalization.

The chapters in Part II are both extremely informative and illuminating with regard to this particular aspect of the global–local nexus. Lowell Dittmer's chapter on globalization and the AFC shows how the state as a dominant institution in East and Southeast Asia was a full participant in the outcome of the crisis. Through their ambivalent relationship to globalization (based on a combination of acceptance and rejection), political leaders in these countries made political–cultural exceptionalism both a tool and a relevant factor in explaining the outcome of the crisis. Dittmer thus allows for the state to take an active role in the interpretation of globalization. Rather than being helpless victims in a process entirely beyond the control of the political élite in these societies, he shows how the Asian states have simultaneously been both enthusiastic globalizers (and modernizers as part of that picture) and beneficiaries of economic globalization. Here Dittmer points to the existing structural problems in these societies as part of the explanation for the AFC, for example a high reliance on external capital, weak regulation, a poorly developed banking system, cronyism, and lack of transparency. The fact that a number of Asian regimes have responded to the AFC and to increased social unrest with nationalist rhetoric also illustrates how identity has indirectly affected the role and the power of the state. The idea of the nation-state is, in other words, still a powerful and inspirational notion in times of crisis, despite its weakening role. All these factors add up to a more complex picture of Asia than that of the innocent prey of financial globalization.

A more complex picture also seems to suggest that modernity, and its notions of unity and universality on thought and the world, has become more difficult as "the rest" have started to talk back. This brings us back to the earlier discussion of globalization and its relationship with modernist and Marxist approaches. As succinctly pointed out by Aswini Ray in Chapter 3, if globalization is viewed as interweaving linkages of factors of production, consumption and lifestyle, then it is at least as old as the global expansion of the European civilization through proselytization, trade, commerce, mass migration, industrial capitalism and colonialism. Globalization in today's South Asia (and other parts of Asia) can, in other words, only be properly understood if analyzed in the broader context of colonialization, decolonialization and the cold war legacy. This becomes clear when reading Ray's chapter, in which he points to a number of contradictions that have their origins in the distorted developments of the colonial era, such as the relatively developed state apparatus in comparison to the predominantly indigenous civil society, or the urban–rural sociological disparity between metropolitan centers and the rest of the country.

What Ray's chapter demonstrates most clearly, however, is the difficulty and resistance from the West when "the rest," as represented by India, has talked back, insisting on its own version of modernity. The Indian preference for indigenous developmental priorities, based on self-reliance, has thus stood in stark contrast to Western agencies' pressures to globalize and pursue a policy of export-led growth. Of particular interest here is how the relative strength of democratic institutions of governance has positively affected India's ability to resist Western pressures and allurements to globalize, at least up to a particular point. This is where Ray turns to the novel dimensions of globalization in the form of time and space compression, as global pressures have been more difficult to resist at times when the state and democratic institutions are weakening. The fact that protest against globalization and political reform has increased as a result of accentuated income disparities shows how "the rest" are talking back, not only globally but also locally. India's progression toward weaker governments consisting of political parties representing regional and sectional interests is thus interesting in many respects, but particularly because it shows the inadequacy of theoretical approaches to globalization which disregard the real consequences of modernity and structural inequalities.

Ray is here drawing our attention to the fact that colonialization has been and still is an important part of globalization; that modernization is inseparable from globalization, and that consumerism is almost invariably following in its footsteps. This is similar to Sklair's discussion of the spread of a "culture-ideology of consumerism:" "[T]he specific task of the global capitalist system in the Third World is to promote consumerism among people with no regard for their own ability to produce for themselves, and with only an indirect regard for their ability to pay for what they are consuming" (1991: 131). Ray's chapter thus illustrates Alan Scott's (1997: 11) claims that there may be an incompatibility between the logic of market relations (free exchange between rational egoists) and social relations (built upon trust and reciprocity between social actors), the former tending to undermine the latter. The contradiction lies in the fact that the former, the market, must eventually rely upon the latter, the trust, which the market undermines. Scott's argument is that various social forces, such as demands for wage increases, change into demands for social wage (welfare, unemployment benefits) as protection from market forces. These demands are directed toward the nation-state at the same time that the state is weakening, which eventually results in some form of market curtailment. Ray's chapter portrays the logic of capital versus the logic of politics, where the former seeks to escape capital control while the latter seeks to curtail it. In Scott's words, this shows how much work on globalization and globalization theory has underestimated the contradictory character of social change (Scott 1997: 11–13).

Though Ray does not come from an explicitly postcolonial perspective in the sense of postcolonial criticism as an important field of the social sciences, it is interesting to note certain overlaps in argument. Postcolonial criticism thus accounts for the way in which identity is constructed by proceeding from imperialism as its main object of analysis, where imperialism is a practice of domination rather than just a textual strategy. It is thus about locating knowledge as a historically constituted site at which the process of "othering" takes place. Such location is necessary in order to demonstrate that eurocentrism has been, and still is, the precondition for our vision of the Other (see Keyman 1997: 189; Bhaba 1986: 150). Without going into the details of postcolonial discourse, it is important to be aware of the fact that we as academics must constantly question not only our epistemological and ontological foundations, but also the social construction of ourselves as structured by certain socioeconomic realities. Constructing a multifaceted picture of Asia and Asian societies must necessarily mean a reconstruction of ourselves in relation to others.

Contesting notions of democracy and civil society in Asia

Understanding democracy and culture in Asia: possibilities and obstacles

All the chapters in Part III are concerned, in various ways, with the social construction of democracy and civil society in line with the argument given above. Hence they all question and problematize liberal thought, liberal institutions, and the way liberal democracy has been used, both as an analytic tool and in practice. The simple and straightforward argument is that liberal democracy needs to be problematized together with the assumptions connected to it. Edward Friedman's chapter is, in this respect, a telling example of how we must question not only liberal democracy as such, but also the idea that anti-democratic forces are mostly to be found and explained from a non-Western perspective. The belief among French authoritarian Catholics that democracy required a Protestant culture is not very different from the belief among many Chinese that democracy and human rights are alien discourses. This wish for a nonexistent East–West binary— both in a Western and a non-Western context—is analyzed throughout Friedman's writings. How Hindus saw Europeans as intolerant, repressive and authoritarian thus demonstrates how a cultural stream of tolerance and reconciliation is part of Hindu discourse. However, this must be put in the light of the historical construction of caste, religion, and other identity patterns as exclusionary and often repressive categories. As Friedman argues; "[H]omogenizing East or West does a disservice to the complexity of both."

Friedman's chapter also reflects the simplicity involved in much literature on democracy. The assumption that once a certain democratic framework is in place a democratic content will more or less automatically follow is refuted time and again in Asia. Both South Korea and Indonesia are good examples of this misconception. Thus, Geir Helgesen talks about how formally democratic South Korea is more democratic in theory than in practice, while Robison is more concerned with the emergence of a predatory democracy in Indonesia. Of particular importance for Helgesen's argument is the observation that despite the strong institutionalization of democratic rituals in South Korea, these rituals are still deeply embedded in the traditional social order. Liberal notions of individual freedom, freedom of choice and political pluralism as supreme good are not supported by the present shared morality in Korea. Thus, even if people are positive toward democracy and human rights they are, at the same time, unwilling to give up Korean traditional values, such as the belief in order and a morally upright leader.

What Helgesen really does in his chapter is to place at the forefront the issues of tradition and modernity. Perhaps the real question is what form democracy is allowed to take, that is, what kind of alternatives to liberal democracy are there and can there be? The general attitude is that Korean democracy must take traditional culture as its point of departure, which implicitly makes the distinction between tradition and modernity obsolete. Helgesen's discussion of South Korea thus opens up new forms of social practices, including other forms of good governance, but without rejecting democratic content. Implicit in this view is that liberal democracy as a universally applicable political model has no future.

Richard Robison's chapter also problematizes issues of "old" and "new" as he demonstrates how the same power relations and institutional forms that defined the Soeharto regime are being reproduced in the new democracy. What is emerging in Indonesia today is a predatory democracy characterized by a range of parties and power centers competing for money and resources. Corruption has increased and gangsters, thugs and militias have gained in importance as a result of politicians and parties no longer being able to call on the repressive state apparatus to enforce their will. The incumbent ruling classes remain intact at the price of democratic reform. Thus, Robison shows how structural factors have been more important for political rule in Indonesia than leadership change, at least in the short run. Robison's chapter also questions the simplicity in associating democracy and markets with increased globalization, as it must be remembered that international investors flourished for decades in Indonesia under the most authoritarian regimes. This, together with the hesitation among today's investors to re-enter and their longing for the "good old days" of Soeharto, are excellent examples of the irony of moral arguments which take as their point of departure East–West dichotomies. The "modern" is thus not by definition the "moral." The emphasis on democratic form and content are often conveniently used in a nonlinear and strategic fashion.

Another assumption made in the democracy literature—the role of the middle class as an advocate for democratization—has also been highly contested in Asia. Robison, for instance, questions the naturally progressive nature of the middle class and civil society. In fact, the middle class in Indonesia did not decamp to a new liberal alliance but stuck to the predatory Soeharto agenda. The resistance to liberal political and market reforms has thus played a pivotal role in shaping the new democracy in Indonesia, demonstrating the strength rather than the weakness of the middle class, both under authoritarian rule and under the present form of democracy. A strong middle class is not, in other words, the same as one in favor of liberal democracy.

One aspect to note when discussing both democracy and the middle class is how the point of reference remains liberal democracy. This may actually constitute the root of the problem. Form has been more important than content, which could possibly explain why democracy has been, and still is, difficult in practice. Moreover, liberal democracy is often seen as the most desirable outcome without any reflection upon the difficulties involved in implementation. The import of formal institutions such as parliament, regular elections and other formal requirements is not enough for democracy to be consolidated. To re-emphasize Friedman's words: "if a democracy is not indigenized to fit particularities of culture, history and society, democracy will never flourish." The question then is the extent to which democracy can be allowed to vary with regard to form, and the need to realize that even if form differs (as it already does in many democracies in the Western hemisphere), democratic content such as freedoms and respect for human rights could remain. These discussions all point to the interrelationship between authority, identity and ideology where, again, identity becomes the missing link in the vast literature on democracy and democratic change.

Another common assumption problematized in Robison's chapter and at heart of Kristina Jönsson's argument is how liberalization commonly equals democratization and how both processes are viewed as unidirectional. Here Jönsson shows that liberalization is promoted in both Vietnam and Laos, especially in the economic sphere, at the same time that few signs of democratization can be seen. The two processes can co-exist but their relationship is more complicated than often presumed as liberalization tends to open up opportunities for new groups challenging the current regime without these groups necessarily opting for democratic development. Thus, the leadership may allow for a more open system, at the same time as a multiparty system is rejected. Moreover, the economic benefits from globalization are spread very unevenly, which supports Jönsson's claim that a more pluralistic system in Vietnam and Laos may actually result in pressure for the political supremacy of new interest groups, namely those benefiting from globalization.

Jönsson's chapter is significant in that it points to the one theme running through the first four chapters of Part III —the mixed effects of (especially economic) globalization as benefiting certain groups at the expense of others, both in authoritarian and democratic systems. This is related to the earlier discussion of how increased inequalities and insecurities (economic and otherwise) may create a foundation for identity-based conflict or result in demands for change, especially in more authoritarian societies. However, the opposite seems to be equally true. Thus, as long as authoritarian regimes are able to provide the "goodies" or aid economic progress in general, no change in a more democratic direction is called for. All the chapters in this section demonstrate how this situation varies substantially across the states in Asia and how calls for democratic change have different meanings as we move from one cultural, economic and social context to another. This is where Friedman's argument—that Eastern and Western culture are not mere categories of an analytical social science—becomes important. The fact that cultural arguments are simplified and often used as political arguments is merely another piece of evidence of how culture in reality is complex and multistranded. All societies are built upon multiple cultural layers. The actual cementing process of cultures is never complete as cultures are always exposed to diffusion and changing economic, political and social relations, as demonstrated by the chapters in this volume (see also Kinnvall 1995). The problem with cultural relativist arguments is not only that they glorify culture, but also that culture is presented as unidimensional. The Asian value debate is a good example of this. In its attempt to cement certain aspects of myth-making the debate simultaneously shows how the reinterpretation of culture is endless.

Asia cannot, in other words, be constructed in unidimensional terms, but must reflect the multifaceted nature of culture as being a mixture of impulses of past and present in real and constructed forms. Culture does not stand in isolation but should be interpreted as a blend of modernity and tradition, especially today when people look for security in a changing world by using the past to make sense of the present. This implies that there are many different kinds of modernities to be found worldwide, a theme returned to below, but they are rarely discussed in a comparative manner. The different chapters in this volume all account for the various consequences of a particular contextual modernity at the same time as together they create a richer comparative picture of an Asian economic, political and social landscape.

Understanding national and transnational civil society: going beyond the current debate

This richer picture is amply provided by both Hugo Dobson and Anders Uhlin in their chapters on Japan, and Malaysia and Thailand, as they question the simplicity with which these societies are often described and interpreted. Hence, Dobson shows how Japan with its top-down democratization today includes bottom-up democracy as well, as globalization has led to an increase in both NGOs and NPOs. Once held up as an example of how to modernize rapidly without the associated social dislocation and still maintain a strong national identity, the Japanese system of today is blamed for social ills and the many scandals among politicians and bureaucrats. The growth of civil society in Japan can thus be seen as a response to the failure of traditional forms of governance. In this sense Dobson gives credit to the view of civil society as a promoter of democracy from below. This is similar to Uhlin's claim that in Thailand there has been political opportunities for civil society to expand under democratic regimes, particularly since the early 1990s. The fact that Thailand today has a large number of NGOs which are active and able to influence politics reinforces the notion of civil society as the upholder of democracy. Obviously the area in which a civil society group or a social movement is involved may affect the relationship between state and society. Some issues, such as human rights, may be viewed as more controversial than others (such as the environment), thus making conflict more possible.

However, in line with Helgesen's argument earlier, Dobson cautions us not to automatically assume that such a civil society, even when emerging as a result of failed state policies, will be free from either traditional or anti-democratic tendencies. Dobson thus problematizes the assumption that a vibrant civil society will automatically promote democracy by arguing that nonstate actors may be undemocratic and working against democracy. The notion that a bottom-up civil society always exists independent of the state is likewise invalidated in Dobson's chapter. Hence, he notices how the Japanese government has realized the importance of NGOs in a number of issue areas, such as those concerning refugees, poverty and the environment, as well as their role as important actors in conflict prevention. This refutes the often-romantic liberal idea of a "free" civil society in opposition to the state.

These latter aspects are further illustrated in Uhlin's chapter as he criticizes the idealized view of civil society in liberal theory. In connection with Malaysia, he clearly shows how the strengthening of civil society does not automatically lead to more democracy even if an expanded civil society gives more political space for political struggles. The political space created by the AFC, for instance, proved short-lived as the state increased repression. Increased repression, in turn, has produced an atmosphere and the need for a more transnational civil society, often in opposition to global forces. Uhlin's claim that civil society in these societies has embraced or resisted globalization, or tried to promote alternative forms of globalization, is therefore of particular significance. The emergence of a transnational civil society in Southeast Asia can, from this perspective, be viewed as a response to negative aspects of globalization, such as environmental degradation and the trafficking of women and children. The focus on transnational civil society is thus important as it brings a novel dimension to the global–local nexus. Local, intimately experienced phenomena such as gender bias, repression of political, religious or other views, environmental pollution, and the spread of HIV/AIDS can be addressed at the global level when the local(e) proves an obstacle. This opens up the possibility of the global, the opportunities, rather than limiting it to its negative effects. The fact that transnational civil society is stronger in Malaysia than in Thailand also shows how the globalization of the local becomes a strategy, perhaps the only one available at times, in the struggle against repressive politics at home. Here it is important to re-emphasize, as Uhlin does in his chapter, that transnational mobilization may expand at the expense of local mobilization.

Both these chapters show how global–local linkages affect democratic developments by providing alternative ways of expression and action. Within this process the role of the state is uncertain and the state can be weakened and strengthened at the same time, depending on the area or issue. If weakened economically, for instance, the state may compensate through more or less repressive political measures. However, if civil society has difficulties domestically, groups may turn toward transnational arenas in order to promote pluralism and democracy. But they may also be directed toward nationalism, chauvinism and other less attractive options. Globalization, as Friedman argues, fosters both democratic and nasty forces, and "... while democratization is a universal potential, challenges to democracy are also universal...."

This section illustrates how the construction of Asia in times of globalization contains a conflict between embracing or rejecting globalization, as the positive aspects are difficult to separate from the negative. Globalization, moreover, challenges the concepts of East and West, of North and South, of the first and the third worlds. The preoccupation with culture in many societies in Asia and the struggle to find one's own identity is often a reflection of this challenge. Within this process there is the temptation to look at the "old democracies," disregarding indigenous historical processes, despite the fact that there is no homogeneous Western democracy to copy. The relationship between democracy and political development in Asia is thus problematic, but our understanding will not be enhanced unless we give up the uniform picture provided in much democracy and transition literature in favor of a diverse, particular but also more accurate, description of these societies. Such a more comprehensive picture can only be provided if identity and culture are taken fully into account.

Explaining identity in Asia: the missing link

As argued in the introduction to this chapter, globalization can foster openness, exchange and mutual benefits, but it can also strengthen chauvinism
and nationalism. Changes come quickly, and people search for old roots to
hold on to when they feel lost in the new world. This process tends to occur
at both a state level and at an individual level. Hence political leaders in
some states, such as China and Malaysia, may try to complete the building
of a centralized state by emphasizing those aspects particularly Chinese or
Asian in their efforts to construct a strong national identity—often in relation to a demonized West. This centralized discourse exists at the same time
as these states attempt to compete economically in the new age of globalization in an arena where the centralized state is commonly questioned. Thus,
at the state level several projects are running parallel and some states are
behaving in what seems to be a contradictory manner. At an individual and
group level, the search for a one-dimensional identity may occur as a
response to a real or imagined feeling of being marginalized culturally,
economically and/or politically. It can also take place in opposition to a
hegemonic state discourse where individuals or (minority) groups feel that
they have little power to influence such a discourse. Both case scenarios
reflect a way to find security in a rapidly changing world, as also argued in
the introduction. Hence, regardless whether localism is good or not, it is a
strategy to cope with globalization.

The chapters in Part IV give different but complementary perspectives of
these aspects of globalization and democracy by relating them to issues of
identity, citizenship, and culture. Identity, we argue, provides the missing
link in discussions of globalization and democracy and has not been properly accounted for in much of this literature. As the discussion in previous
chapters has shown, however, issues of culture and identity are very much
present when analyzing economic, political and social change in Asia. If we
revisit these chapters, we soon discover certain "identity themes." At a quick
glance we can distinguish at least five such themes.

First, the issue of whether globalization leads to homogenization or fragmentation of culture is really about identity as being universal (we are all the
same) or particular (we are all different in some respect). Second, when
discussing the reasons behind institutional democracy in, for example, South
Korea, Taiwan and Indonesia as compared to China, Vietnam and Laos, the
actual discussion is about competing versions of institutional rule, beliefs
and ideas in the hands and minds of political leaders and the people they
represent (or fail to represent). What is contested are those beliefs and myths
on which the state structure should rest, and which make it possible to argue
that the identity of the state is at risk.[1] Third, the tendency to think in terms
of dichotomies, such as West versus East, modernity versus tradition, colonialization versus decolonialization, transnational versus national, state
versus nonstate actors are all about identity and culture. Value judgments

are essential to these dichotomies considering superiority or inferiority, inclusiveness or exclusiveness, good or bad, and so on.

These same issues are involved when discussing institutionalized aspects of identity, such as citizenship. Using modernity as an example, it is easy to see how it has always needed the presence of the "Other" in order to realize itself; what is not modern has been viewed as the "Other" of modernity. Those aspects not considered modern have had to join modernity by becoming one with it globally. "Universalizability is for modernity what proselytizing is for many religions" (Alam 1999: 7). The problem with the terminology of modernity is of course that it is based upon an ahistorical and essentializing treatment of culture as either "traditional" or "modern." Modern becomes a picture of the West, rather than modernity as such. Here we need to emphasize, as Featherstone (1995: 84) has done, that many different kinds of modernity can occur at the same time—global modernities—as different contexts may experience different patterns of modernity.

The fourth theme, the development of uneven structural patterns between various groups and regions in relation to global forces, is also about identity and often about identity conflict. As argued by Jabri (1996: 121), "identity becomes the essential link between the individual and mass mobilization for conflict." Unequal power relations and structural inequalities are thus intimately linked with calls for one-dimensional identities. This involves the "othering" of the Other as in "the West" as alien or "the East" as romantic, modernity as demoralizing or tradition as picturesque, Christians as oppressive or Muslims as dogmatic, and so on. At times of uncertainty and rapid change, such essentialized identity patterns often gain predominance, or become trump card identities (see Oommen 1997; Calhoun 1994) in the construction of the enemy Other, be it within or between societies. Fifth and finally, identity is present in the authors' interpretation of local events in the light of global forces.

Identity and culture are thus central to all the chapters of this book, but are explicitly analyzed in Part IV. Hence Bishnu Mohaptra discusses the growing politicization of ethnicity in India. In doing so he rejects both the primordialist and the overly instrumentalist view of ethnicity and ethnic mobilization. Ethnicity is neither merely an outburst of irrational sentiment in the public domain, nor the result only of a deliberate creation. Rather, by using examples drawn from the experiences of India, Mohaptra demonstrates how ethnic mobilizations have highlighted social cleavages and the feelings of marginality experienced among various ethnic groups in these societies. This argument makes the important leap from identity to citizenship, discussing issues of inclusion and exclusion. Of particular interest in this regard is Mohaptra's appreciation for the postmodern celebration of diversity, while, and in our view correctly, lamenting its insensitivity to the unequal power relations or hegemonic structures in a society. This is similar to much postcolonial critique. For Homi Bhaba, for instance, it is essential to question both the modernist and the postmodernist failure to account for how the colonial subject is historically constructed in order to reveal "the limits of Western metaphysical discourse." In the case of much postmodernist writing, Bhaba's argument is that though these discourses take an anti-Western perspective they keep eurocentrism as their reference point. In doing this they fail to explore the historical and discursive construction of otherness as an outcome of a different materiality and history of colonial culture (Bhaba 1986: 150).

Shamsul A. B. takes a similar perspective in his discussion of globalization in relation to development, decolonialization, and the modernization project. The fact that many societies, such as Malaysia, consist of both hunters-and-gatherers and corporate headhunters points to the need to understand the historical construction of unevenness in development. Shamsul's argument illustrates how globalization and democratization are both historical and contemporary in nature and closely connected to colonialization. Similar to Bhaba's claims, Shamsul shows how colonial knowledge deconstructed indigenous knowledge in favor of the European model of modernization and development. The rejection of this development project unites a number of so-called new social movements, or identity-based interest groups. What is particularly interesting in Shamsul's text is his claim that increased tension between the local–particular and the global–universal has led to the globalization project slowly swallowing the development project. Rather than resulting in demands for democratization, this has been followed by increased calls for so-called cosmopolitan localism (in Malaysia, Chinese minority fundamentalism), where the assertion of diverse localism is viewed as a universal right.

Claims by Chinese minorities is evidence of a particularly important aspect of identity politics, that is, the questioning of uniformity in the global project. The Chinese case is especially interesting in another respect as well, as it displays a recent tendency to encourage ethnic interaction, networking and bonding for reasons of social, economic and political nature. The transnational character of such interaction may indicate a trend by which it becomes even more difficult to disregard issues of identity in the forms of diasporas, refugees, migrant workers, multiple citizenships, and so on. Shamsul's more general discussion of the rise of fundamentalism in Southeast Asia also illustrates how the essentialization of identity unifies the group as it provides both comfort and identifies scapegoats. The wish to return to simplicity and traditional behavior as the world becomes more complex is further illustrated by Shamsul's discussion of fundamentalism. Here the issue of who gets to decide what tradition *is* accentuates the role of myth-making and convincing storytelling for the fundamentalist discourse and thus for identity-building. Finally, we should emphasize Shamsul's claim that being NGOized is not the same as being developed or globalized. It is a sign, however, that national governments and international institutions have lost much of their legitimacy in an increasingly global world.

This loss of legitimacy could, of course, result in different kind of conflicts than those occurring in an era characterized by the dominance of states and state power. As argued by Ang,

> globalization and cultural flows should not necessarily be understood in terms of a set of neat linear determinations, but instead viewed as a series of overlapping, overdetermined, complex and "chaotic" conditions which, at best, can be seen to cluster around key "nodal points." This has led, "not to the creation of an ordered global village, but to the multiplication of points of conflict, antagonism and contradiction."
>
> (Ang in Barker 1999: 41)

The interaction of the global and the local may, in other words, take unexpected turns. This is perhaps especially true for authoritarian societies, with the idea of a homogeneous society challenged by hybrid forces. Vivienne Shue, in her chapter on China and the challenge of Falun Gong to the Chinese state, relates a story of how ideas, values and external influences pass through prisms of local contexts. Similar to Shamsul, Shue discusses the fact that some enjoy the fruits of globalization while others suffer from it. Her story confirms what has been discussed in most of the chapters in this volume, that is, how economic developments and globalization create counter reactions. What is particularly interesting in Shue's account, however, is her argument that hybridity in policies may backfire for governments in authoritarian societies. The state-sponsored belief that it is possible to blend old ideas (of socialism) with new ones (of market reform) has left the government exposed to a similar search for pre-communist cultural roots.

Deteriorating sovereign authority and the state's capability to define and pursue its own ends have, in other words, put pressure on the Chinese state. However, the fact that the state is deteriorating in one sphere does not necessarily mean that the authoritarian state is disappearing. It may, in fact, provoke an even more hard-line political response. Here, Shue's chapter shows how the state may have diminished internationally and nationally, but how it still has remained strong and even strengthened its authoritarian policies in relation to certain groups in society. This adds an important dimension to the discussion in the introduction regarding the weakened role of the state in light of liberalization and market forces. It also goes counter to the liberal belief that increased economic liberalization will eventually result in democratization. Instead it supports Jönsson's claim that these are two related, but still different, processes. At the same time it is important to note the increasing difficulty with which the Chinese state is maintaining its hegemony in cultural affairs. As modernization has replaced class struggle, the Chinese regime has been more or less forced to rely on state-sponsored cultural nationalism that glorifies the past, Asian values, and other cultural constructions in its efforts to find a "national" culture. This implies that if culture is understood through the principle of state sovereignty it can only refer to the diversity of national cultures. Such a unity of the nation is constructed in a narrative form in which stories, images, symbols and rituals represent "shared" meanings of nationhood. National identity, in other words, becomes a way of unifying cultural diversity (see Walker 1993: 177).

This aspect of Shue's chapter is particularly interesting as it shows the volatility of identity politics, especially when such politics are state-sponsored. Hence traditional culturalists and postmodern nativists have all reacted against the negative image of Chinese political culture, thus resulting in a cultural revival. The fact that Chineseness has become contested challenges the state version in two respects. First, it defies the image of "shared" meanings of nationhood; second, it breaks down the attempts to unify cultural diversity. In the case of Falun Gong, it also threatens the state's monopoly of moral truth, leaving China caught between Western ideals and values and popular mysticism and magic. This prevents the Chinese regime from providing a picture of order and continuity in a chaotic world, a picture that it needs if it is to renew its hegemony in cultural affairs.

This emphasis on the world as chaotic and anarchical, with sovereign states as the solution to a disorganized chaos, continues to provide an illusion of national (and cultural) homogeneity. But it is and remains an illusion, despite its obvious appeal. As argued by Stuart Hall:

> Instead of thinking of national cultures as unified, we should think of them as a discursive device which represents difference as unity or identity. They are cross-cut by deep internal differences, and "unified" only through the exercise of different forms of cultural power.
>
> (Hall 1992: 297)

National cultures do not, in other words, have fixed beliefs, only fixed interpretations of those beliefs. Nationalism, but also religion as the Falun Gong example shows, may work as alternative sources of legitimacy upon which incumbent regimes as well as opposition movements may draw. It is through this dialogue that both nationalism and religion help to make sense of the core problems in human life—failure, insecurity, alienation, suffering and loss. At the same time it is important to remember and re-emphasize Mohapatra's claim that communities, despite their fragmented essence, are not fictitious, but often represent marginalized, disempowered minorities, whose only resource may be "strategic essentialism." Nationalism and other identity construction may, in other words, constitute a response to an exclusive hegemonic discourse and politics.

The use of nationalism as a main component in the reconstruction of local identities is also at heart of Michael Jacobsen's chapter on Minahasa identity formation. Jacobsen's focus, however, is on the subnational level. His chapter illustrates how the resurgence of local identities embedded in cultural idioms in many parts of the world has produced a diversity at subnational level. It is interesting to note how nationalism works similarly at both the subnational and the state level. The conflicting perceptions of what "authentic" culture is in the Minahasa case is thus not very different from the struggle over Chineseness as delineated in Shue's chapter. Both cases involve incorporating the past in the present in order to prepare for the future.

Even in other respects there are similarities between the state and the subnational level. Akin to Dittmer's description of the role of the Asian states in the AFC, the Minahasa do not see themselves as victims of globalization. Instead they use globalization processes to promote their own agenda *vis-à-vis* the state. This would suggest a very instrumentalist reading of Minahasa identity. However, Jacobsen is careful to make at least three distinctions that challenge any pure instrumentalist view. First, he views identity as a project, as a process of becoming rather than one of being. Second, he links identity to social organization, making it situational and fluid in content and therefore politically potent. And finally, he discusses the difficulties for the Minahasa in probing their identity because of Christianity and the New Order nationalist ideology. The fact that this elusive Minahasa identity is now being gradually replaced by a more culturally specific identity which can be used by the Minahasa politicians to mobilize an otherwise heavily depoliticized population is evidence of a fundamental aspect of identity politics: the creation of a political community.

The creation of a political community is an important component when discussing identity conflict, as the process of defining an external and feared "Other" is most likely to occur in cases when a religious or nationalist collectivity claims that it also is a political community (Oommen 1994; Kinnvall 2002), thus posing a threat to the larger community—to the Indonesian state in the case of the Minahasa. The potential for nationalism thus exists in any stratified society where one group is dominant over another, but it is usually not realized until some members from one group (ethnic or otherwise defined) attempt to move into the economic and political space occupied by another group (see Brass 1991; Horowitz 1985). The wish of the Minahasa to remain dominant in provincial affairs could thus create counter reactions locally, as well as in the changing state of Indonesia. Nationalism may very well become that multicultural and multidimensional project described by Jacobsen, a project that is embedded in both a nationwide and an international context. However, the extent to which such a transition will be smooth and relatively painless is yet to be seen, as illustrated in the chapter by Robison.

All these chapters show the volatile nature of the relationship between the global and the local in Asia. It is within this relationship that Asia can be crystallized, not as an entity or a unified body of thought but as a loosely configured pattern of societies that are both real constructs and vague contours on the political map of the world. The vagueness is in the fluidity of borders, people, and the movement of goods and capital, while there is a certain permanence to the actual map, the local(e). Not that the local is forever the same, but it is contextual in its historical construction of social relations which shape and influence values and traditions. It is at this nexus of the global and the local that identity becomes the missing link, as without the concept of identity we fail to understand the cultural underpinnings of social relations. Without social relations we have no institutional arrangement of political rule, such as democracy or authoritarianism; neither do we have any movement of people, commodities, values or ideas in the form of globalization. Social relations make society. Ignoring the cultural dimension of social relations means that we must remain within the binary world of opposites, of essentialized categories and cultural stereotypes instead of acknowledging how the global–local nexus works to challenge such simplified views. All the chapters in this volume have shown, time and again, how culture, identity and the structural components of social relations are essential for analyzing recent developments in world politics, but they have also all illustrated how such analyses cannot be made without a serious reconsideration of the impact of historical categories and dichotomies for us as academics in explaining such politics.

Note

1   When discussing group, nation or state identity it remains important to abstain from the common tendency to treat any of these as unequivocally bounded actors with a set of individual attributes. If by deconstructing the group (nation, state) we end up with a reification of the very category of self; a given self with a certain number of properties, then we must question whether an actual deconstruction process has occurred.

References

Alam, J. (1999) *India: Living With Modernity*, Delhi: Oxford University Press.
Barker, C. (1999) *Television, Globalization and Cultural Identities*, Buckingham: Open University Press.
Bhaba, H. (1986) "The other question: difference, discrimination and the discourse of colonialism," in F. Barker (ed.), *Literature, Politics and Theory*, London: Methuen.
Brass, P. (1991) *Ethnicity and Nationalism: Theory and Comparison*, London: Sage Publications.
Calhoun, C. (ed.) (1994) *Social Theory and the Politics of Identity*, Oxford: Blackwell.
Featherstone, M. (1995) *Undoing Culture: Globalization, Postmodernism and Identity*, London: Sage Publications.
Giddens, A. (1990) *The Consequences of Modernity*, Stanford: Stanford University Press.
Hall, S. (ed.) (1992) *Modernity Its Futures*, London: Polity Press.
Horowitz, D. L. (1985) *Ethnic Groups in Conflict,* Berkeley: University of California Press.

Jabri, V. (1996) *Discourses on Analysis: Conflict Analysis Reconsidered*, Manchester: Manchester University Press.

Keyman, F. (1997) *Globalization, State, Identity/Difference. Toward a Critical Social Theory of International Relations*, Atlantic Highlands: Humanities Press.

Kinnvall, C. (1995) *Cultural Diffusion and Political Learning: The Democratization of China*, Lund: Lund University Press.

—— (2002) "Nationalism, Religion and the Search for Chosen Traumas: Comparing Sikh and Hindu Identity Constructions", *Ethnicities,* Vol. 2, No. 1.

Oommen, T. K. (1997) *Citizenship, Nationality and Ethnicity*, Cambridge: Polity Press.

Scott, A. (ed.) (1997) *The Limits of Globalization*, London: Routledge.

Sklair, L. (1991) *Sociology of the Global System*, London; Harvester Wheatsheaf.

Walker, R. B. J. (1993) *Inside/Outside: International Relations as Political Theory*, Cambridge: Cambridge University Press.

Index

Page references for notes are followed by n